HISTORIC PHOTOS OF
LOS ANGELES

TEXT AND CAPTIONS BY DANA LOMBARDY

TURNER
PUBLISHING COMPANY

One of the early movie pioneers of Hollywood was Mack Sennett (1880–1960). He founded Keystone Studios in 1912 with history's first totally enclosed film stage and studio, which still exists. Mack Sennett Productions became famous for slapstick comedies with wild car chases and pie fights, and for the Sennett Bathing Beauties such as these young women photographed on an L.A. beach about 1917.

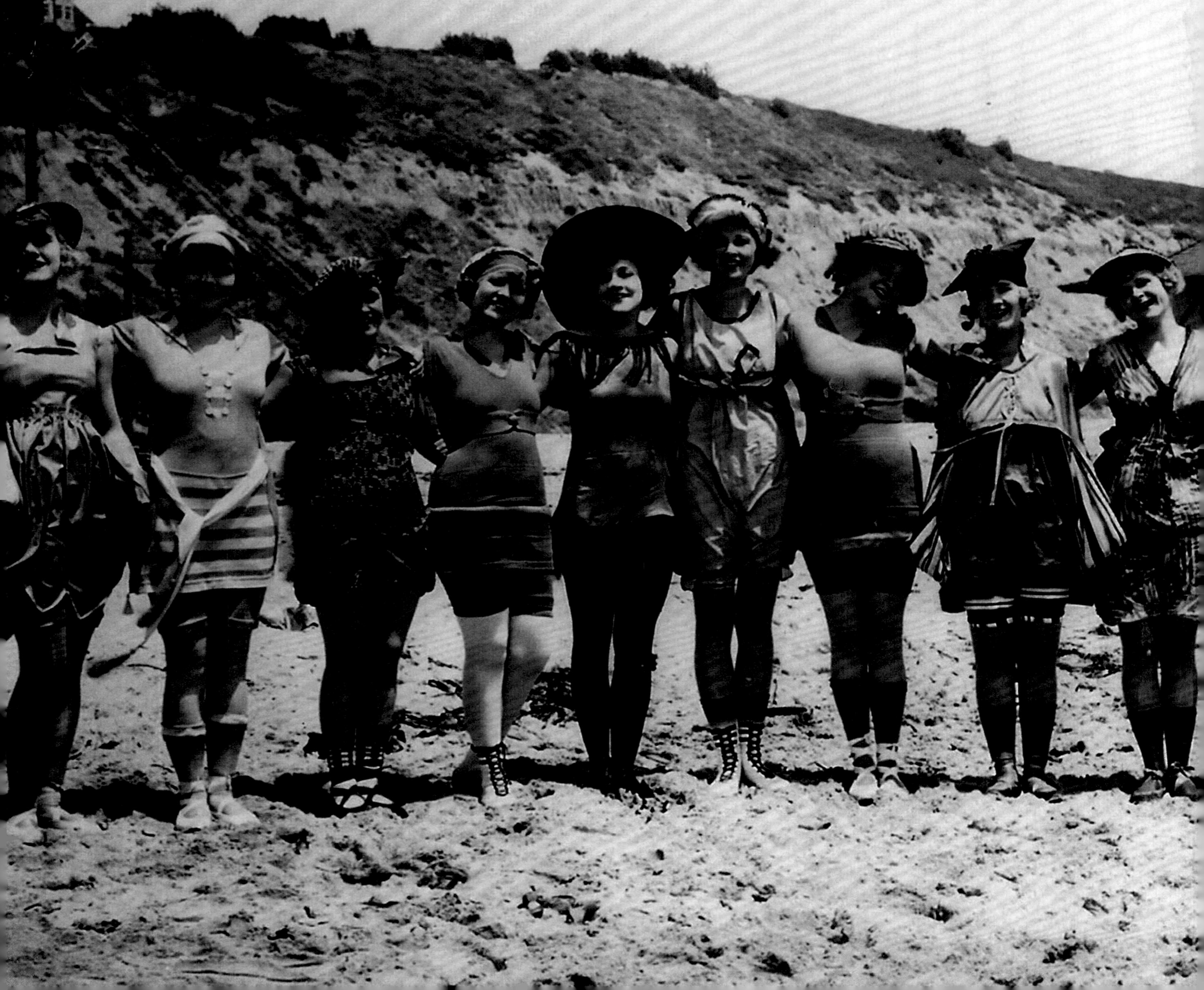

HISTORIC PHOTOS OF LOS ANGELES

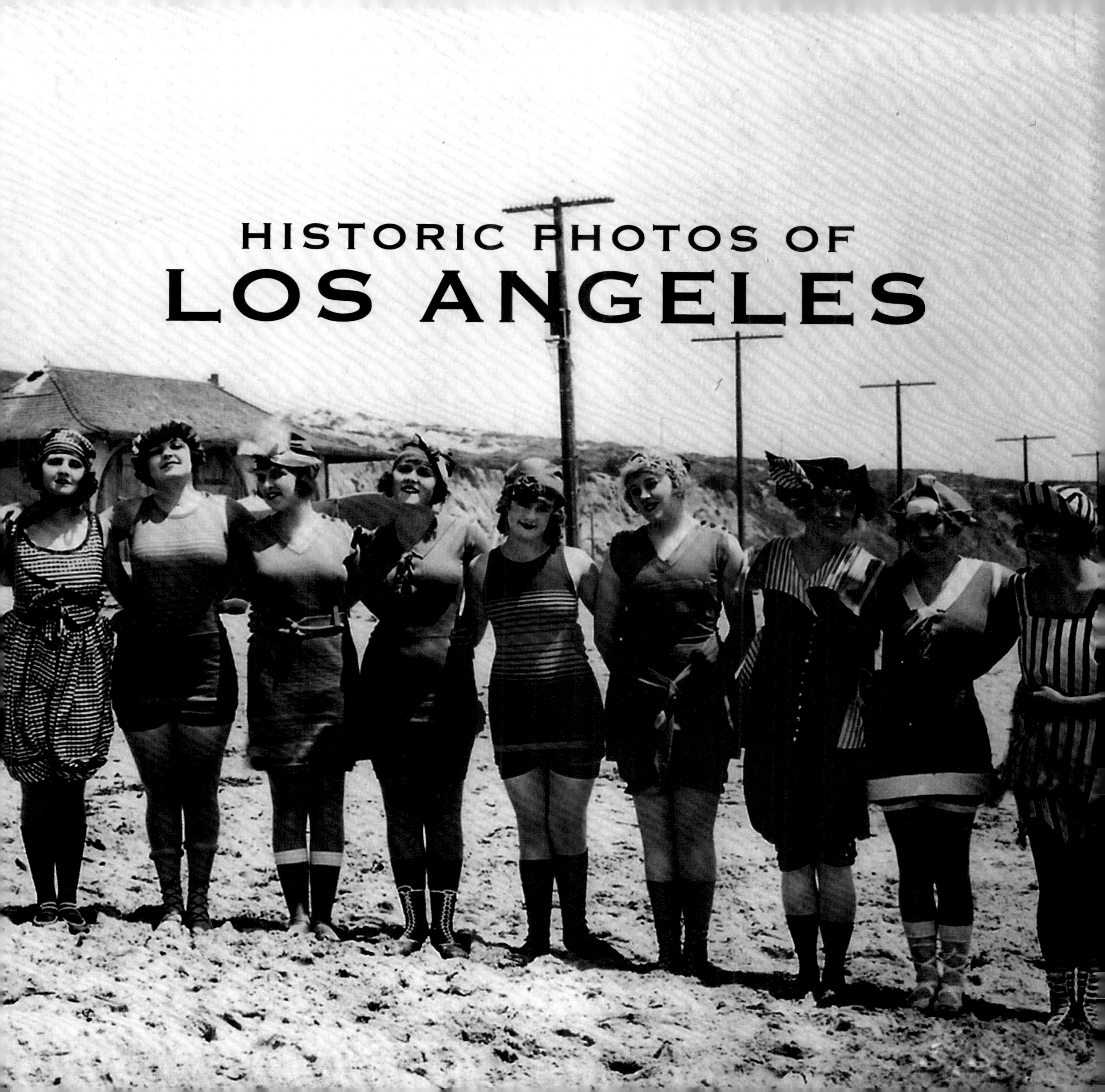

Turner Publishing Company
200 4th Avenue North • Suite 950
Nashville, Tennessee 37219
(615) 255-2665

www.turnerpublishing.com

Historic Photos of Los Angeles

Library of Congress Control Number: 2007929596

ISBN: 978-1-59652-374-6

Printed in China

09 10 11 12 13 14 15—0 9 8 7 6 5 4 3

Contents

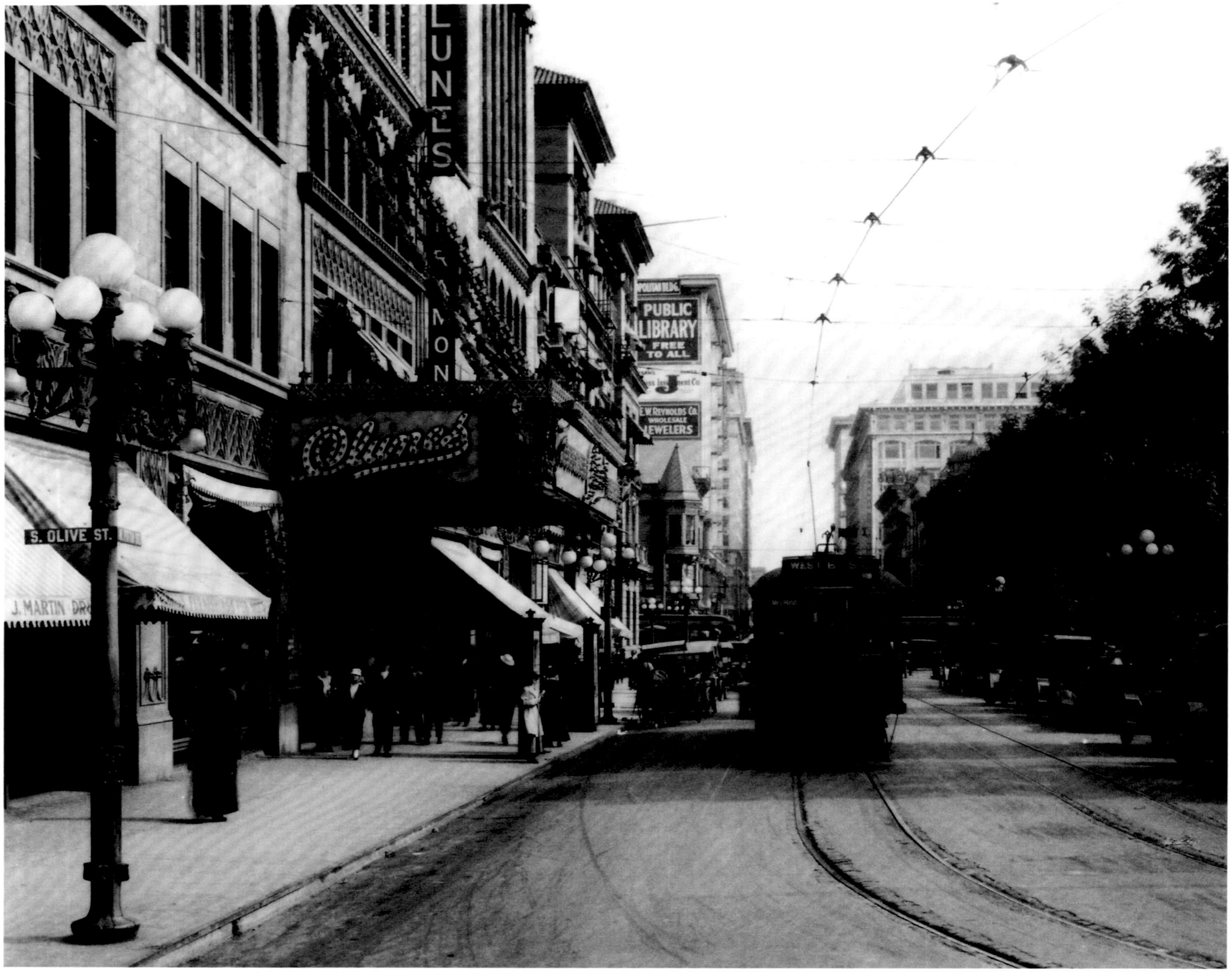

Fifth Street in Los Angeles. Harris Newmark (1834–1916), one of L.A.'s entrepreneurs and philanthropists, wrote about advertising excesses during one of the early real estate booms in his *Sixty Years in Southern California, 1853-1913,* published in 1916: "If every conceivable trick in advertising was not resorted to, it was probably due to oversight."

Acknowledgments

With the exception of cropping images where needed and touching up imperfections that have accrued over time, no other changes have been made to the photographs in this volume. The caliber and clarity of many photographs are limited by the technology of the day and the ability of the photographer at the time they were made.

This volume, *Historic Photos of Los Angeles,* is the result of the cooperation and efforts of many individuals, organizations, and corporations. It is with great thanks that we acknowledge the valuable contribution of the following for their generous support:

The Bancroft Library, University of California, Berkeley
Korean Heritage Library, University of Southern California
Library of Congress
Los Angeles Public Library
National Archives
Southern California Library for Social Studies and Research
University of Southern California, USC Special Collections

We would also like to thank the following individuals for valuable contributions and assistance in making this work possible:

Michael Hanlon
Bill Jaffe
Howie Muir

This book is a tribute to my family and memories of Los Angeles. Most important, it is for Anne and Iggy, who help me chase my dreams. —*Dana Lombardy*

PREFACE

I grew up in Southern California. My immediate and extended family lived in various Los Angeles and San Diego suburbs, and many family members still live in both cities. Every time I return I look forward to sampling the tremendous variety of great restaurants. Although I can still navigate the familiar freeways and main streets of L.A., each subsequent visit seems to require more and more time to travel from one part of town to another, due to the continuing increase in traffic on those highways.

When the opportunity was presented to write this book, I wondered what might be possible for the text beyond a collection of captions for a broad selection of old photos. Was it possible to write a story about L.A. through the presentation of these sometimes unrelated pictures? I considered it a challenge.

In this book you will read about how the phenomenal growth of Los Angeles occurred, transforming a desert into a dynamic metropolitan super-city. From the 1910s on, there are regular reminders of the city's movie industry and entertainment celebrities, plus examples of L.A.'s tradition of architectural experimentation. These are all things for which Los Angeles is world famous.

The notorious side of L.A., the corruption and crime that accompanied this rapid growth, is also presented in words and photos. The disasters—both natural such as earthquakes, and man-made such as the race riots—can also be found in this volume.

What you won't see in this book is a nostalgic tribute to a beloved city. People will readily recognize songs like "California Girls" and "California Dreamin'," but after "Hooray for Hollywood" appeared in 1937, no song specifically about Los Angeles attained the status of a popular standard, as occurred for San Francisco, Chicago, and New York. This seems a bit odd, considering that Los Angeles (Hollywood, actually) claims to be "the entertainment capital of the world." Most of the nice things about L.A., such as the beaches, gorgeous sunsets, and beautiful weather, are often qualified or counterbalanced with a disparaging remark by critics about some negative aspect of the city—traffic congestion, poor or nonexistent urban planning, air pollution, and so on.

The "City of the Angels" may be the most maligned large city in America—at least in the descriptions of many literary and sociological sources. Other big American cities also suffer from corruption, crime, and areas of urban decay. However, in L.A. these problems seem exacerbated by the perceived hypocritical and phony social façade and relentless promotion, or "hype," of Hollywood specifically and Los Angeles in general.

I did not intend to write a controversial book about Los Angeles. However, the recurring negativity about L.A. in the twentieth century is readily apparent from the magnitude of critical opinions and disdain in the writing of the famous, the talented, and the influential. To ignore this would present an incomplete picture of Los Angeles.

Perhaps this negativity stems from the disappointment that follows high expectations. Los Angeles attracts dreamers as well as schemers. Angelenos love their sunshine, beaches, movies, celebrities, cars, and freeways. These icons of L.A. and the sometimes less than successful interaction between nature, civilization, and various groups of people in the city's sprawling vastness inspired a diverse collection of writers. These writers' words, and the photos in this book, combine to create a fascinating, if not always favorable, portrait of America's second largest city.

—Dana Lombardy, Author

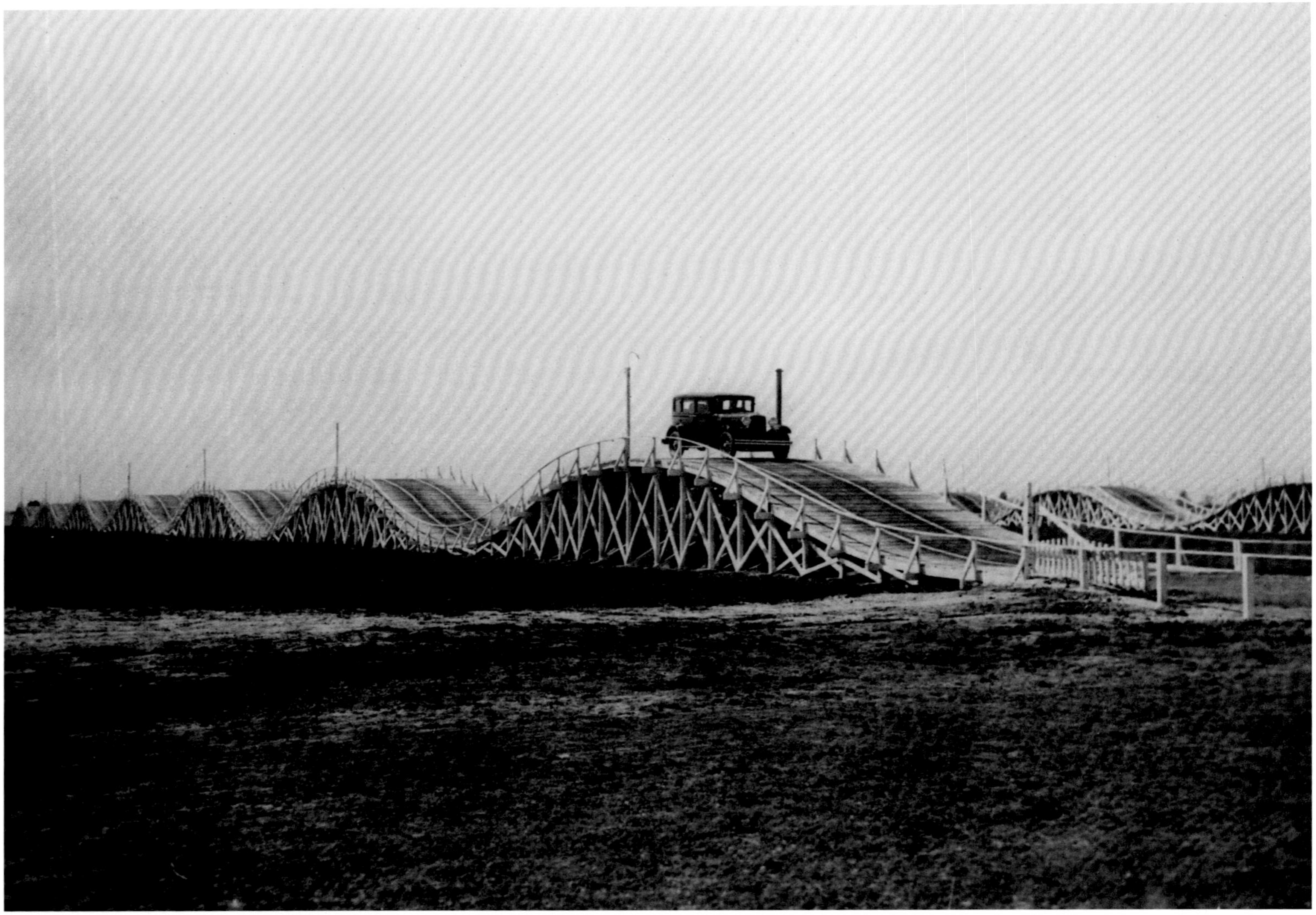

Americans went crazy for their cars in the 1920s. This is an unusual automobile course at Los Angeles photographed by a visiting French team for World Wide Photos. Architect Frank Lloyd Wright (1867–1959), for one, embraced the automobile as a revolutionary, liberating force. Wright built several houses in the Los Angeles area, including the Hollyhock House in Hollywood and the shops at Anderton Court in Beverly Hills.

A Sleepy Pueblo Becomes an American Town

(1870–1899)

The area that became known as California was first sighted by Spanish navigator Juan Rodríguez Cabrillo in 1542, and was named for a mythical land described in a popular Spanish novel by Garcia Ordóñez de Montalvo. California's first Spanish mission, at San Diego, was established in 1769.

In 1781 a British army surrendered at Yorktown, Virginia, an event that led to the independence of the American colonies. That same year Los Angeles was founded by Spanish governor Felipe de Neve as El Pueblo de Nuestra Señora la Reina de los Ángeles de Porciúncula (the Village of Our Lady, the Queen of the Angels of Porciúncula). California, and the small village of los Ángeles, became part of Mexico in 1821 following its war of independence against Spain.

California was first inhabited by various Indian tribes, then seized by Spanish conquistadors, then conquered again by United States military forces in 1847. At the end of the Mexican-American War, in 1848, Los Angeles and California became part of the United States. On January 24, 1848, James W. Marshall discovered gold at Sutter's Mill, starting the California gold rush that attracted settlers to the state in large numbers.

Five months before California achieved statehood in 1850, Los Angeles was incorporated as an American municipality. In the 1850 U.S. census, the L.A. population of 1,610 was mostly Mexican. Twenty years later, as the first bridge was built over the Los Angeles River, the population had only grown to 5,728, compared to San Francisco's 149,473.

Among the reasons for this disparity in size were that the Spanish founded Los Angeles in the middle of an empty, semi-arid coastal plain that had no suitable harbor (unlike San Francisco and San Diego) and that L.A. depended on an unnavigable river that suffered through droughts and flooding. Northern California also had the lure of gold.

The situation of Los Angeles as a backwater small town eventually started to change. The first railroad line to reach L.A., the Southern Pacific, arrived by 1876. The Santa Fe Railway followed in 1885. Tens of thousands of acres of open land attracted a new wave of settlers to California. Los Angeles was poised for its first big population explosion.

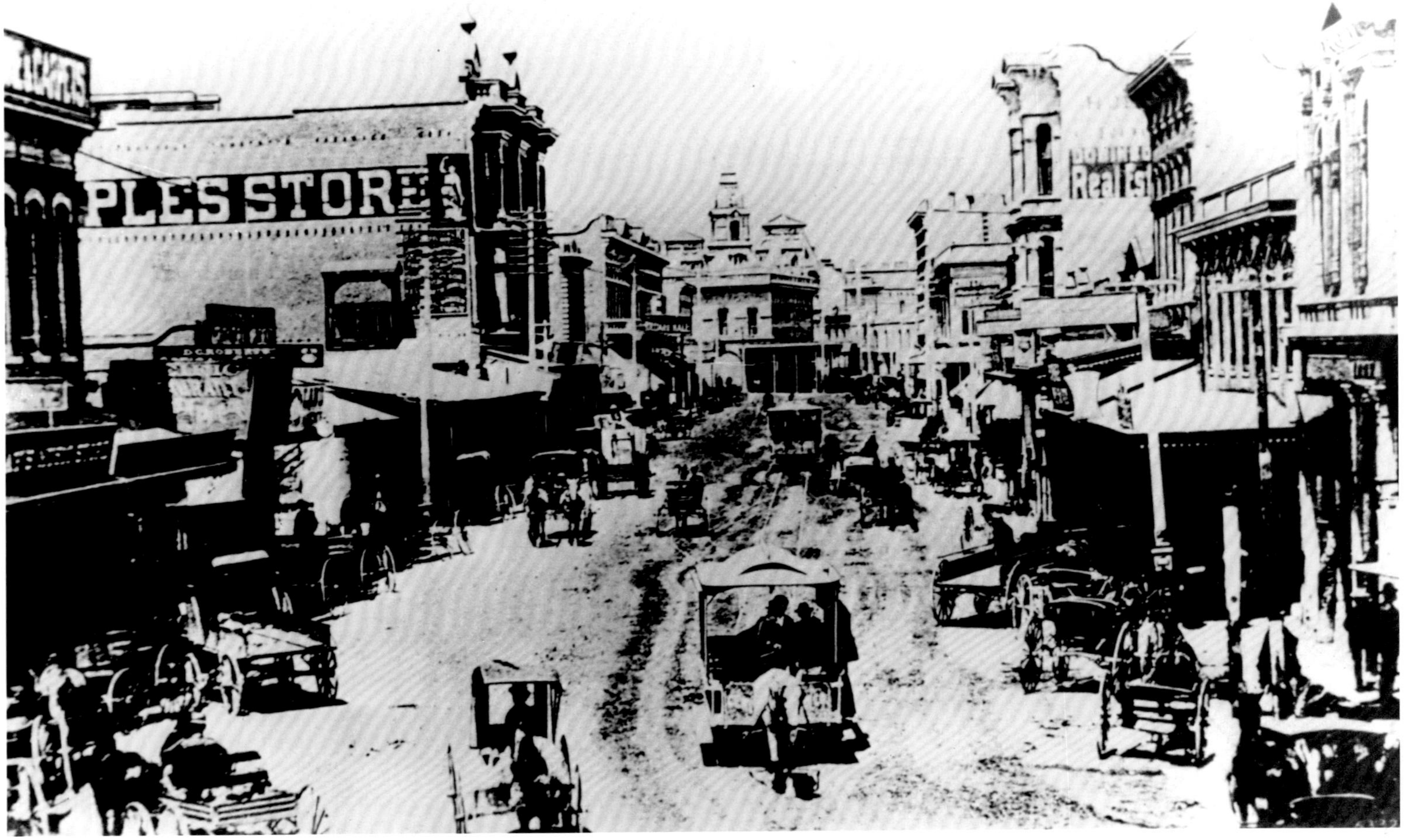

In 1879, Los Angeles was a small frontier town of unpaved roads, horse-drawn carriages, and about 11,000 people.

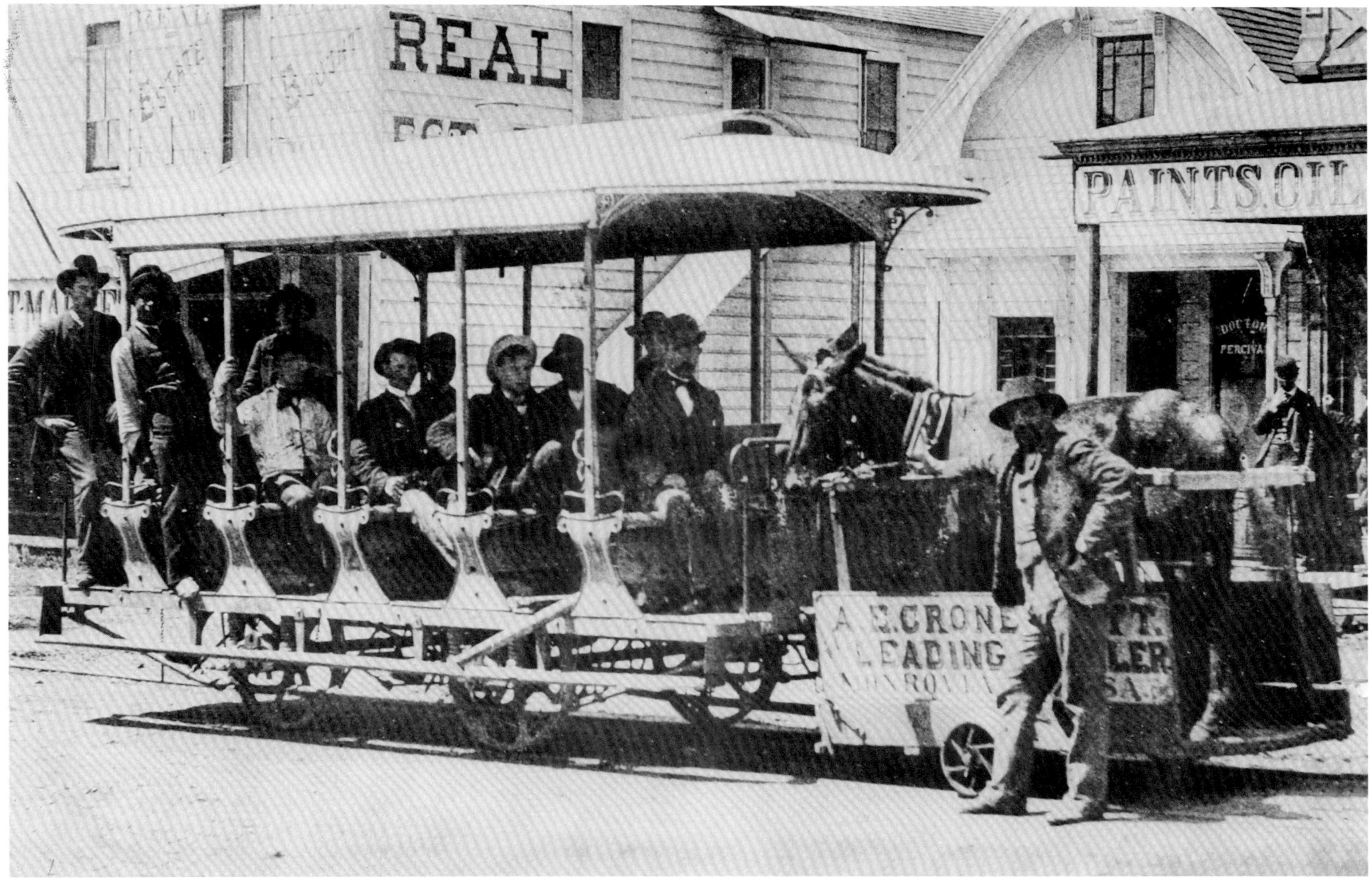

This is the first Los Angeles streetcar. By 1877 L.A. had a horse-drawn car line that was the city's "interurban" rail system.

An early photo of the Wolfskill Orange Grove, Los Angeles. The Washington navel orange was first brought to the L.A. area in 1873, and this variety helped develop California's citrus industry.

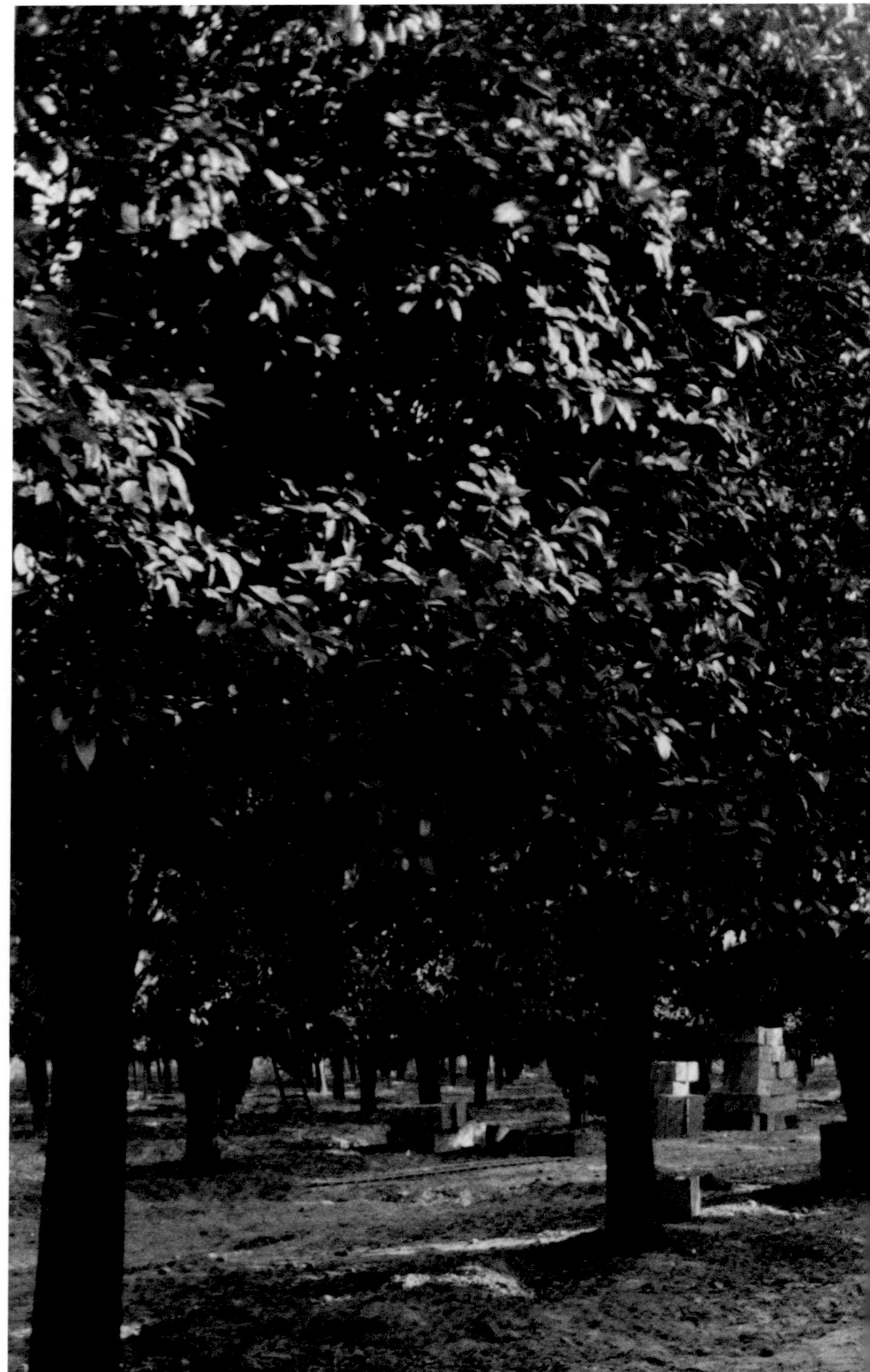

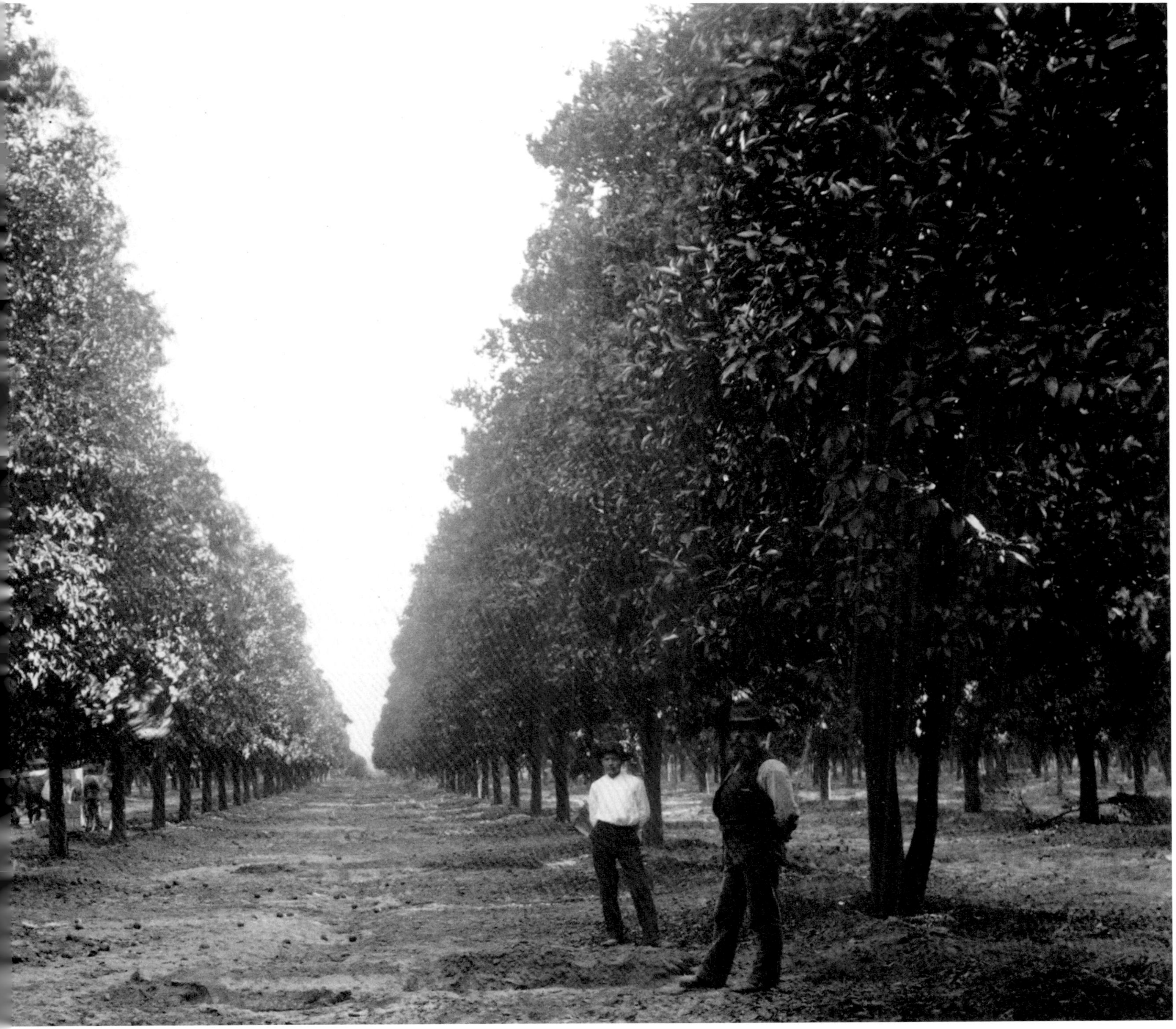

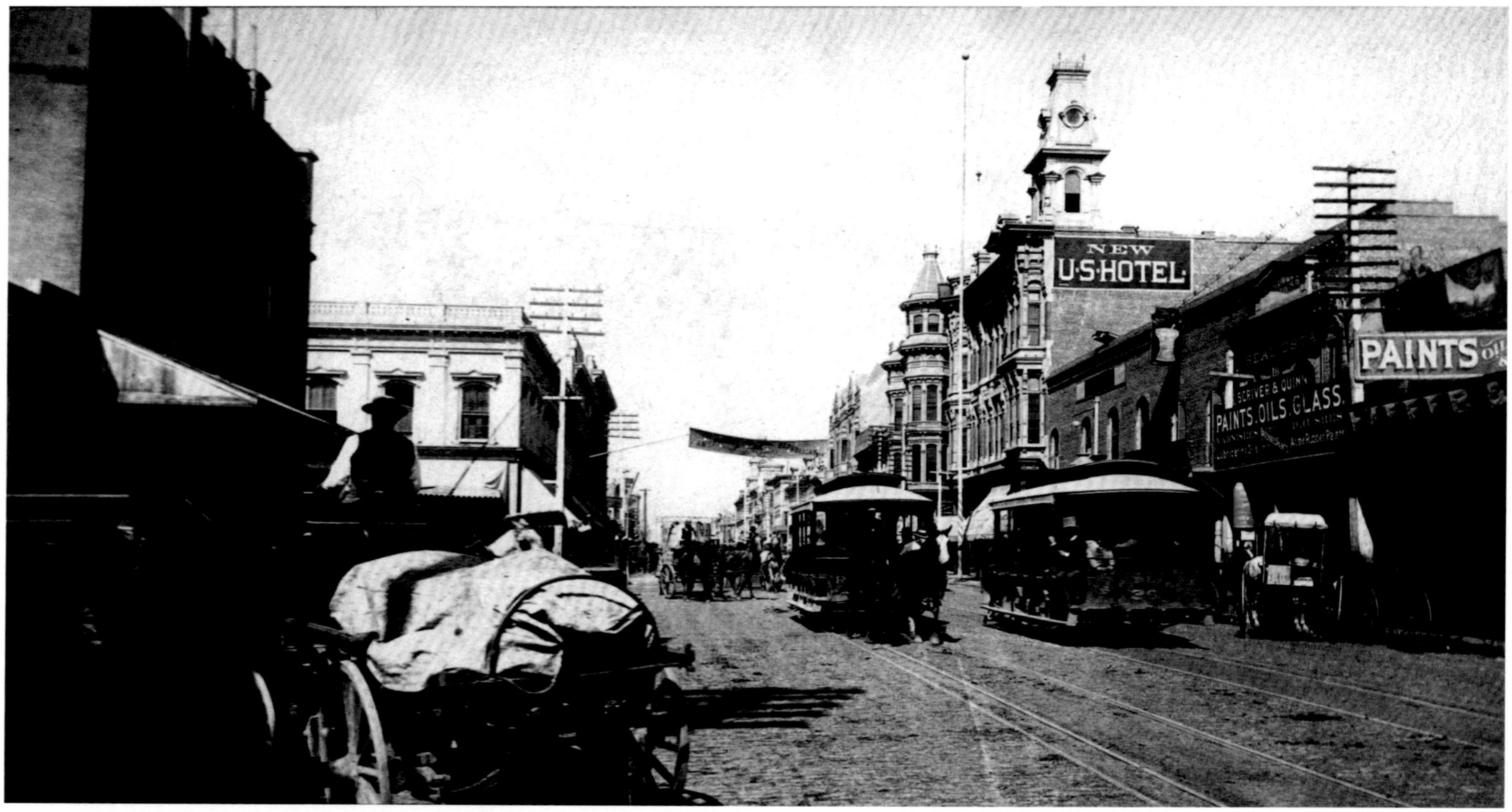

Main and Requena streets in the 1880s. Helen Hunt Jackson (1830–1885), activist for Native Americans, visited Los Angeles and wrote about the early history of the city in her story "Echoes in the City of the Angels" that appeared in the *Century* magazine in 1883: "Greedy traders from all parts of the world added their rivalries and interventions to the civil and military disputation." Her opinion was that the Indians, Spanish, and Mexicans were robbed of their lands, expressed in her famous novel *Ramona,* published in 1884. Jackson prepared a report that called for massive government aid. A bill incorporating her advice passed the Senate but died in the House of Representatives.

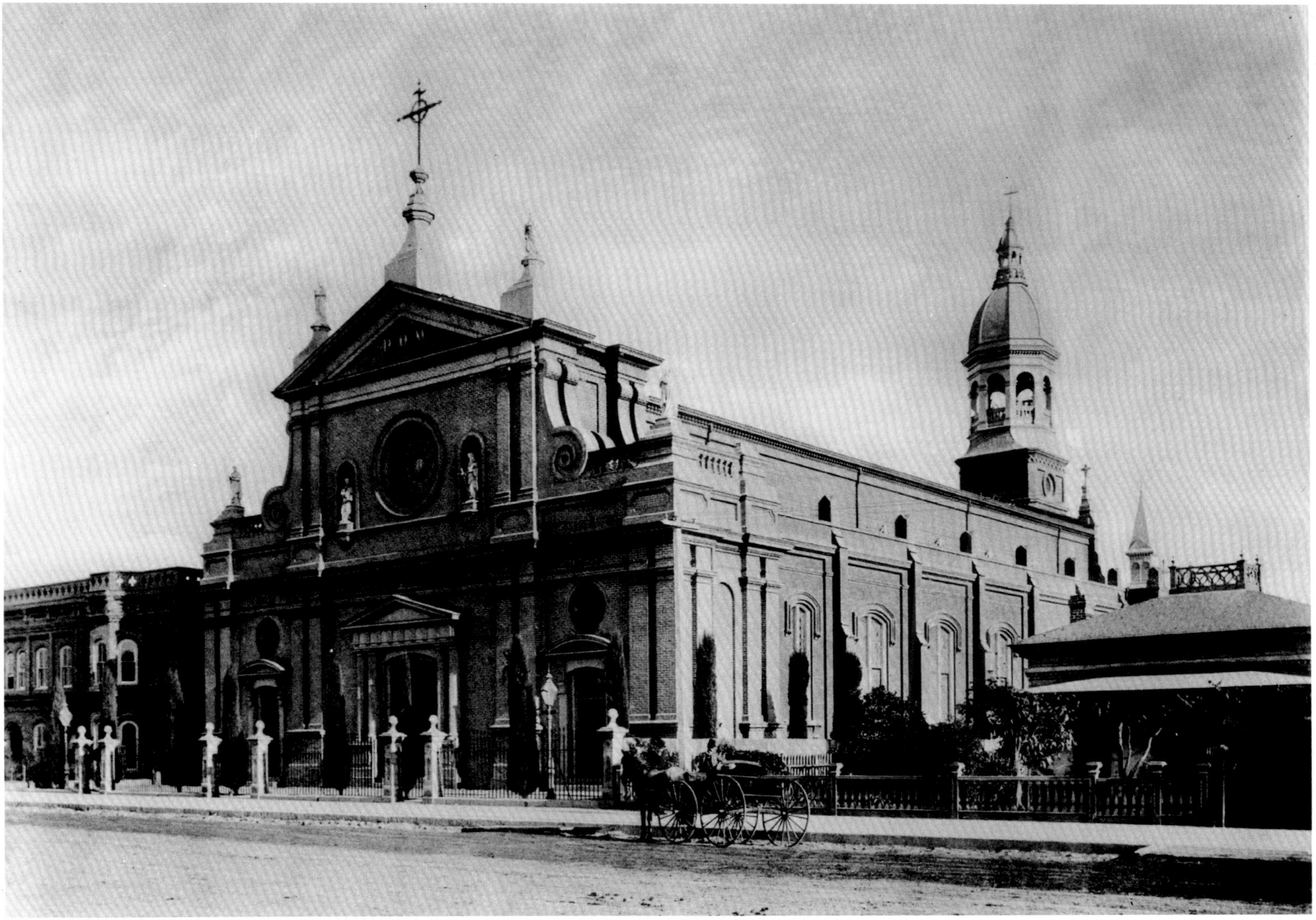

St. Vibiana's Catholic Cathedral, located at Second and Main streets in Los Angeles, was dedicated in 1876. As of 2008 it is the seat of the Los Angeles Archdiocese.

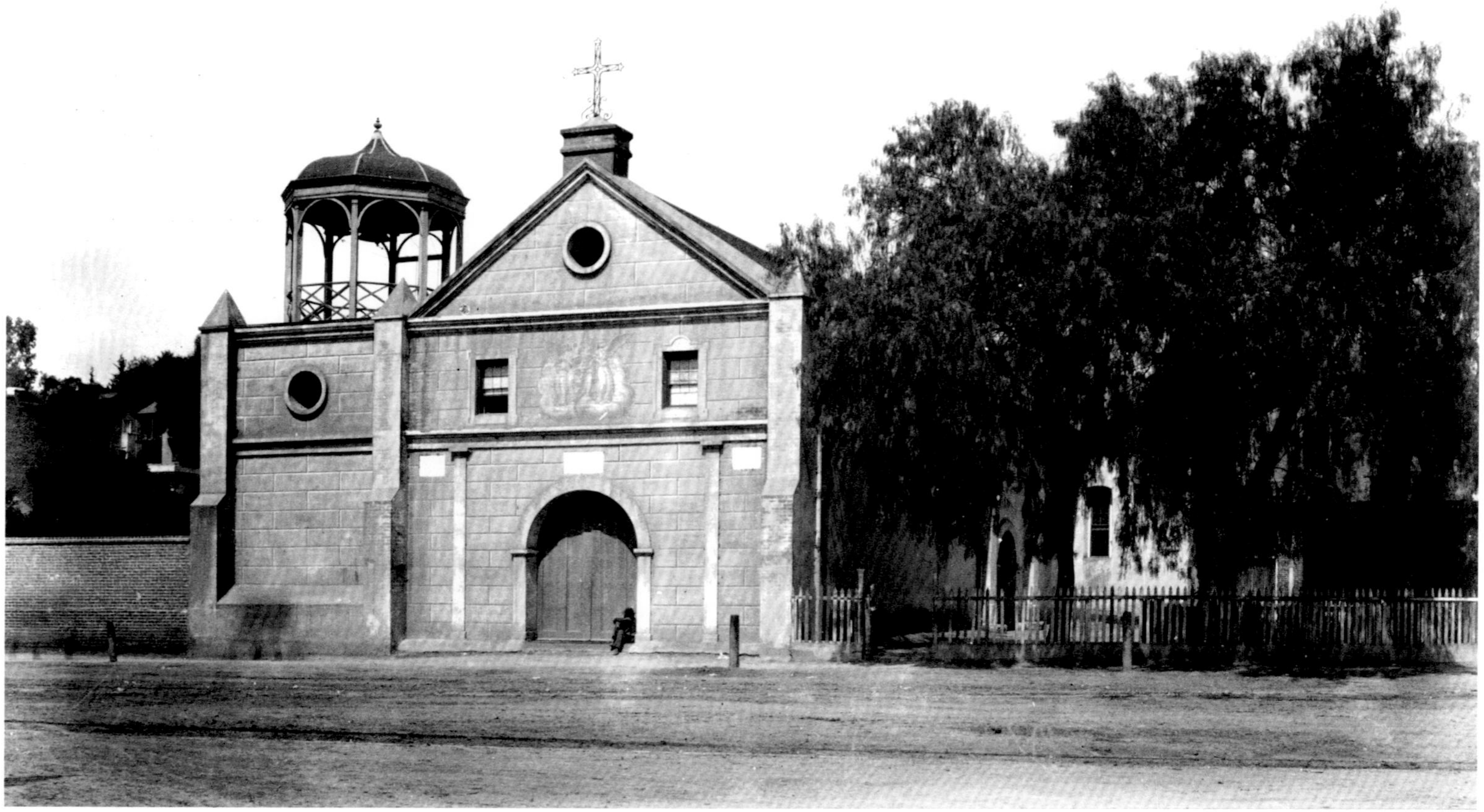

The Church of Our Lady of the Angels was built in 1821, the year that Mexico won its independence from Spain. It is the oldest building in Los Angeles.

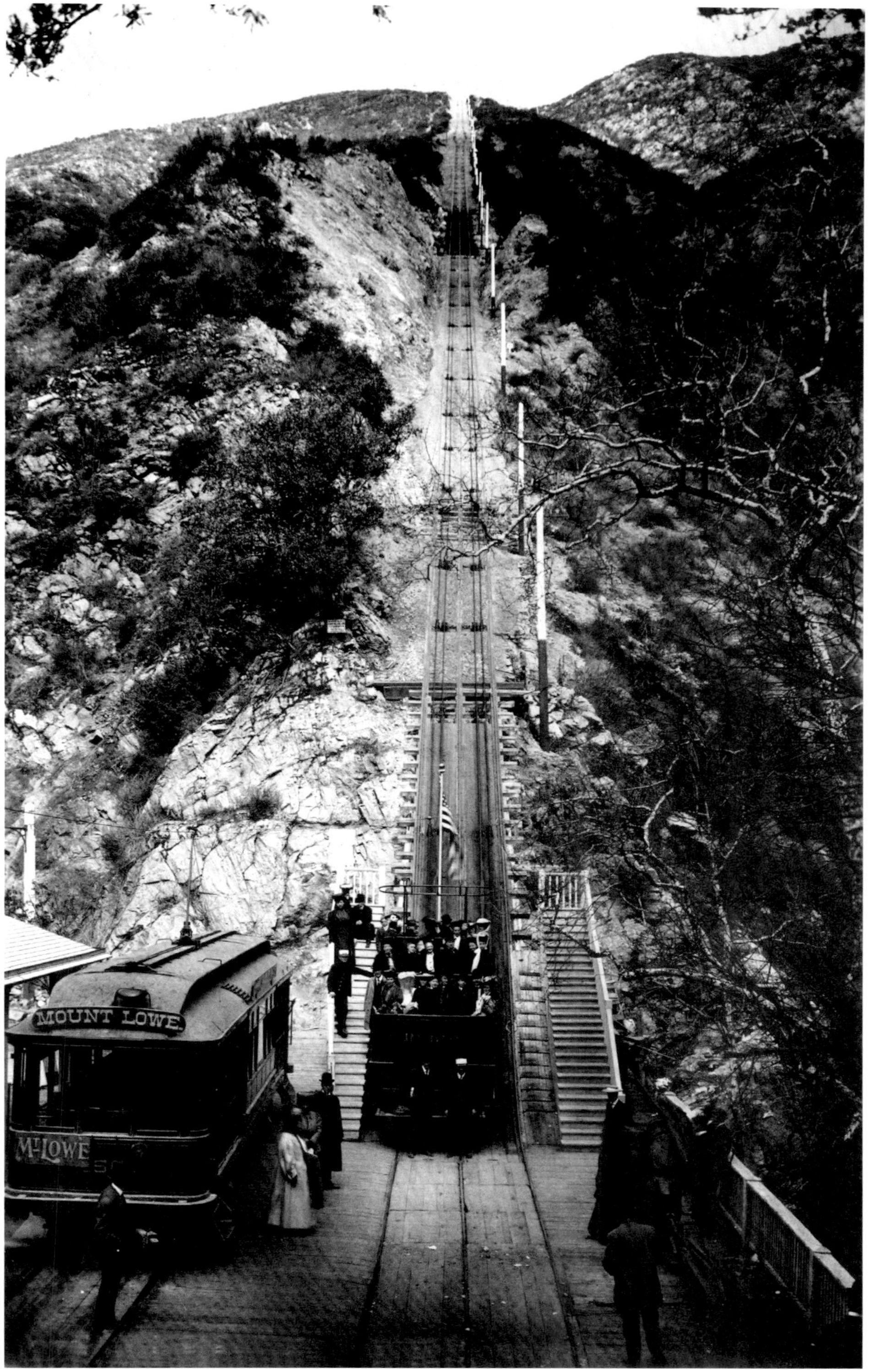

A Pacific Electric interurban car connects with the 3,000-foot Mount Lowe incline around the turn of the century. In 1889, the Los Angeles Cable Railway opened with a line extending over the First Street Viaduct into Boyle Heights.

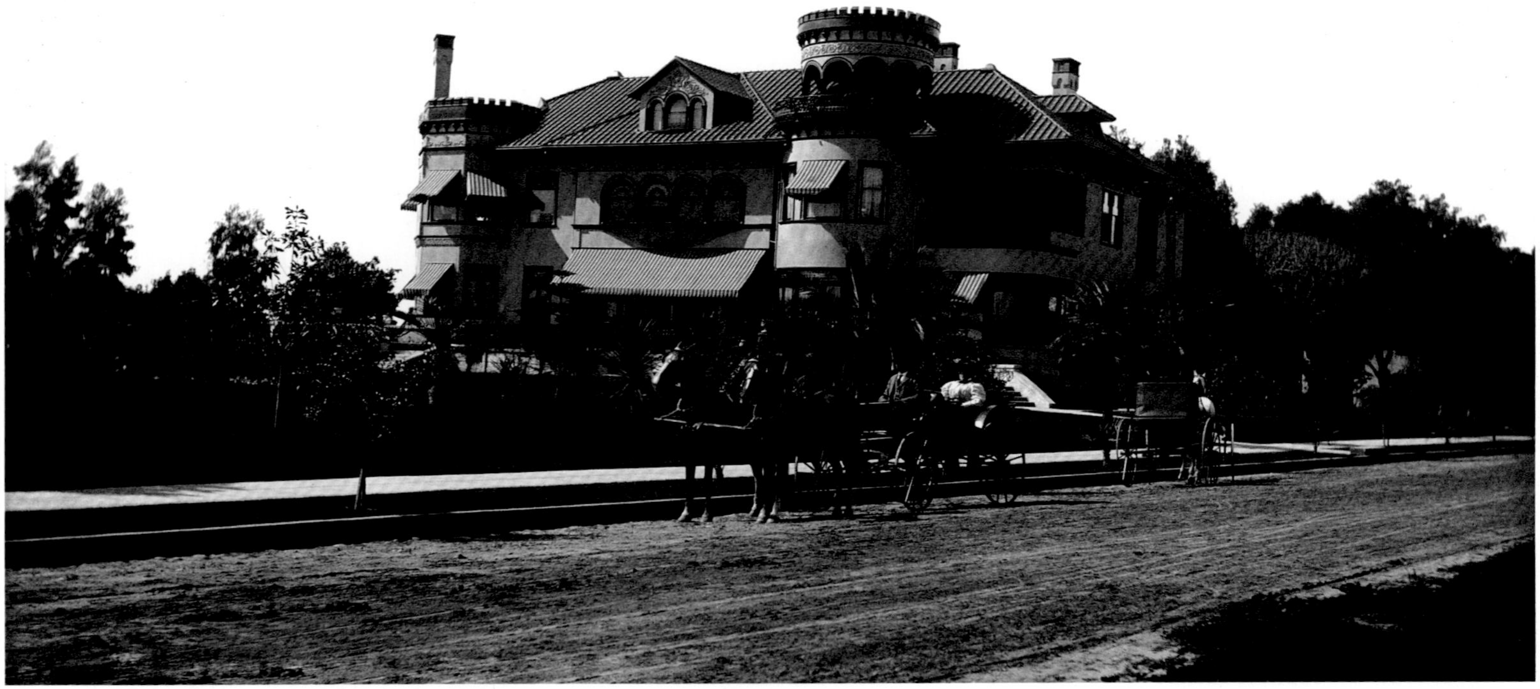

A stately Victorian mansion in L.A. features palm trees—a flora that became a famous Southern California trademark.

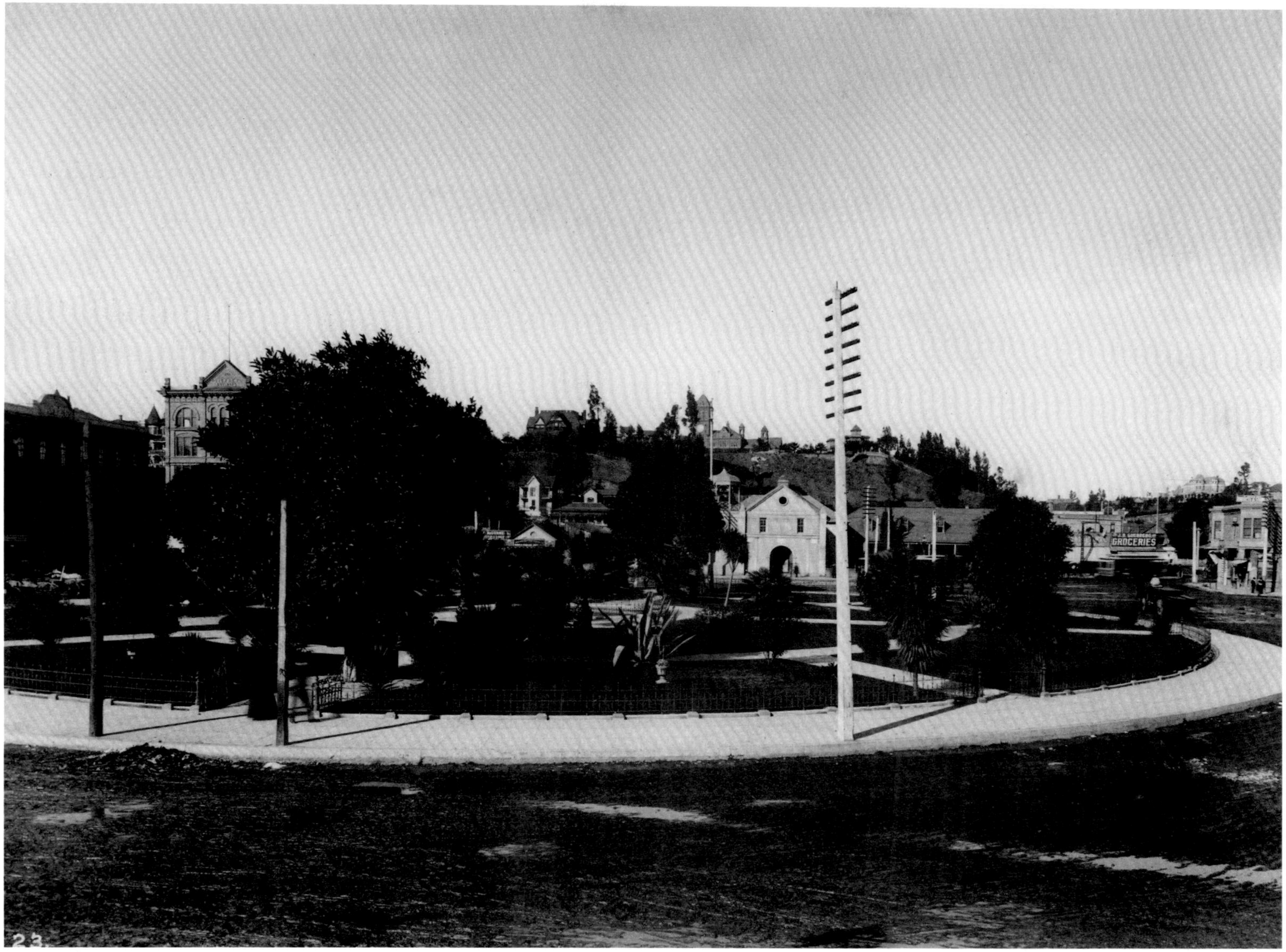

L.A.'s first park, seen here in 1890, was located in the center of Pueblo de los Angeles, founded by Spanish Governor Felipe de Neve in 1781. The park was later named Los Angeles Plaza.

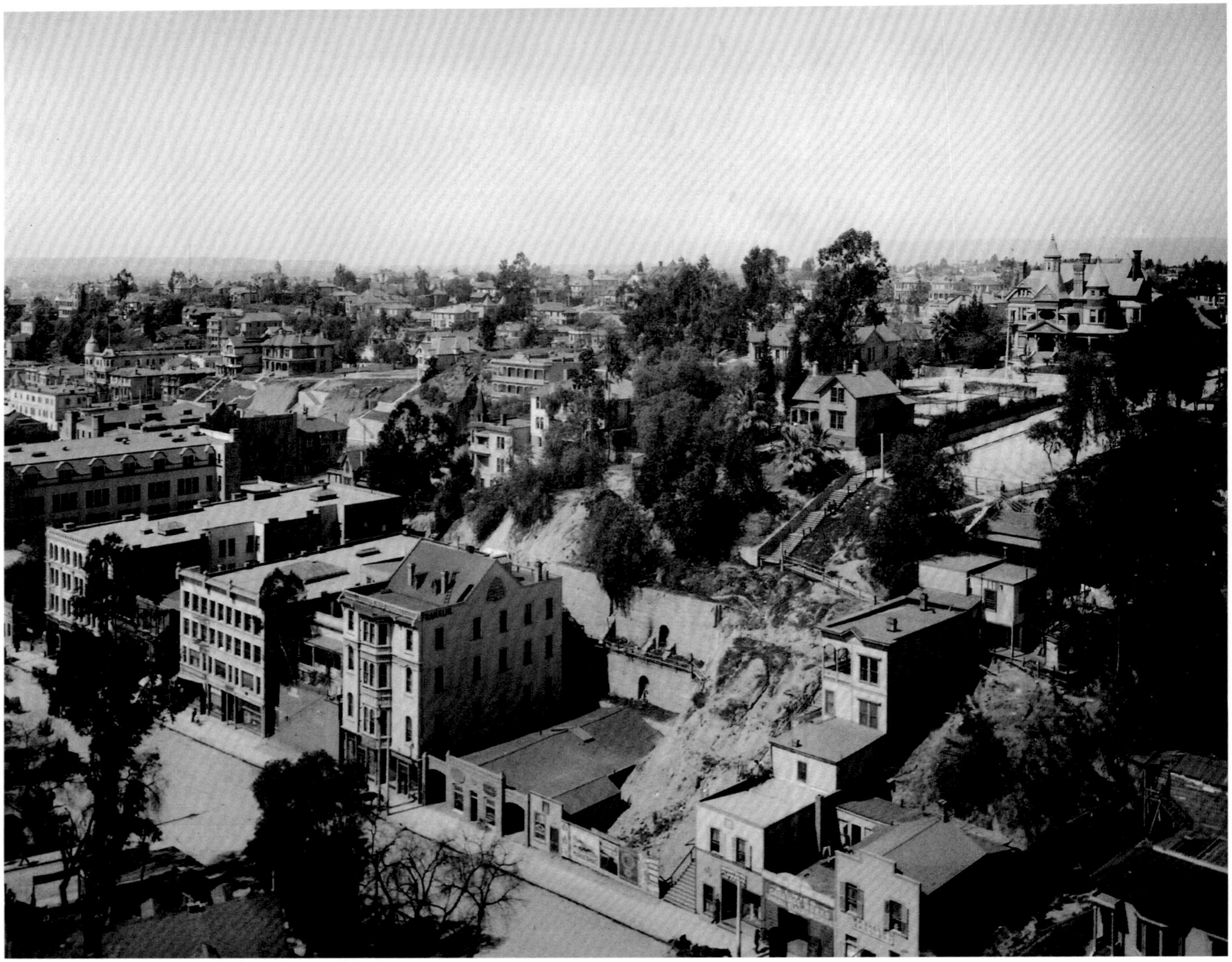

A general view of Los Angeles as it appeared in the late 1800s. Several hundred thousand Chinese immigrants arrived in California to work in the Northern California gold rush area or to help build the transcontinental rail line. Only 4,424 Chinese had settled in L.A. by 1890, since further immigration had been stopped by the Chinese Exclusion Act of 1882. Large-scale Chinese immigration did not occur again until after 1965. After the Chinese Exclusion Act took effect, Japanese immigrants were recruited to fill the need for cheap labor, and L.A. had a significant "Little Tokyo" area by the early 1900s.

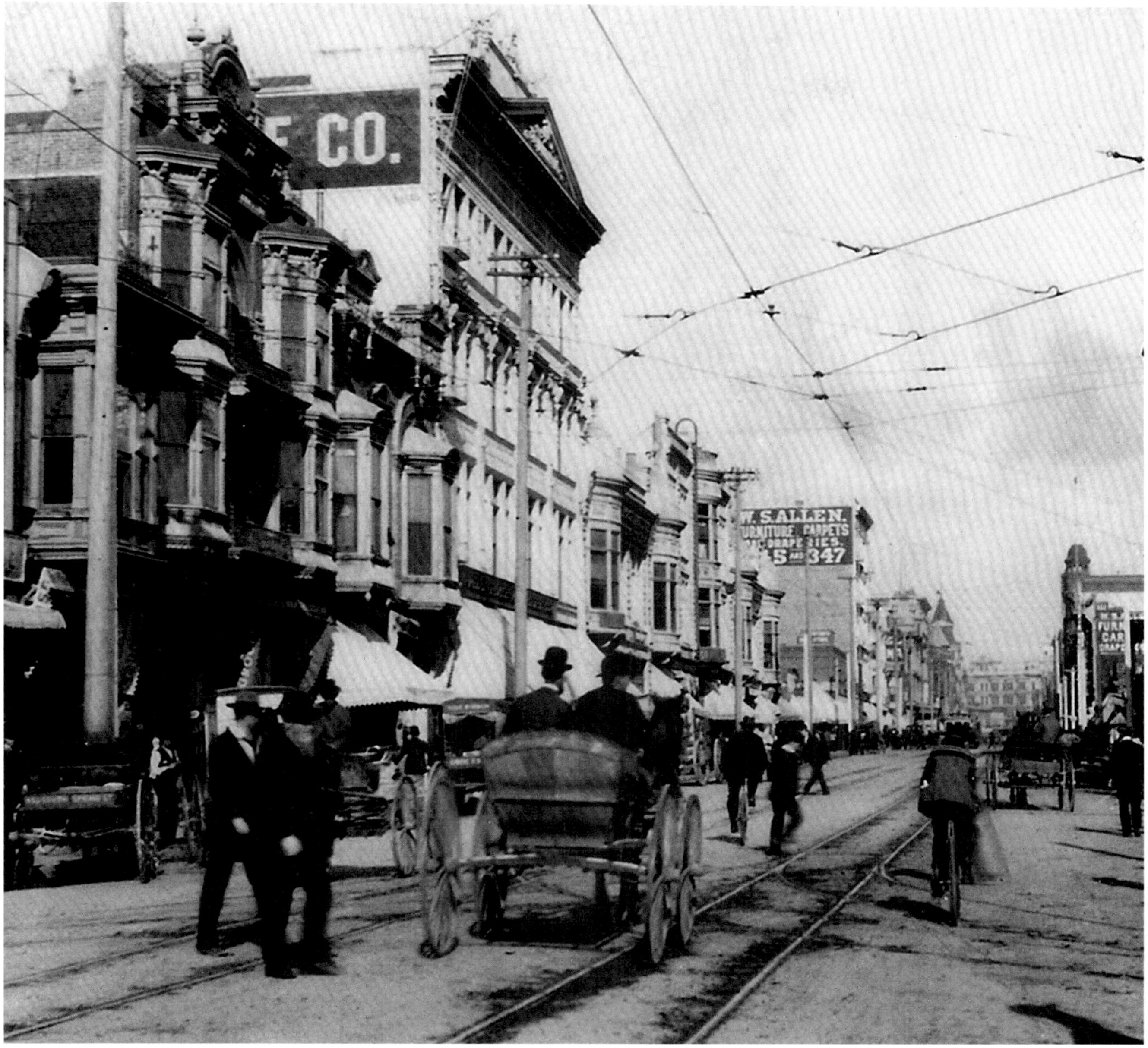

Spring Street in Los Angeles as it was shown on a stereo card intended to be viewed with a stereoscope to provide the illusion of a three-dimensional image. This technique of viewing photographs was very popular in the mid-1800s.

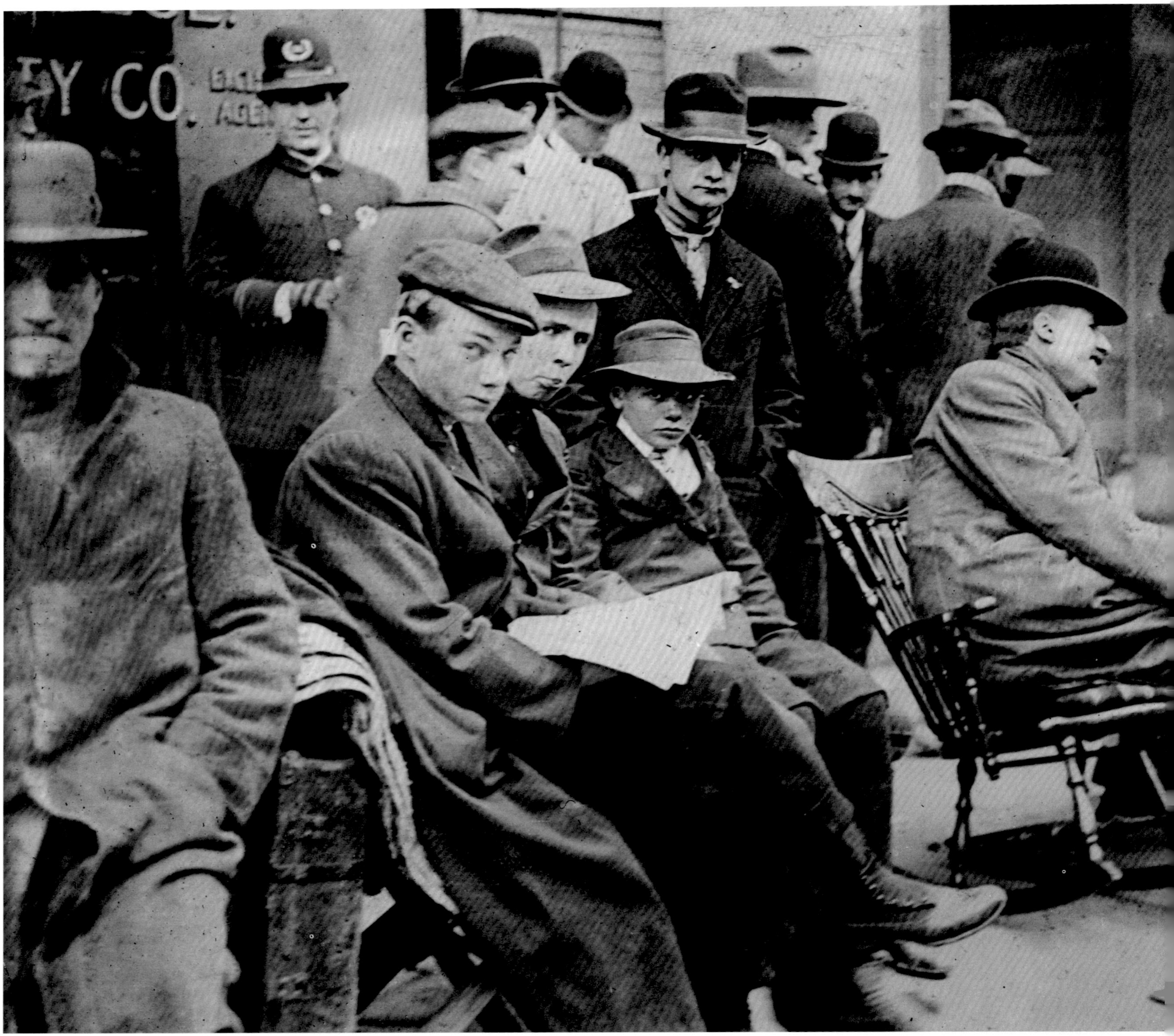

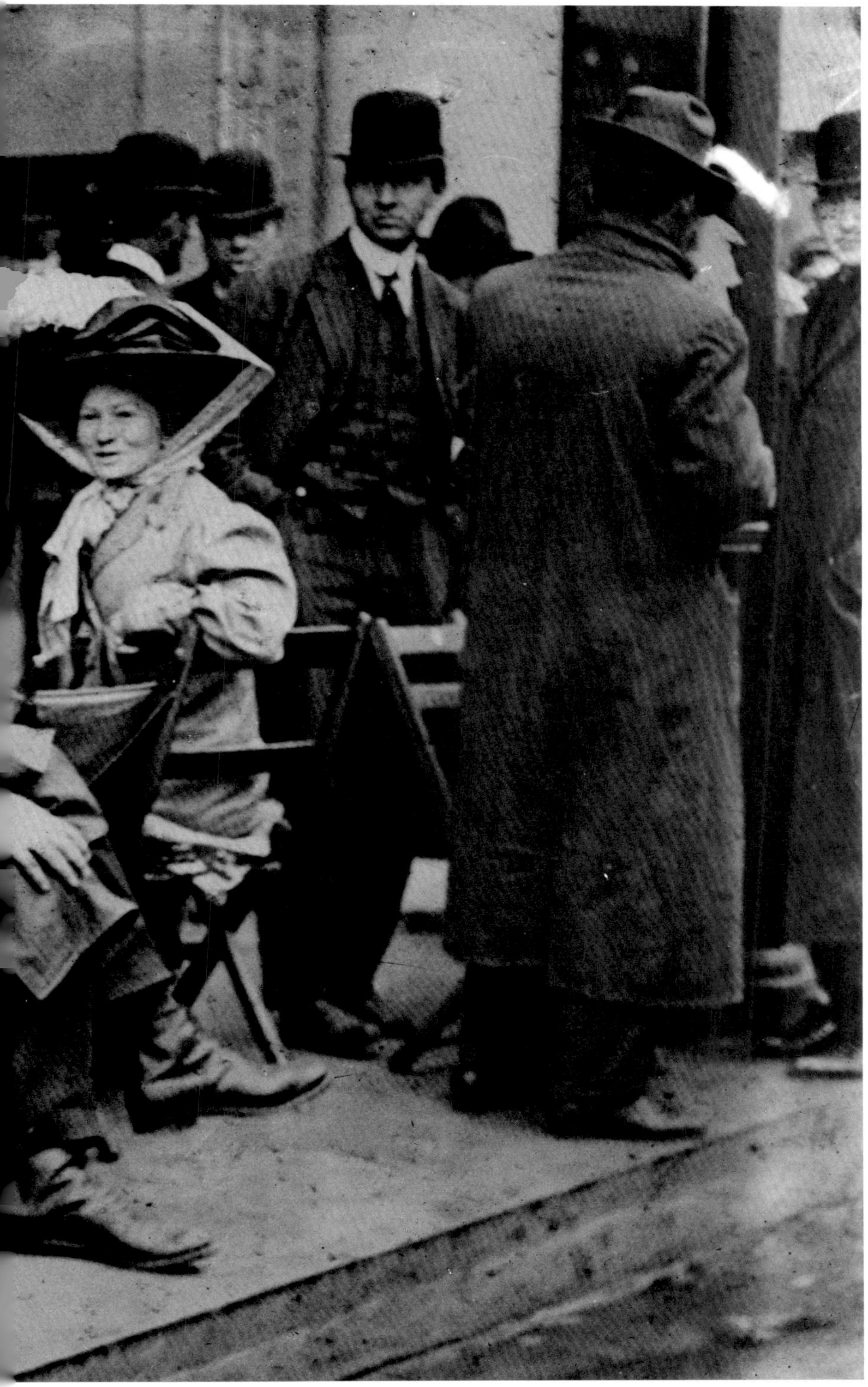

Some standing, some seated, people wait to file Yuma Land claims in Los Angeles, around 1900. Land runs or land rushes were events where previously restricted land of the United States was opened for homesteading on a first-come basis, or by lottery, or was sold by bid. The most famous of these was the Oklahoma Land Run of 1889, but others took place, including for areas seized from the Yuma Indian tribe in California and other states.

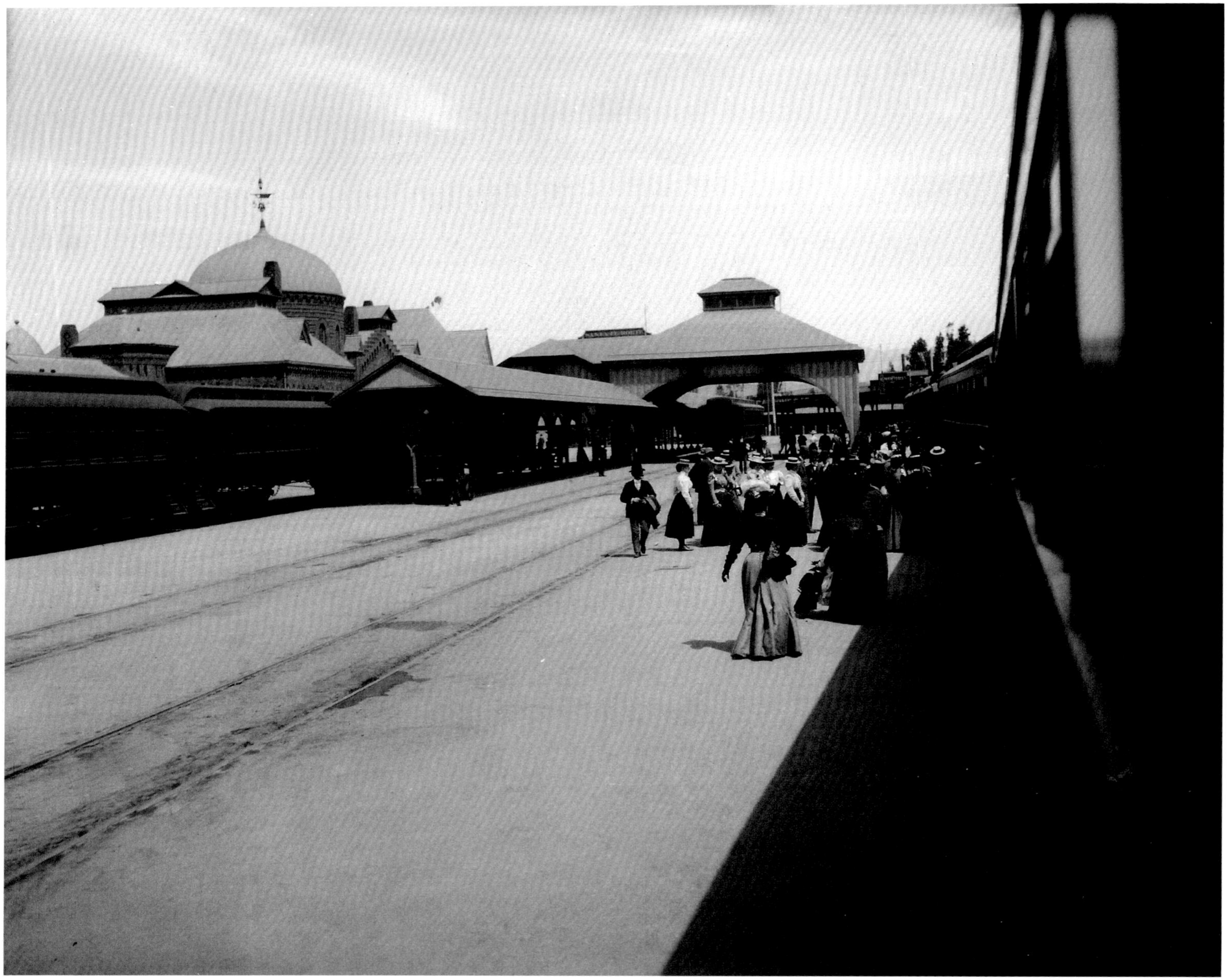

Travelers board the overland for departure from Los Angeles, around 1890. During this period, the arrival of the railroad lines dramatically transformed the city. In particular, the 1890s to 1920s were described by one sociologist as a "golden era" for African Americans in Los Angeles. Migrants from the South and Southwest found better opportunities for home-ownership and employment in parts of Los Angeles.

Defeating Rival San Diego for West Coast Dominance

(1900–1909)

The railroads brought thousands of people to Southern California, but it was not initially clear whether San Diego or L.A. would be the beneficiary. Business and political leaders in L.A. skillfully explained to Central Pacific railroad executives and San Francisco business interests that a rail line into L.A. did not jeopardize their dominance in Northern California. Instead of being an asset, San Diego's excellent harbor was presented as a potential threat to San Francisco's position on the coast. This lobbying succeeded in getting the Southern Pacific to construct branches to L.A. that gained the city an edge over San Diego that it never relinquished. By 1900, Los Angeles had more than 102,000 people, compared to San Diego's 17,700 residents.

The history of Los Angeles can be measured in its cycles of real estate booms (originally called "bubbles") that saw huge increases in population. The first bubble was in 1887, and during that decade L.A. grew from just over 11,000 to more than 50,000 residents. The 1906 boom was fed partly by the southern migration of survivors of the famous San Francisco Earthquake.

Many ethnic groups became part of the evolving cultural patchwork of Los Angeles. By 1904, the city saw an influx of Russian Molokans, a sect of the Russian Orthodox Church, who fled Russia to avoid persecution and military conscription during the Russo-Japanese War. At the same time, Japanese immigration also grew dramatically until halted by the Exclusion Act of 1924. The Workmen's Circle/Arbeiter Ring, a Yiddish cultural and political organization, established its Southern California headquarters in downtown L.A., where it served Jewish labor unionists and activists.

Regardless of which period of Los Angeles history is studied, one critical element is always prominent: water. The repeated real estate booms were not possible without it. Los Angeles Water received its franchise in 1868 and was the most successful company of its kind, capable of providing water to more than 300,000 people by the 1890s. In 1902 the city acquired the company and assumed sole responsibility for supplying water in L.A.

To secure additional water for the future, a study by Superintendent William Mulholland (1855–1935) concluded that an aqueduct from the Owens River, more than two hundred miles north, was feasible. Public land for the aqueduct was acquired with the help of President Theodore Roosevelt, and a 1907 bond issue passed by a ten-to-one vote. Los Angeles was preparing for phenomenal growth.

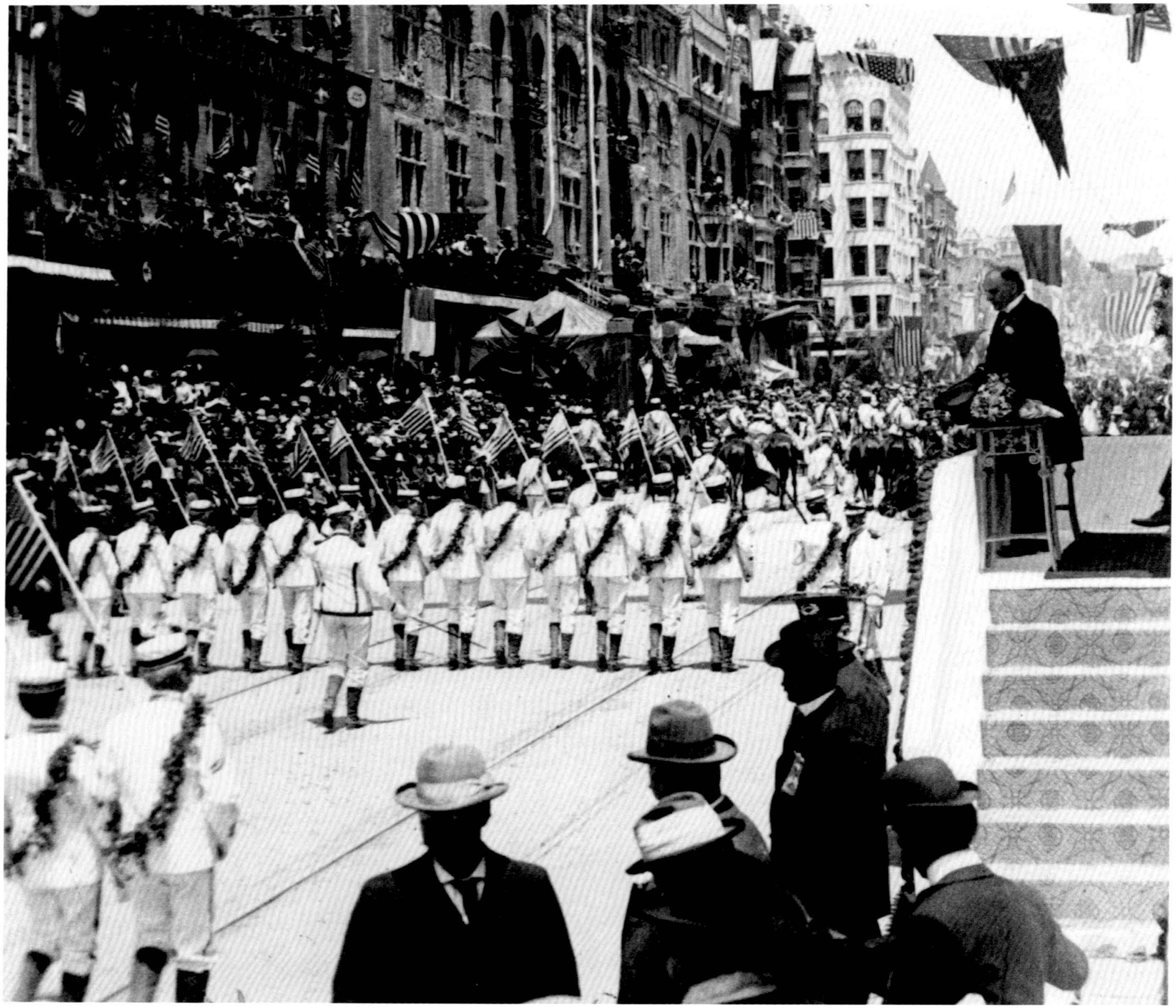

This is a stereo card photograph of a reception held in Los Angeles for the recently reelected President William McKinley. McKinley served one term as the twenty-fifth president of the United States, but before he could finish his second term he was assassinated by an anarchist in 1901. Vice-president Theodore Roosevelt succeeded him.

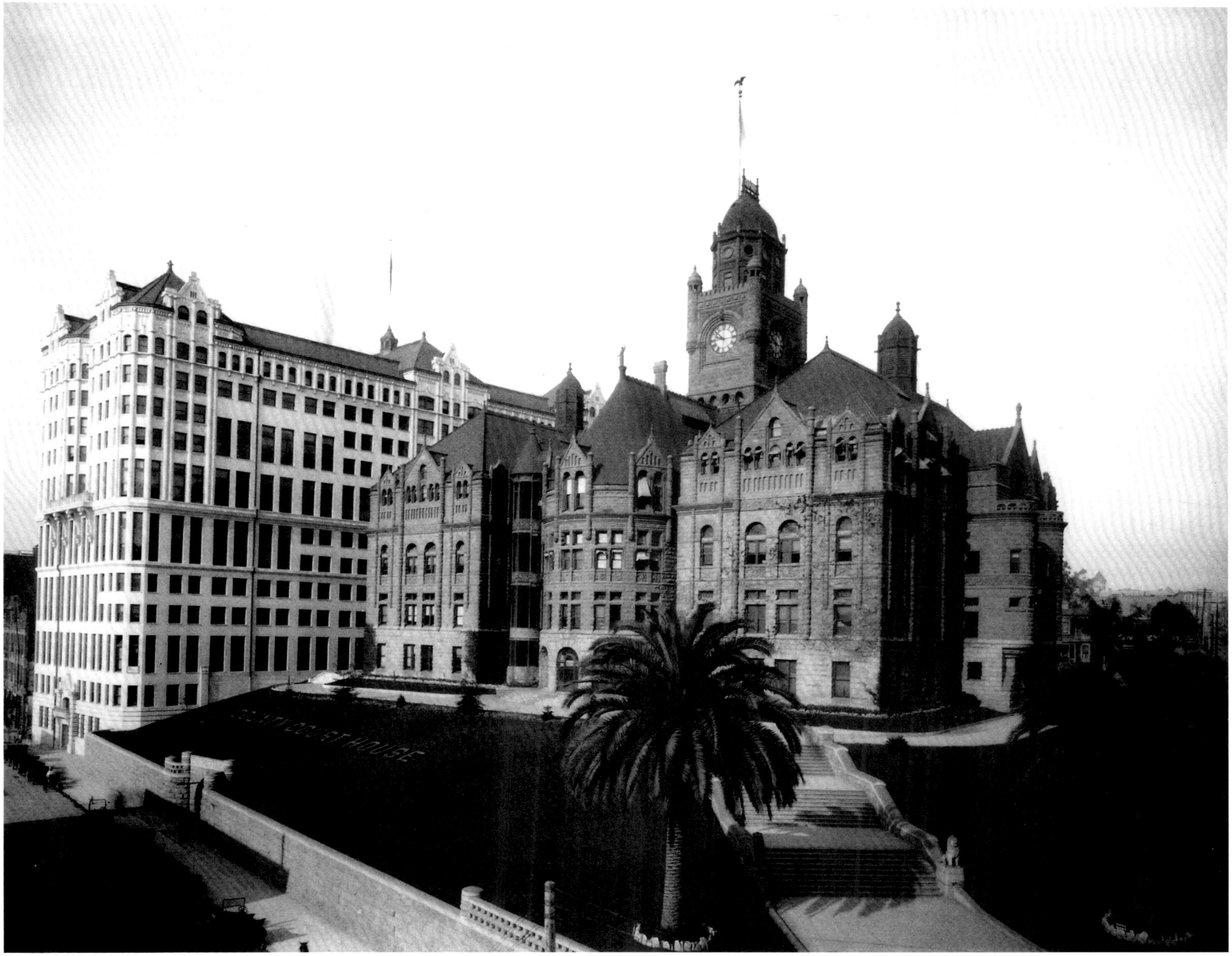

Los Angeles Court House and Hall of Records in the early twentieth century. L.A.'s drive to obtain more water for future growth was not always seen as positive. Mary Austin (1868–1934), writer and poet, described the conflict between developing a desert terrain and conserving diminishing water resources in her story "The Land" (1909). Austin lived in the Owens Valley where the "notorious" plan to divert water from the Owens River destroyed many farming communities.

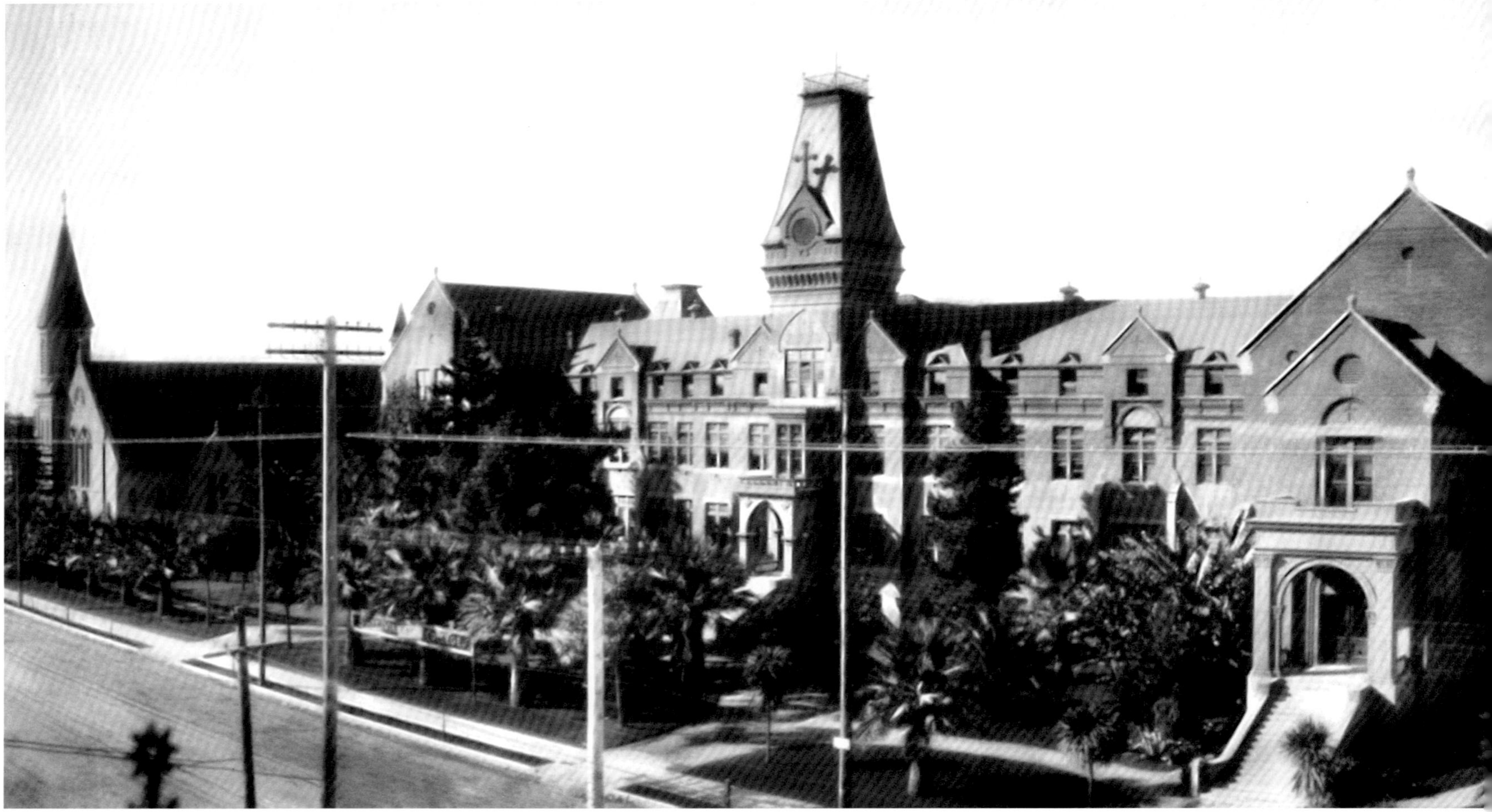

A panorama view of St. Vincent's College around 1908. The school was founded in Los Angeles in 1865 at the behest of the Roman Catholic Archdiocese Bishop Thaddeus Amat, a member of the Vincentian order. In 1917 the school moved and in 2008 was known as Loyola High School of Los Angeles, a Jesuit preparatory school for young men.

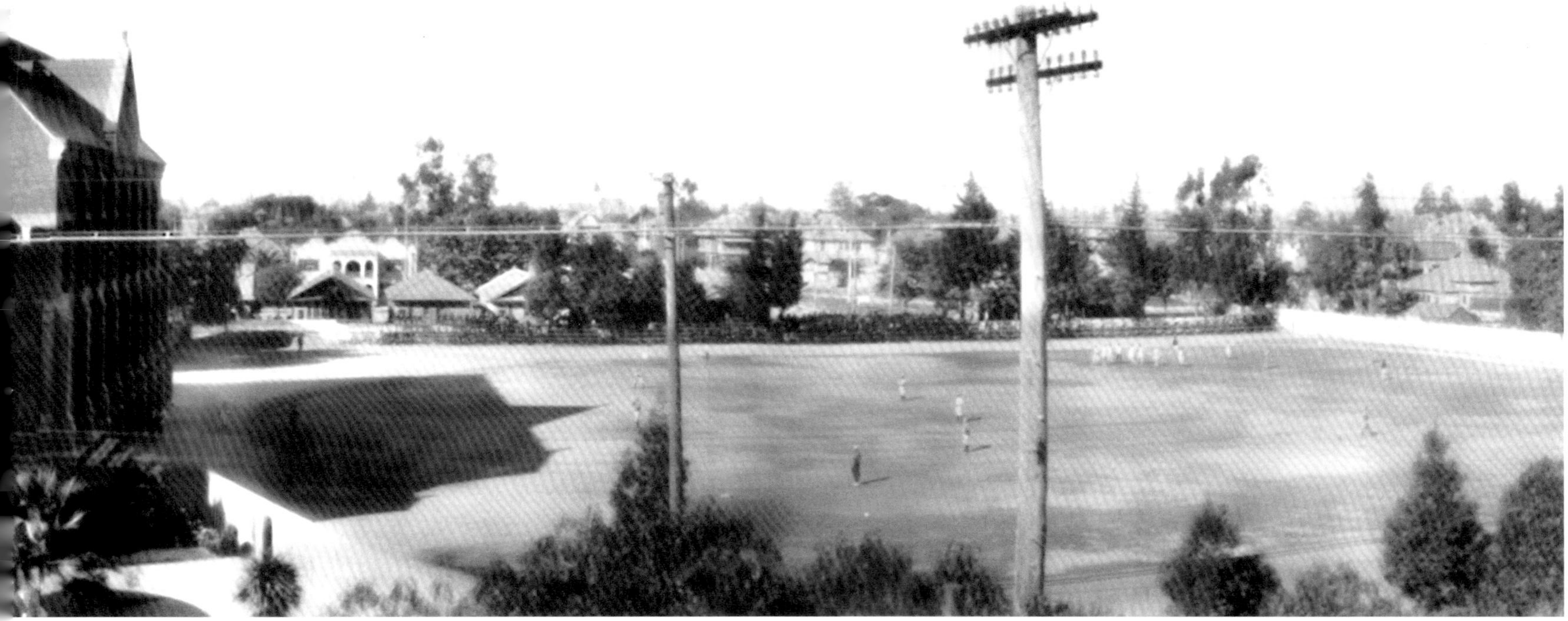

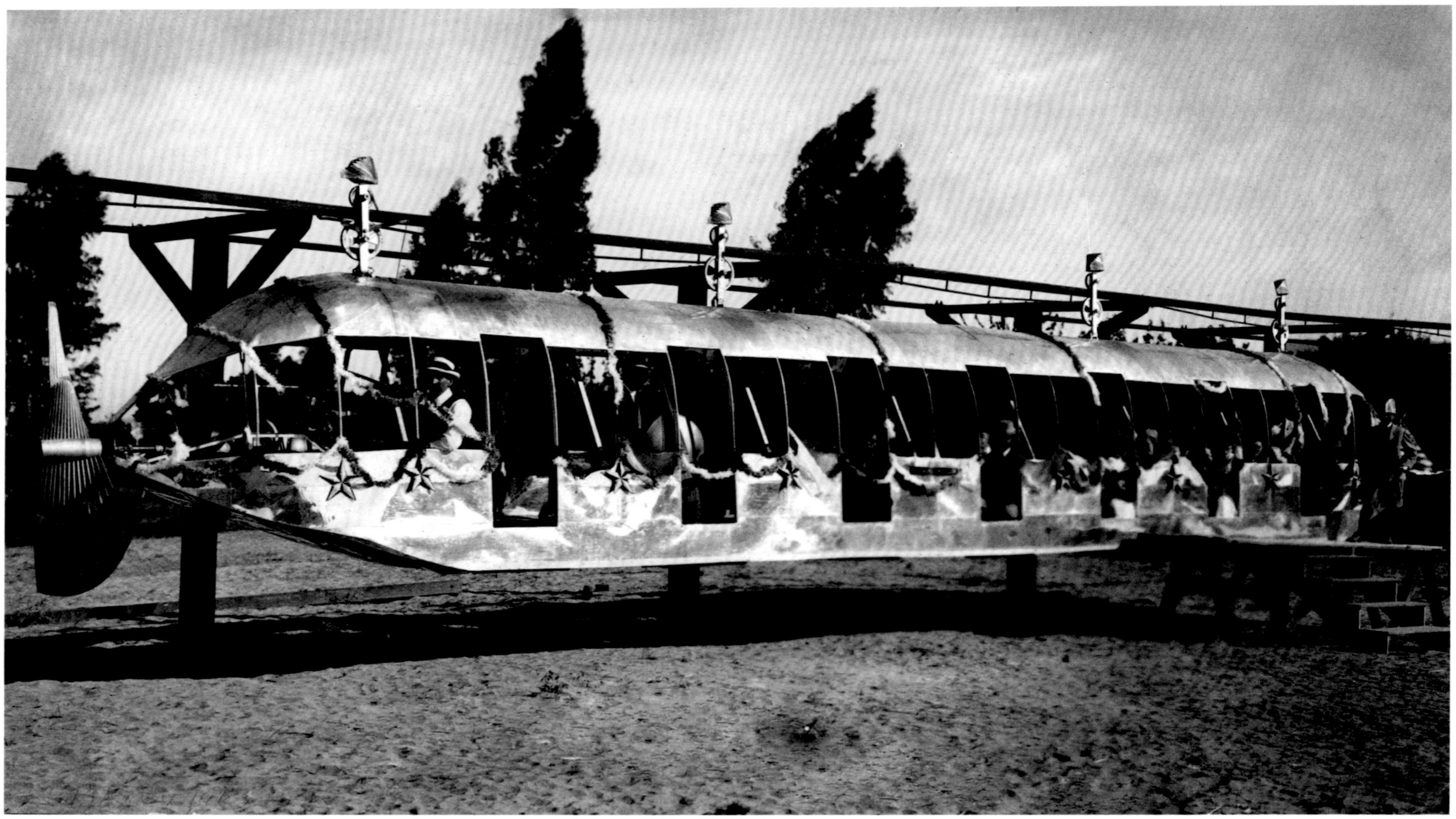

California's reputation for novel and progressive ideas grew along with its population. This 1904 photo shows Joseph Fawkes at the control of his "Aerial Swallow" (derisively called "Fawkes's Folly"), a short-lived experimental monorail conveyance in Burbank.

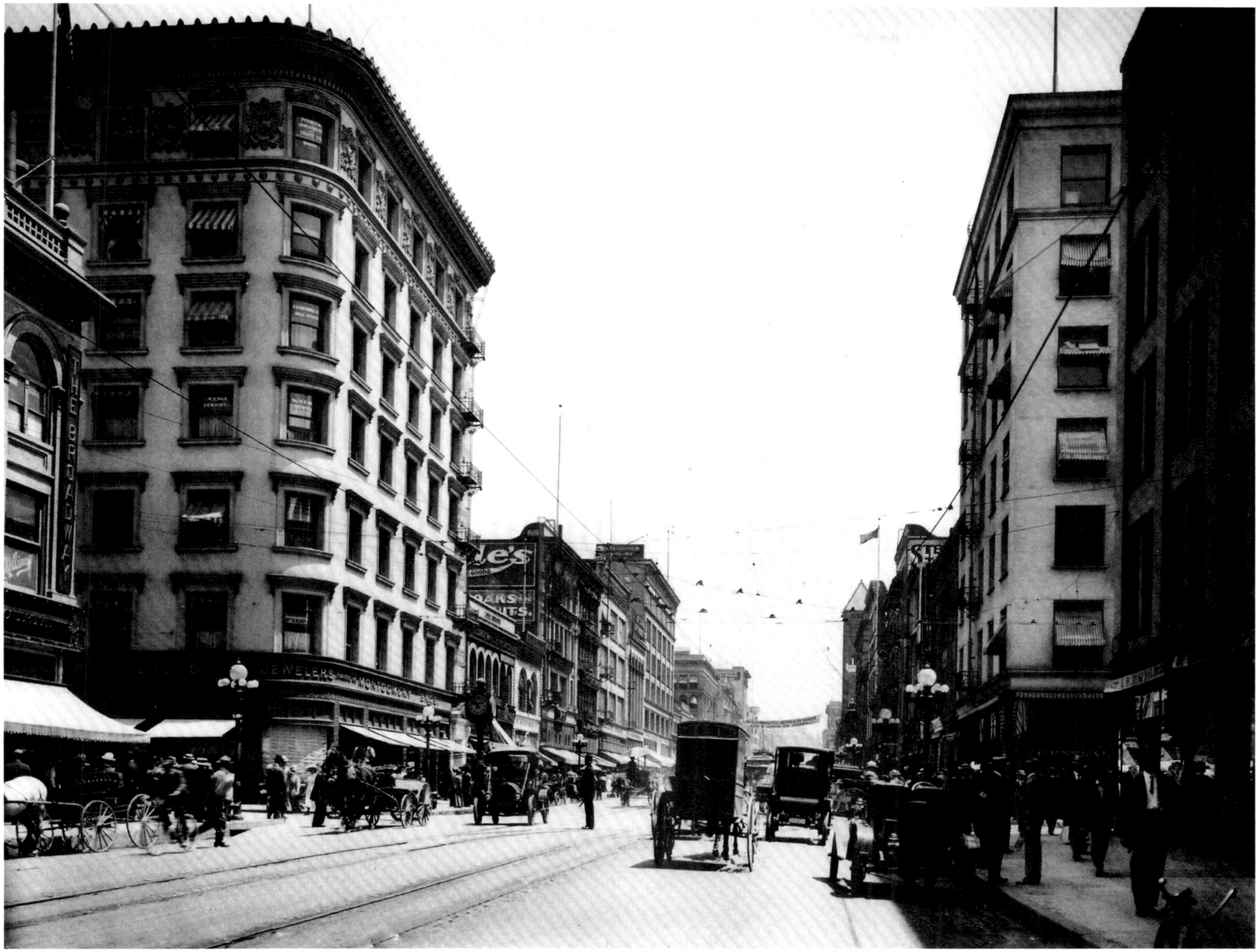

Some of the first automobiles in America appear in this Los Angeles photograph of Broadway looking north from 4th Street. Due in large part to Henry Ford's (1863–1947) innovative, assembly-line production techniques, ownership of motor cars expanded dramatically over the next several decades.

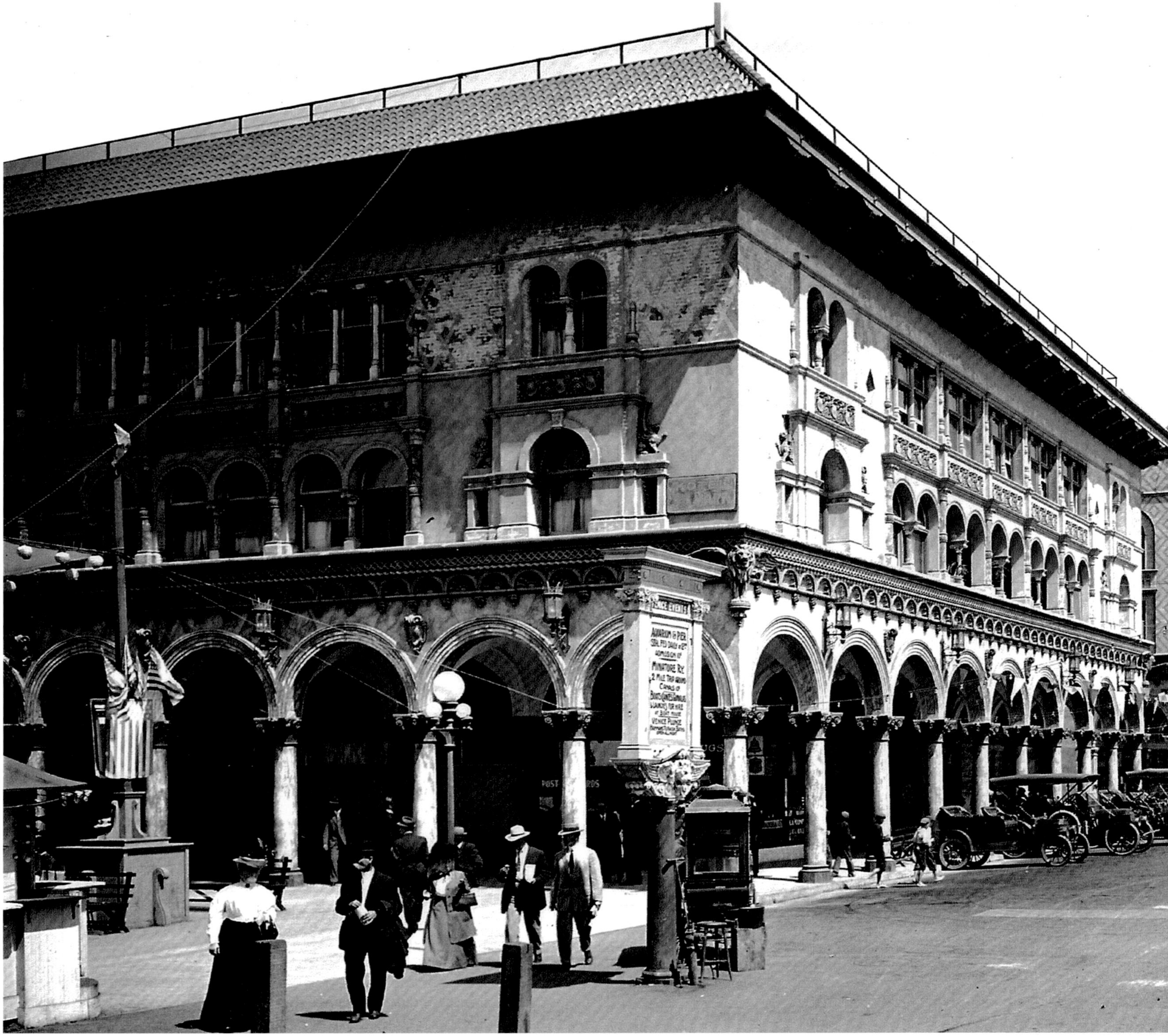
AQUARIUM & PIER
MINIATURE RY.
2 MILE TRIP AROUND
CANALS OF
VENICE PLUNGE

Southern California, with its beautiful weather, was often compared to Italy, "A Mediterranean land without the marshes and malaria." Venice, California, was built by Abbot Kinney (1850–1920), a wealthy tobacco mogul, to resemble its Italian namesake. By 1906 the resort and amusement park was completed, and it became known as the "Coney Island of the Pacific." With the Hotel St. Mark at left, this Venice street scene could easily pass for the famous European city of the same name.

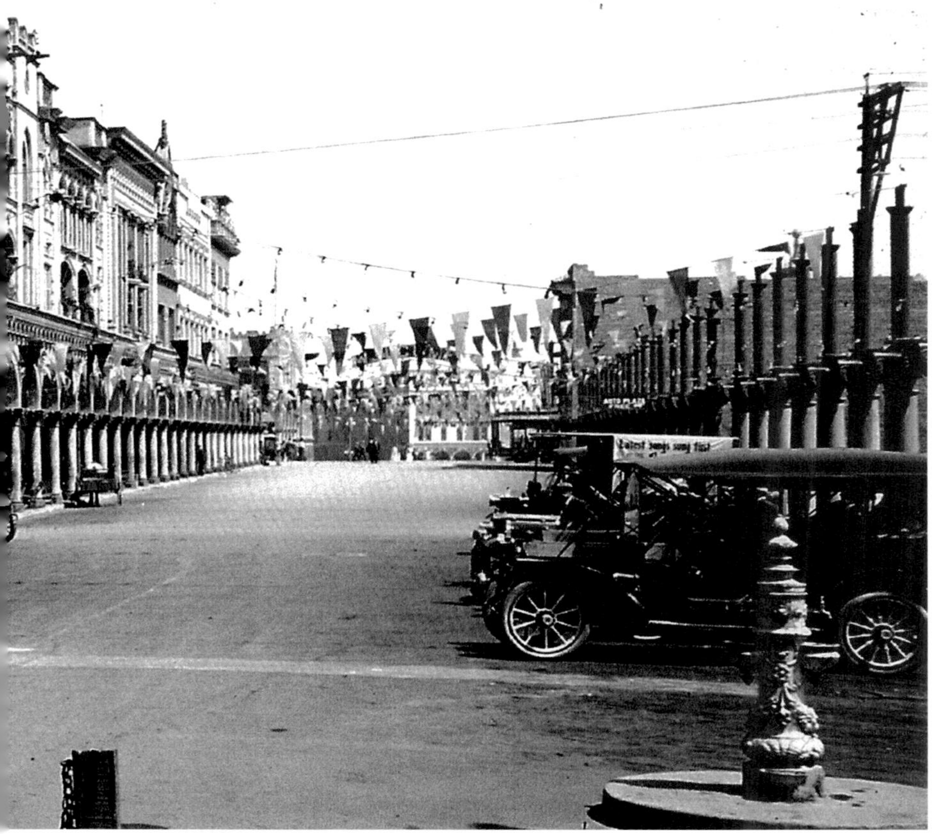

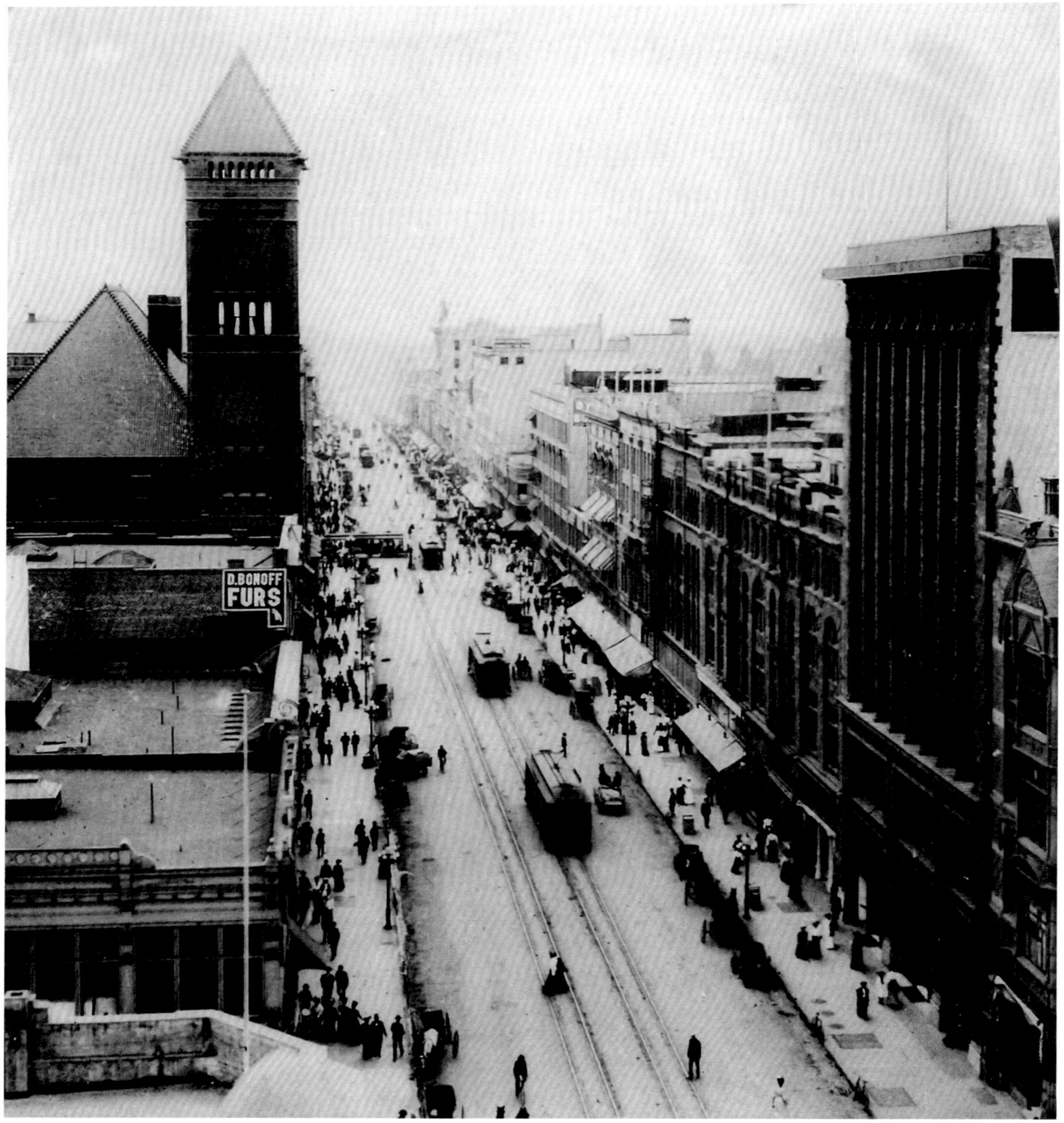

A stereo-card view of Broadway in Los Angeles as seen from the Chamber of Commerce Building. The Chamber of Commerce displayed the Coronel Collection, donated in 1901 by Doña Mariana, the widow of Don Antonio Coronel, which contained relics of the Spanish and Mexican regimes in California.

The Rise of Hollywood and the Great War

(1910–1919)

By 1910, Los Angeles was the seventeenth-largest city in the United States, with a population of 319,198—about as many residents as lived in New Orleans or Washington, D.C. In 1850, L.A. consisted of an area of 28 square miles. Sixty years later the city had increased in area to more than 100 square miles—more than double the size of San Francisco but with a hundred thousand fewer people. Residents could live in such widespread suburban sectors of Los Angeles because the city had an impressive streetcar and interurban rail system.

While the 1906 earthquake retarded subsequent growth in San Francisco, winter tourists continued to pour into Los Angeles, and the city's manufacturing increased by 100 percent in the decade prior to 1910.

The decade 1910–1919 saw several important milestones. In 1913, the 225-mile aqueduct consisting of conduits, tunnels, and ditches was completed, connecting the Owens and San Fernando valleys. Los Angeles now had enough water for one million people.

By 1915, more than 60 percent of all U.S. film production was done in the Los Angeles–Hollywood area. Filmmakers were lured to the West Coast by the Los Angeles Chamber of Commerce with promises of cheap labor, inexpensive land on which to build studios, varied landscapes to serve as backdrops for many genres of film, and sunshine—the last factor essential in the days before indoor studios and artificial lighting.

President Woodrow Wilson strove to keep the U.S. neutral and out of "the war to end all wars" that started in 1914, but Germany's return to unrestricted submarine warfare, sinking ships without warning, and America's ties to the Allies drove Wilson to military intervention. In 1917, the U.S. entered World War I on the side of the Allies, fighting alongside the forces of France and Great Britain.

The end of the Great War in 1918 saw the migration of tens of thousands of people to the United States. One such group was the Armenians, who were persecuted and victims of massacre in Turkey. In 2008, L.A. had the second-largest Armenian diaspora community in the world, after Moscow, Russia.

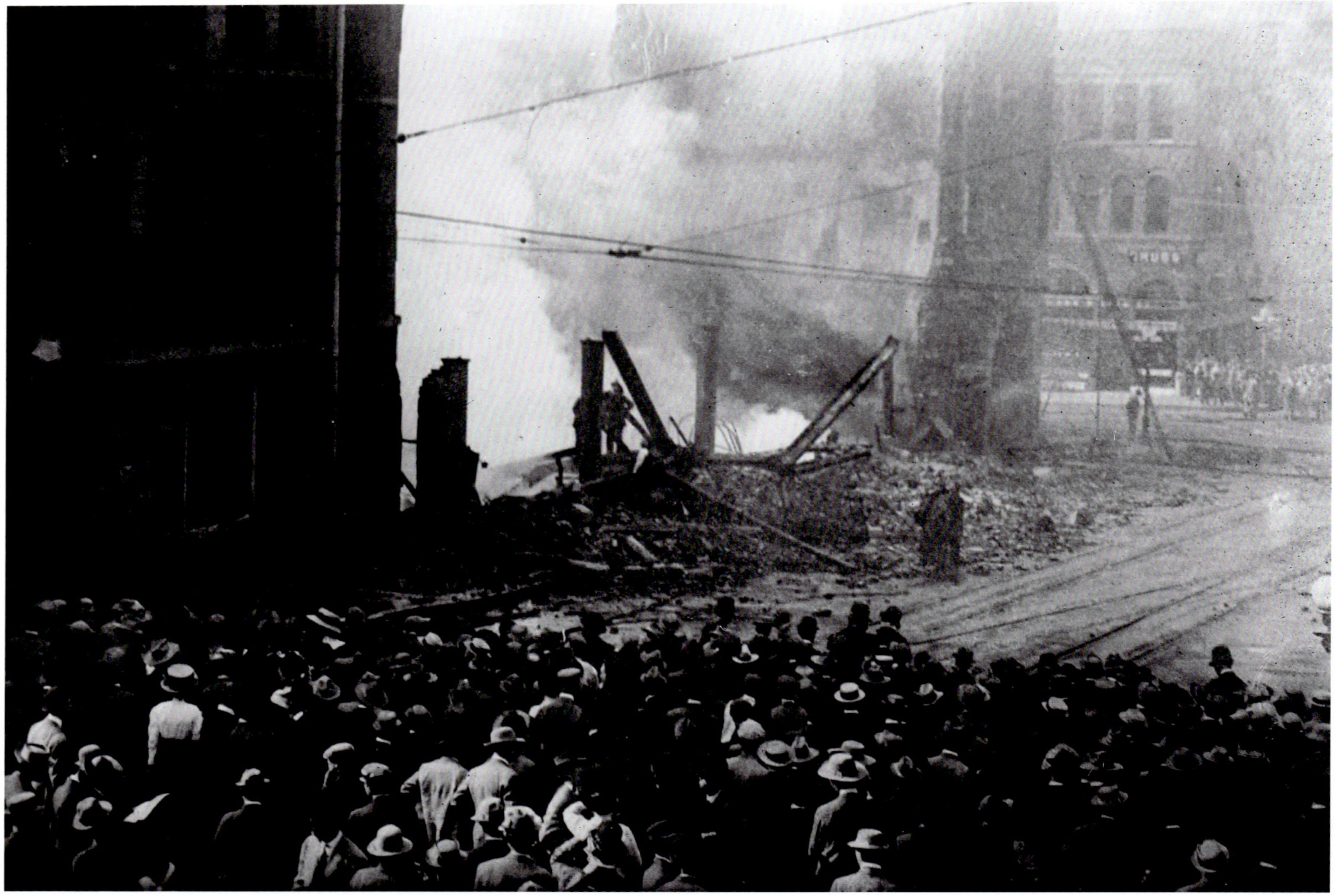

This wreckage is all that remained of the *Los Angeles Times* building after dynamite was detonated at the anti-union newspaper on October 1, 1910. Twenty-one employees were killed and many more injured in the explosion and fire. James and John McNamara, Irish American trade unionists, were arrested and initially pleaded not guilty. The unions hired Clarence Darrow (1857–1938) as their lawyer.

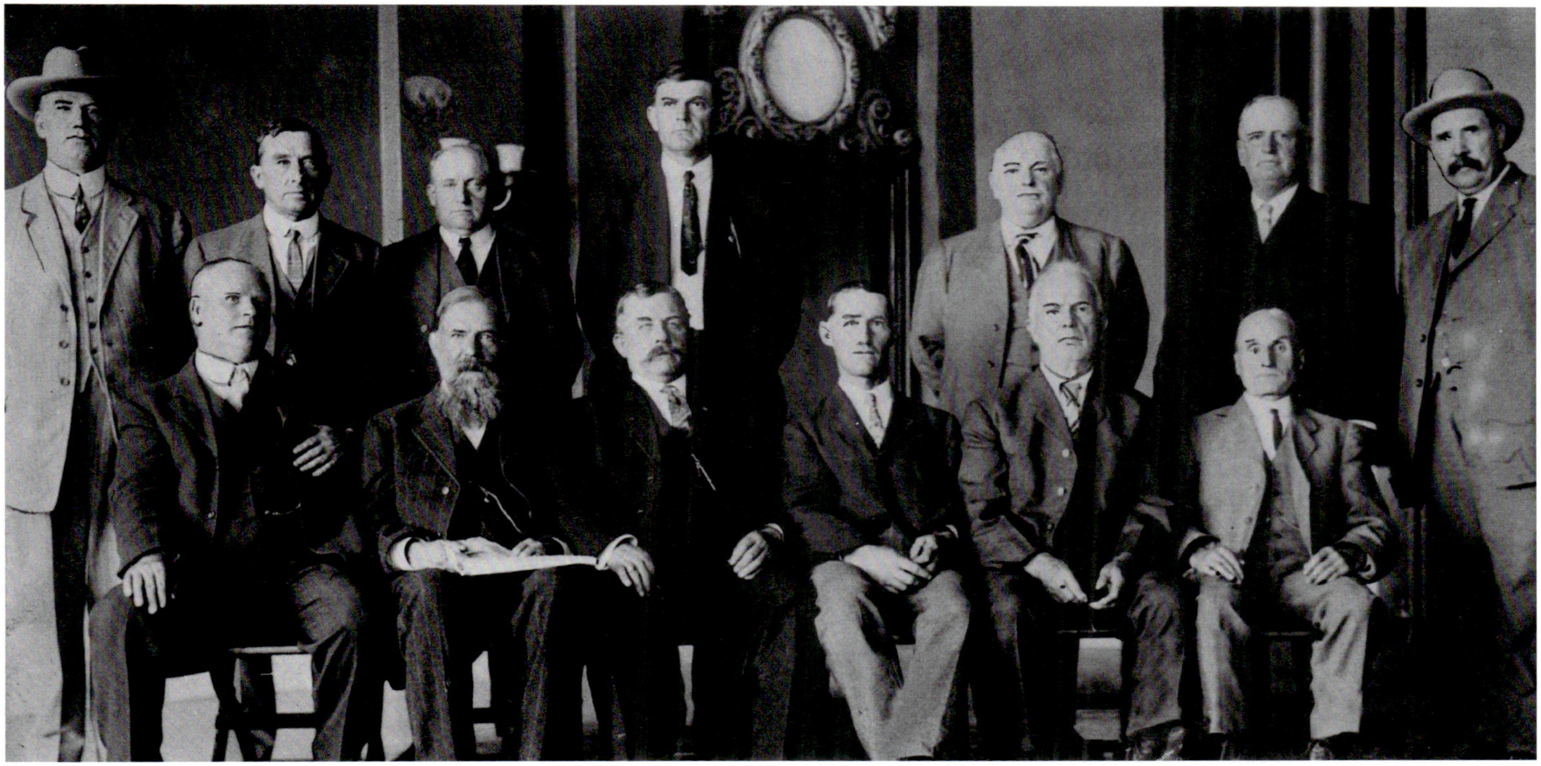

Overwhelming evidence against the McNamara brothers for destroying the *Los Angeles Times* building caused them to change their plea to guilty. The outcome of the McNamara case destroyed Socialist candidate Job Harriman's chances of being the next governor of California. Because no trial occurred, prospective jurors, such as these "talesmen" (a person who is summoned under a "writ of tales"), were not needed.

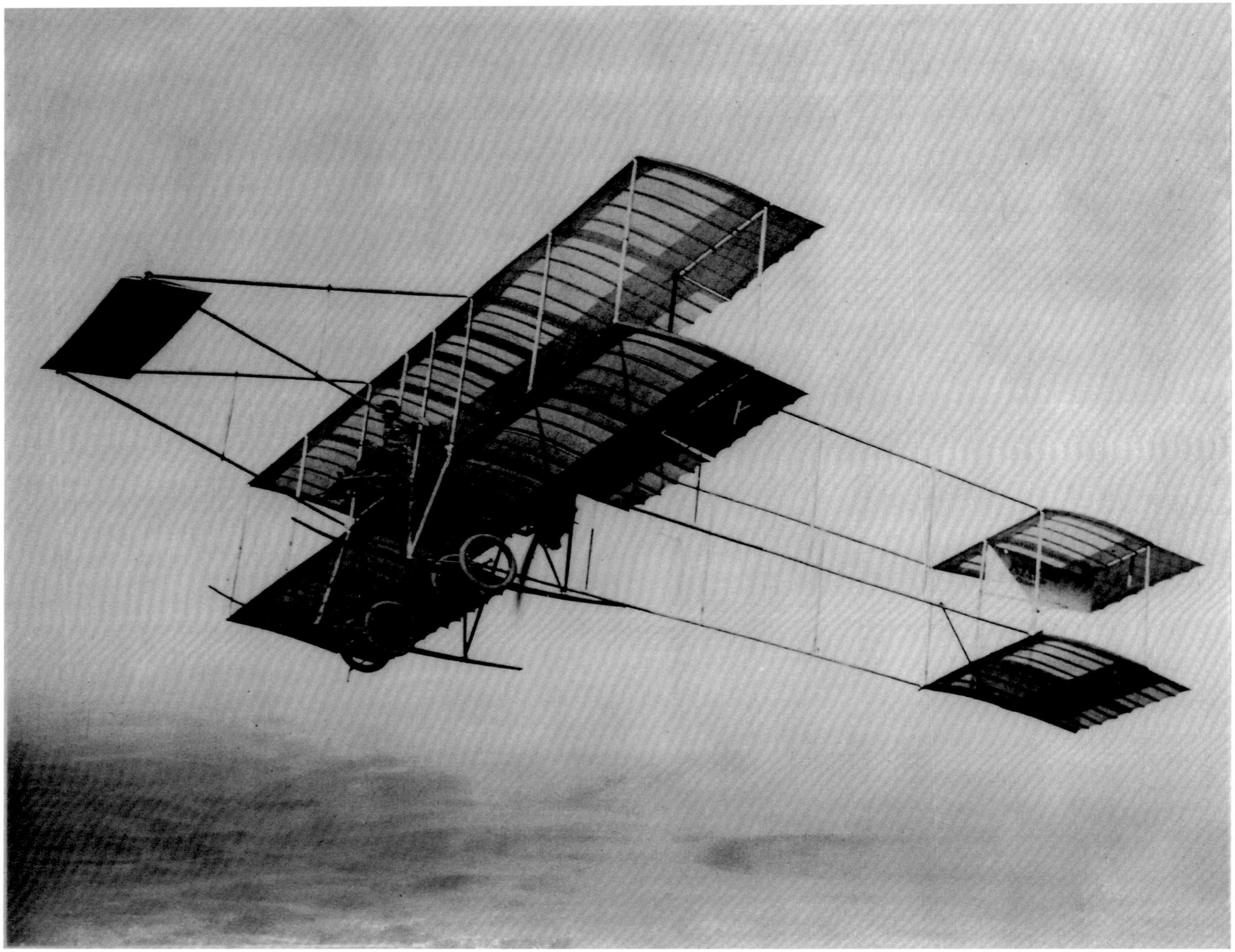

Americans Orville and Wilbur Wright are credited with inventing and building the world's first successful airplane and making the first controlled, powered, and sustained heavier-than-air human flight on December 17, 1903. Daredevil pilots soon followed to capture the public's imagination. One of these was French aviator Louis Paulhan (1883–1963), shown in this photo, who won $10,000 in prize money and the title "King of the Air" for establishing a new altitude record of 4,165 feet at the Los Angeles Air Meet in January 1910.

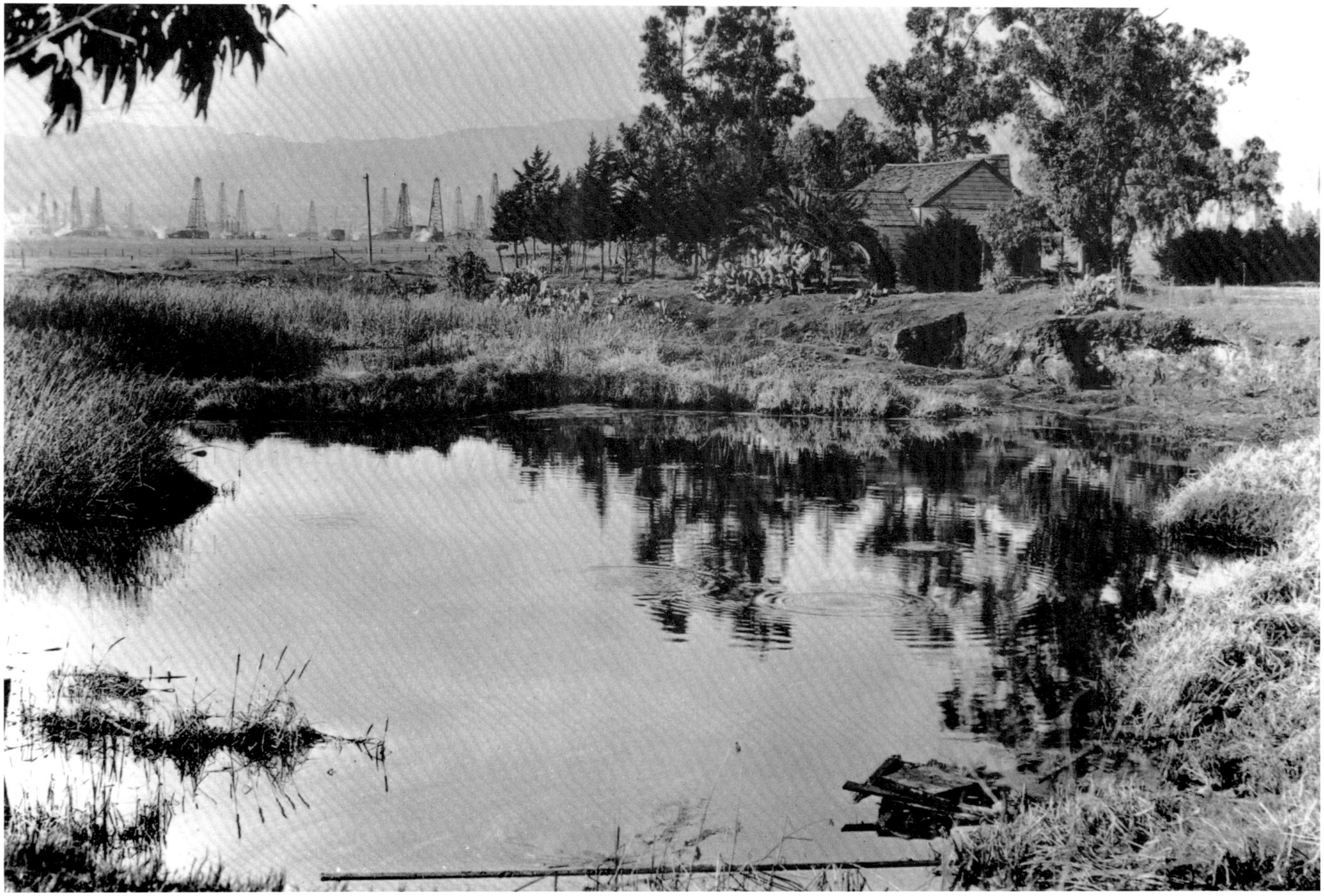

View of a tar pit and the Hancock ranch house about 1910, with oil fields in the distance. The cluster of tar pits, located in Hancock Park with the George C. Page Museum in the heart of Los Angeles, became famous as La Brea Tar Pits. Asphalt, called "tar" ("brea" in Spanish) seeped up from the ground in this area for thousands of years, creating sticky pools that trapped animals and plants. The asphalt preserved the remains, providing a valuable collection of fossils from the last ice age.

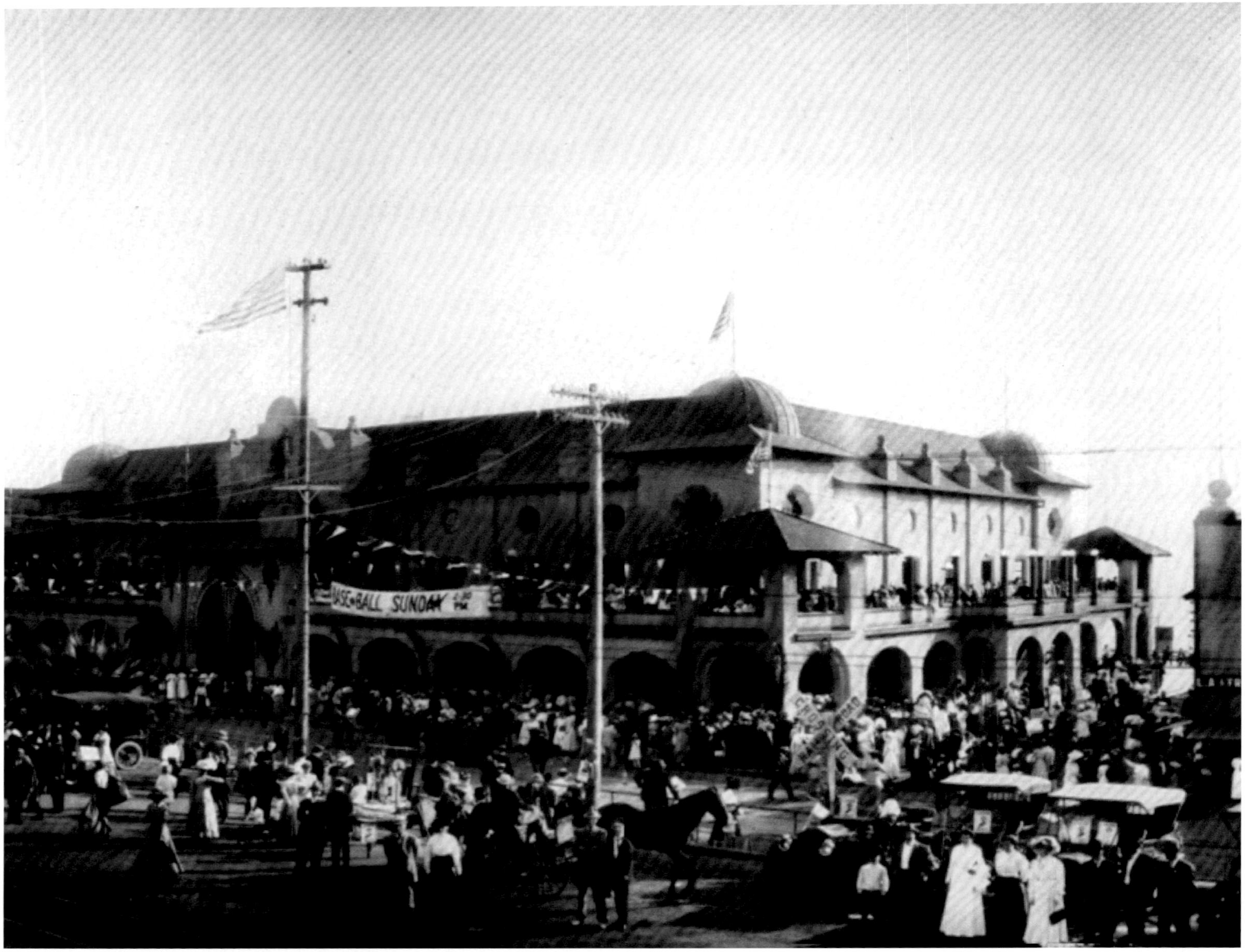

Los Angeles became a winter tourist haven for people escaping the cold, snow, and ice of the Midwest. Coastal areas like Redondo Beach, shown here, were popular destinations.

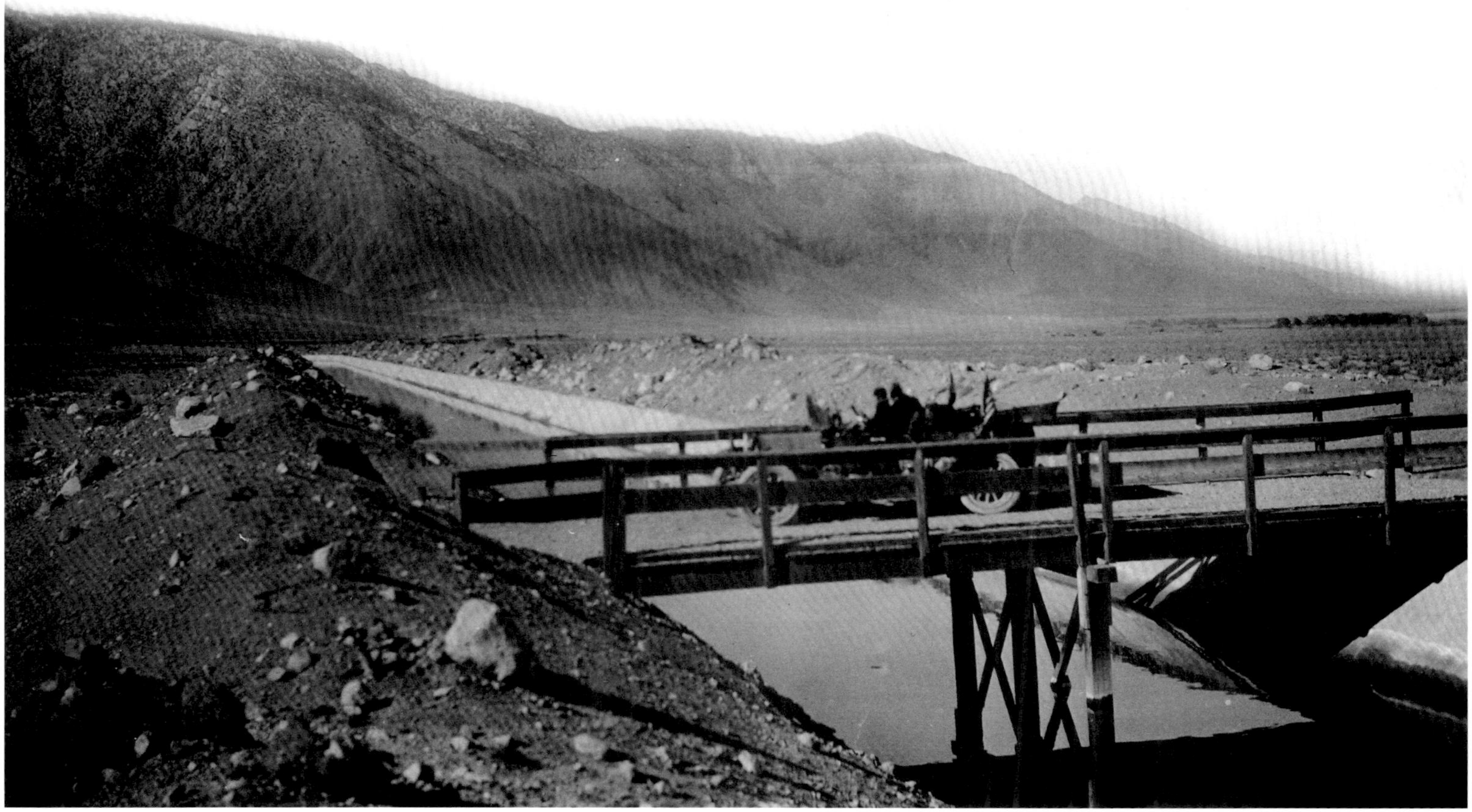

A car crosses the Los Angeles aqueduct in the Owens River valley in November 1912. L.A. financed and built the 225-mile project to bring vital water to the Southern California area, providing the key ingredient for incredible growth for the next twenty years.

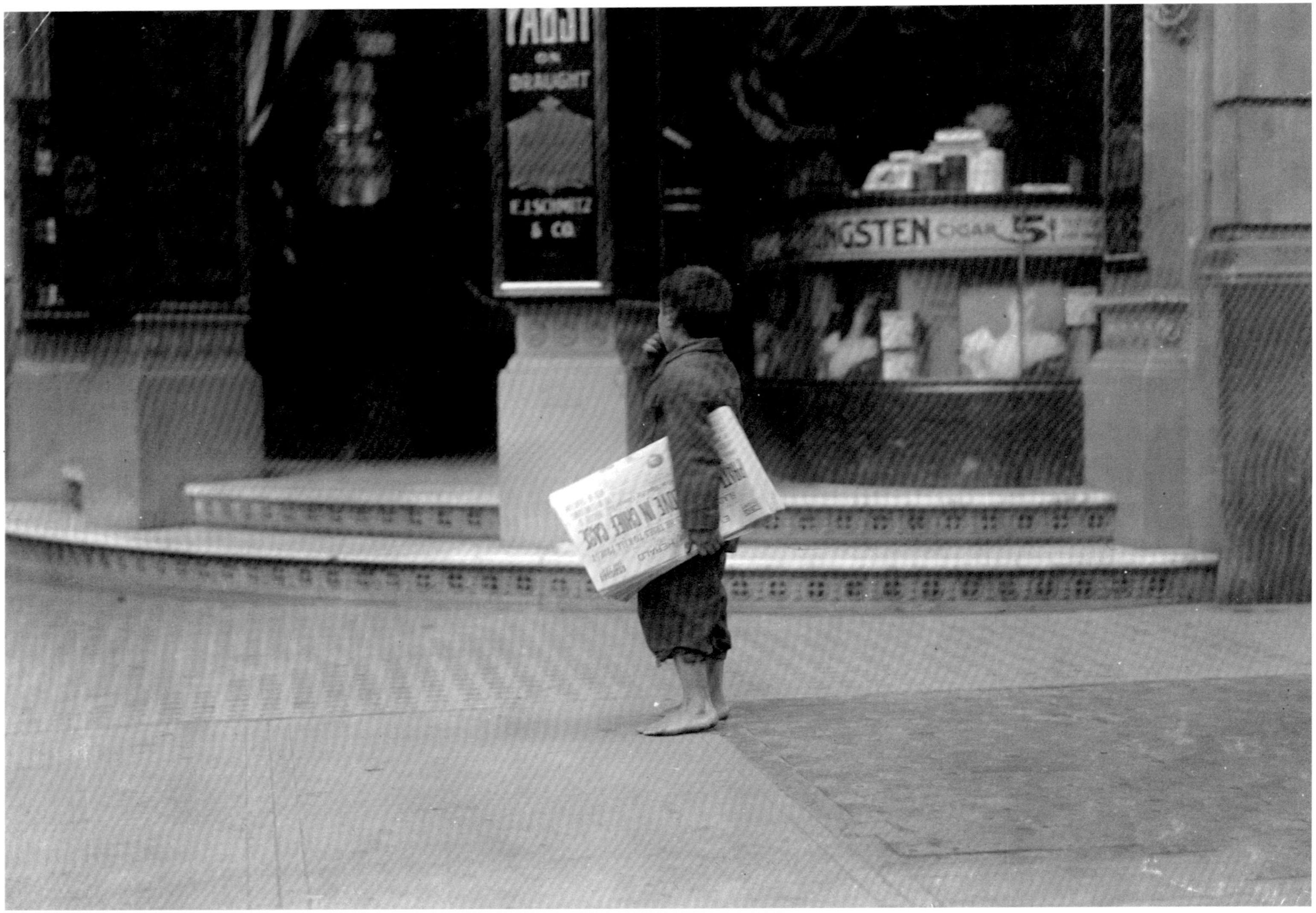

A barefoot newsie sells papers to earn a few pennies. The fierce competition for circulation motivated newspapers to practice "yellow journalism"—a type of reporting that featured scandal-mongering, sensationalism, jingoism, and unethical and unprofessional writing.

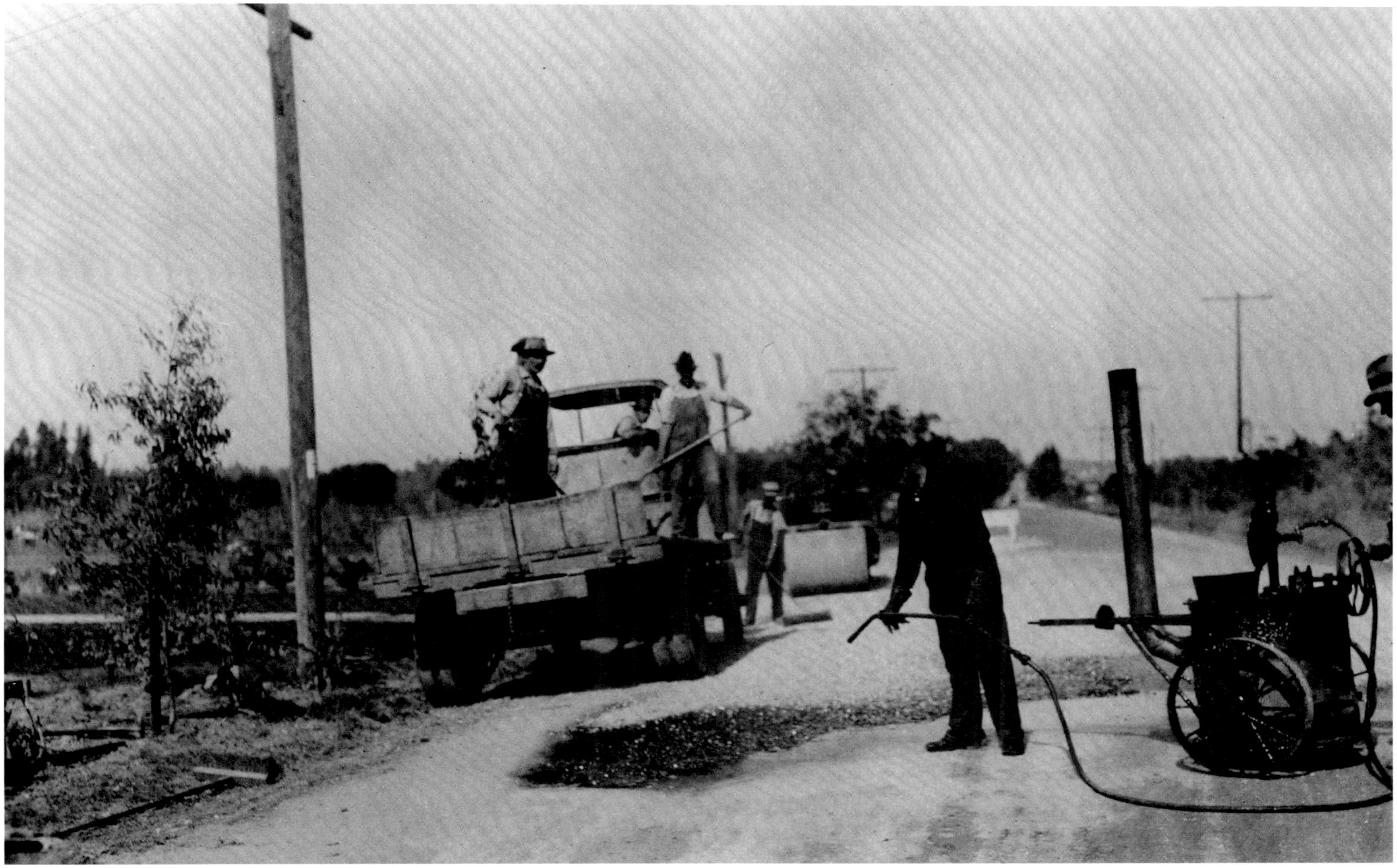

Automobile ownership in America increased tremendously during the second decade of the twentieth century. Private cars and business-owned trucks kept repair crews like this "heavy maintenance" squad constantly busy. The crew here is placing a three-inch-deep patch on oiled macadam around 1915.

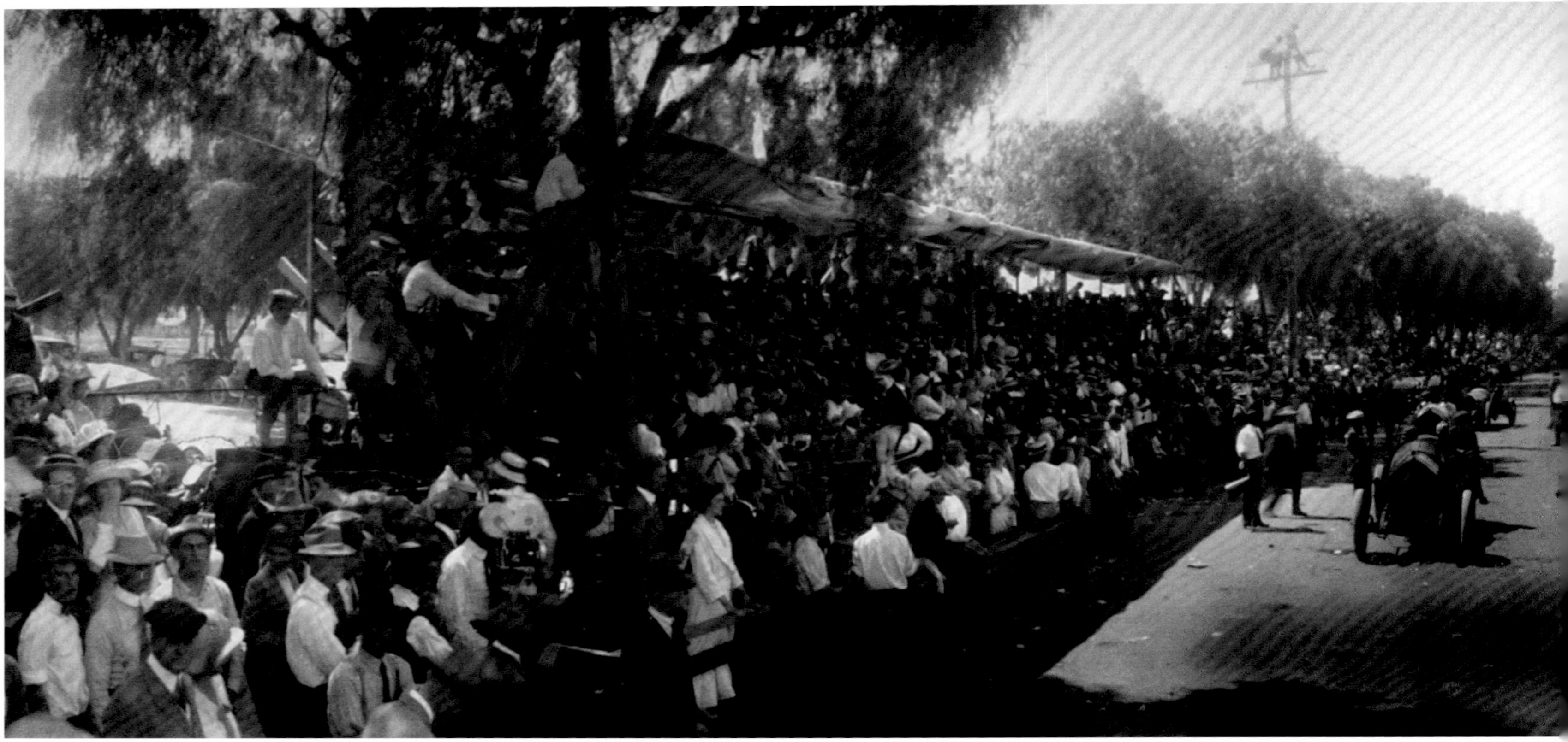

Within a few years after the automobile was invented, car races became popular. This panorama view shows the start of a "medium and heavyweight" auto race at the Corona Speedway around 1913.

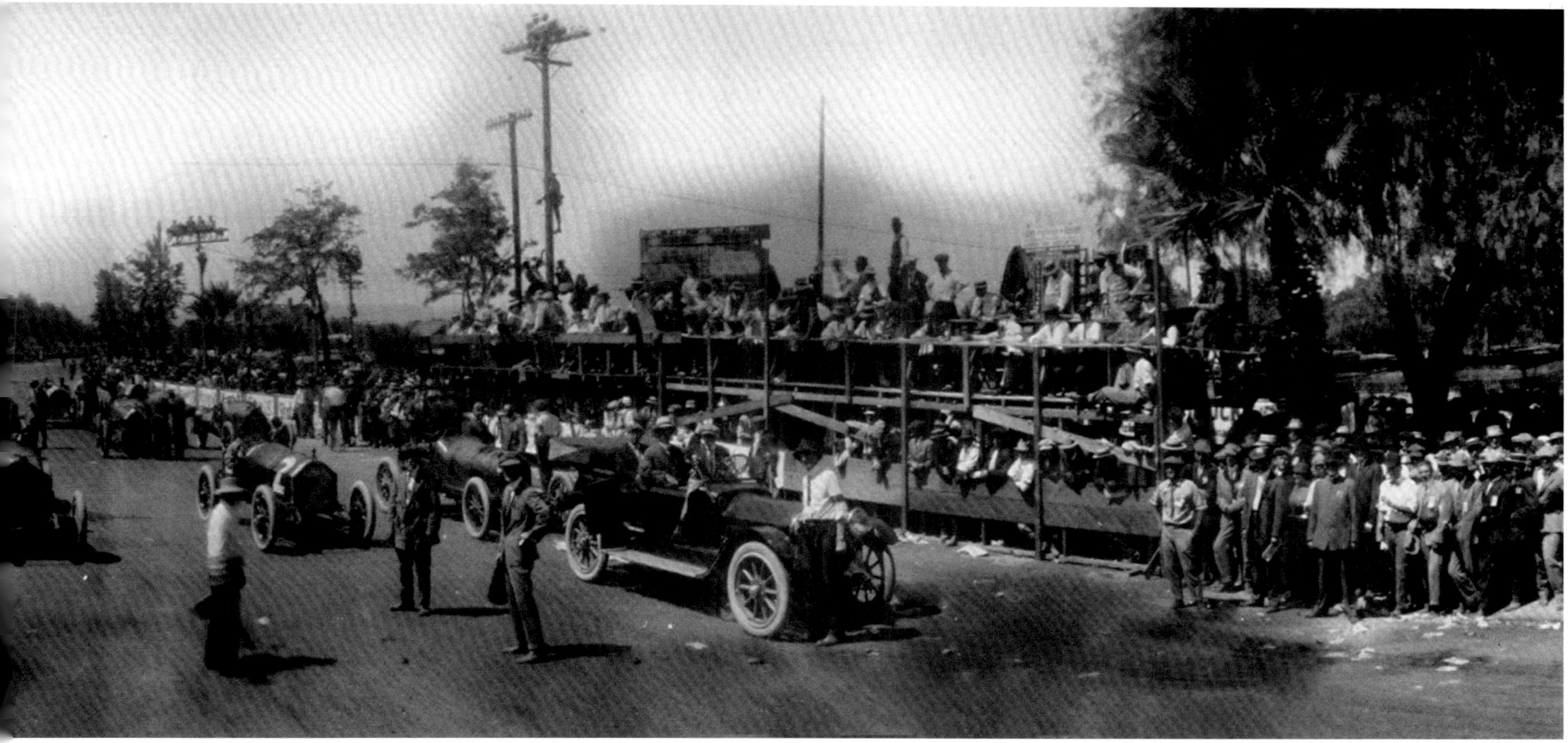

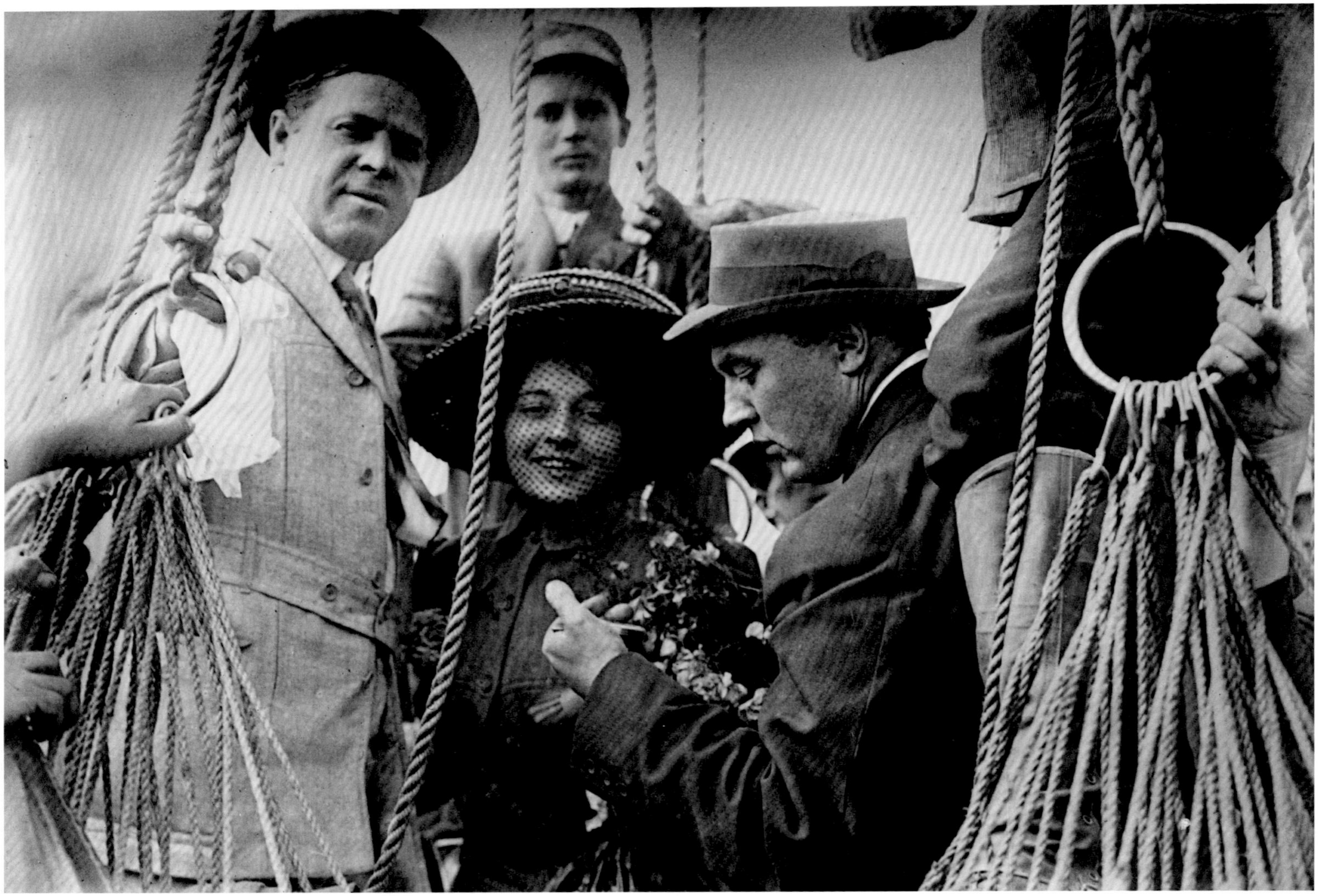

One of America's earliest news picture agencies was the Bain News Service. George Grantham Bain (1865–1914) created a business that documented sports events, celebrities, crime, strikes, disasters, political activities, and so on, from the 1860s through the 1930s. The bulk of the collection covers life in New York City, but other cities were included. This Bain image shows C. A. Coey and his bride in Los Angeles in the 1910s.

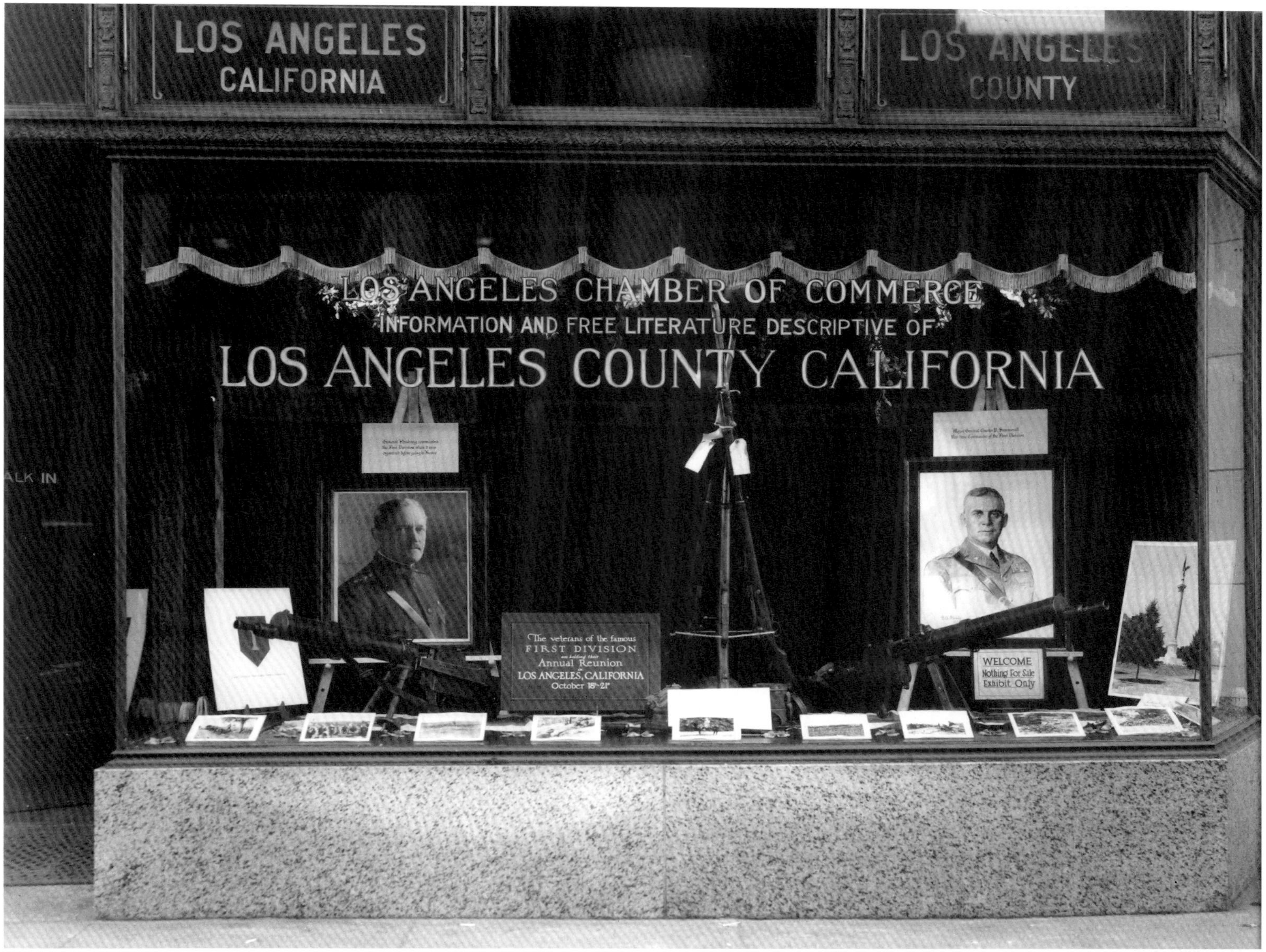

After President Woodrow Wilson delivered his "war message" speech on April 2, 1917, Congress declared war against Germany. By June, the first American military units arrived in France, including the First Division. A window display for a First Division reunion appeared in the office of the Los Angeles Chamber of Commerce.

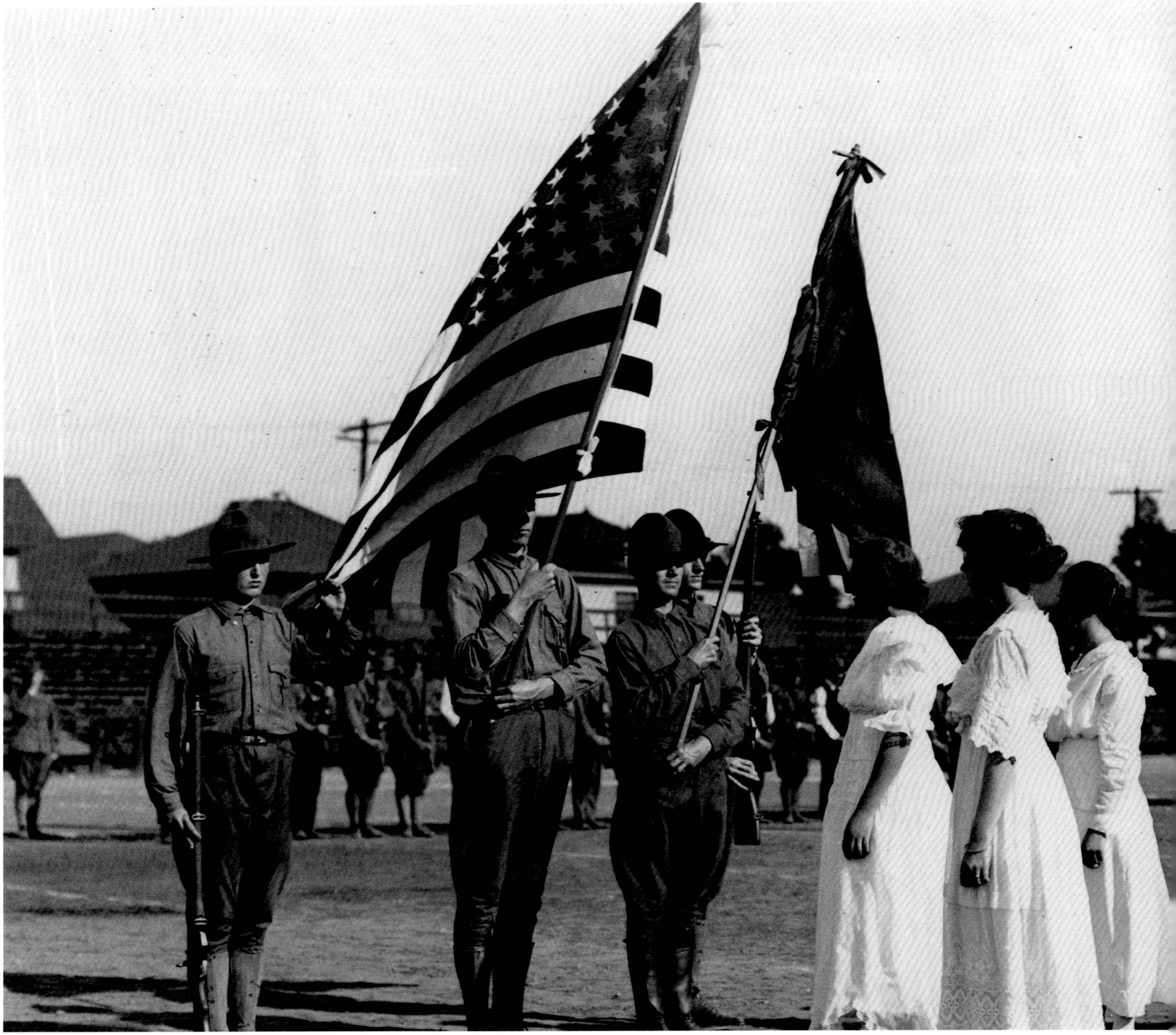

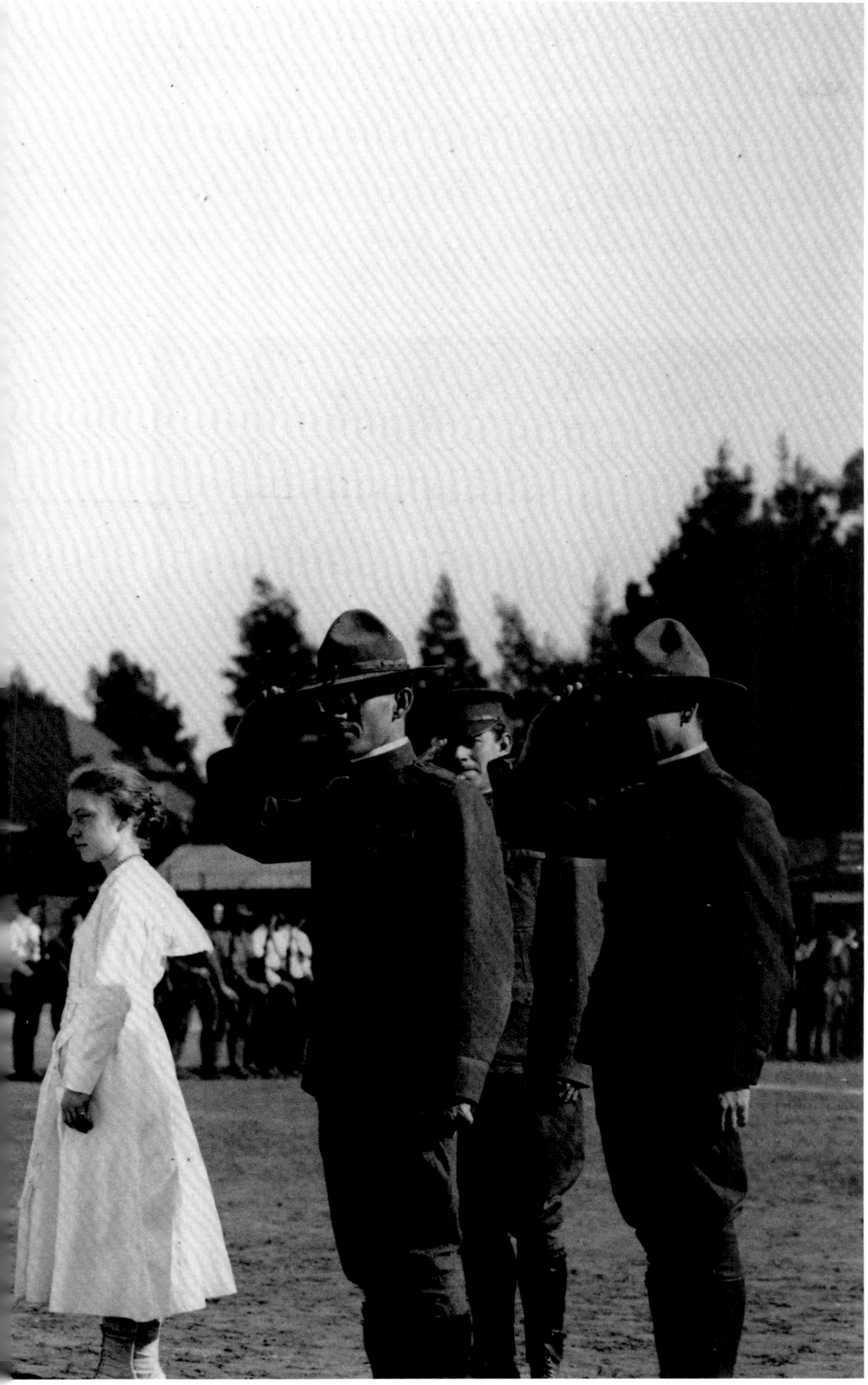

Presentation of the colors and standard of the USC (University of Southern California) Battalion to a committee of women students. The American Expeditionary Force (AEF) sent to fight in Europe lost 116,708 soldiers of the nearly six million dead lost by the Allied powers as a whole. Following the war, more than 650,000 Americans died in the influenza pandemic of 1918–1919.

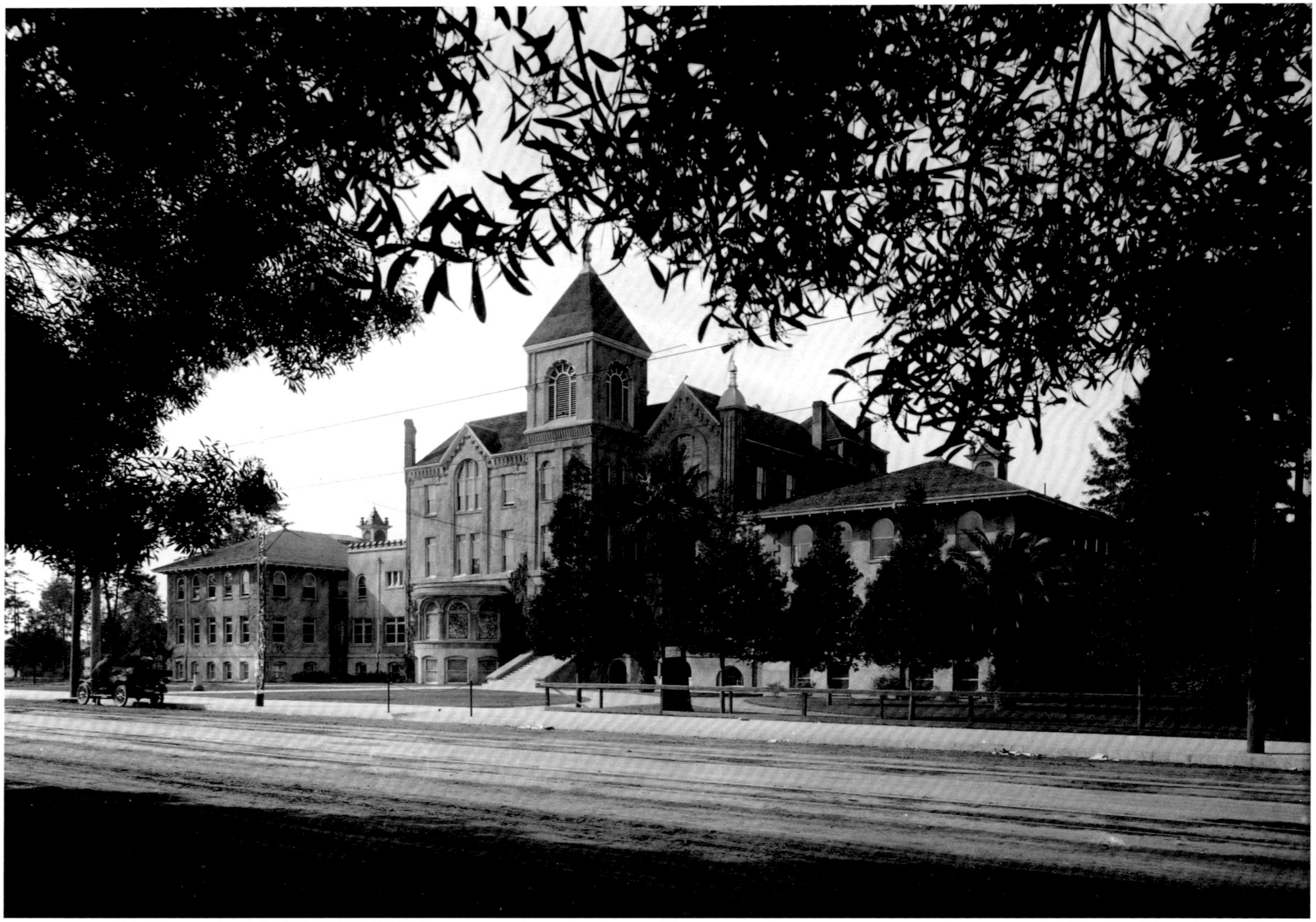

The University of Southern California, commonly referred to as USC, was founded in 1880, making it California's oldest private research university. This photograph from the 1910s shows the Administration Building of the College of Liberal Arts at USC. The school consistently ranks among the top American colleges, with students from all 50 states as well as more than 115 countries.

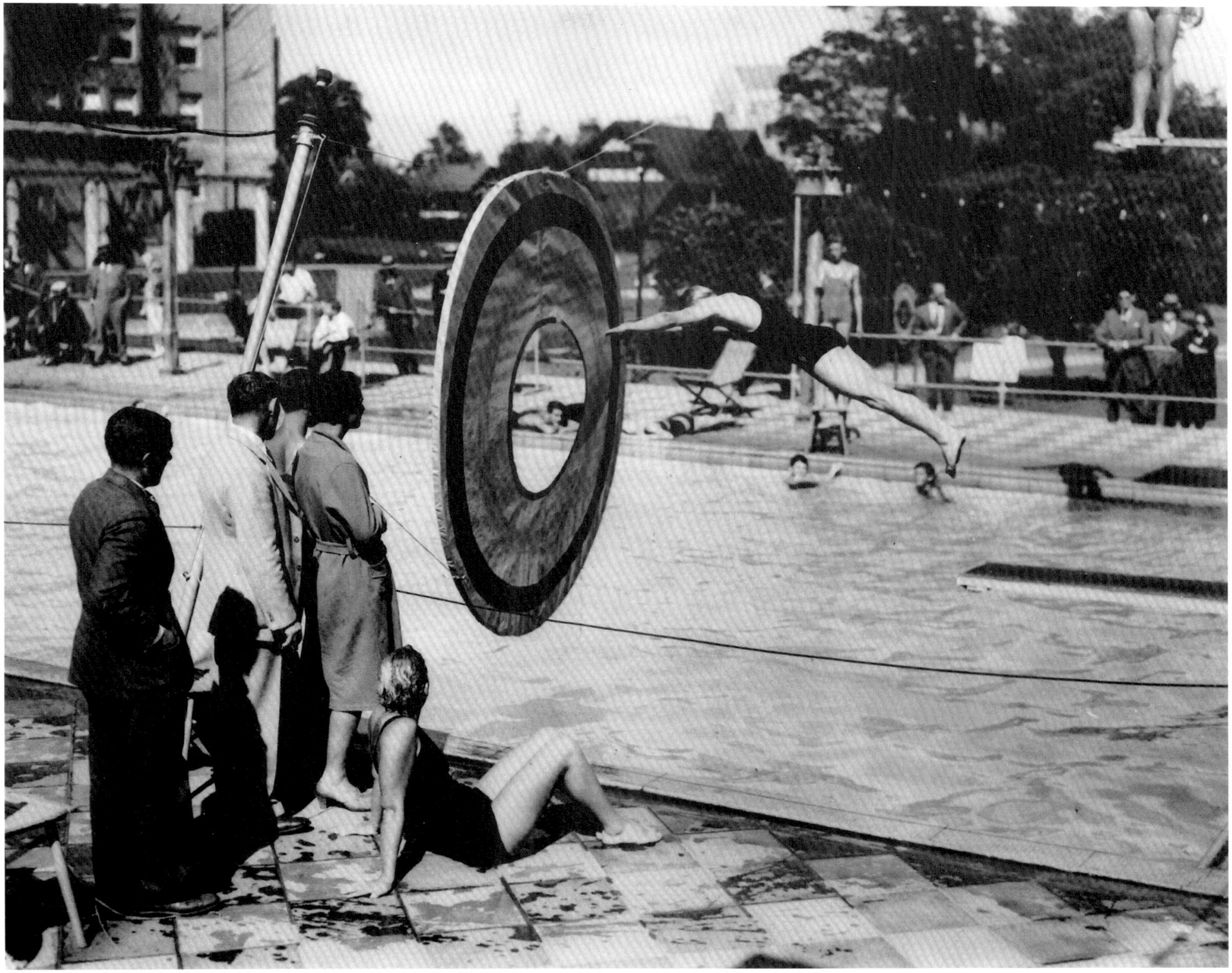

In this acrobatic "target diving" stunt in Los Angeles, Johnny Riley, national 10-foot-diving champ, takes flight as a "human arrow."

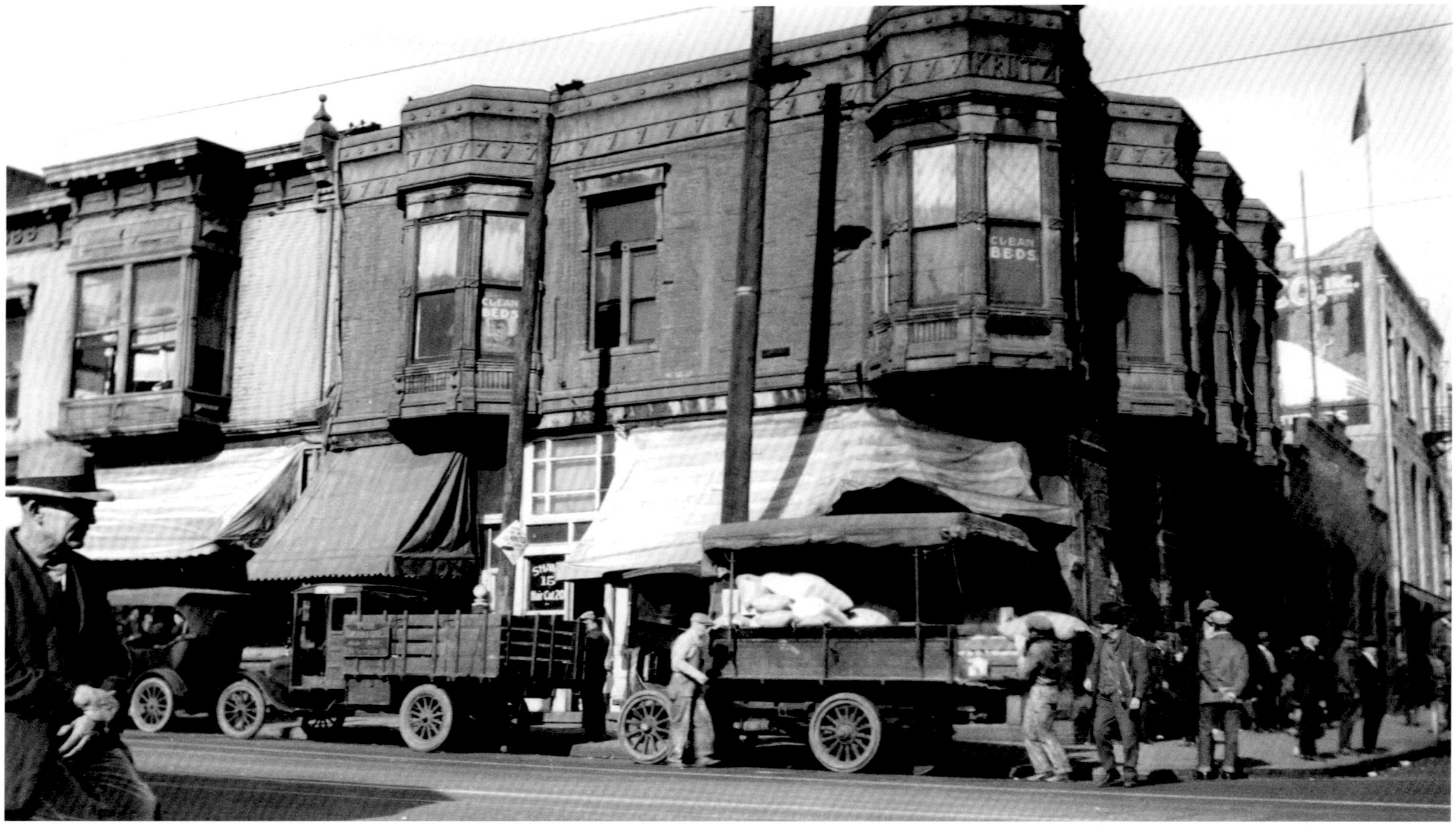

A scene at 2nd and Los Angeles streets in the 1910s. Stewart Edward White (1873–1946) wrote adventure travel books based on his experiences in the American West. He settled in California, and in his 1910 novel *The Rules of the Game*, White examined the way that Los Angeles shamelessly promoted itself. He portrayed L.A. as a city where everything is bigger and stranger, with large numbers of clairvoyants, palm readers, and fake healers—"crazy" cults and "newfangled religions."

The tower of Los Angeles City Hall can be seen in the background as a Hispanic woman obtains water at a fountain on Olvera Street, an area described as a "Mexican shopping lane." In 1910, Mexican immigration to Los Angeles increased dramatically as many people fled the turmoil and violence of the Mexican Revolution, the first large revolution of the twentieth century. Reaction to the tide of illegal immigrants from Mexico led to the 1913 California Alien Land Law that prevented ownership of land by "aliens ineligible for citizenship."

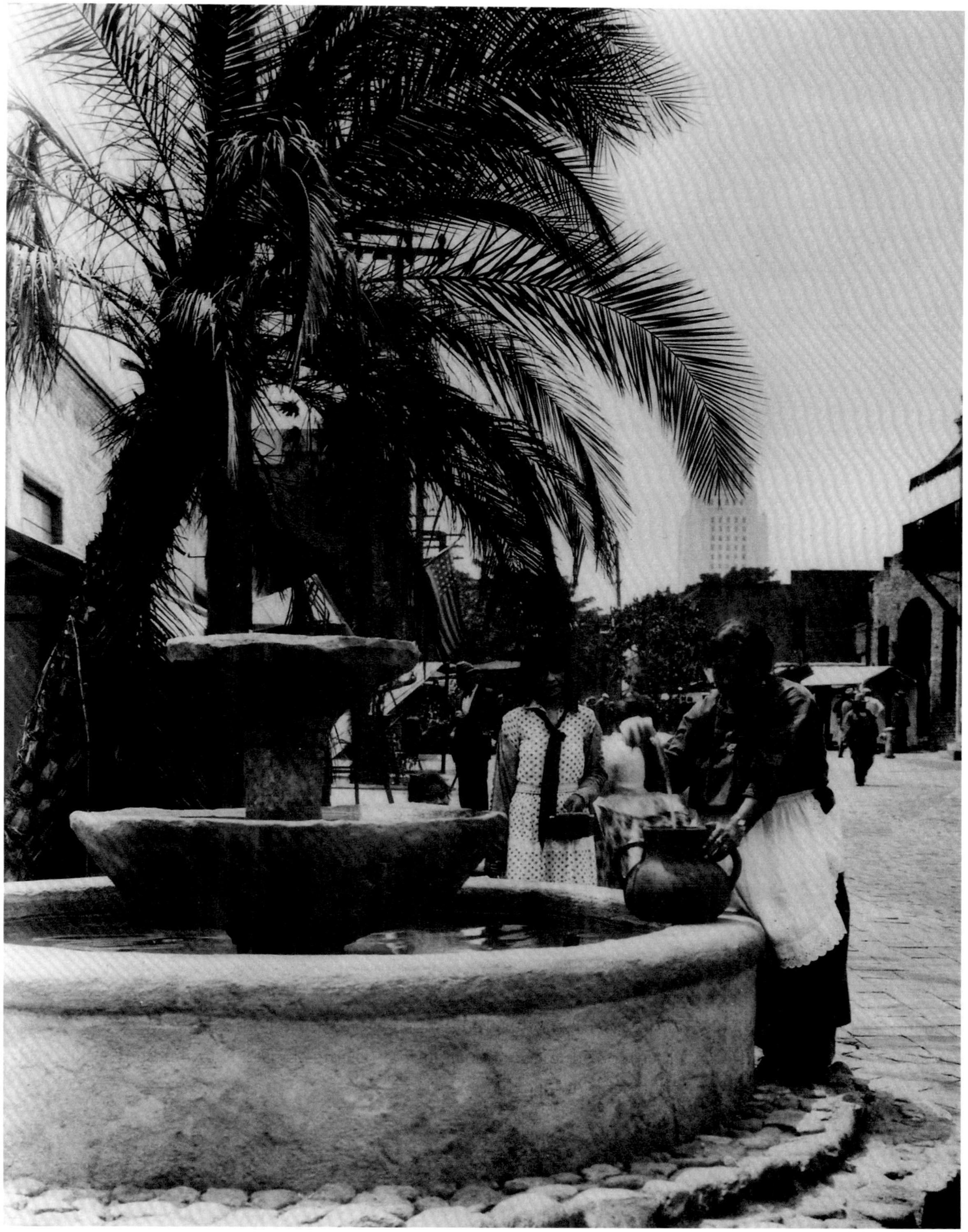

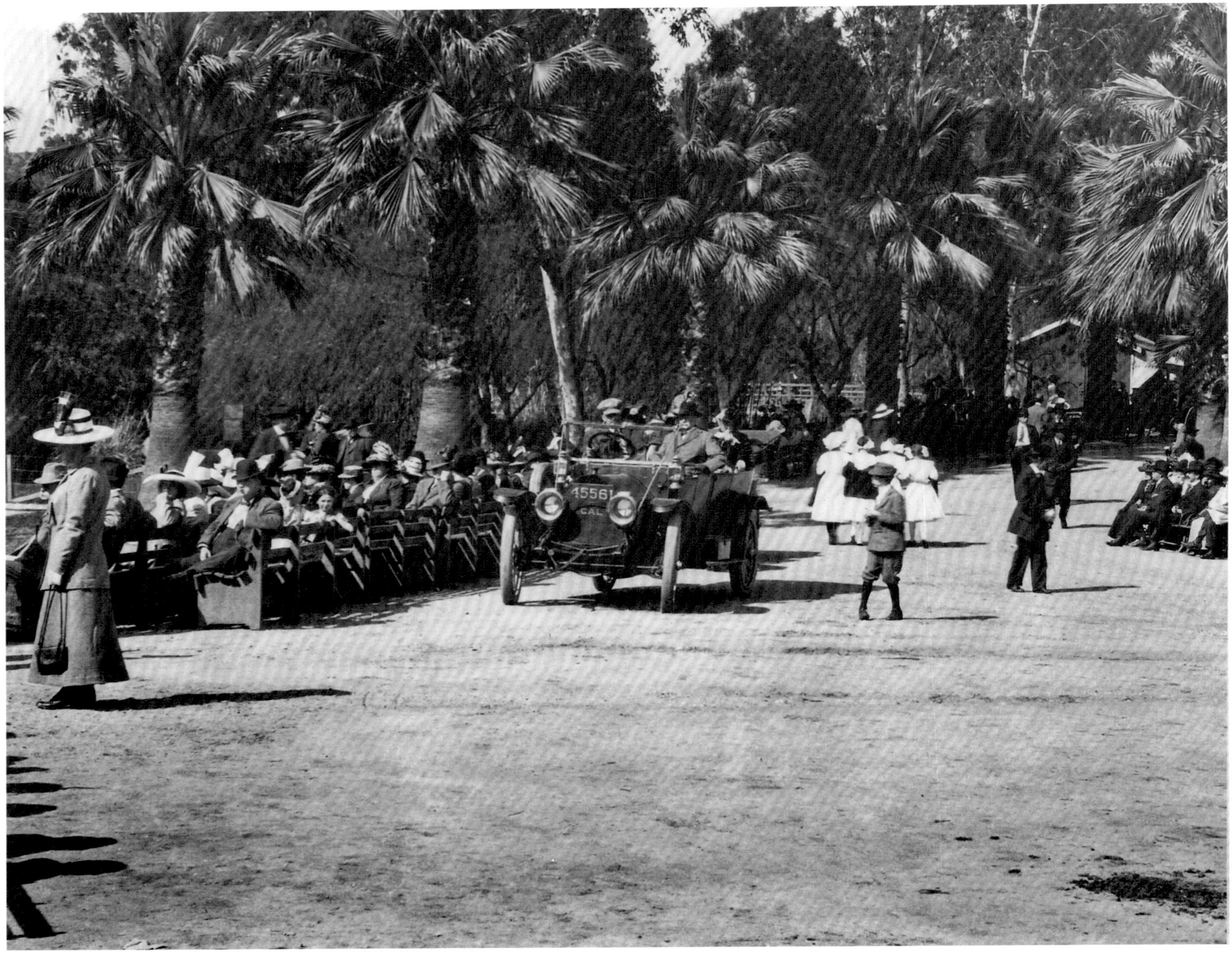

An early photo of Lincoln Park, initially called East Los Angeles Park and then Eastlake Park in 1901. It quickly became a major amusement center, and one of its main attractions was the area's first zoological display. In 1917, the L.A. City Council responded to a petition from residents and renamed it Lincoln Park after a local high school.

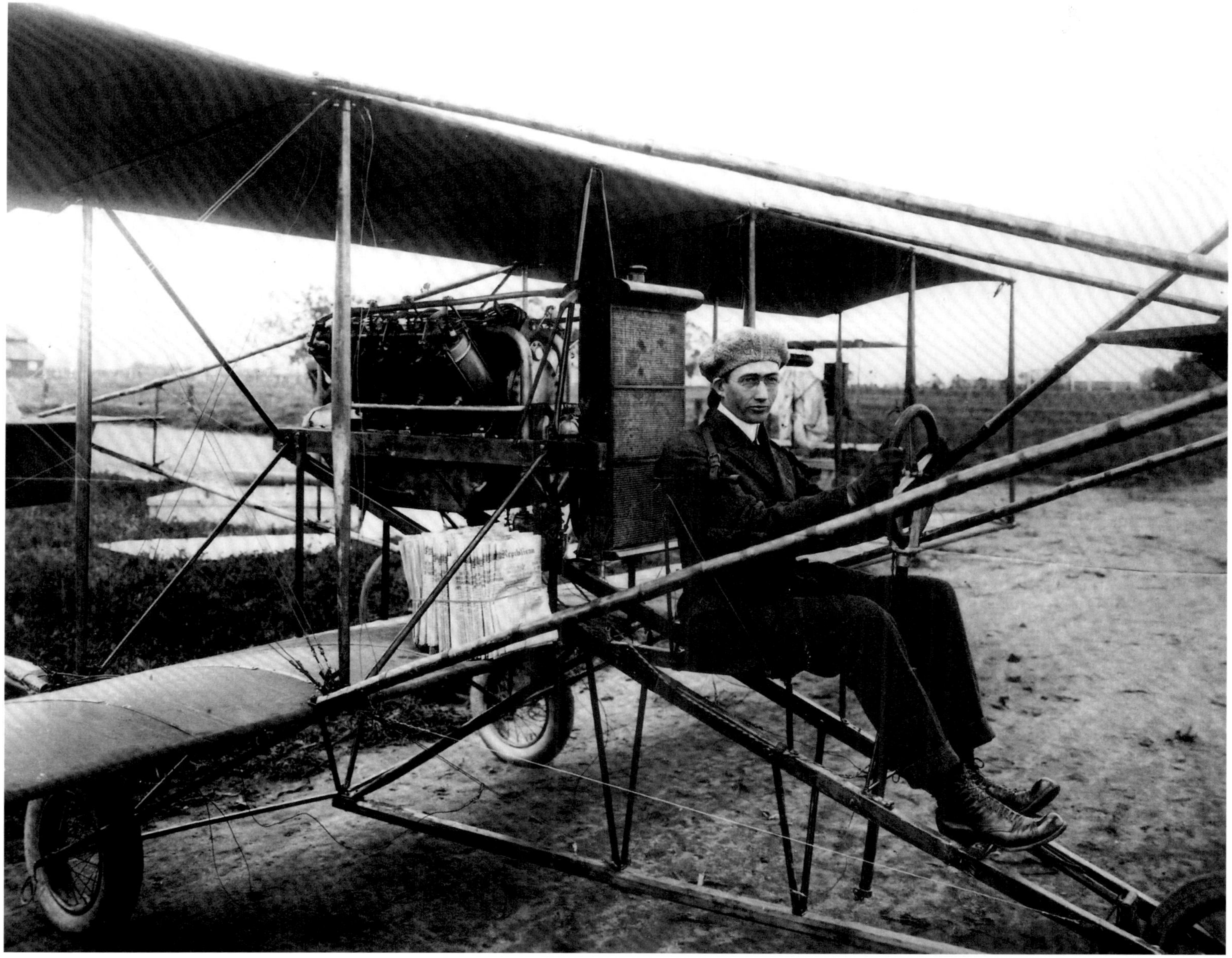

Aviation pioneer Glenn Martin (1886–1955) is shown delivering newspapers to Los Angeles in his airplane in 1911. He founded a company that initially made military trainers in Santa Ana, then eventually relocated to Maryland where he produced military aircraft until after World War II. His company went through several mergers and in 1995 became part of Lockheed Martin, a leading multinational aerospace manufacturer and advanced technology company.

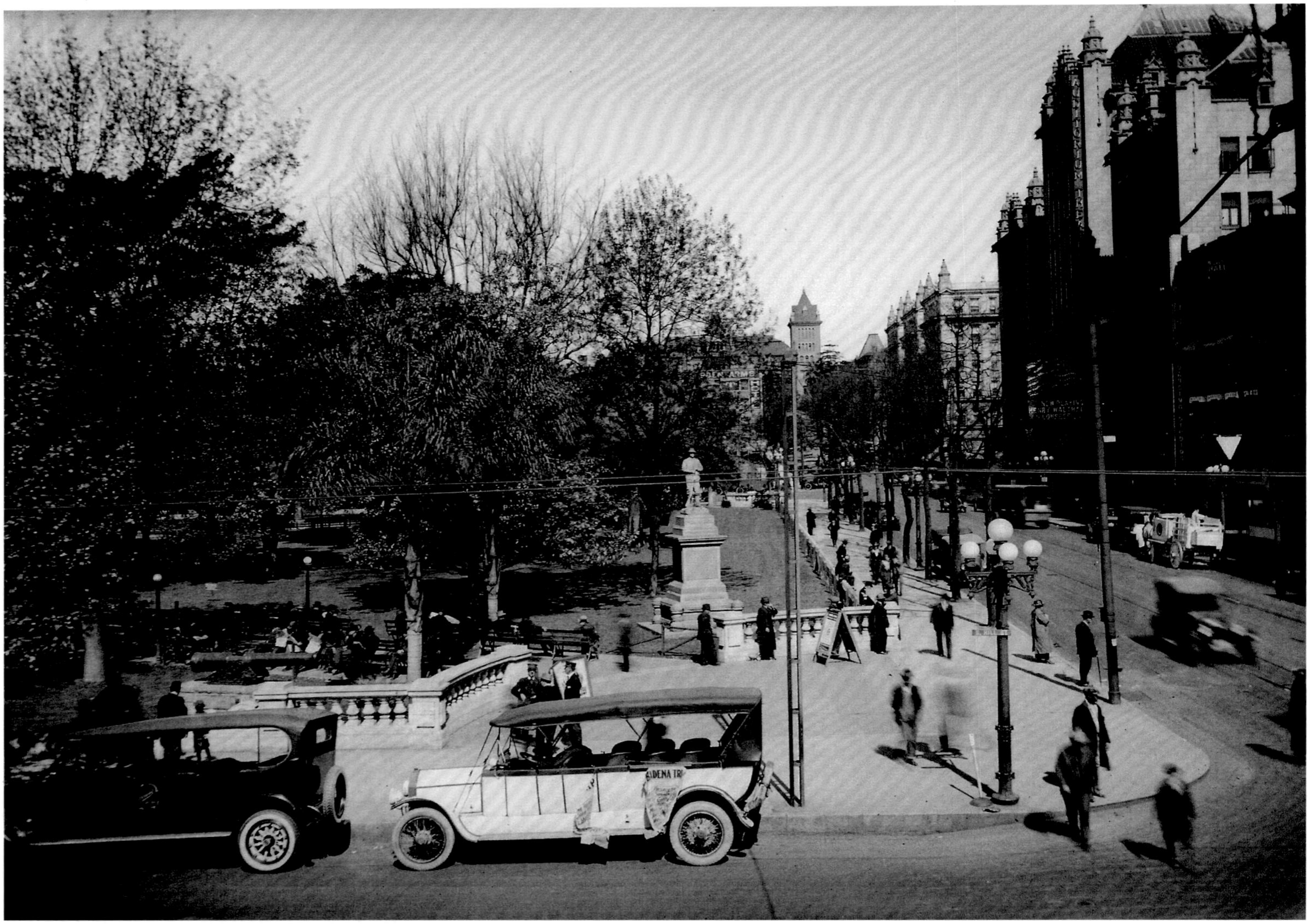

This photo shows Central Park, one of the oldest parks in Los Angeles, with its Spanish-American War Memorial honoring the Seventh California Volunteer Infantry Regiment. The monument, reputedly the first work of public art in L.A., was dedicated in 1900. The park was renamed Pershing Square in 1918 to honor General John Joseph "Black Jack" Pershing, the commander of the American Expeditionary Force that fought in Europe. In 2008 the park was a concrete plaza located on the roof of a parking garage.

The Roaring Twenties, Prohibition, and Gangsters

(1920–1929)

At the end of the Great War, Europe slowly began recovering from the huge financial and human cost of this unprecedented conflict. Across the Atlantic Ocean, the United States economy flourished. Mass production techniques made consumer goods affordable to millions of Americans. The automobile, movie, radio, and chemical industries skyrocketed during the 1920s. Electricity and the telephone became part of most American homes.

Everything seemed to be possible through modern technology. This era was called both the "Roaring Twenties" and the "Jazz Age," the latter term credited to F. Scott Fitzgerald (1895–1940) who wrote *The Great Gatsby* (1925), a novel that highlighted the corruption of the postwar period, new social attitudes, and the growth of individualism. Fitzgerald himself became the archetype of the writer who is seduced and destroyed by Hollywood.

By 1920, with 576,673 people, Los Angeles was the tenth largest city in the U.S., finally surpassing San Francisco. The city's 365 square miles made it the largest metropolitan area in America. During this decade significant numbers of Jewish immigrants and their families moved to Los Angeles from the East Coast and Midwest, eventually making L.A. the largest Jewish community west of Chicago.

Prohibition, an attempt to ban alcohol manufacture, sales, and consumption, became U.S. law in 1920. Many progressives supported Prohibition as a way to eliminate the evils of alcoholism such as domestic violence. Unfortunately, the ban was widely disregarded, and the demand for alcohol was satisfied by criminals when legitimate businesses were no longer permitted to make and sell it. This resulted in gangsters becoming incredibly wealthy and holding some American cities hostage through bribery and terror. Fortunately, unlike Detroit, Chicago, and some other major cities, L.A. did not fall under the control of mobsters during this era.

This period of liberality and fantastic growth ended with the Wall Street crash of 1929. The most devastating stock market collapse in U.S. history began on October 24, and conditions deteriorated rapidly. Many historians consider this the beginning of the Great Depression that would define the next decade and have repercussions even today.

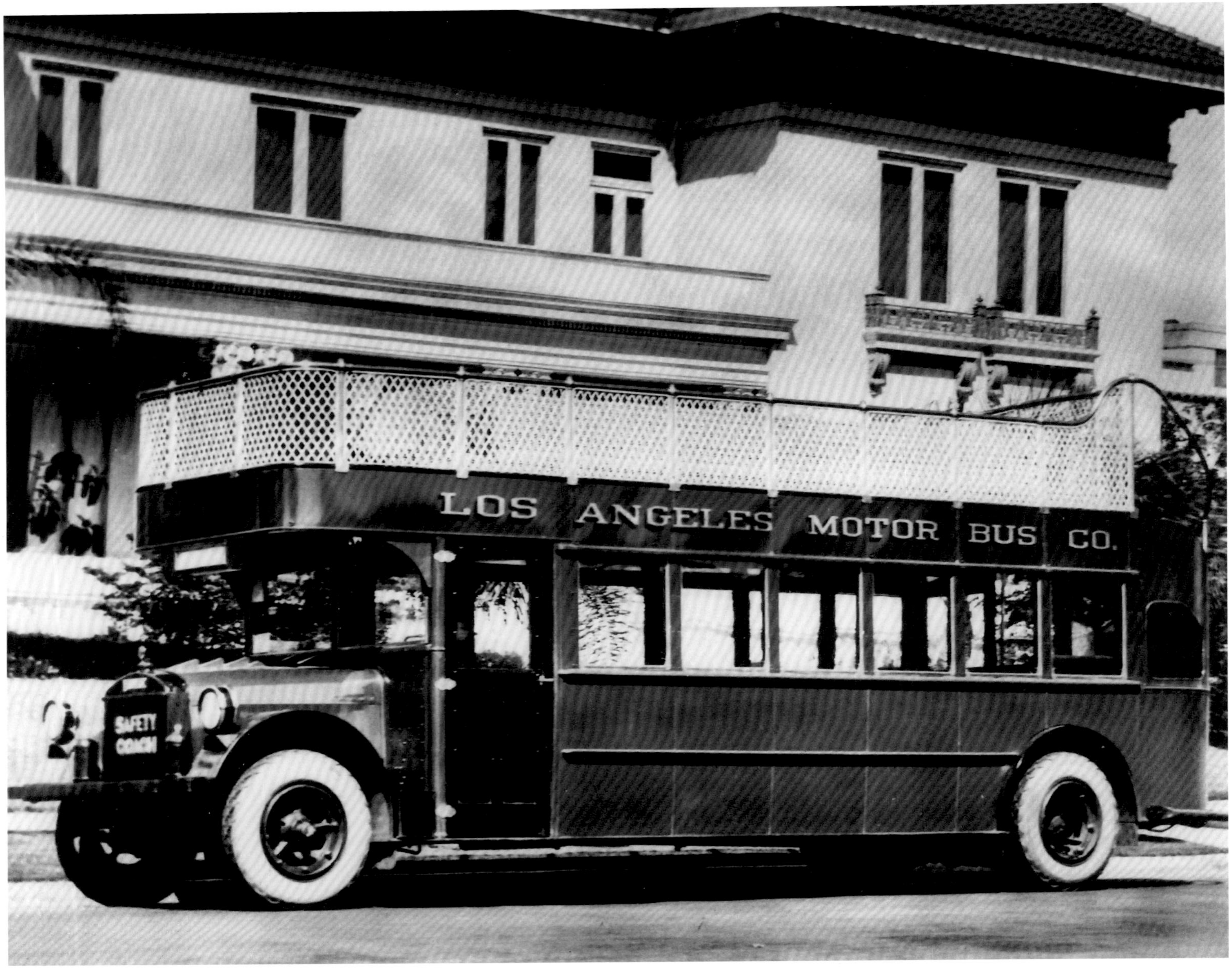

By 1925, every other Angeleno owned an automobile, compared to the rest of the U.S., where there was one car for every six people. Complaints about traffic congestion downtown were offset by public anger over the "rotten" service then provided by L.A. streetcars, according to articles that ran in the Los Angeles *Record*. In most cities, public transportation, like this double-decker motorbus operated by the Los Angeles Motor Bus Company, was still the most affordable and practical, but L.A. residents preferred the convenience and freedom afforded by the automobile.

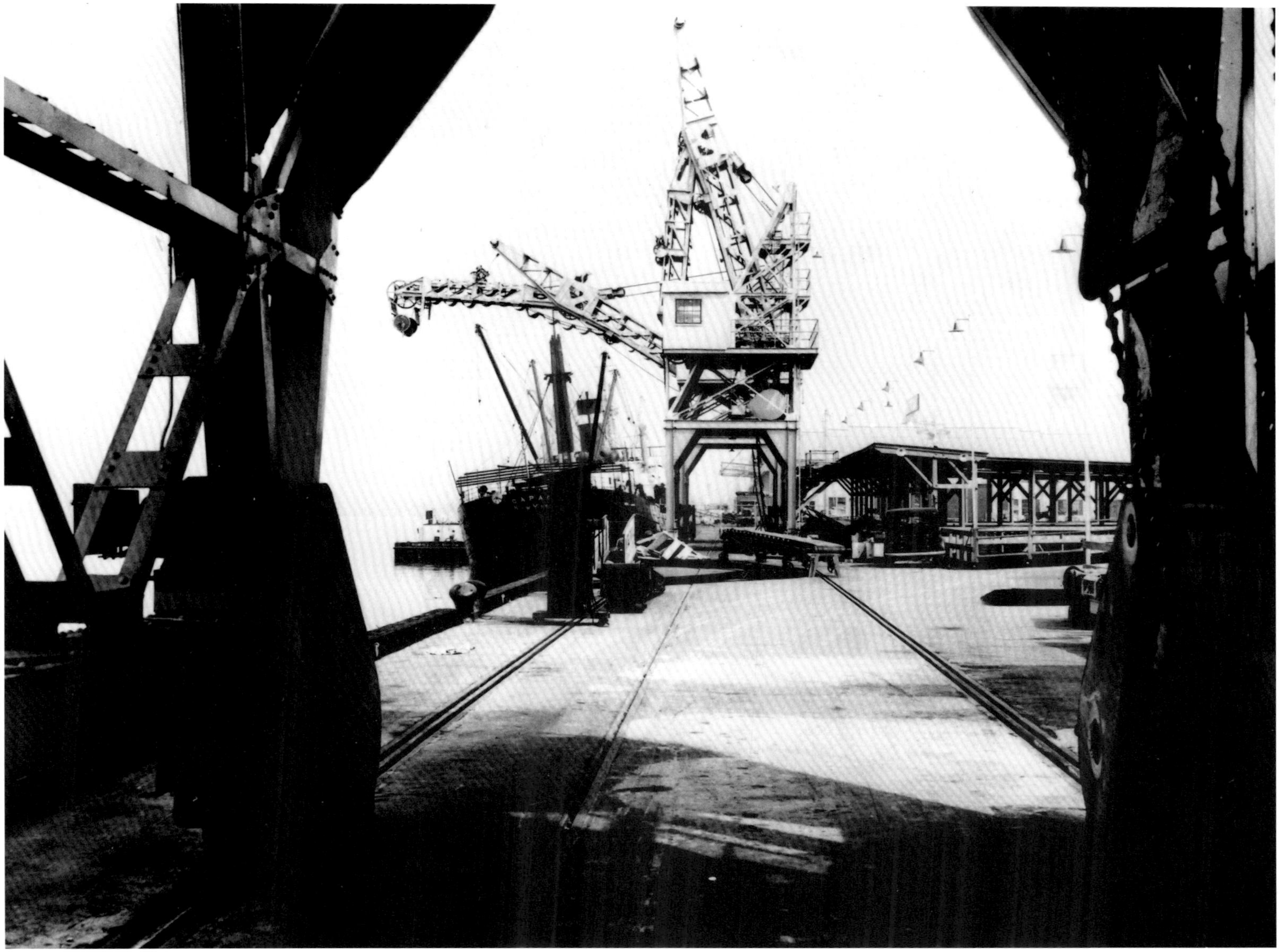

Los Angeles did not originally have a deep harbor like San Diego or San Francisco. In the early 1900s repeated bonds were issued by the L.A. Harbor Commission to create a viable Port of Los Angeles. Over many years the Army Corps of Engineers widened the channel near San Pedro and Wilmington and constructed a deep basin. Here, traveling cranes stand at ready on a Los Angeles pier.

A Congressional party visits the Universal Motion Picture Studio in Los Angeles while on a tour to Panama and Alaska in 1924. Although immorality was presented in burlesque houses and dime novels, many religious groups and other organizations were concerned that moving pictures had much greater influence. Congress was therefore pushed to censor movie content, and a ruling by the Supreme Court confirmed that films were subject to censorship and could not claim protection under the First Amendment.

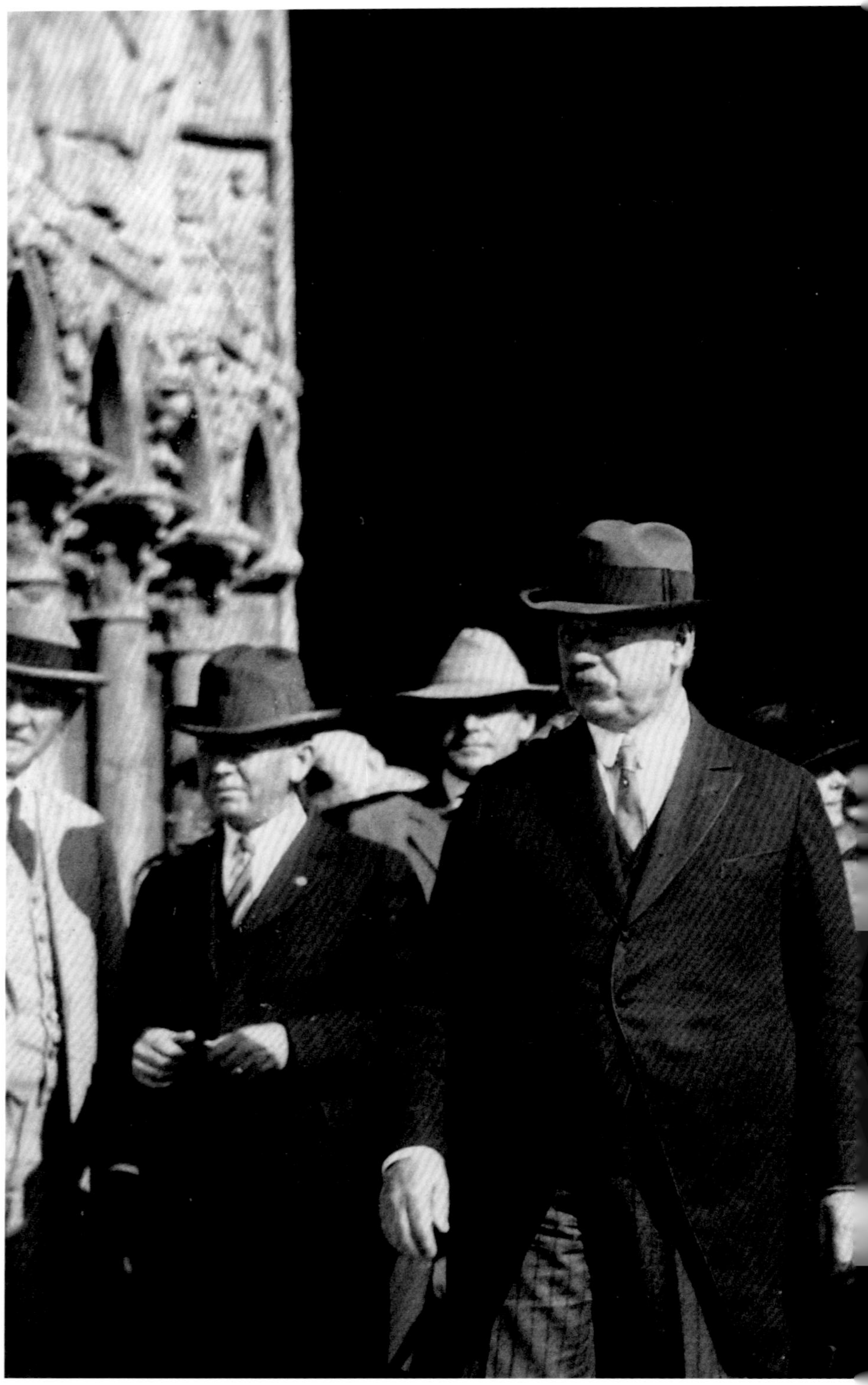

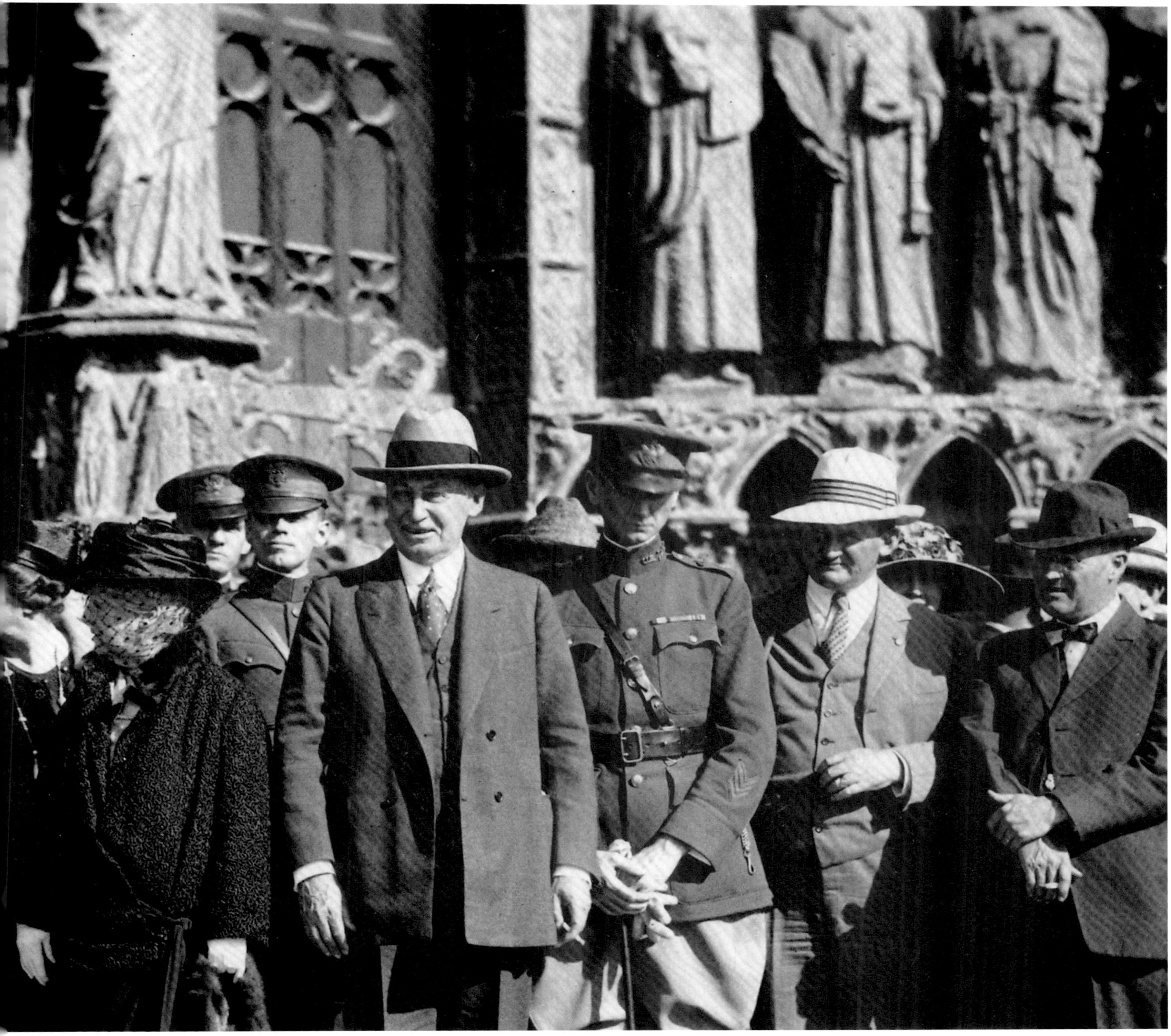

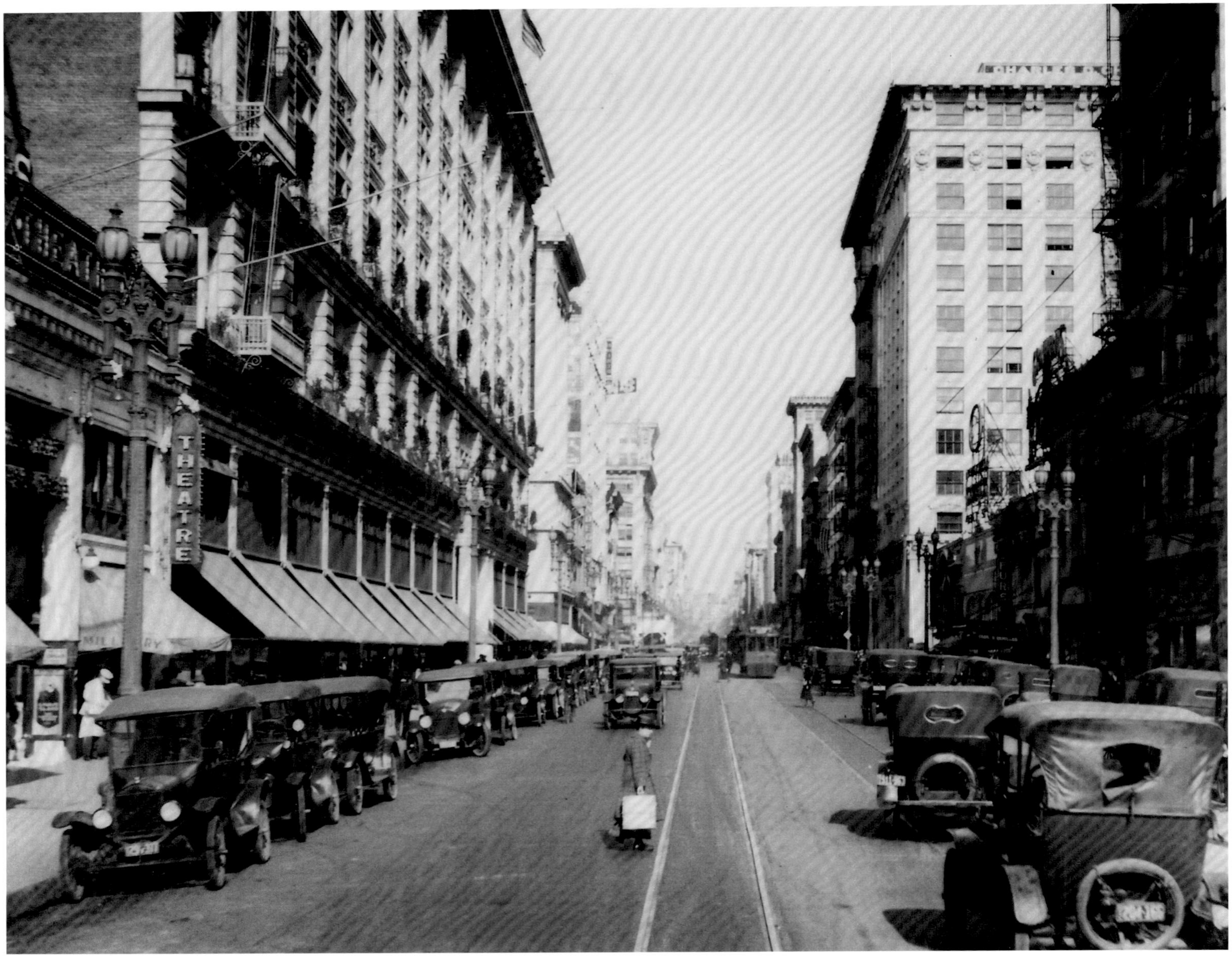

Broadway at 8th Street in downtown Los Angeles around 1920. The dramatic increase in roads and cars created the suburban boom of the 1920s and affected nearly a hundred American cities. This growth was welcomed not only by real estate developers; housing reformers believed that poverty and crime resulted from overcrowding in centralized cities.

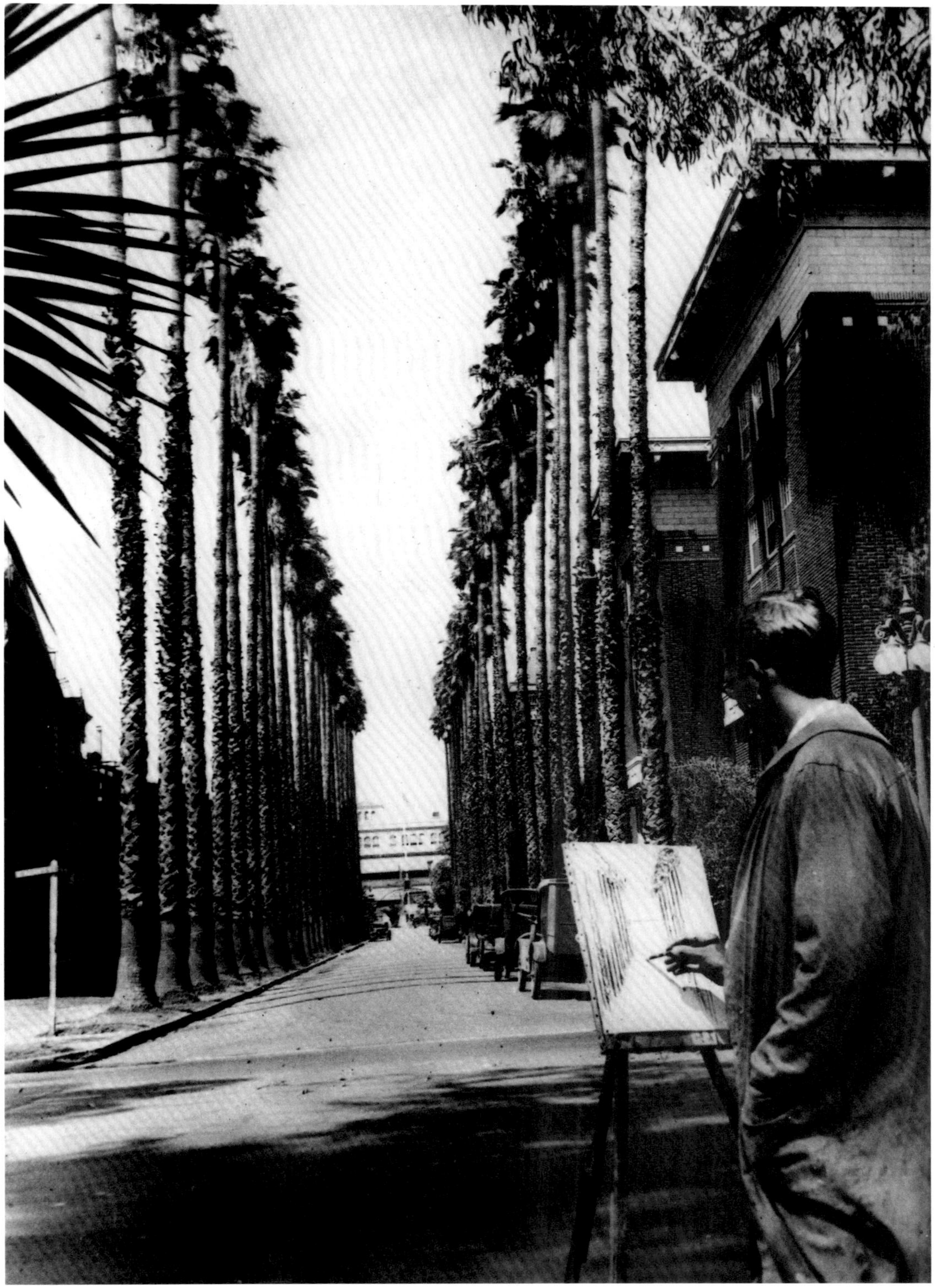

An artist at his easel, Avenue of the Palms in Los Angeles. Louis Adamic (1899–1951), an émigré writer and labor activist from Slovenia, eked out a living in Los Angeles in the 1920s. His bitter view of L.A., expressed through such works as *Laughing in the Jungle,* was that of a remorseless city where dishonest promoters grew rich exploiting deluded idealists looking for a nonexistent paradise. Similar sentiments of Los Angeles would echo in the works of many other writers.

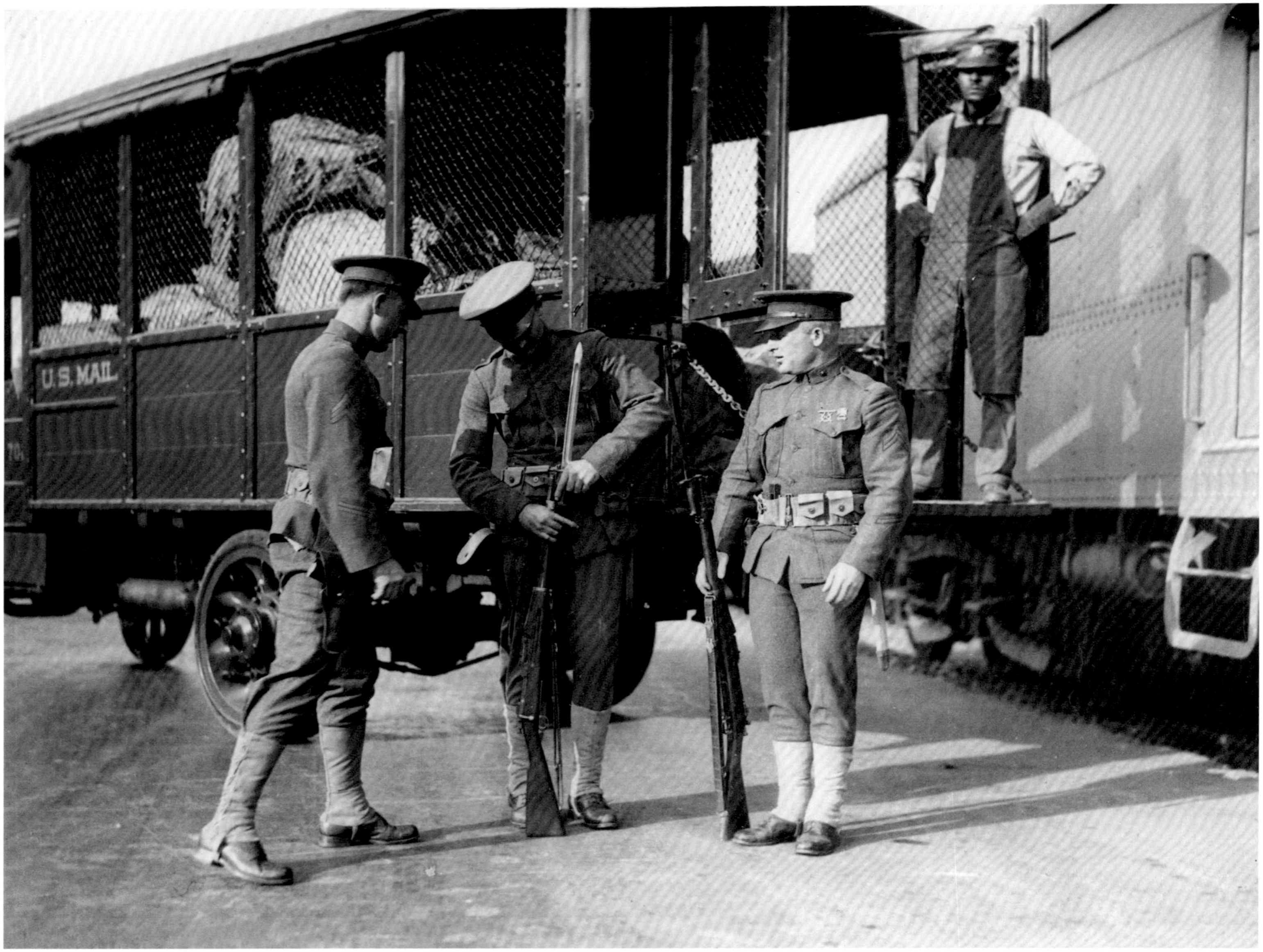

Prohibition unintentionally created criminal networks throughout many American cities. Although Los Angeles was not controlled by gangsters as Chicago was, L.A. still had its share of ruthless thugs, corrupt policemen, and petty crime. In 1926, so many mail robberies occurred that 2,500 Marines were assigned to guard the mail in 23 cities. Marines equipped with semiautomatic pistols, shotguns, rifles, and machine guns guarded the U.S. mail in Los Angeles with instructions to shoot to kill.

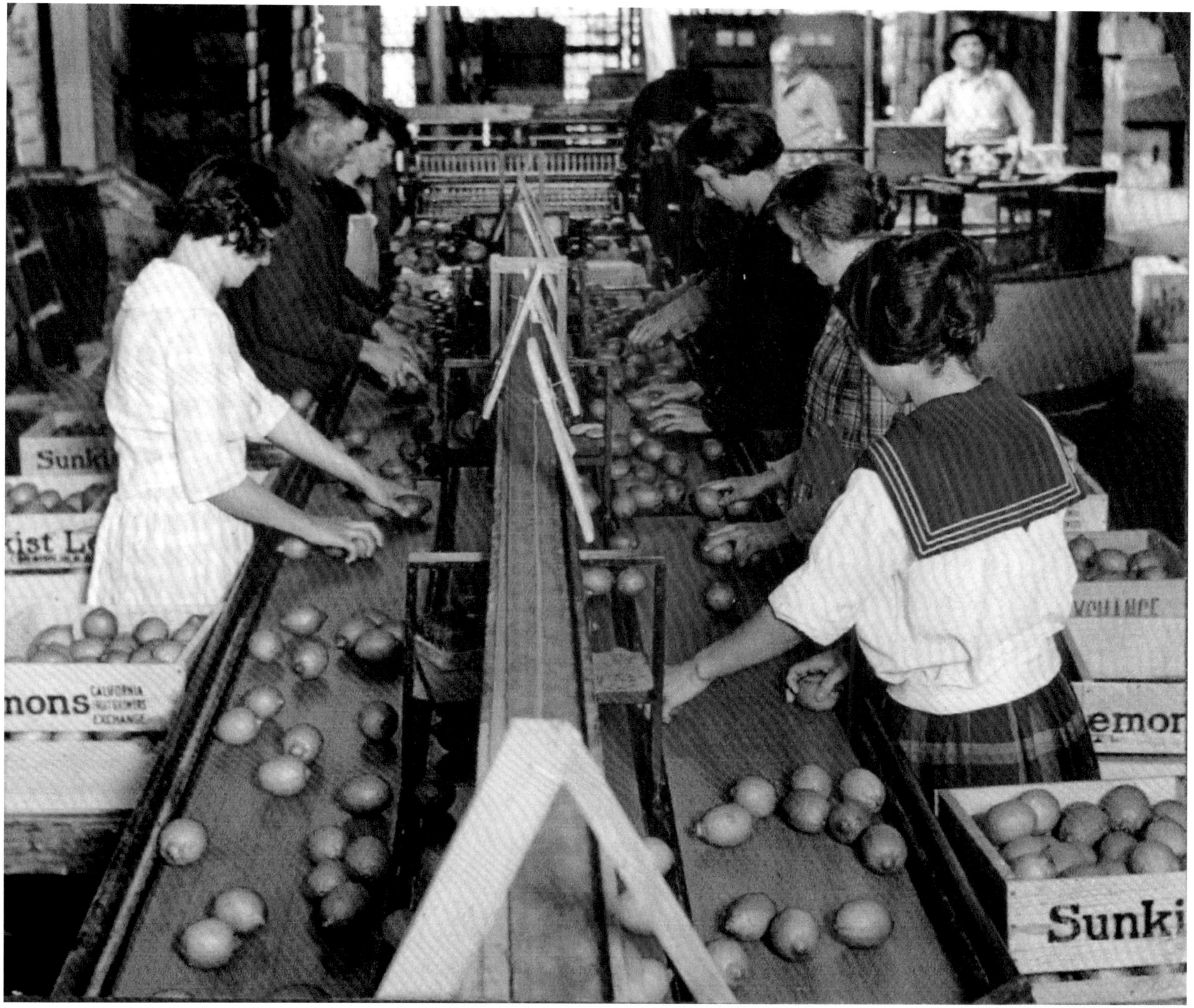

In Lamanda Park, lemons coming from a washer are hand-graded according to their color. Such labor in the 1920s, as today, was often done by migrant workers.

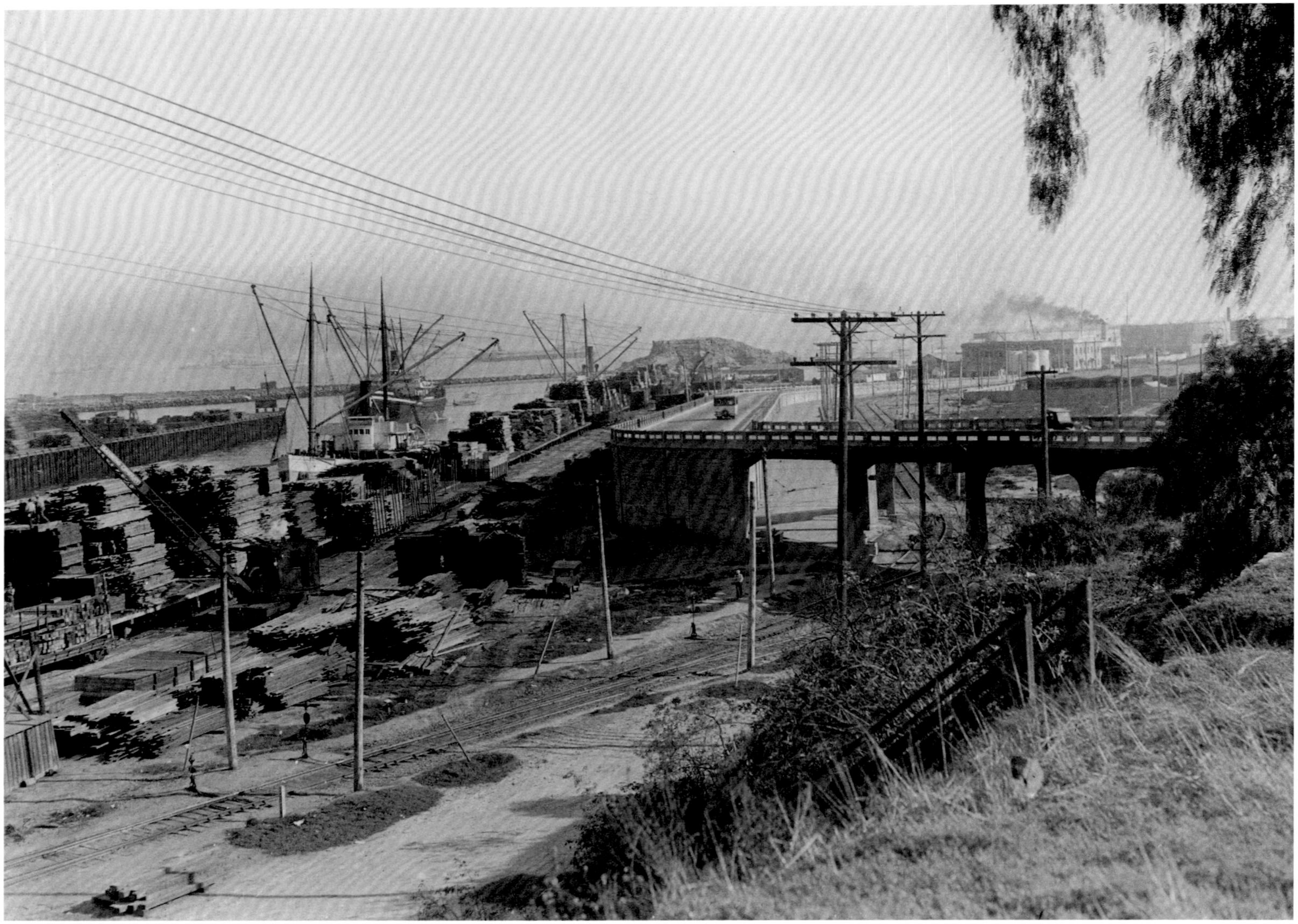

A view of Los Angeles harbor, whose phenomenal growth in this decade made it the second greatest port in America. L.A.'s shipping trade was exceeded only by New York and exports alone during 1926 were more than $100 million, nearly fourteen times greater than exports through L.A. in 1915.

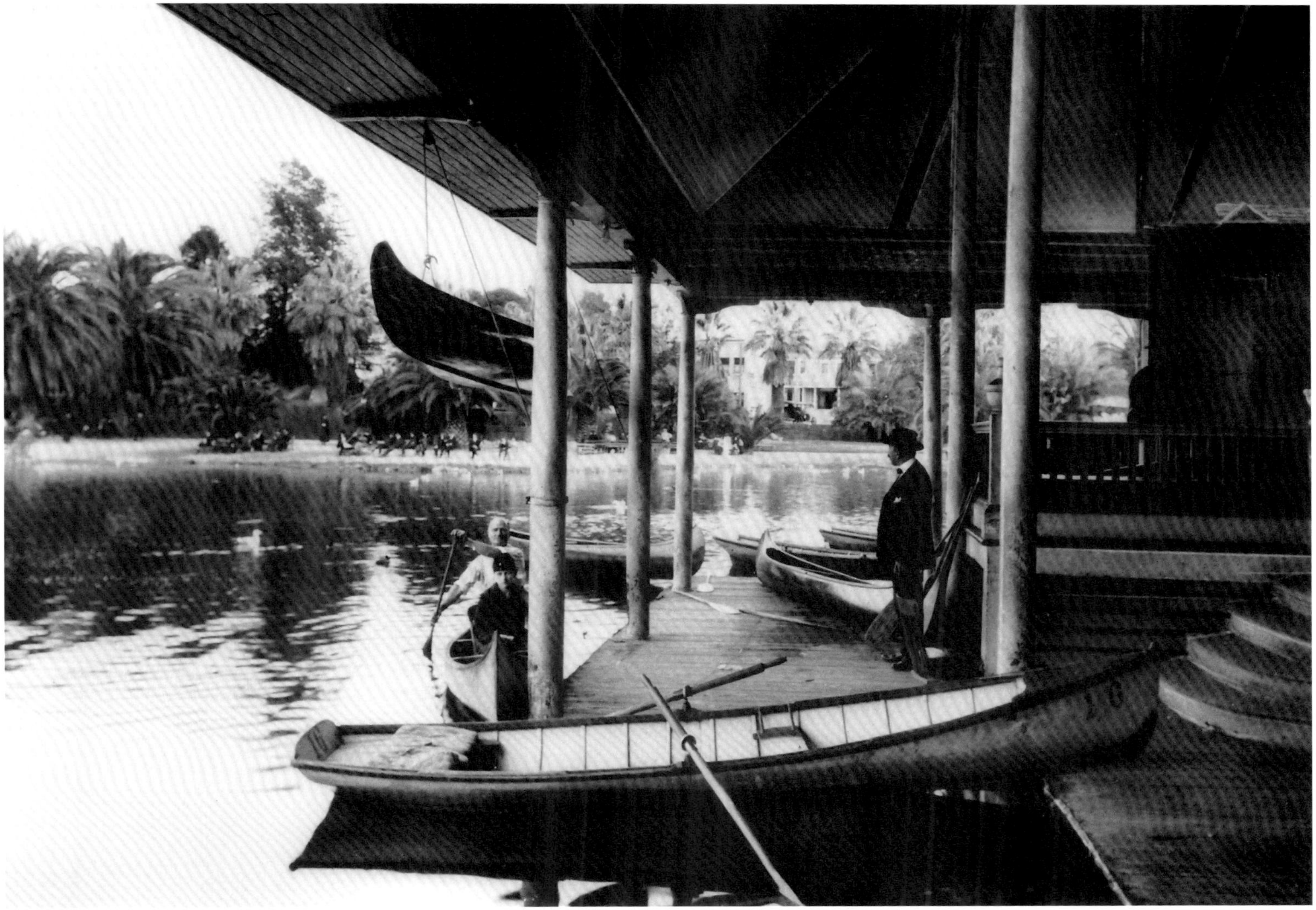

Canoes in the water at Westlake Park. This placid scene belies the stress that the economic boom and rapid expansion of Los Angeles had on the average Angeleno. One woman wondered: "how soon the wheels of progress are going to stop rattling long enough for us to hear ourselves think, catch our breath and develop some sort of cohesive social organism."

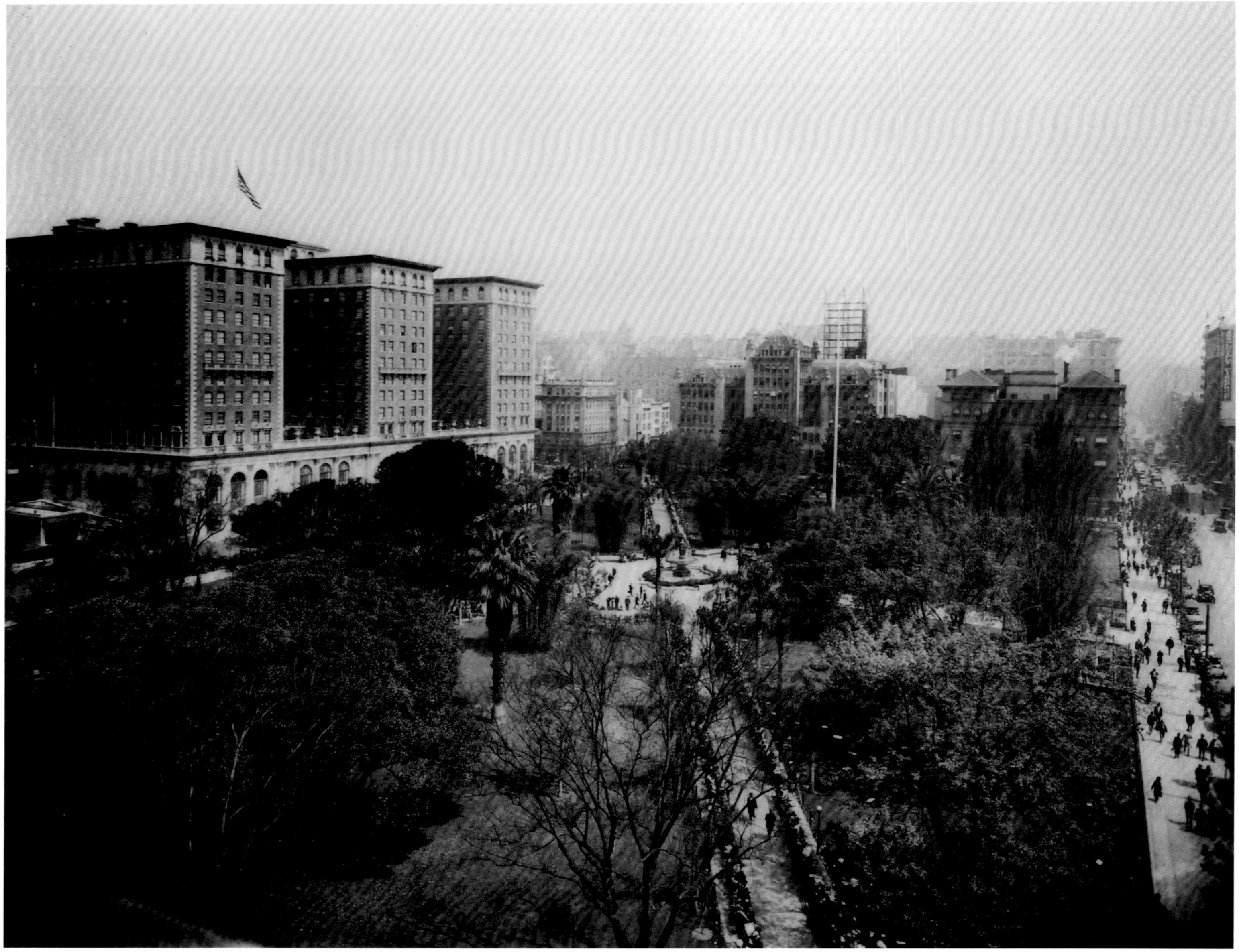

Pershing Square and the Biltmore Hotel in Los Angeles in the 1920s. The nearby Long Beach oil boom was one of the driving forces of L.A.'s dramatic economic growth in this decade. Upton Sinclair (1878–1968) was an author, investigator, and Socialist best known for his 1906 exposé of the meatpacking industry. In 1916 he settled in the L.A. area and wrote a muckraking novel about the corrupting effects of the boom.

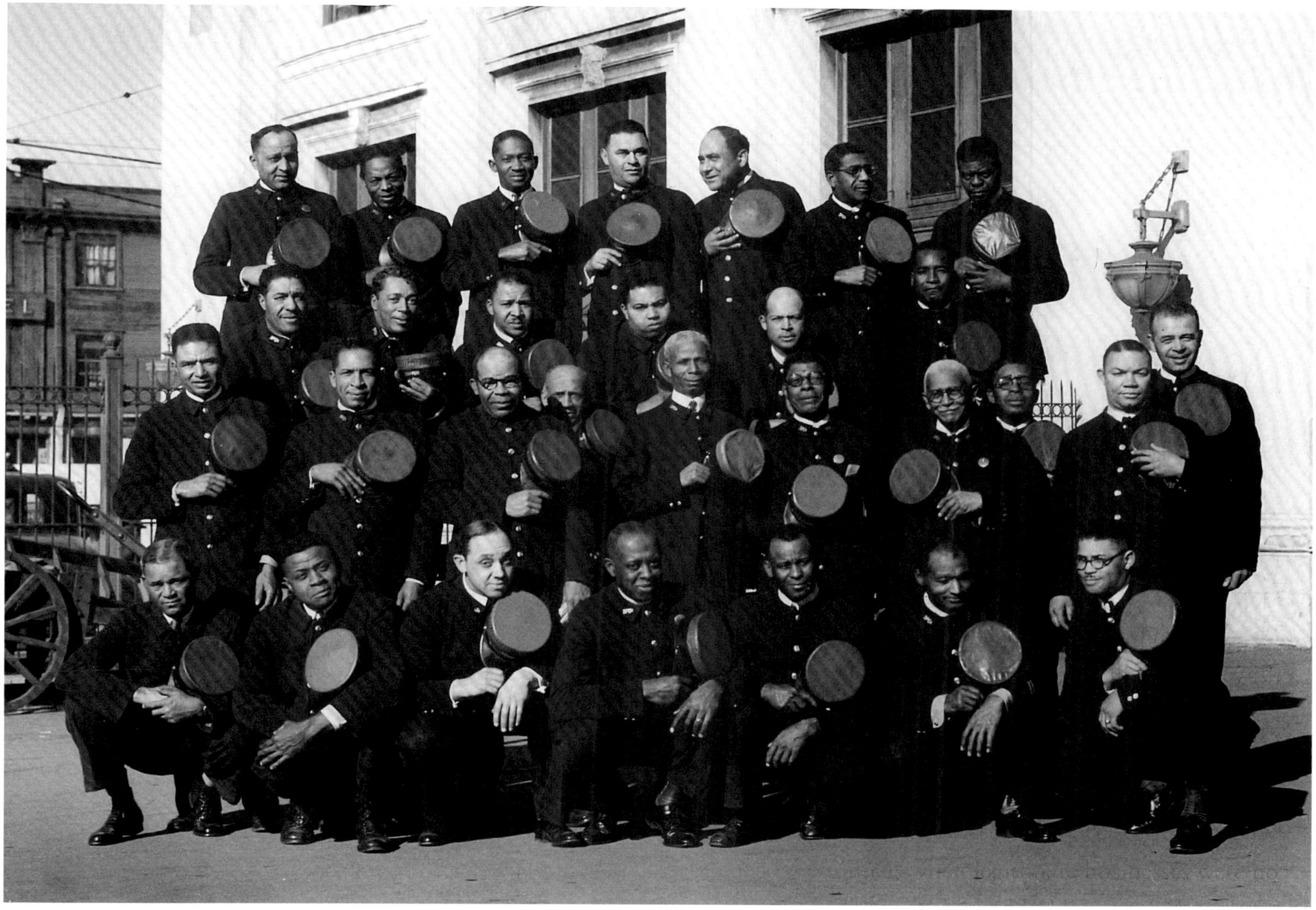

Redcaps employed by the Southern Pacific railroad in Los Angeles in the 1920s. During this decade minorities were treated with more equality in some large American cities (including L.A.), and there was open tolerance of homosexuality. By the end of this decade, L.A. had the largest African American population on the West Coast.

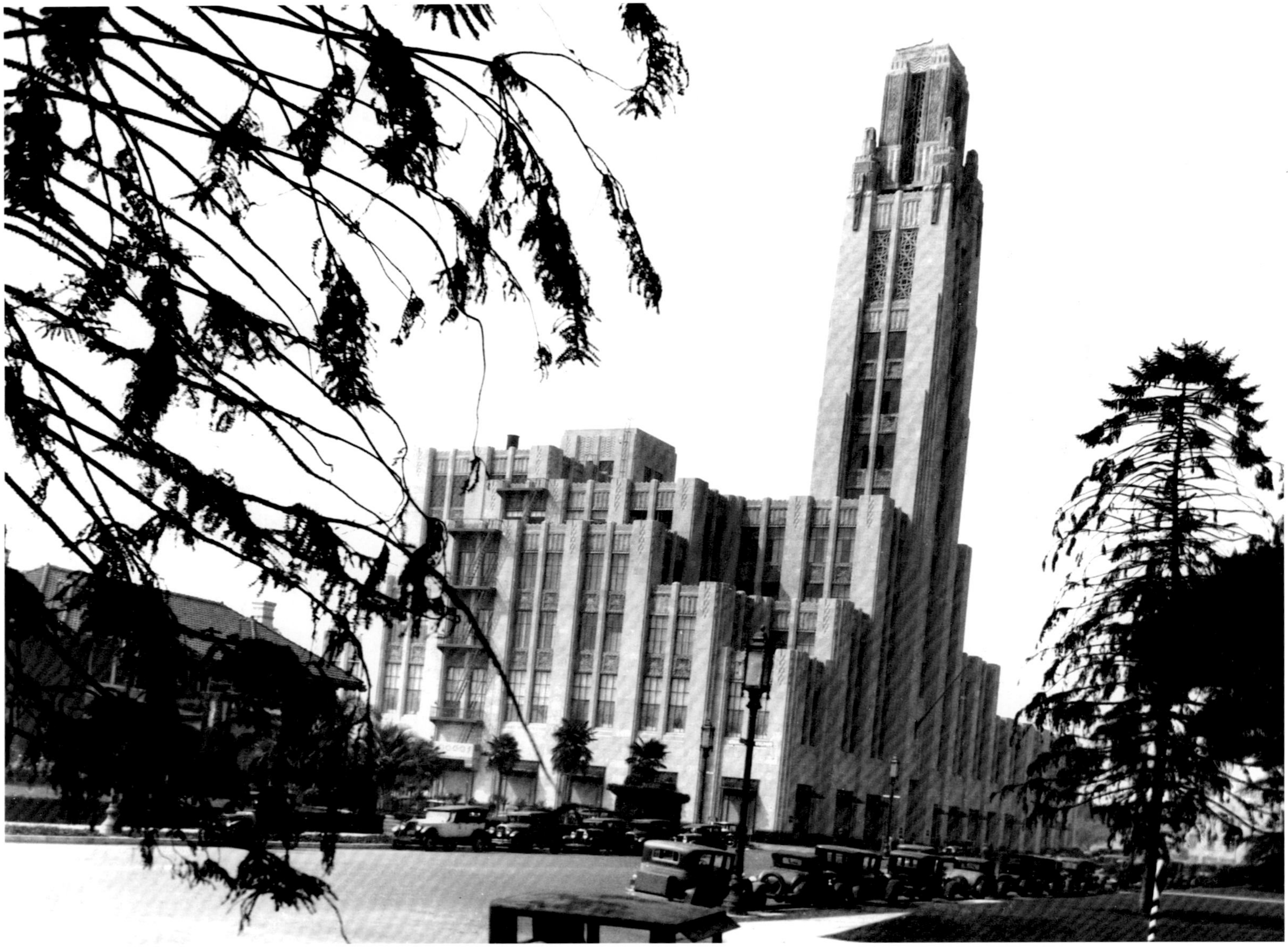

The same month that the stock market collapsed in 1929, Bullock's opened a Wilshire Boulevard retail operation the company claimed was the most beautiful such establishment in the world. The store's brightly illuminated tower could be seen for miles along Wilshire at night.

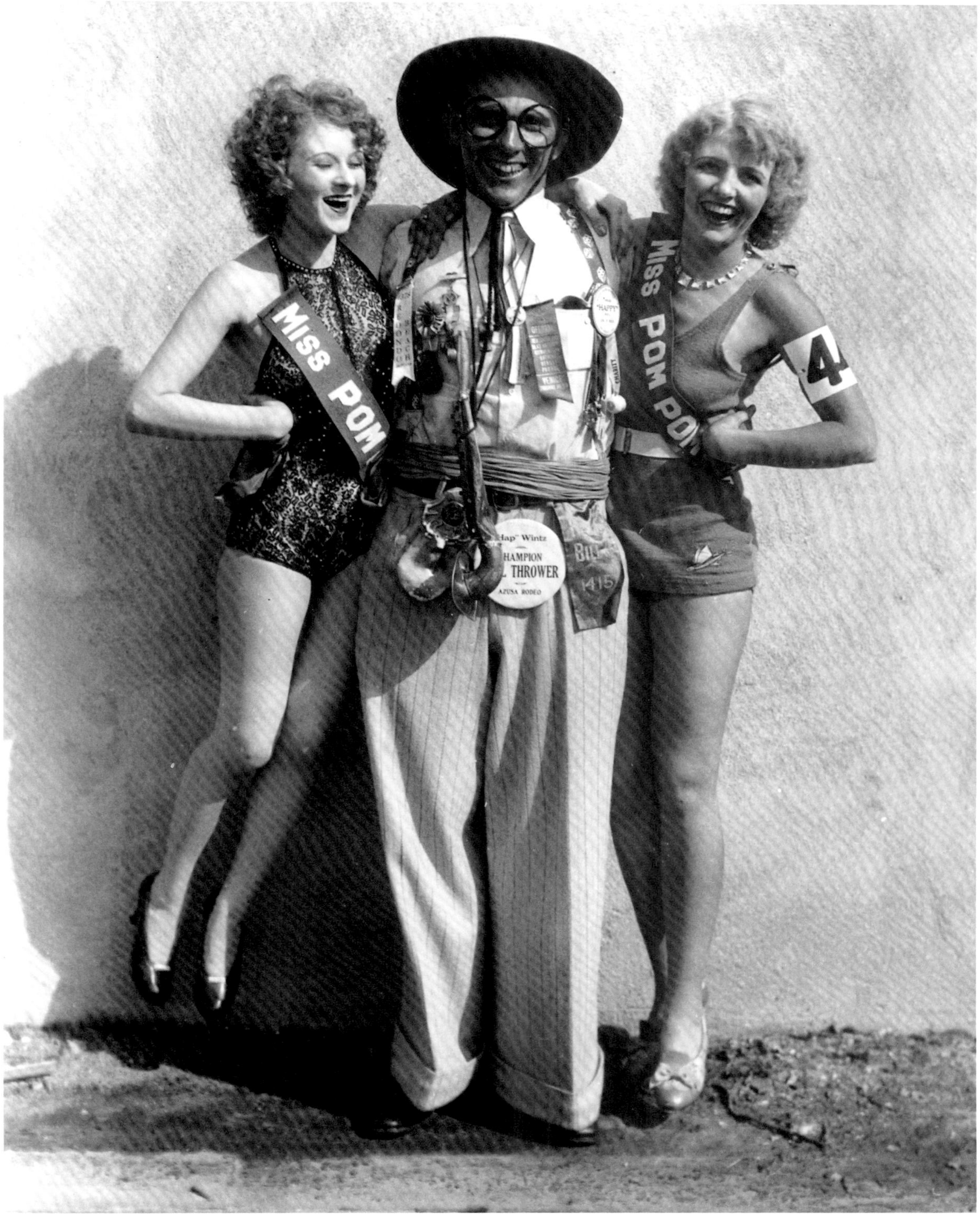

Flanked by two entrants in a "bathing beauty contest," this Elks Lodge member poses during a 1929 Elks convention in Venice.

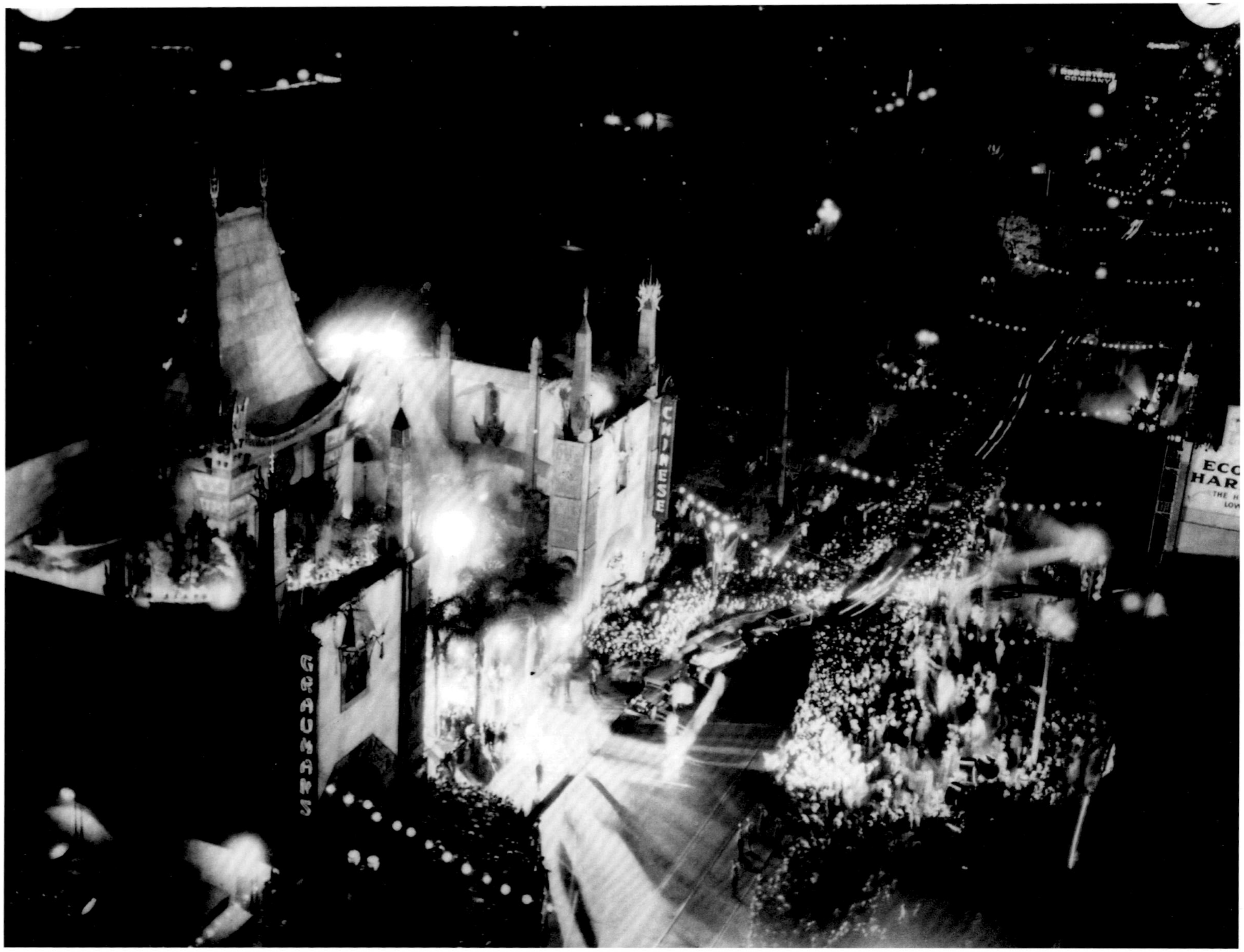

On the night of May 18, 1927, Grauman's Chinese Theatre in Hollywood held its grand opening—touted as the most spectacular theater opening in motion picture history. Thousands of fans lined Hollywood Boulevard to see the movie stars and other celebrities arrive for the opening. *The King of Kings,* directed by Cecil B. DeMille, was the film premiered that night.

The Great Depression and Recovery

(1930–1939)

The greatest man-made economic disaster in history started with the U.S. stock market crash in 1929. Known in America as the Great Depression, it devastated international trade, ruined businesses, and left millions of workers jobless.

After the boom of the 1920s, the economic collapse of the 1930s shattered lives and expectations. Millions of disillusioned people started listening to left-wing and right-wing demagogues who blamed problems on the Jews and other groups, and promised better times under their leadership. One such rabble-rouser was Adolf Hitler, who used terror, skillful oratory, and clever propaganda to become chancellor of Germany in 1933 and then seized power as dictator.

Extremists also preached a combination of hope and hate on the radio in America. When Franklin Delano Roosevelt (1882–1945) was sworn in as the thirty-second president in early 1933, a quarter of the U.S. work force was unemployed, and industrial production was half its 1929 level. Millions were homeless. Roosevelt's New Deal social and economic programs did not end the Depression, but they helped America remain a democracy when other industrialized countries succumbed to fascist or communist totalitarianism.

By 1930, Los Angeles was the fifth most populous city in the United States, with more than 1.2 million residents. By 1934, 300,000 people were unemployed in Los Angeles. Angelenos sought answers by joining the Utopian Society, Epic Movement, and dozens of social movements. Most of these groups were feared as potentially subversive. L.A. police captain William "Red" Hynes had his men break up suspected communist meetings with clubs and tear gas.

President Roosevelt's radio "Fireside Chats" reassured Americans that they would pull through the Depression. However, it was Hollywood that played perhaps the most valuable role in sustaining national morale. Even at the depths of the Depression, 60 to 80 million Americans attended the movies each week. This was not simple escapism. Many movies depicted the grim realities of the era, but they also reinforced the belief that an individual could still succeed and that government could protect its citizens, and they preserved the vision of America as a classless society.

By the end of the decade, massive rearmament policies to counter the threat from Nazi Germany helped stimulate European economies. America was starting to build up its armed forces, too, and government deficit-spending on New Deal programs and the military led to recovery.

Hollywood, seen here in the 1930s, had 200,000 residents of the 1.2 million people who lived in greater Los Angeles. The movie industry made millions of dollars for the studios and star celebrities, but not everyone was happy with the types of movies that were produced. In 1933, Reverend Amleto Cicognani asked fellow Catholics to launch "a united and vigorous campaign for the purification of the cinema, which has become a deadly menace to morals." Nine million Catholics joined the Legion of Decency, pledged to boycott films that the Legion's rating board condemned.

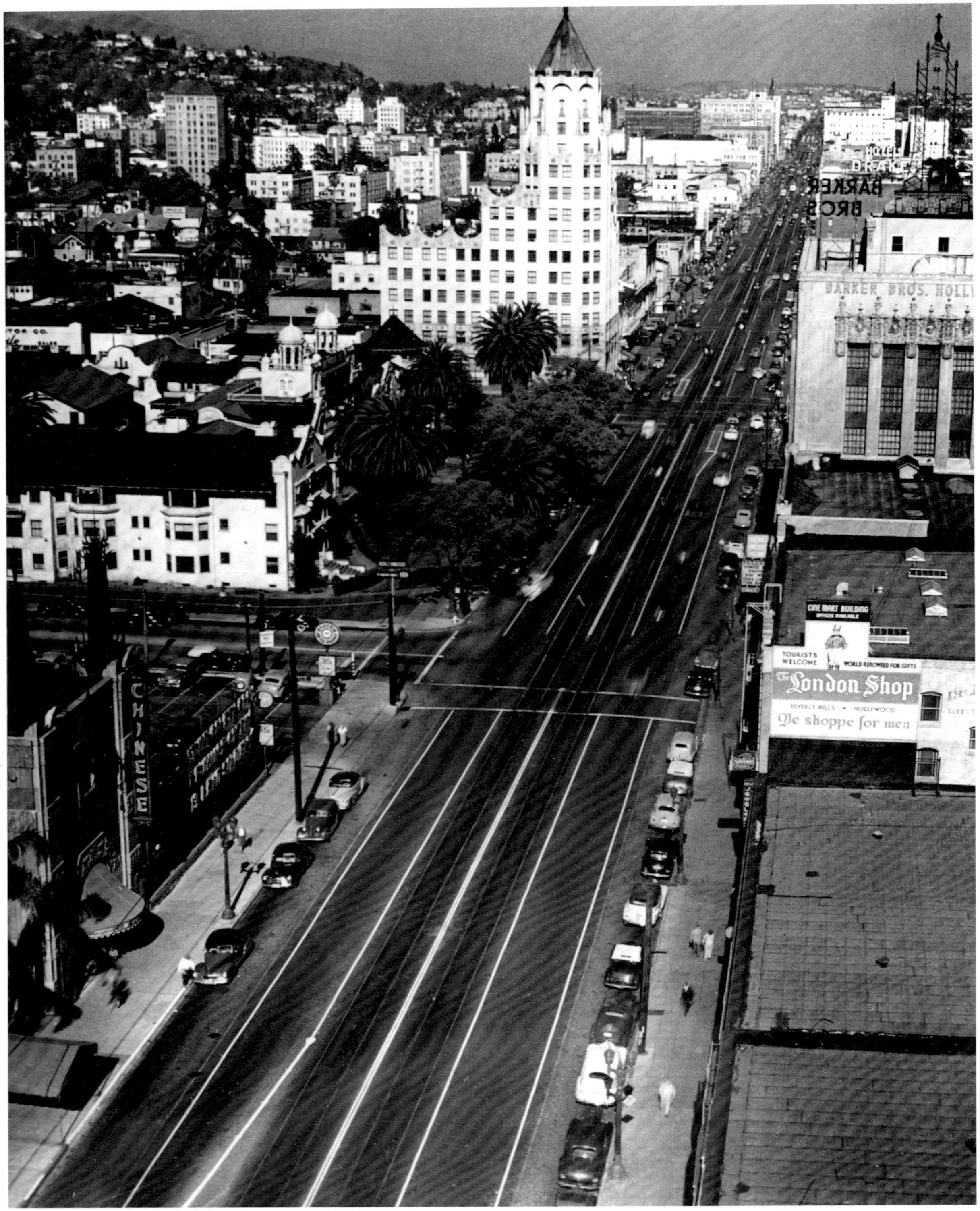

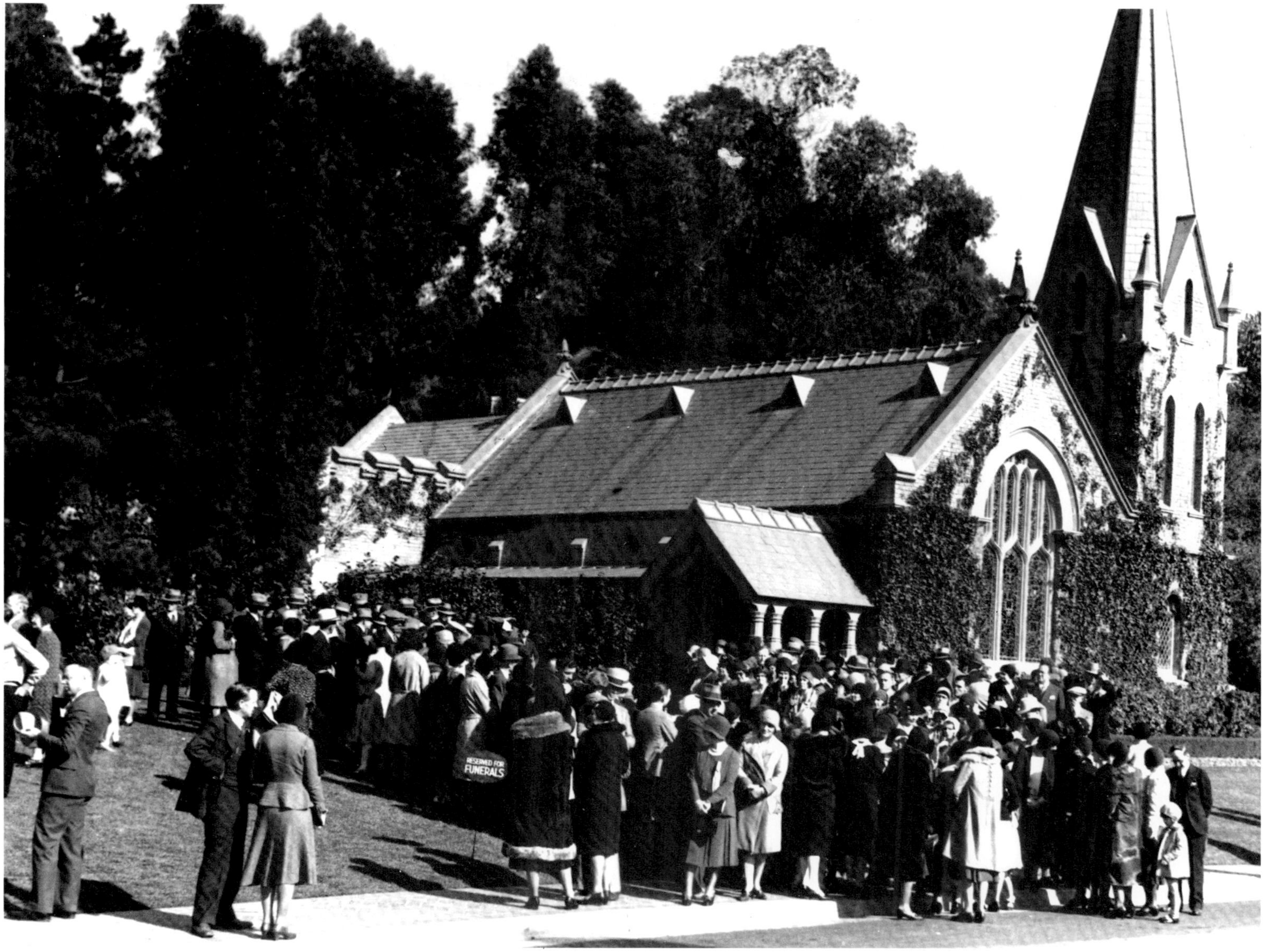

A crowd outside the Church of the Little Flower at the Forest Lawn Memorial Cemetery, where services were conducted for silent film star Alma Rubens (1897–1931). Rubens died January 22, 1931, from pneumonia. Forest Lawn, founded in 1906, was managed from 1917 by Dr. Hubert Eaton. Eaton was an innovator who said that most cemeteries were "unsightly, depressing stoneyards" and designed Forest Lawn to be "a great park devoid of misshapen monuments and other signs of earthly death."

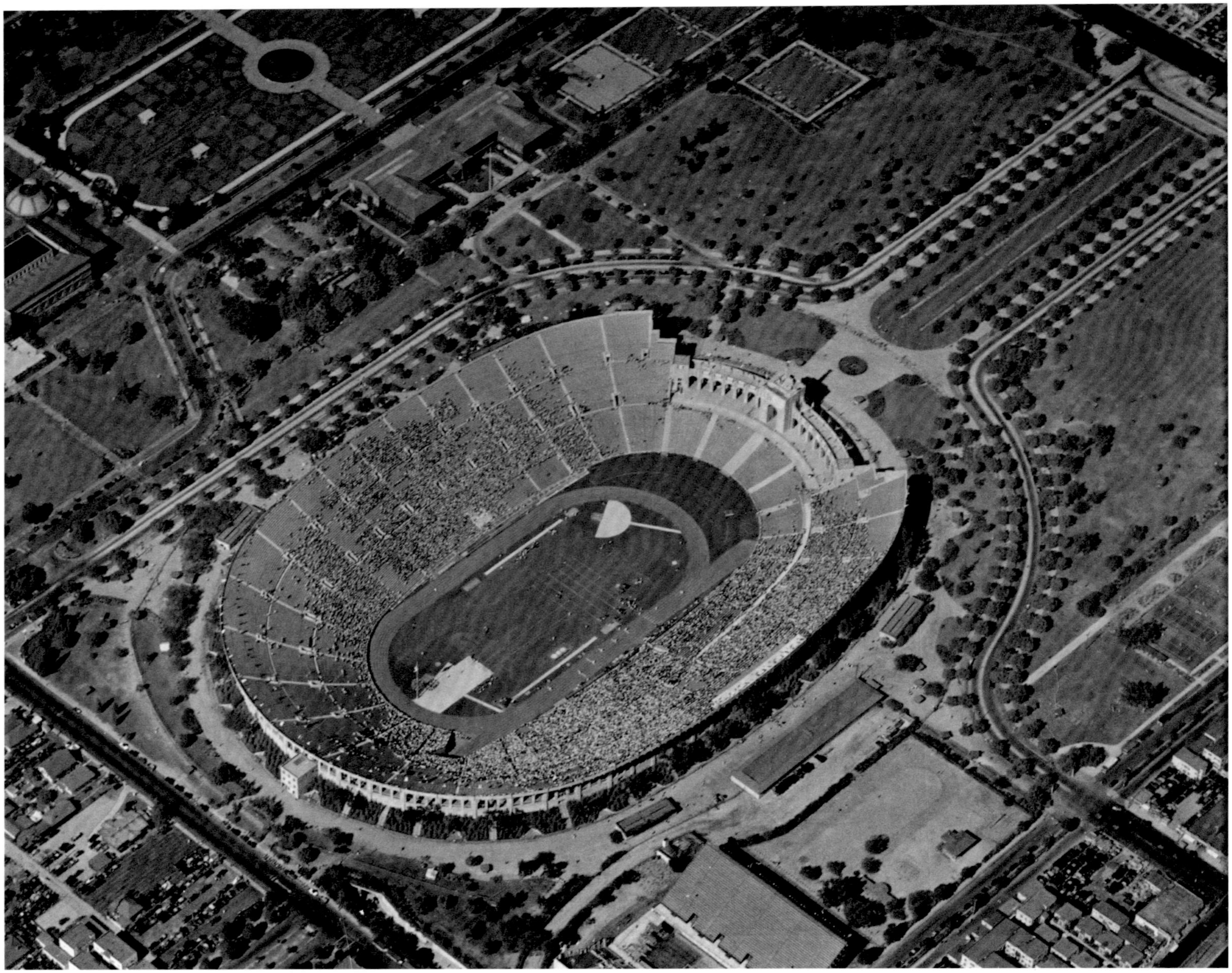

Vice-president Charles Curtis opened the X Olympiad on July 30, 1932, in Los Angeles Olympic Stadium, which was completed in 1923 as a memorial to Great War veterans. Approximately 1,300 athletes participated, representing 37 countries. The 1932 Olympic Games introduced the first photo-finish cameras as well as the victory platform. Los Angeles hosted the Summer Olympics again in 1984.

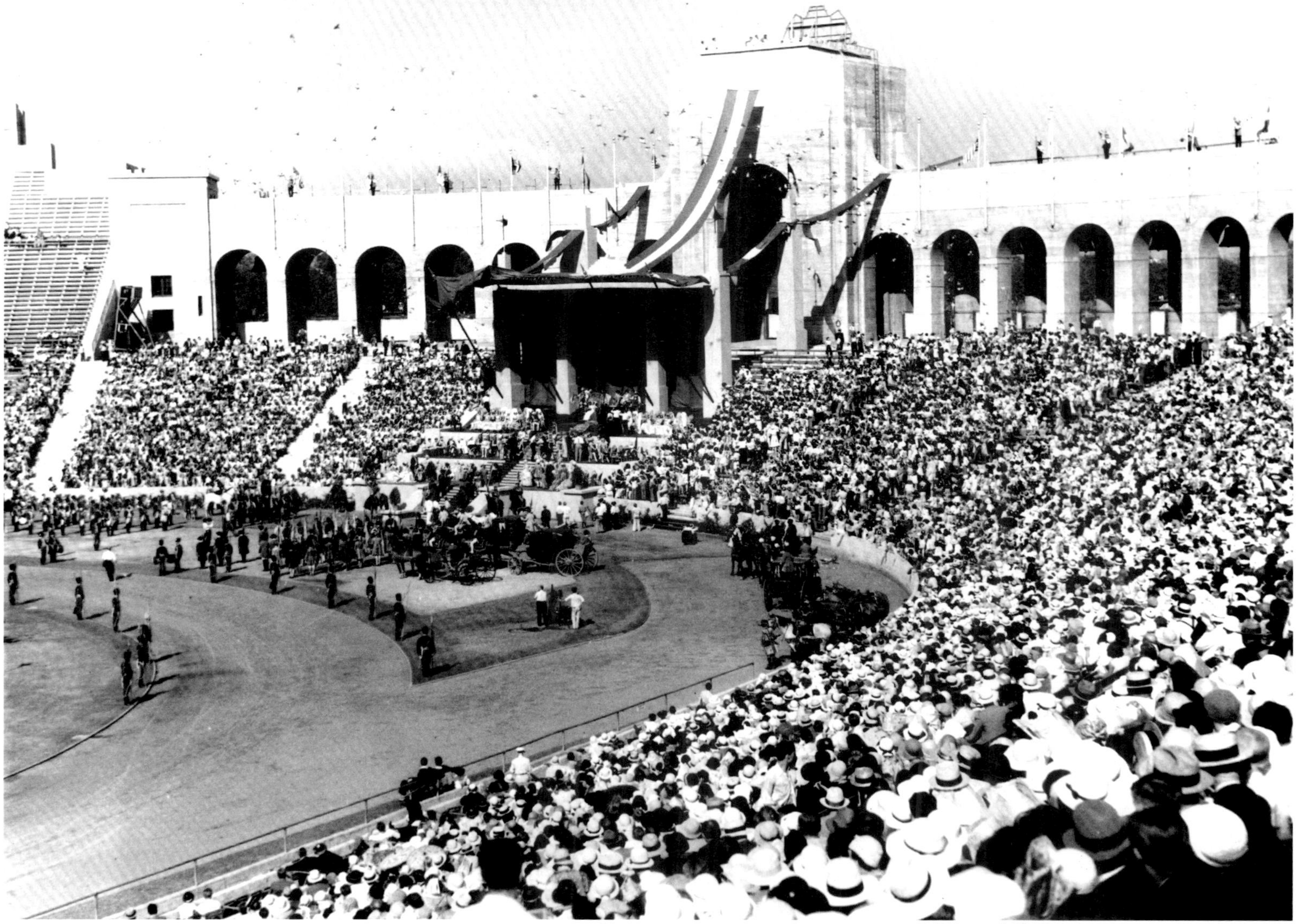

Los Angeles Olympic Stadium hosted many other events, such as the crowning of Mrs. Elizabeth Hicks Green as Queen of La Fiesta de Los Angeles that marked the 150th anniversary of the city. The scene of medieval pomp and ceremony was witnessed by a large crowd that jammed the stadium.

A Los Angeles street scene during the 1932 Summer Olympics. Because these Olympics were held in the middle of the Great Depression, half as many athletes (126 women, 1,206 men) took part as had in 1928. Nevertheless, the level of competition was extremely high, and 18 world records were either broken or equalled. The crowds set records, too, starting with the 100,000 people who attended the Opening Ceremony. The 1932 Olympics were the first to last sixteen days.

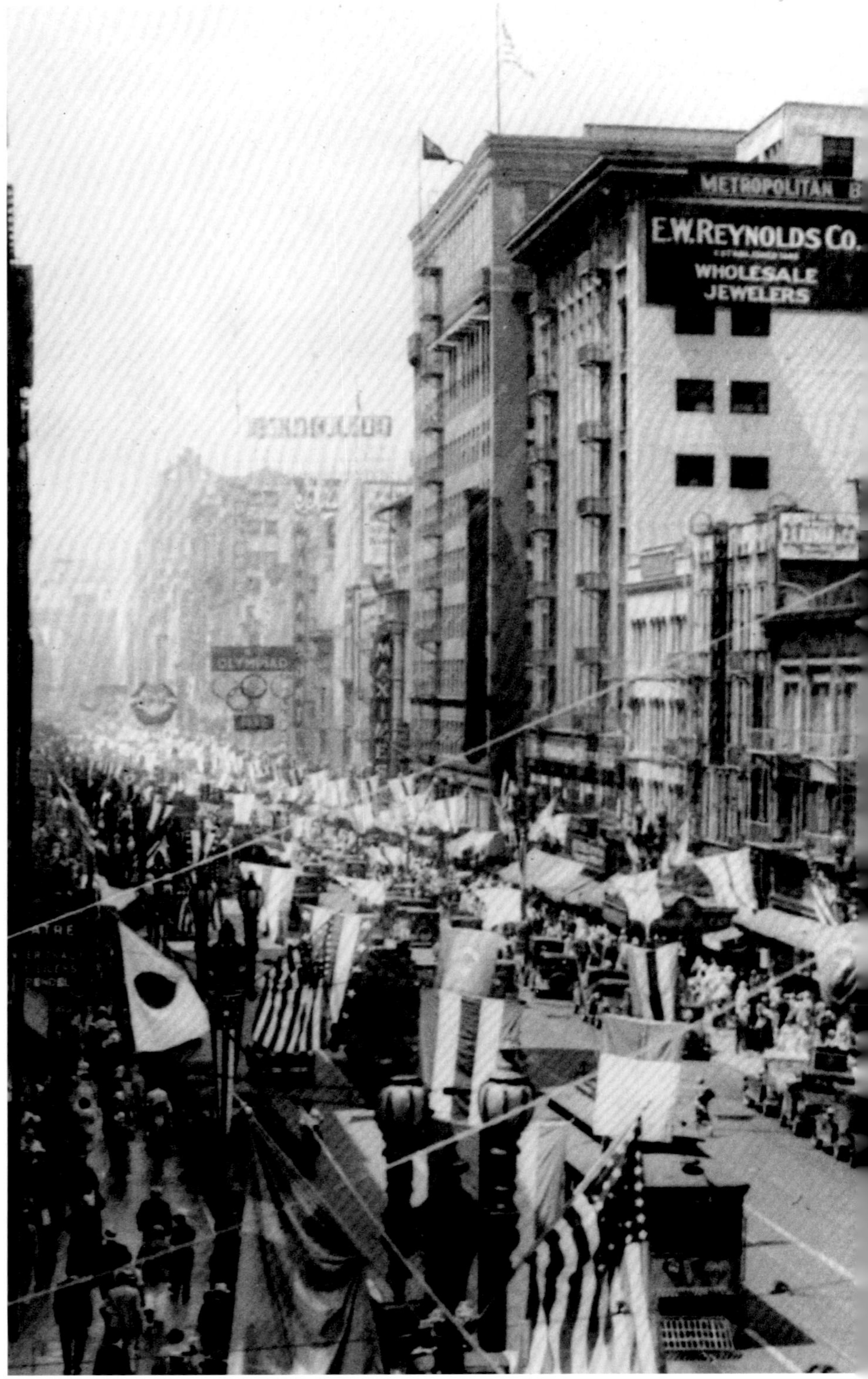

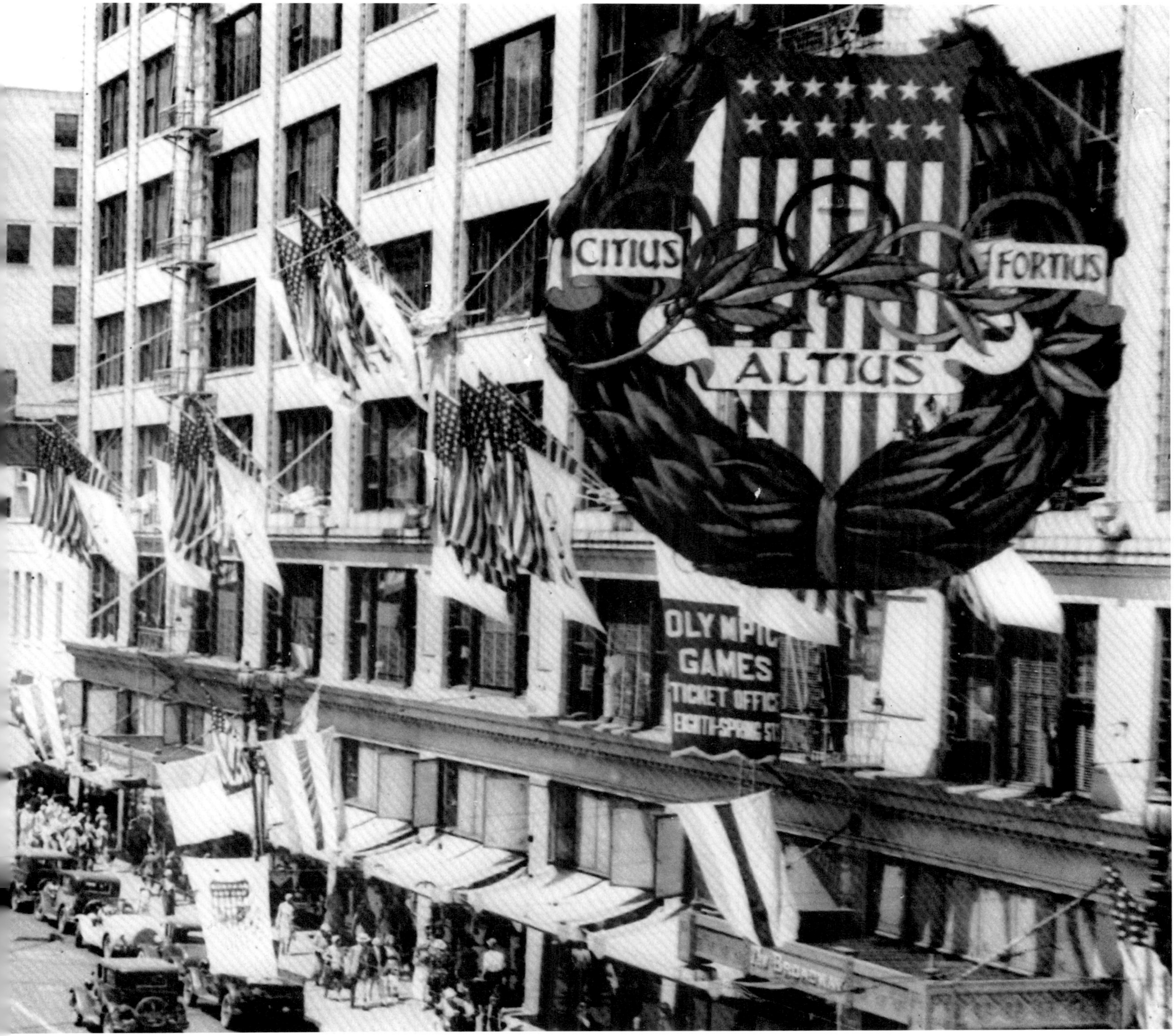
CITIUS
FORTIUS
ALTIUS
OLYMPIC
GAMES
TICKET OFFIC
EIGHTH-SPRING ST

A special telephone exchange was put into service for the Los Angeles Olympic Games. The operators could speak English, German, Spanish, and French.

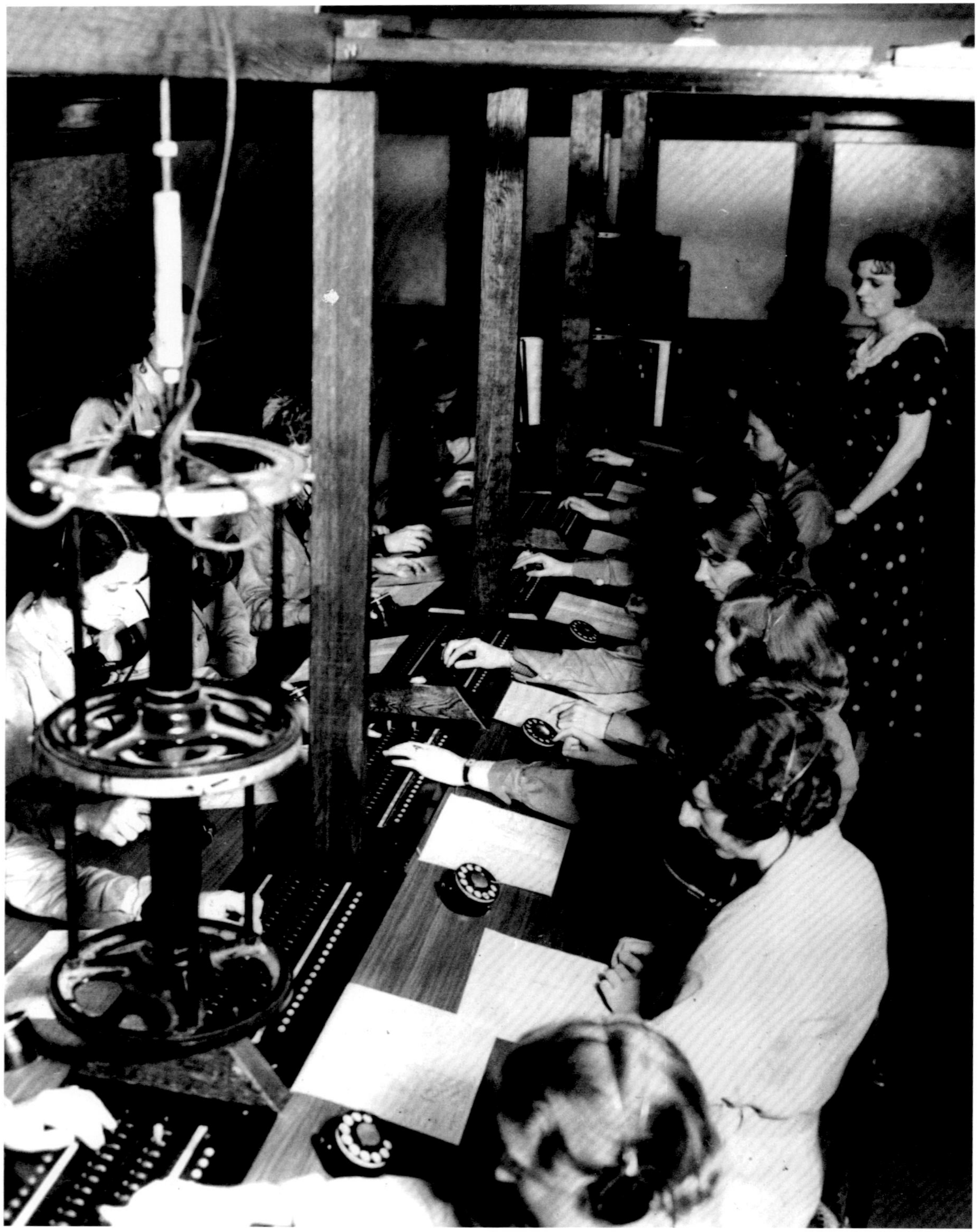

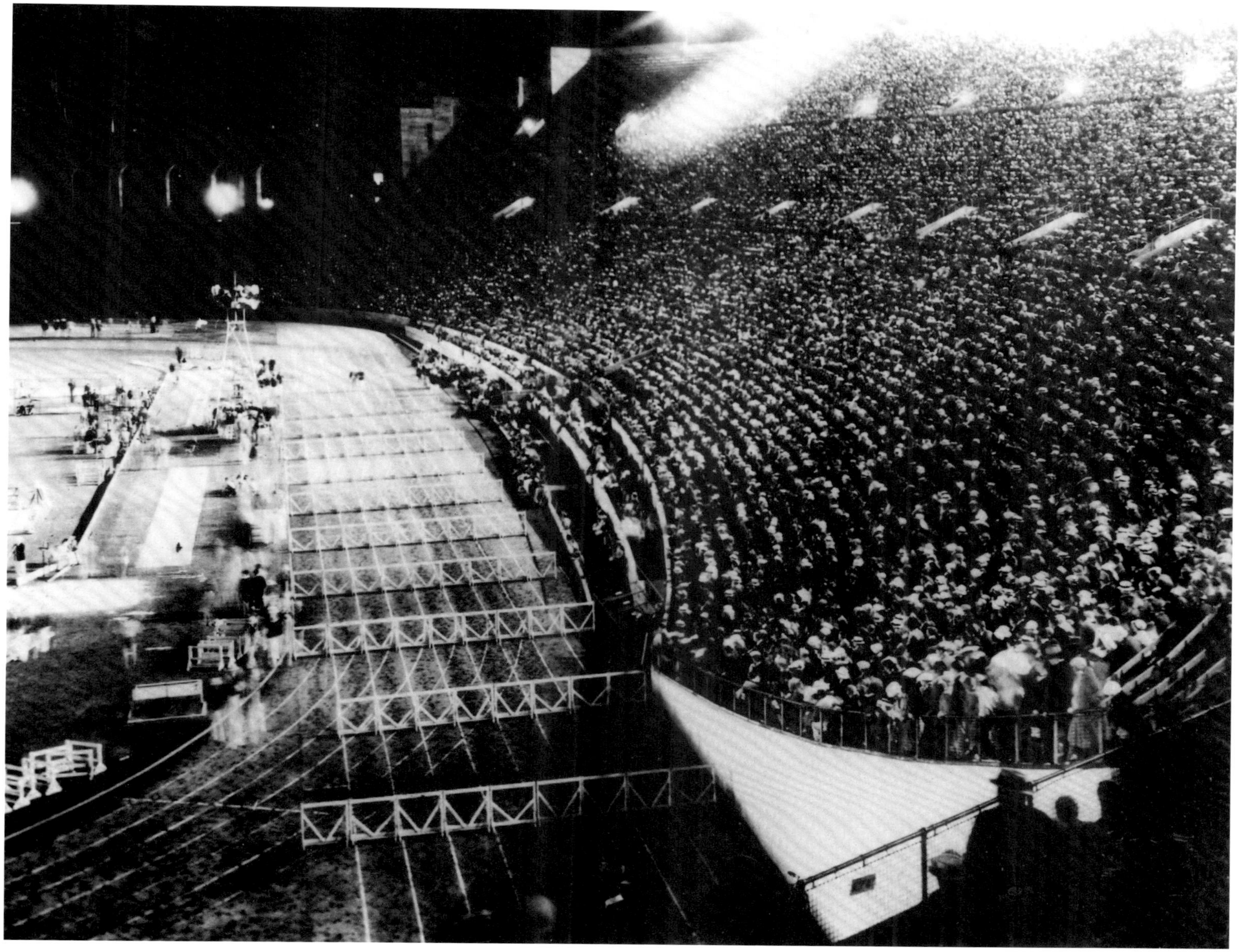

A night event at Olympic Stadium. While mounted on the victory platform during the 1932 Olympic Games, Italian Luigi Beccali, winner of the gold medal in the 1,500-meter race, gave the fascist salute. American Mildred "Babe" Didrikson (1914–1956) made history at the 1932 Olympics. Didrikson won gold medals and set new world records for both the 80-meter hurdles and the javelin, and she won the silver medal in the high jump. Didrikson later became a very successful professional golfer and was considered the greatest woman athlete of modern times.

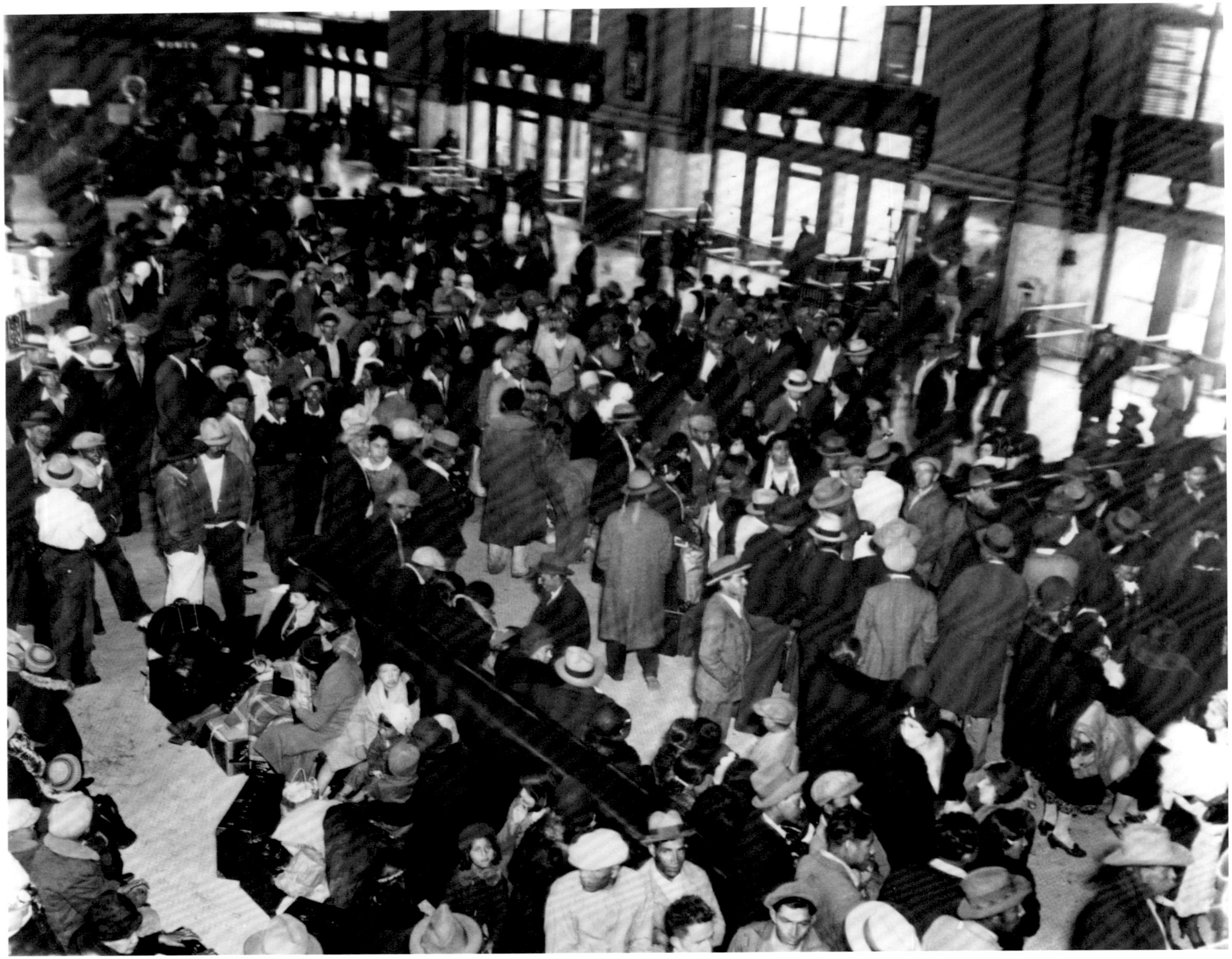

This crowd inside Union Station are some of the Mexican American immigrants deported back to Mexico in 1931-32. Mexicans were exempt from the 1924 Immigration Act that stopped immigration from Europe, and around 900,000 entered the U.S. between 1924 and 1930, some 630,000 illegally. During the Depression, with 25 percent unemployment, the federal government began coercive repatriation. One-third of those living in Los Angeles were encouraged or forced to leave for Mexico.

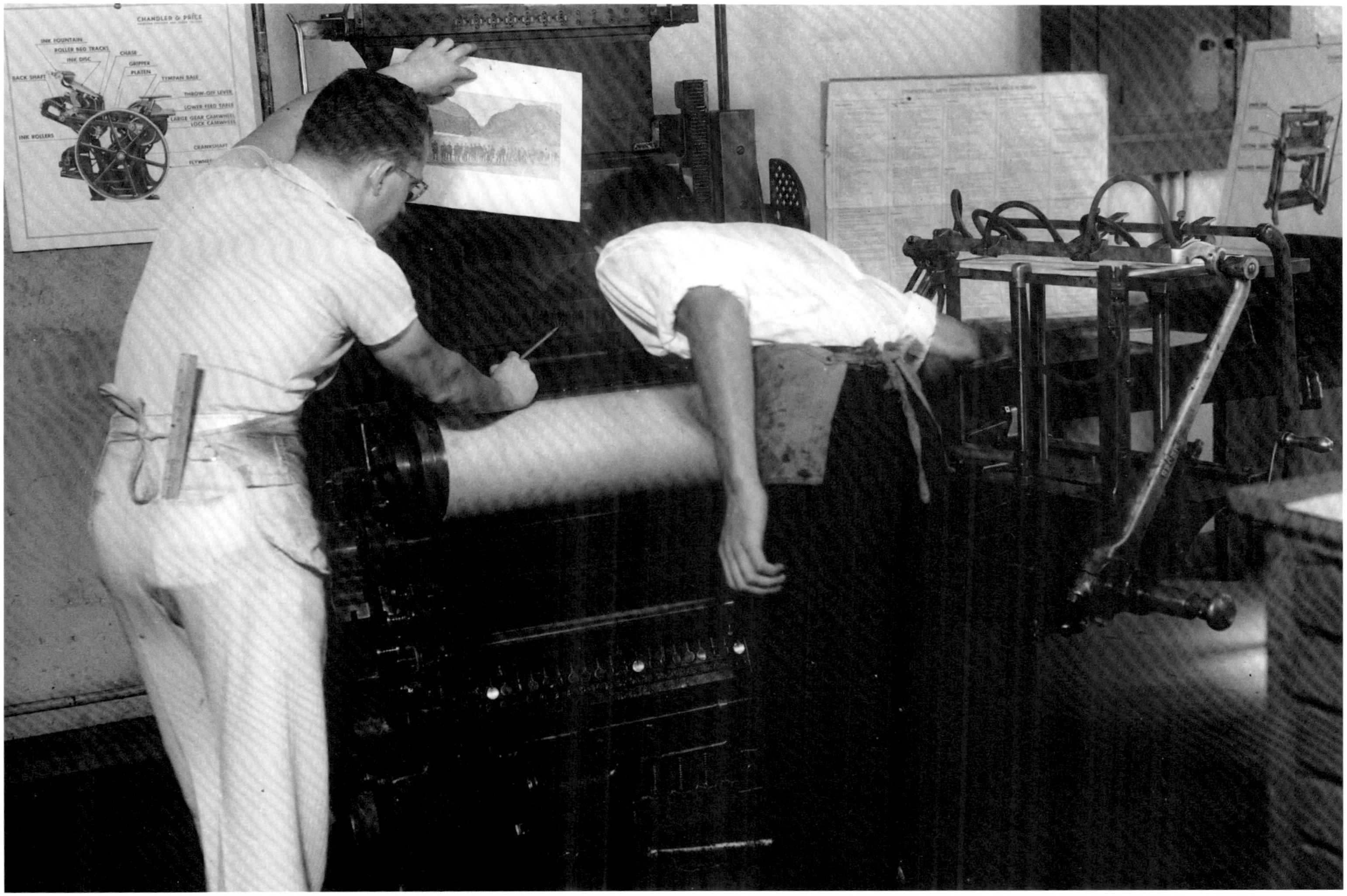

This Los Angeles student received instruction in printing through a Works Progress Administration (Work Projects Administration after 1939) adult education project. The WPA was the largest of President Roosevelt's New Deal agencies, employing millions of people in nearly every part of America. The program was closed down in 1943 during the war production years of World War II.

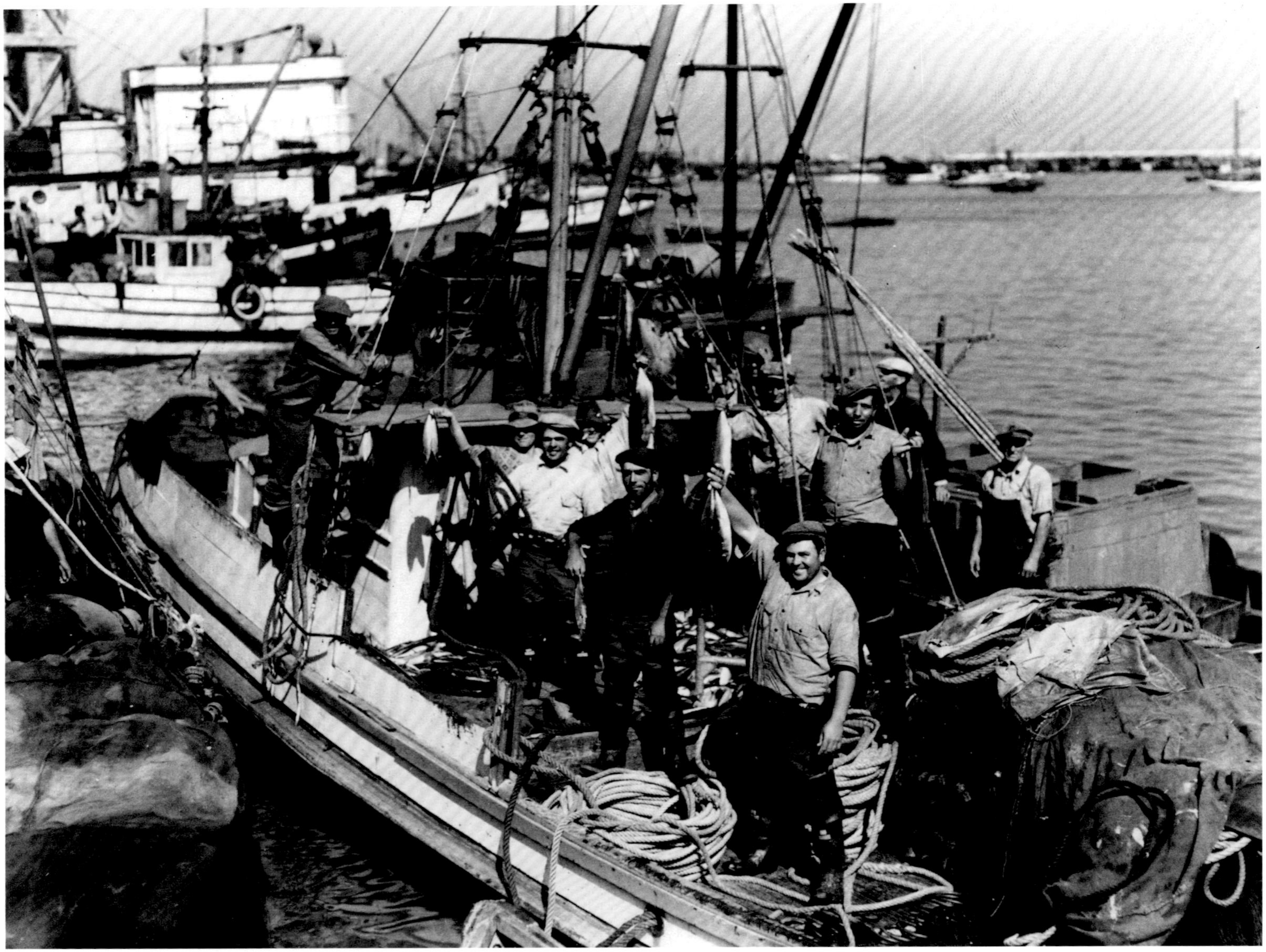

For many decades, Los Angeles harbor was divided into little villages and docks according to ethnic groups or nationalities that spoke little English. Here Russian fishermen proudly display their day's catch.

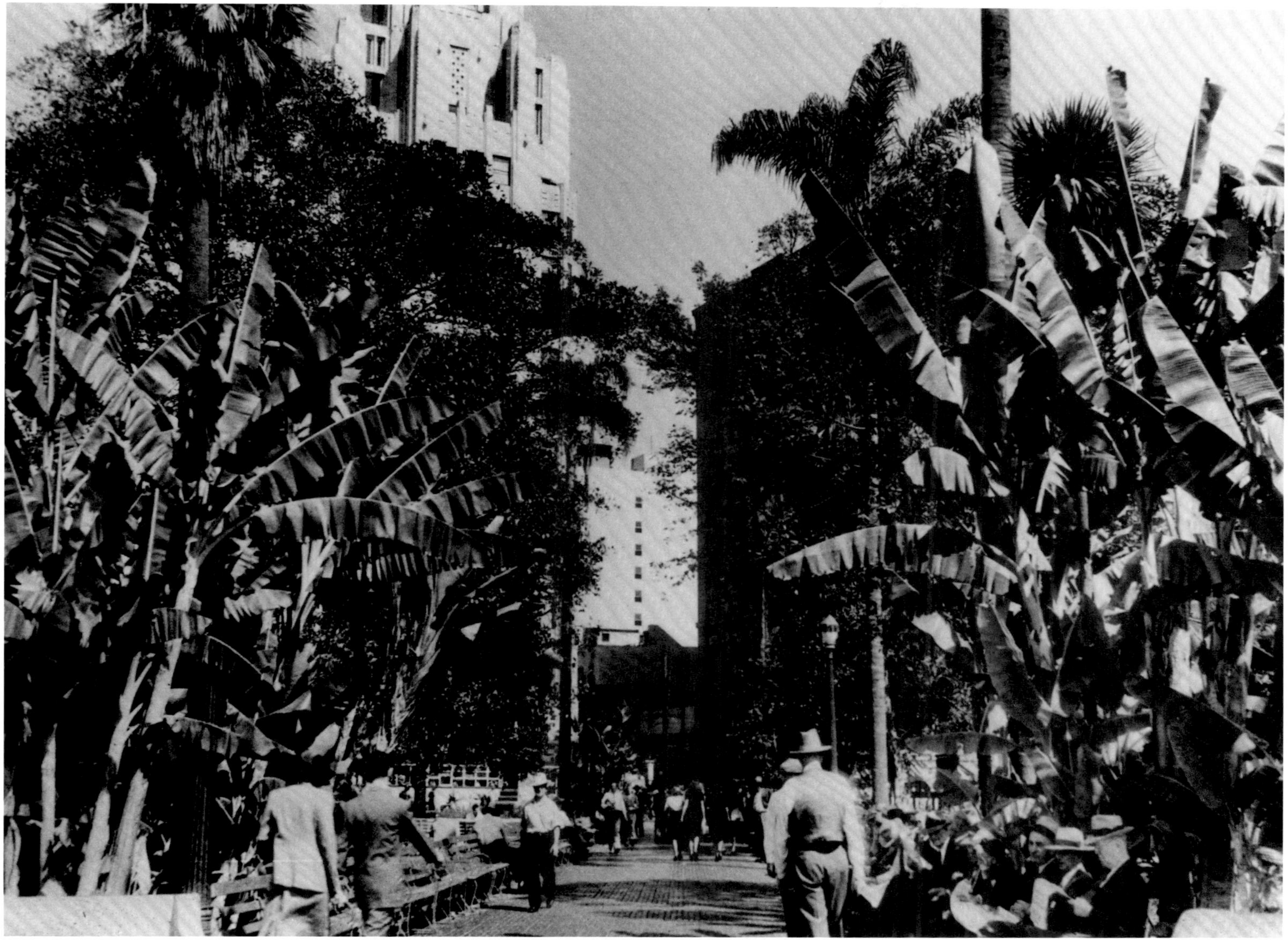

Pershing Place at the center of Los Angeles. Palm and banana trees stand against a background of what would have appeared then as blue sky and white buildings. This is the image of L.A. as utopia. Progressive lawyer and journalist Carey McWilliams (1905–1980) wrote that if this vast metropolitan area could be created by improvisation, propaganda, and boosterism, it did not seem incredible "that a new society might be evoked . . . in which the benefits of the machine age would be shared by all alike."

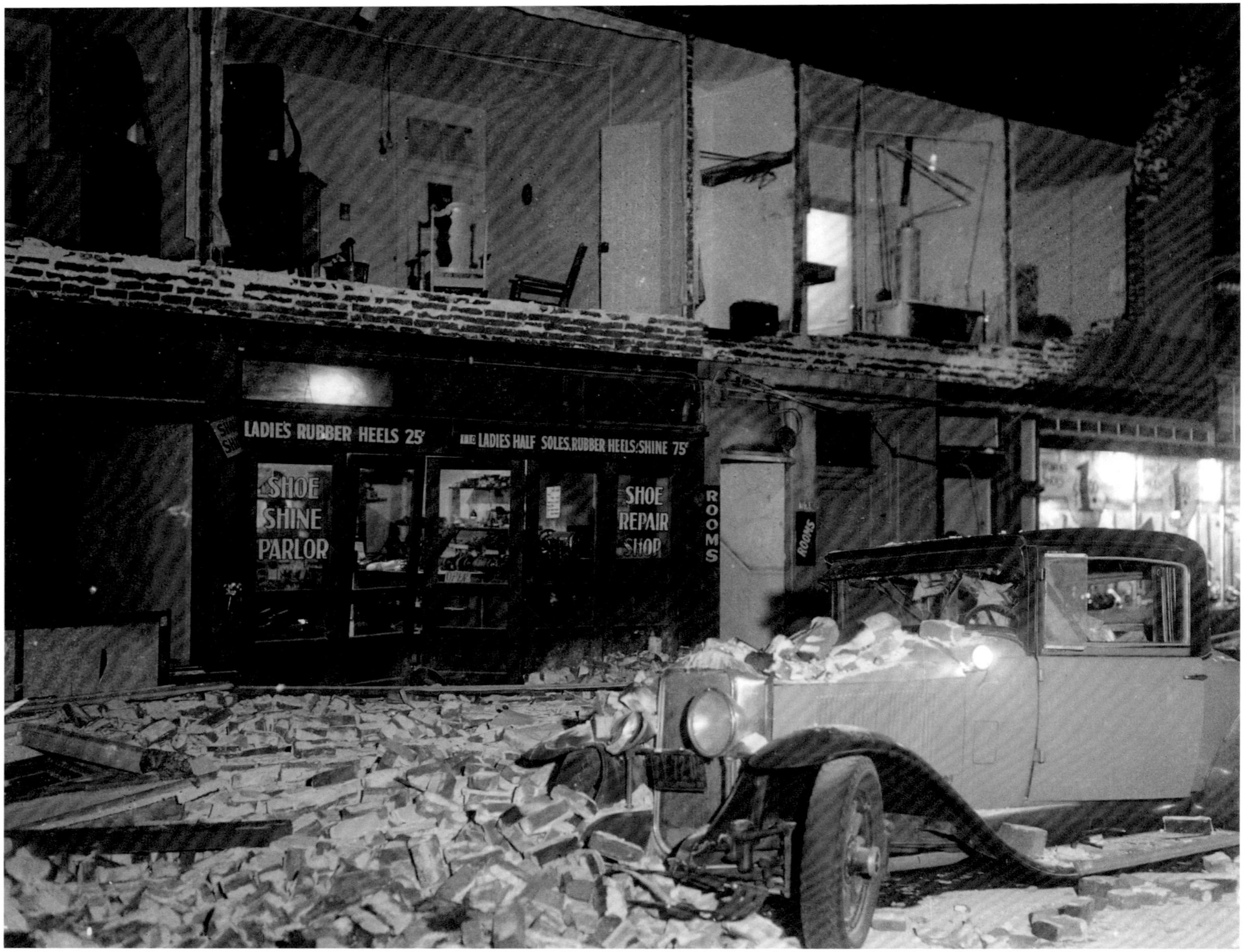

Earthquakes occur in California regularly, but most do little or no serious damage. The earthquake that hit Long Beach on March 10, 1933, registered 6.3 on the Richter scale and resulted in $40 million of property damage. One hundred fifteen people were killed, many when they ran out of buildings and were hit by falling debris. So many school buildings were damaged that the Field Act was passed by the California State Legislature the next month, mandating that school buildings must be earthquake-resistant.

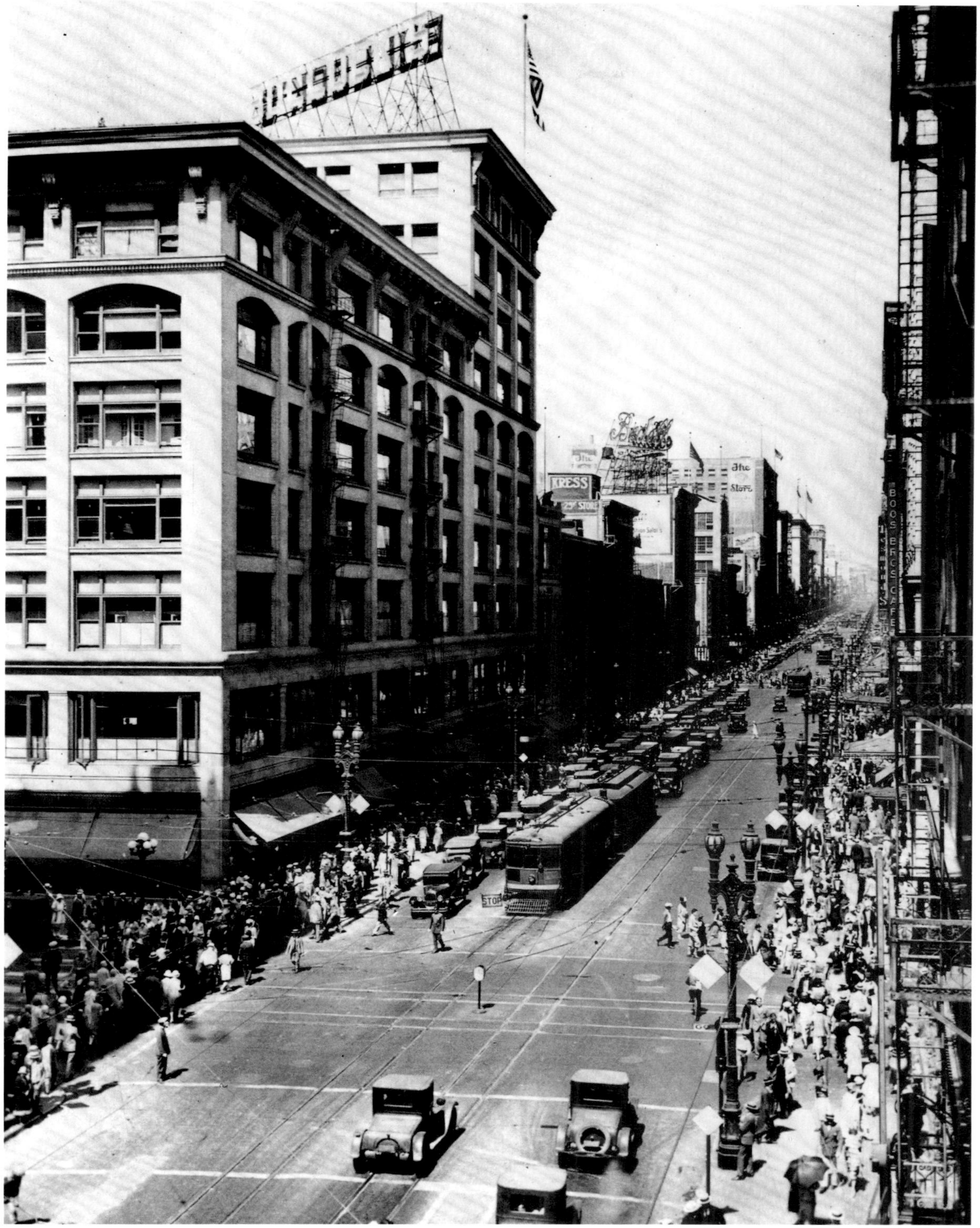

This view of Broadway looking north from West 7th Street shows a major downtown L.A. shopping district. In 1930 the ratio of population in the central metropolitan area to outlying suburbs in most American cities was sixteen to one (as in Pittsburgh) or more. L.A.'s ratio was only three to one, making its structure radically different from other U.S. cities'.

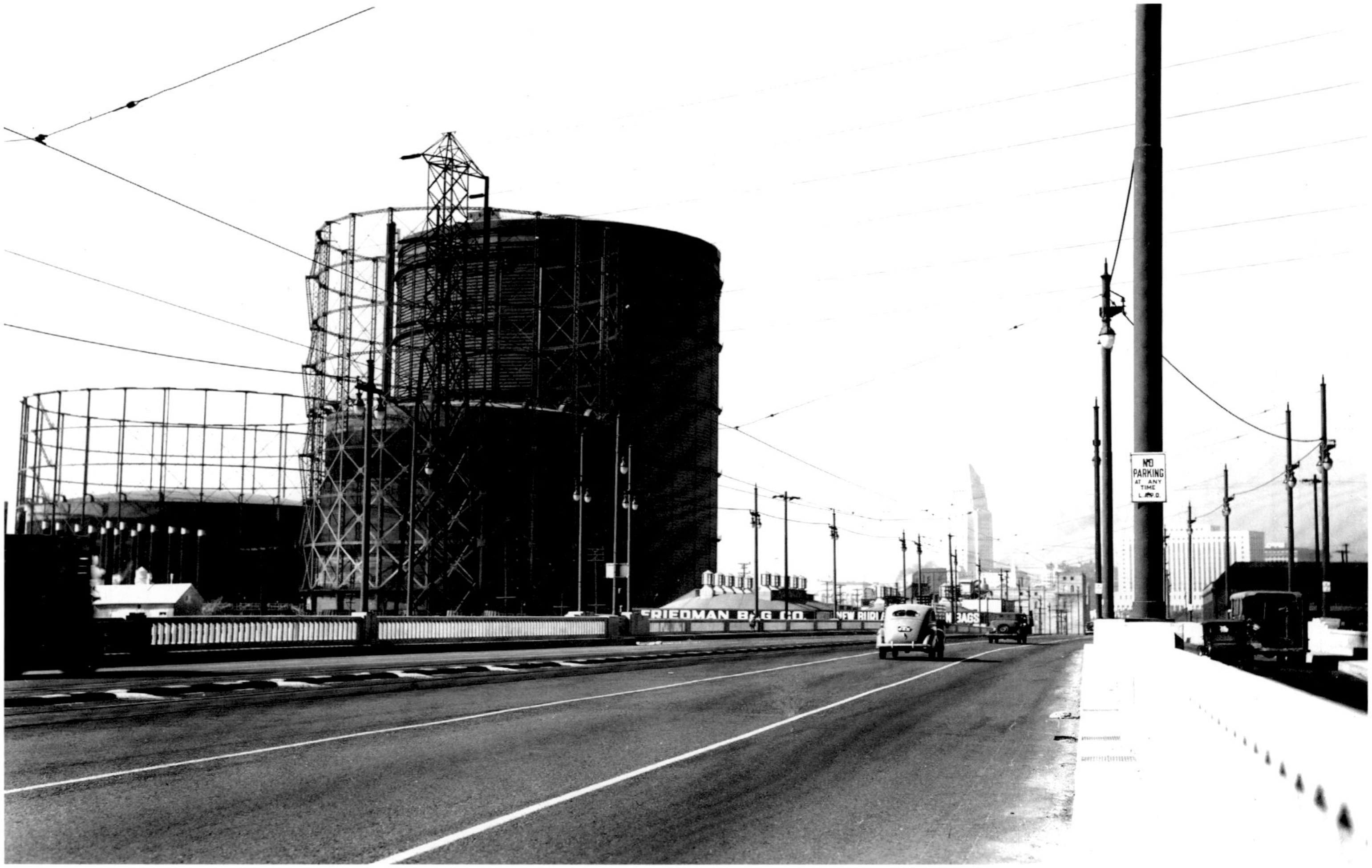

This view toward the center of Los Angeles is from the terminus of Ramona Boulevard. Despite the economic downturn of the Depression, by 1938 nearly 72 percent of the L.A. labor force drove cars to their jobs. Only 20 percent used public transportation, and the remainder walked.

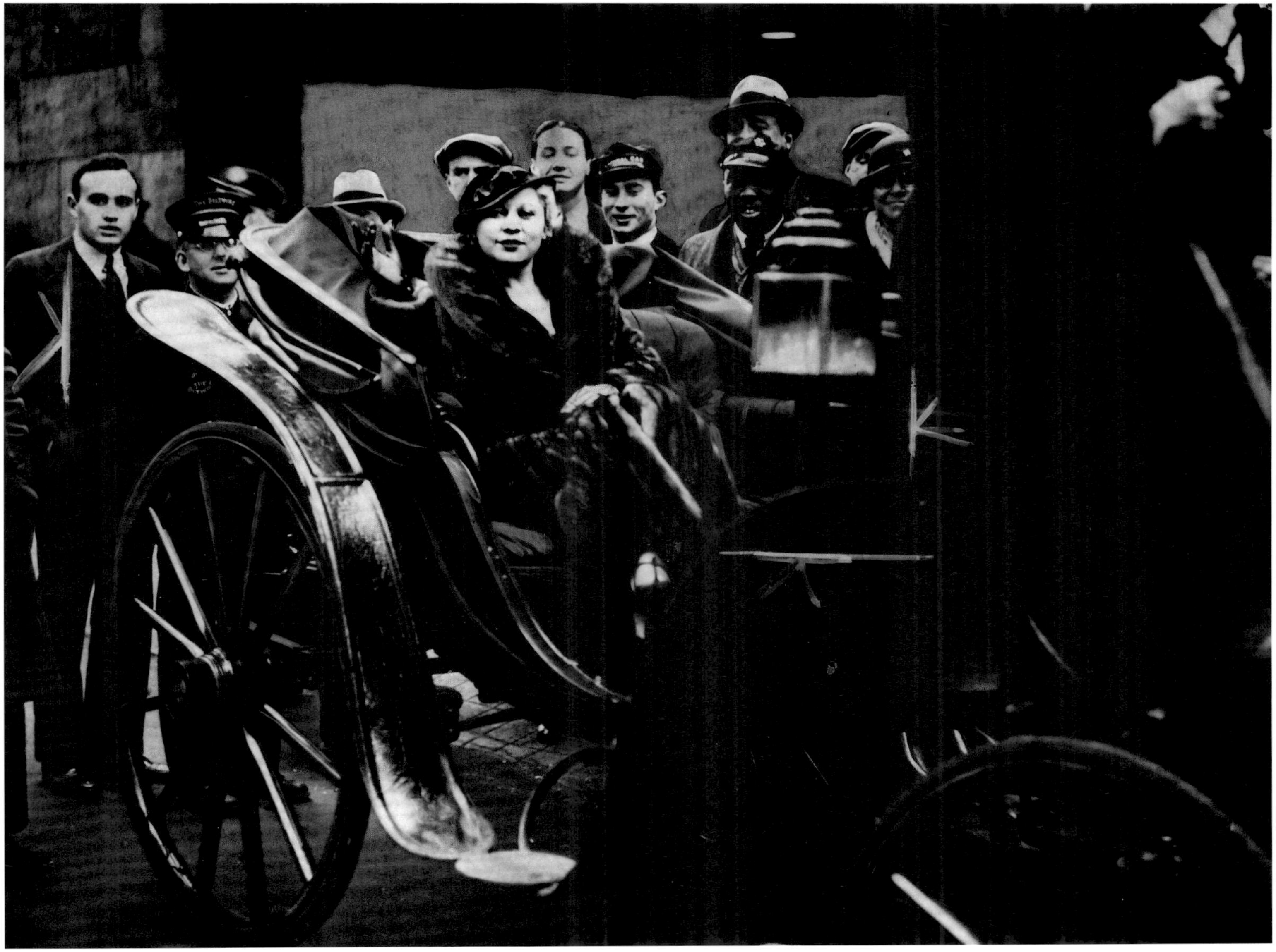

In 1932, comedian, actress, and writer Mae West (1893–1980) started making films. The controversial 38-year-old sex symbol was famous for her outrageous quotes such as "When I'm good, I'm very, very good, but when I'm bad, I'm better." When her cinematic career ended, West continued to perform on stage, radio, and television. "Between two evils, I always pick the one I never tried before."

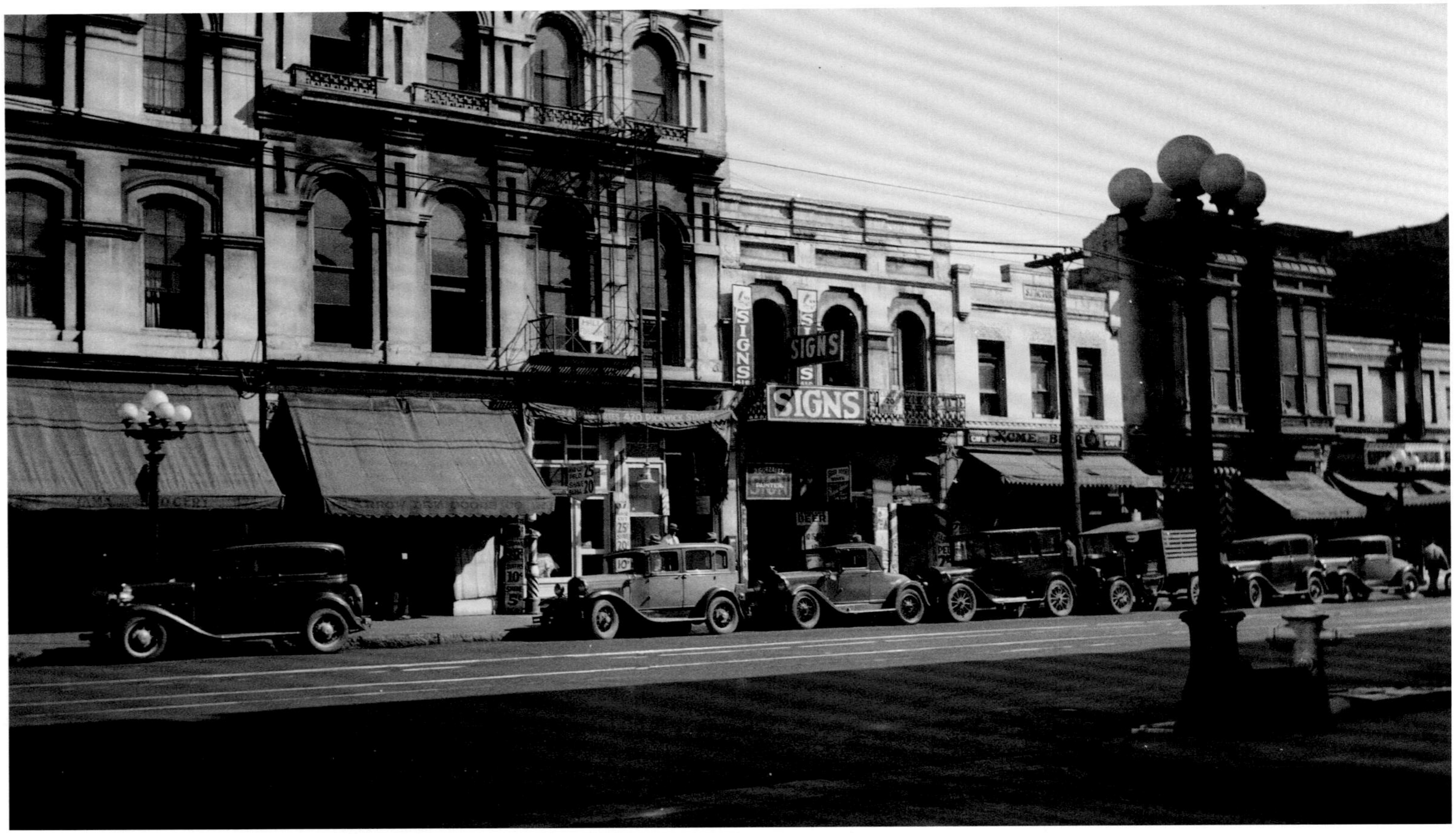

This photo was taken as part of the Historic American Buildings Survey of 1934. The Masonic Temple Number 42 on North Main Street in Los Angeles is the building advertising signs at center. Most Masonic temples in the United States were built between 1870 and 1930 as meeting places for the Freemason fraternal organization. The origins and early development of Freemasonry are a matter of some debate and conjecture. Famous members include presidents George Washington and Franklin Roosevelt.

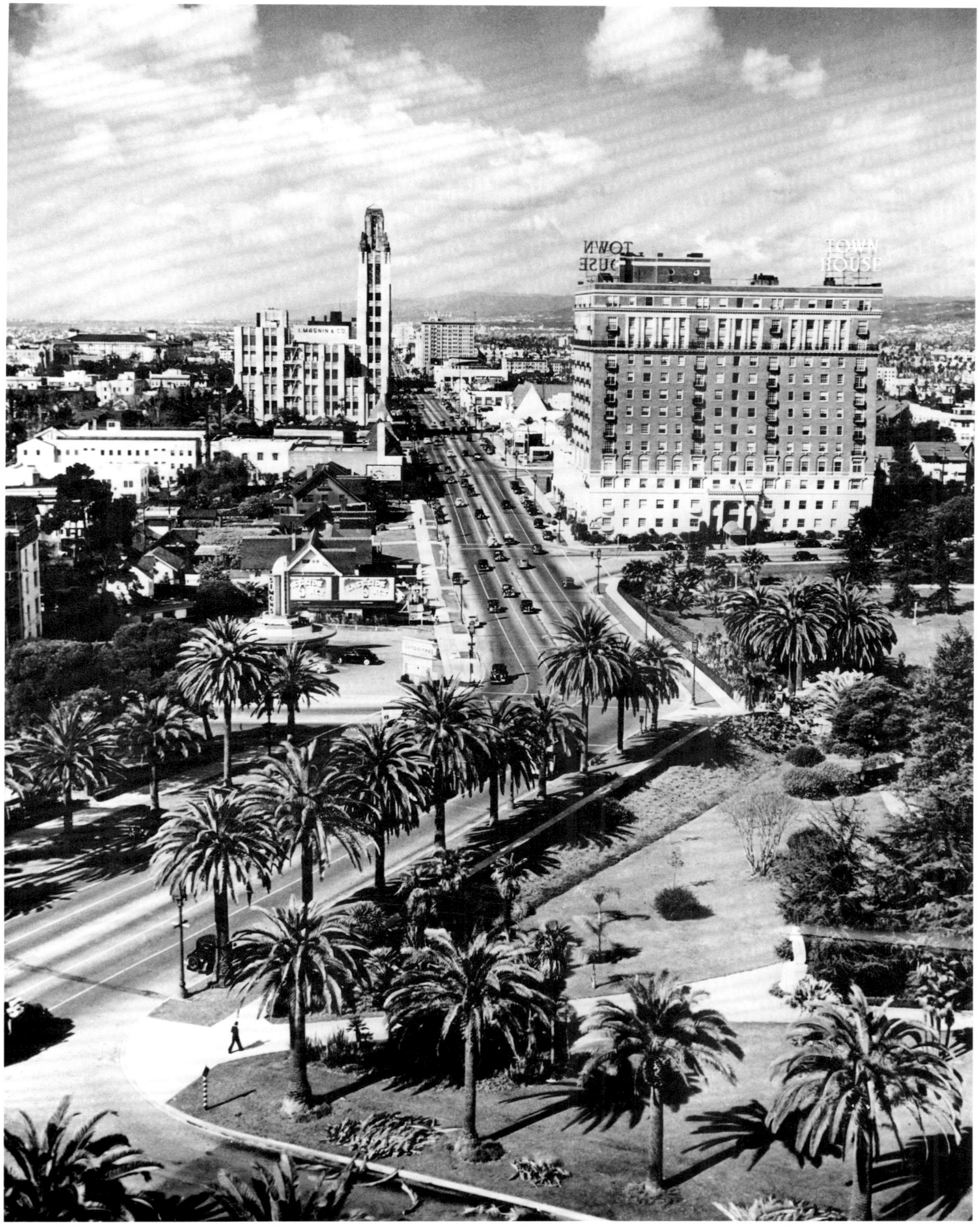

Wilshire Boulevard, looking toward Beverly Hills and Santa Monica, where many famous Hollywood screen stars lived in the 1930s and today. Wilshire was designed to accommodate six cars at a time, as were most of the major Southern California thoroughfares back then.

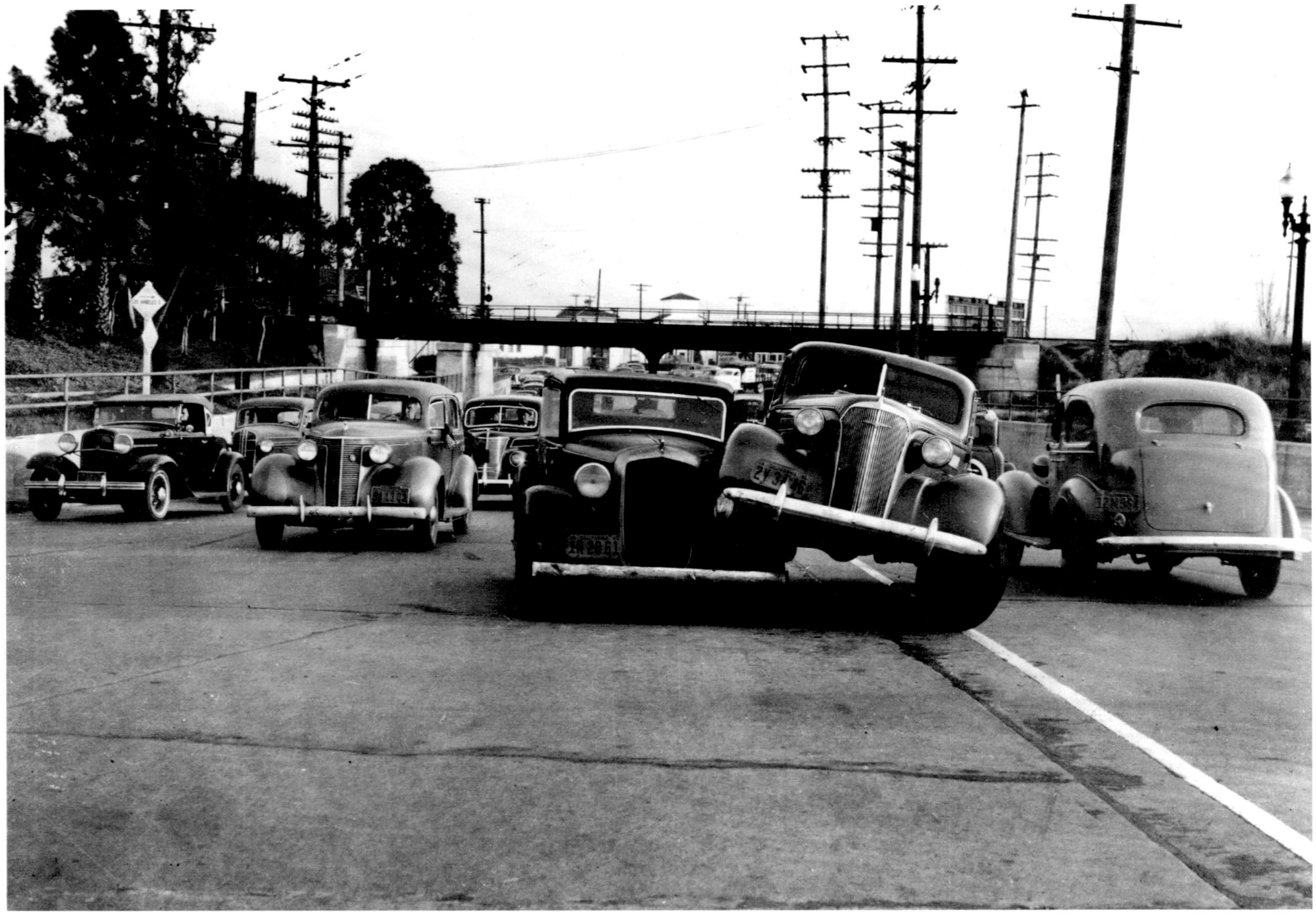

Bandini Underpass in Los Angeles. The Major Traffic Street Plan instituted in the previous decade improved traffic flow for a few years, but it proved inadequate by the early 1930s. The city was unable to decide whether to finance a rapid-transit system, so Angelenos continued to jam the roads with their cars. This congestion led to the rise of suburbs and the decentralization of retail businesses.

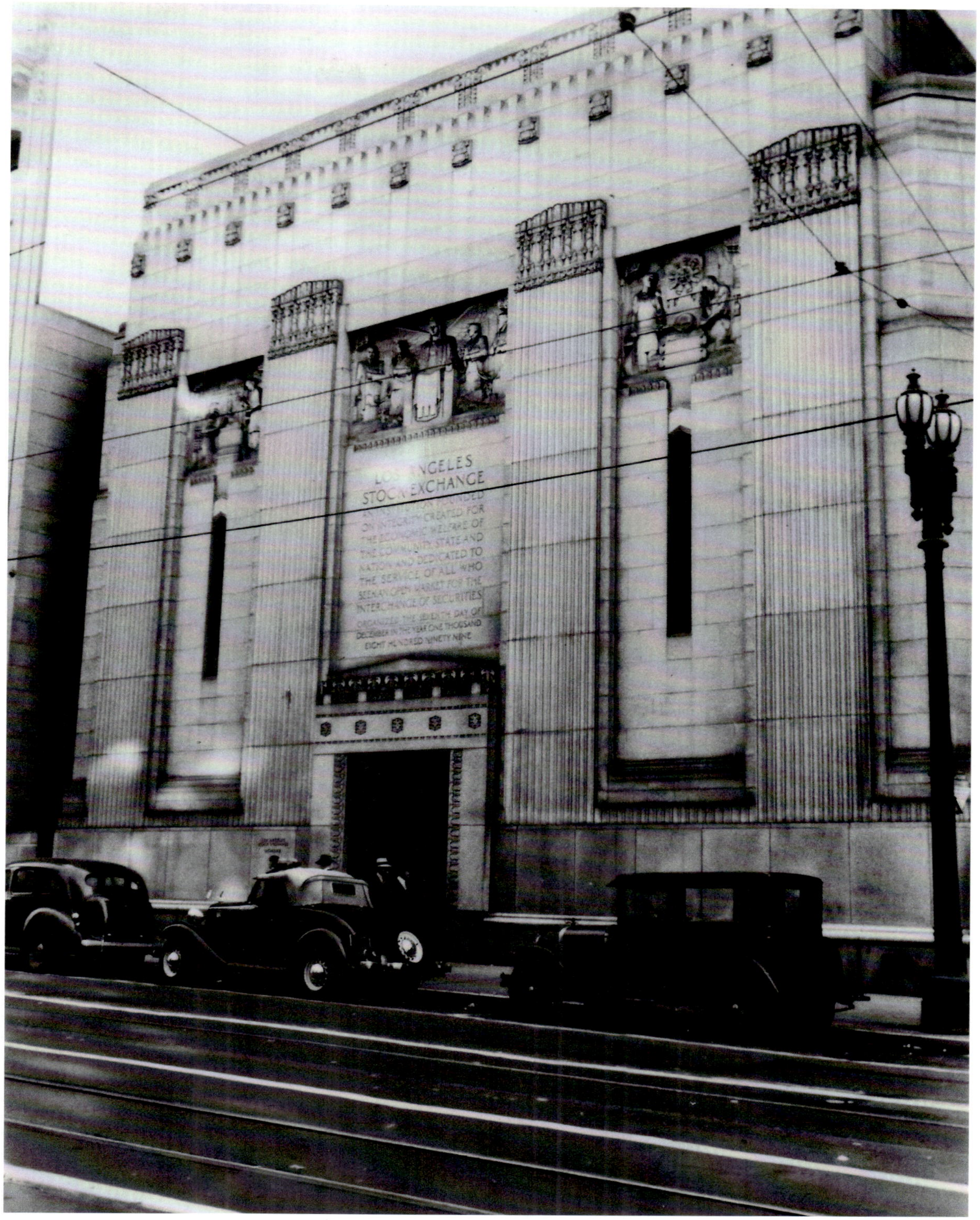

This was the Los Angeles Stock Exchange home office at 639 South Spring Street as it appeared in 1937. The stock market crash of 1929 was not the fundamental cause of the Great Depression of the 1930s, but the stock market collapse and subsequent panic did trigger and mark the start of the economic disaster.

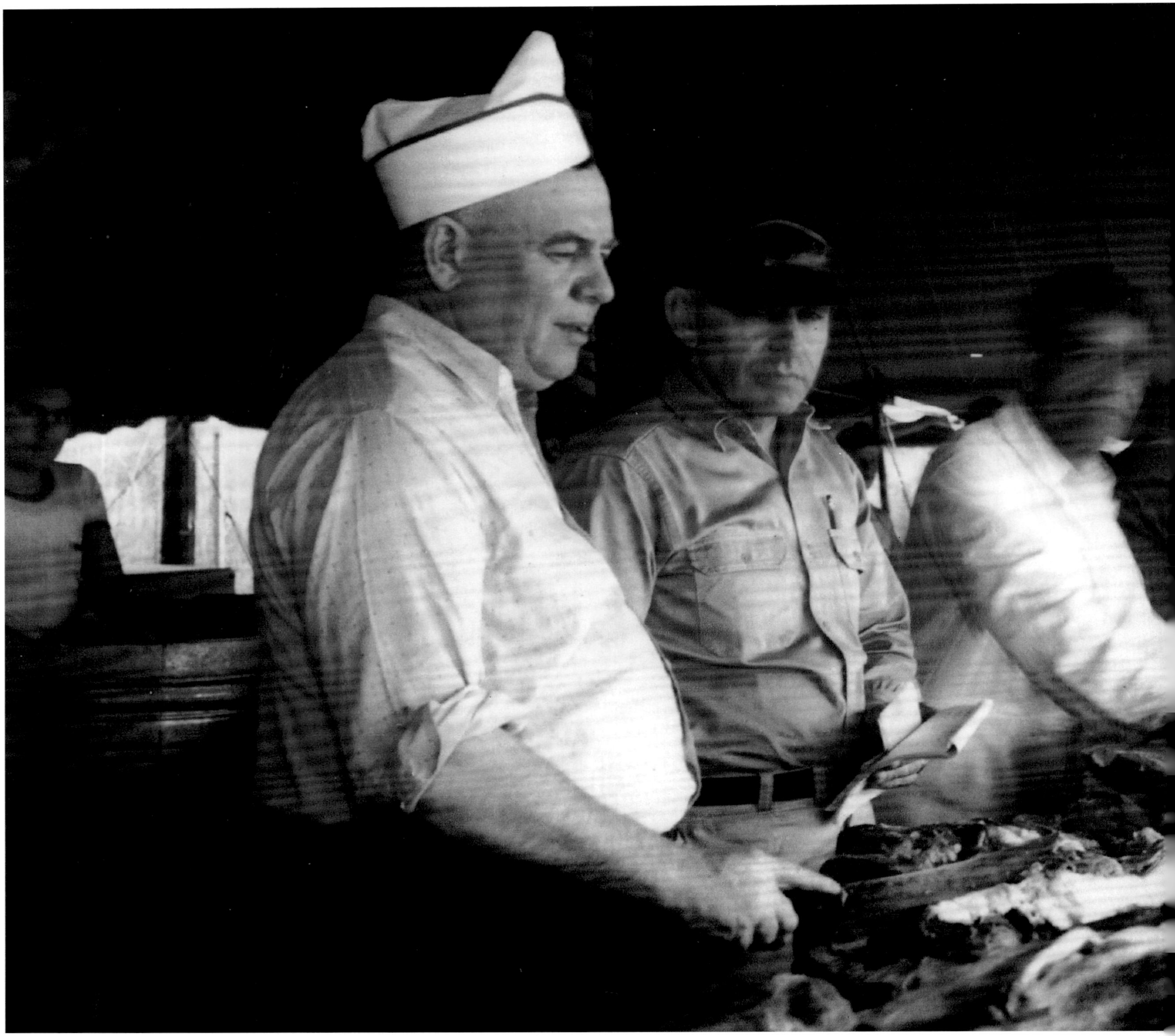

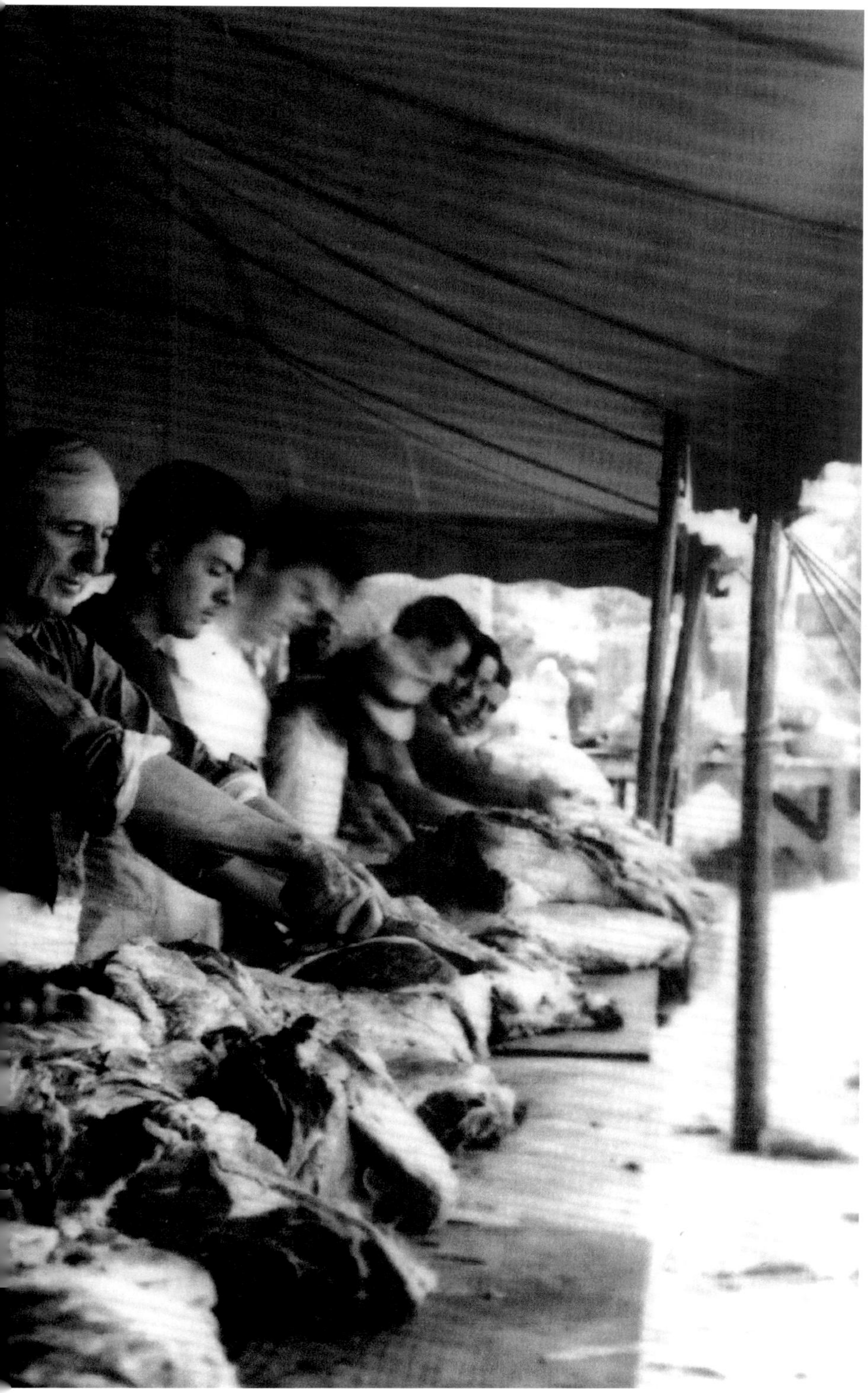

At a Los Angeles Sheriff's Barbecue, beef forequarters are cut into 20-pound hunks. This photo was made as part of the "America Eats" project for the Federal Writers' Project (FWP), one of four New Deal arts programs established in 1935 that compiled local histories, oral histories, ethnographies, children's books, and other works. The most well-known of these publications were the 48 state guides the federal program produced.

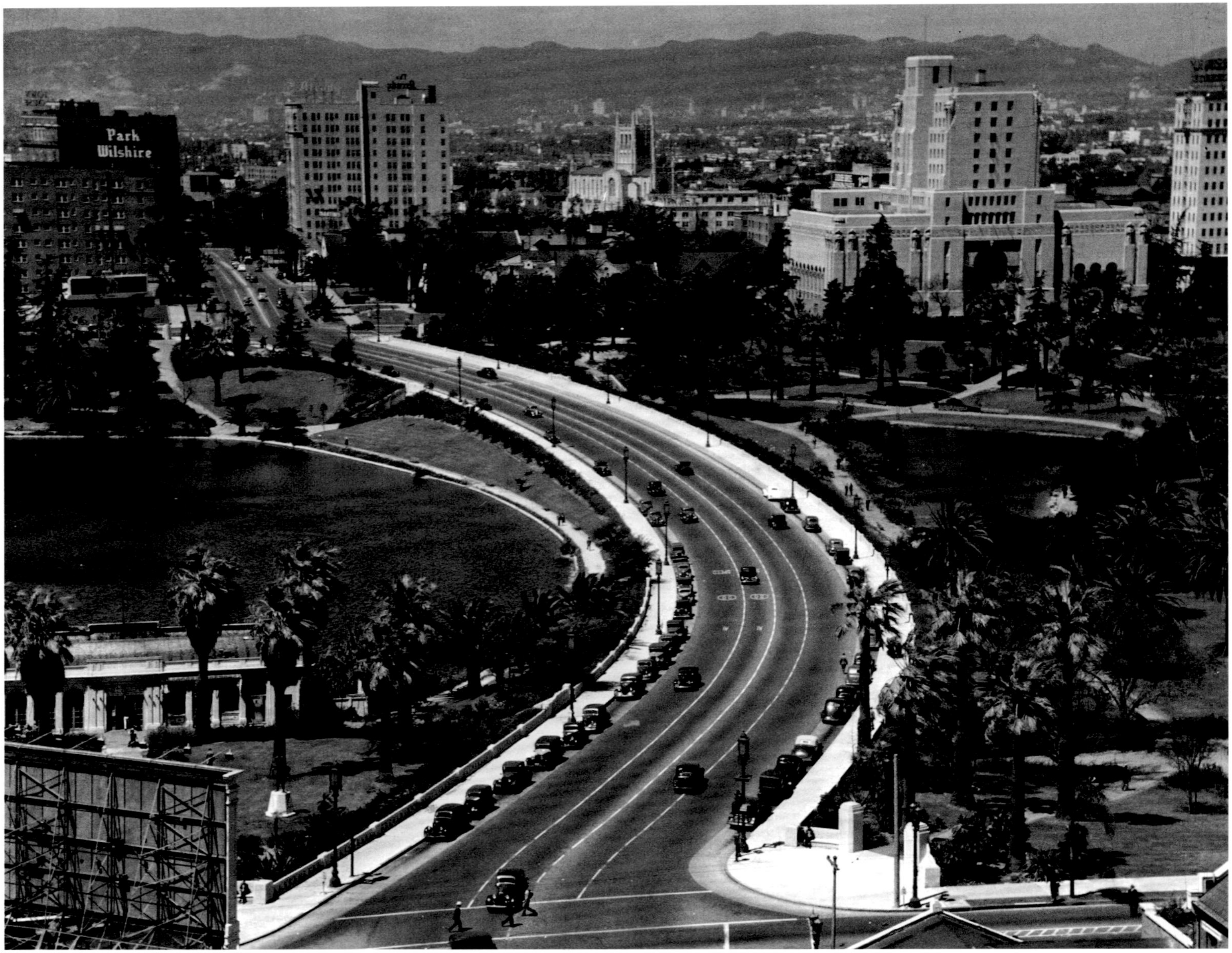

Built in the 1880s, MacArthur Park, crossed here by Wilshire Boulevard, was originally named Westlake Park but was renamed shortly after the end of World War II. Prior to 1930, Los Angeles lacked an adequate number of streets leading into the downtown area. The city therefore built this bridge across the lake and turned Wilshire into one of L.A.'s most important traffic arteries.

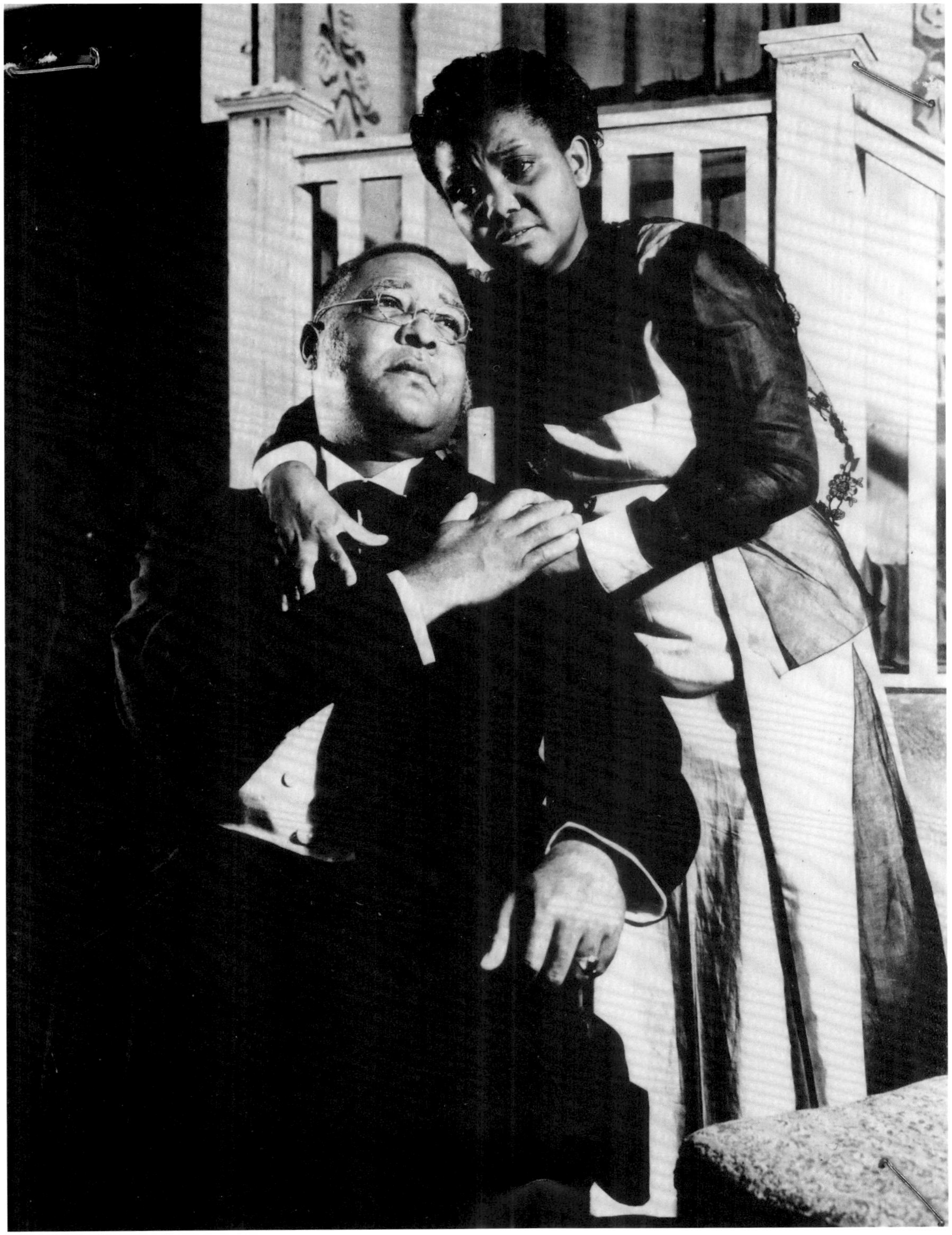

A promotional photograph from the Federal Theater Project stage production *Run Little Chillun* with Jess Lee Brooks (1894–1944) and Ruby Elzy (1908–1943). An African American thespian regarded as an exceptional actor, Brooks worked in 24 movies, including *Dark Manhattan* (1937) and *Gang War* (1940). His co-star Elzy was a pioneer black opera singer who appeared on stage, radio, and film. Her most prominent screen role was in the 1941 *Birth of the Blues* with Bing Crosby.

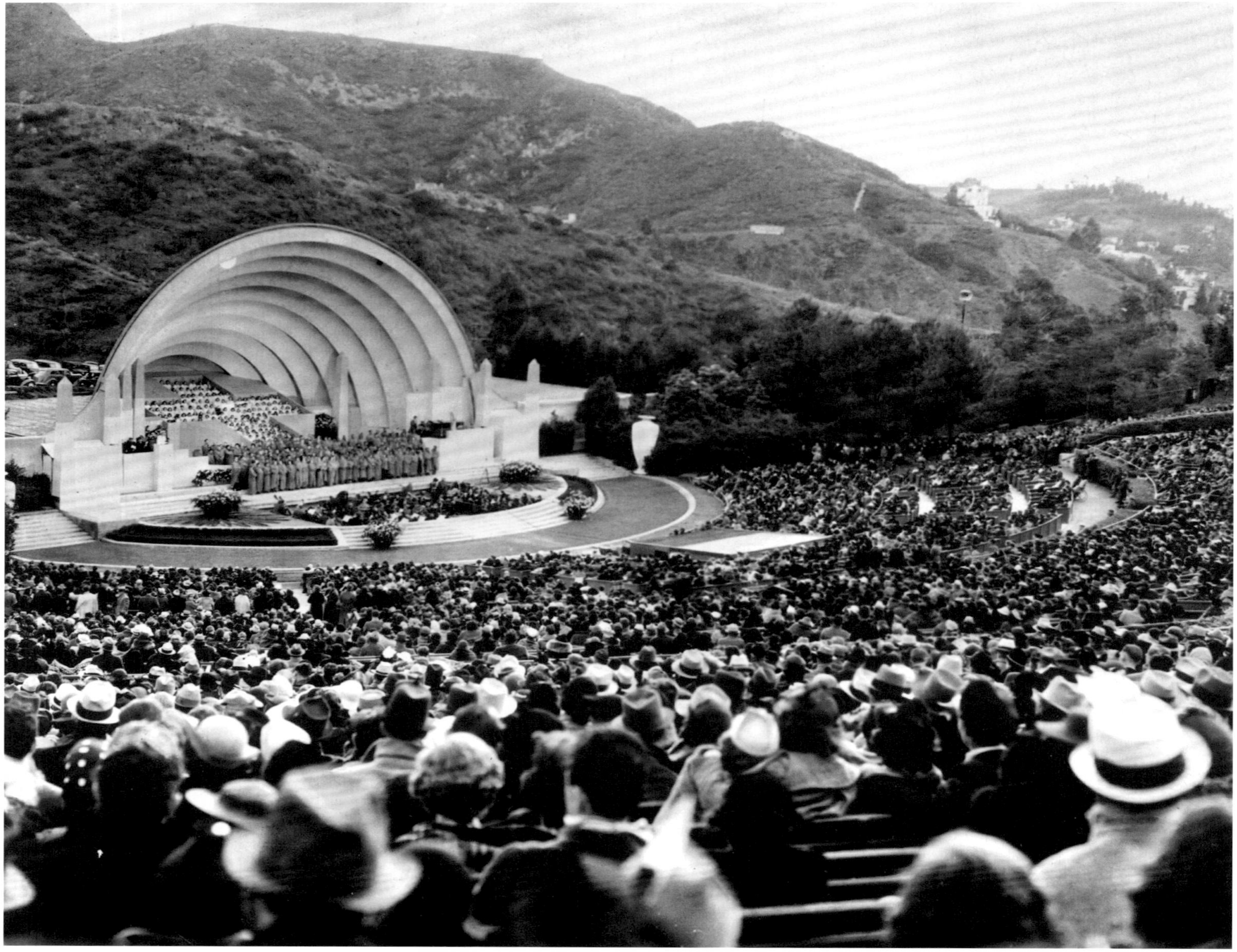

Hollywood Bowl was rebuilt in 1929 with its distinctive set of concentric arches known as the band shell. The Technocracy Movement, advocating a form of society where the welfare of human beings is optimized by widespread use of technology, and other organizations held public events in the Bowl during the 1930s. This is an Easter Sunrise Service featuring WPA Orchestra and Singers.

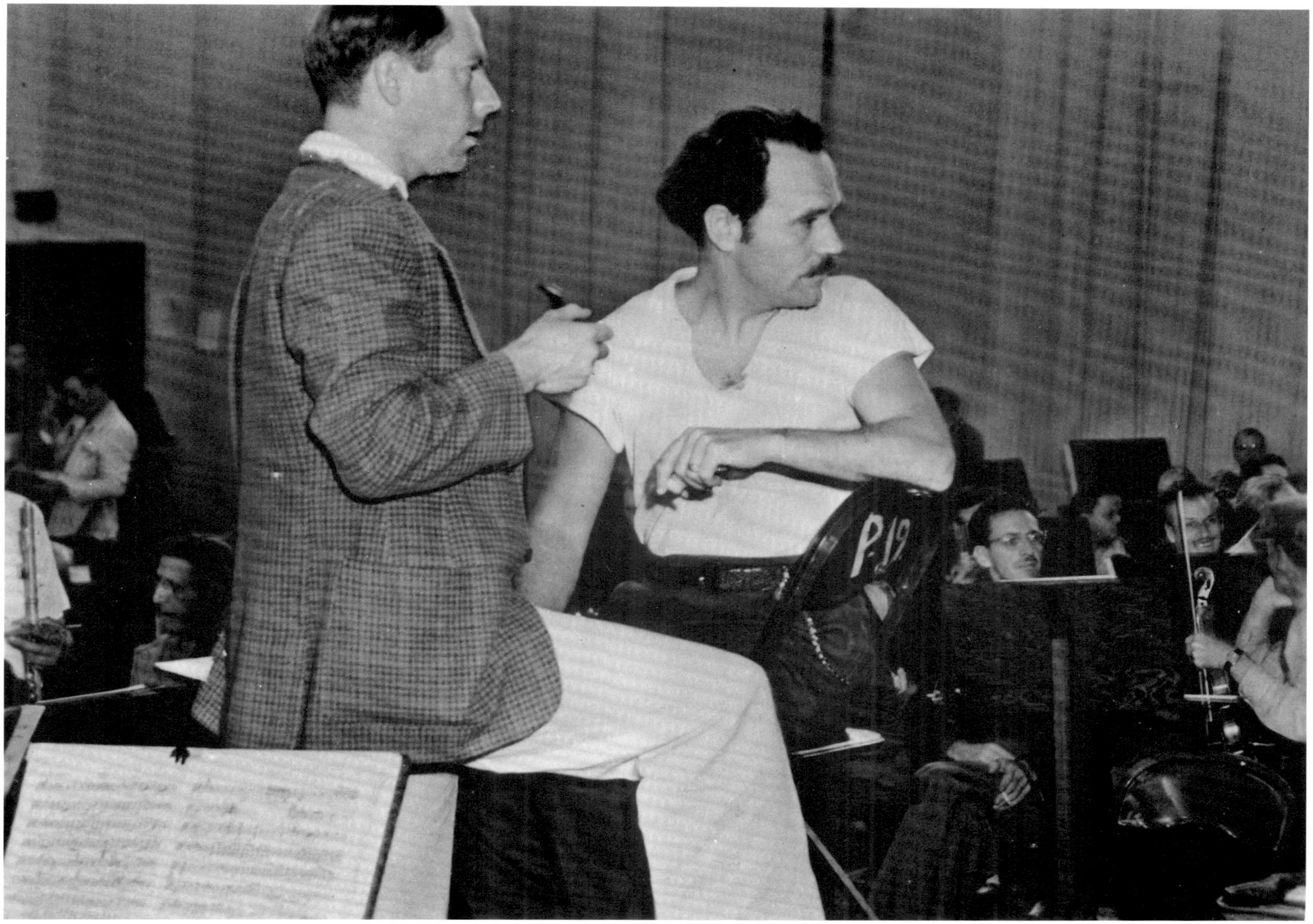

The two men working with the orchestra are Morris Hutchins Ruger, composer, and Gastone Usigli, conductor and general director of the opera *Gettysburg* that premiered at the Hollywood Bowl, September 23, 1938. Ruger (1902–1974) was a composer, concert singer, and music teacher. His works included sonatas, chamber music, chorales, and this opera.

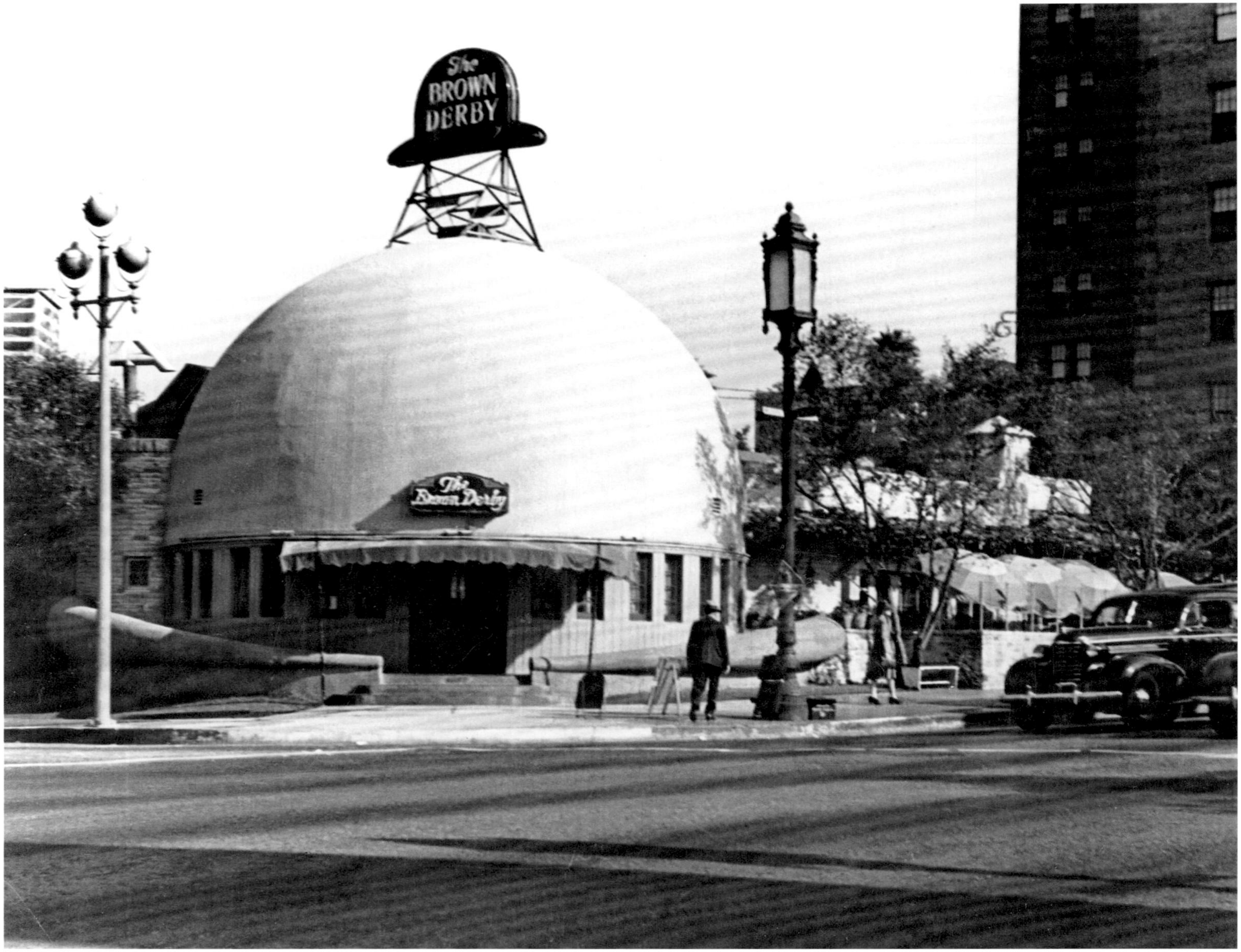

The Brown Derby is an example of novelty architecture and was a landmark Los Angeles restaurant frequented by celebrities during the golden age of Hollywood. There were four Brown Derby restaurants: Beverly Hills, Los Feliz, Wilshire at Alexandria (the one seen here in 1939), and Vine Street in Hollywood. Reputedly, the single greatest legacy recipe of the Brown Derby is the Cobb Salad, invented by and named after one of the owners of the Brown Derby, Bob Cobb.

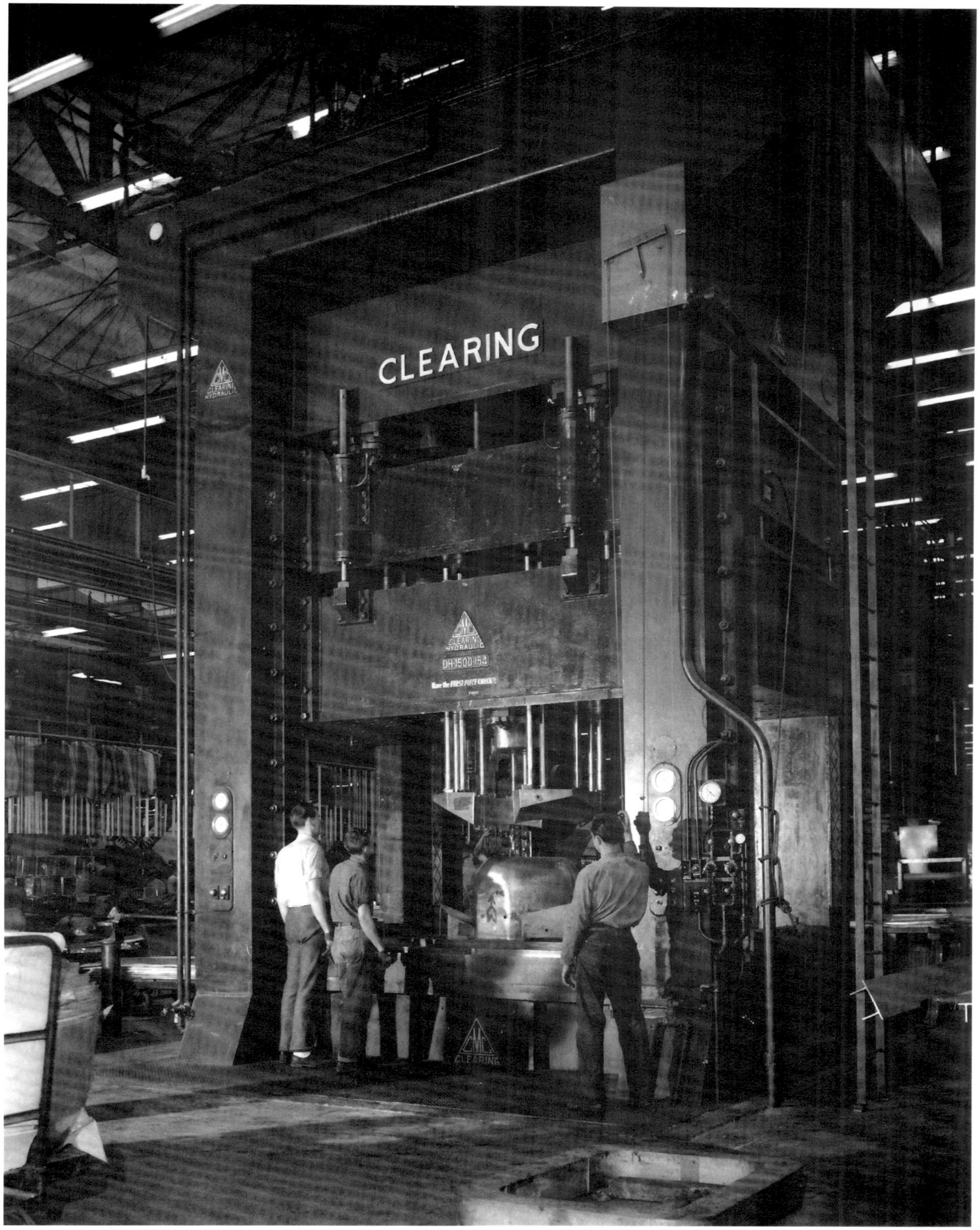

Inside the Vega Aircraft Corporation in Burbank, around the late 1930s. The Vega Aircraft Corporation was a subsidiary of the Lockheed Aircraft Company and was responsible for much of the parent company's production in World War II. The Vega company was first formed in August 1937 as the AiRover Company to produce a new light plane design. It was soon renamed Vega to honor Lockheed's first aircraft design.

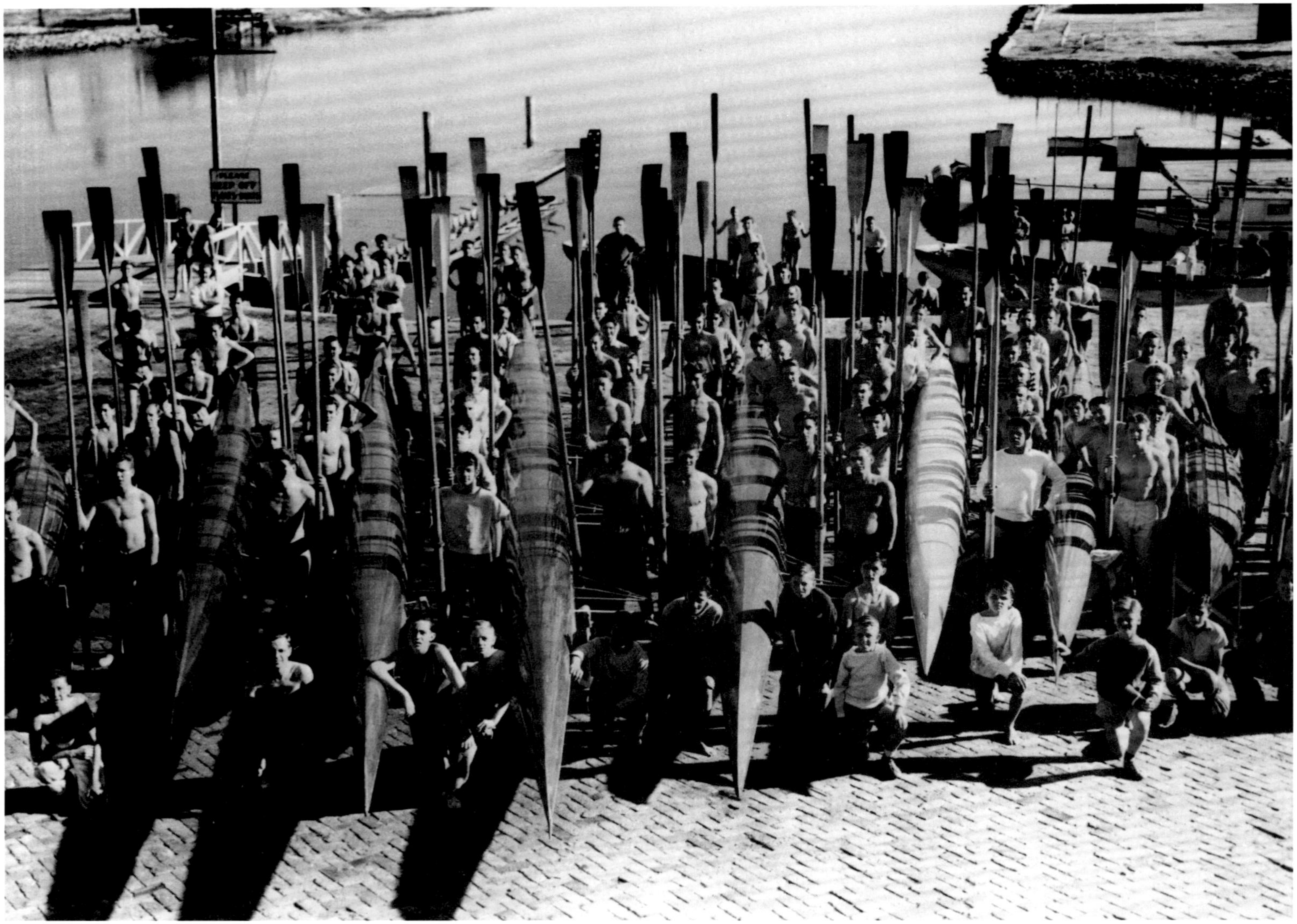

The Long Beach Recreation Commission offered boating activities with the aid of the Works Progress Administration. These high school and junior college students are part of crew groups at Long Beach Marine Stadium in 1936. The young men received instruction and practice in rowing and handling of gigs, navy-type cutters, whale boats, canoes, crew boats, barges, and many other types of boats.

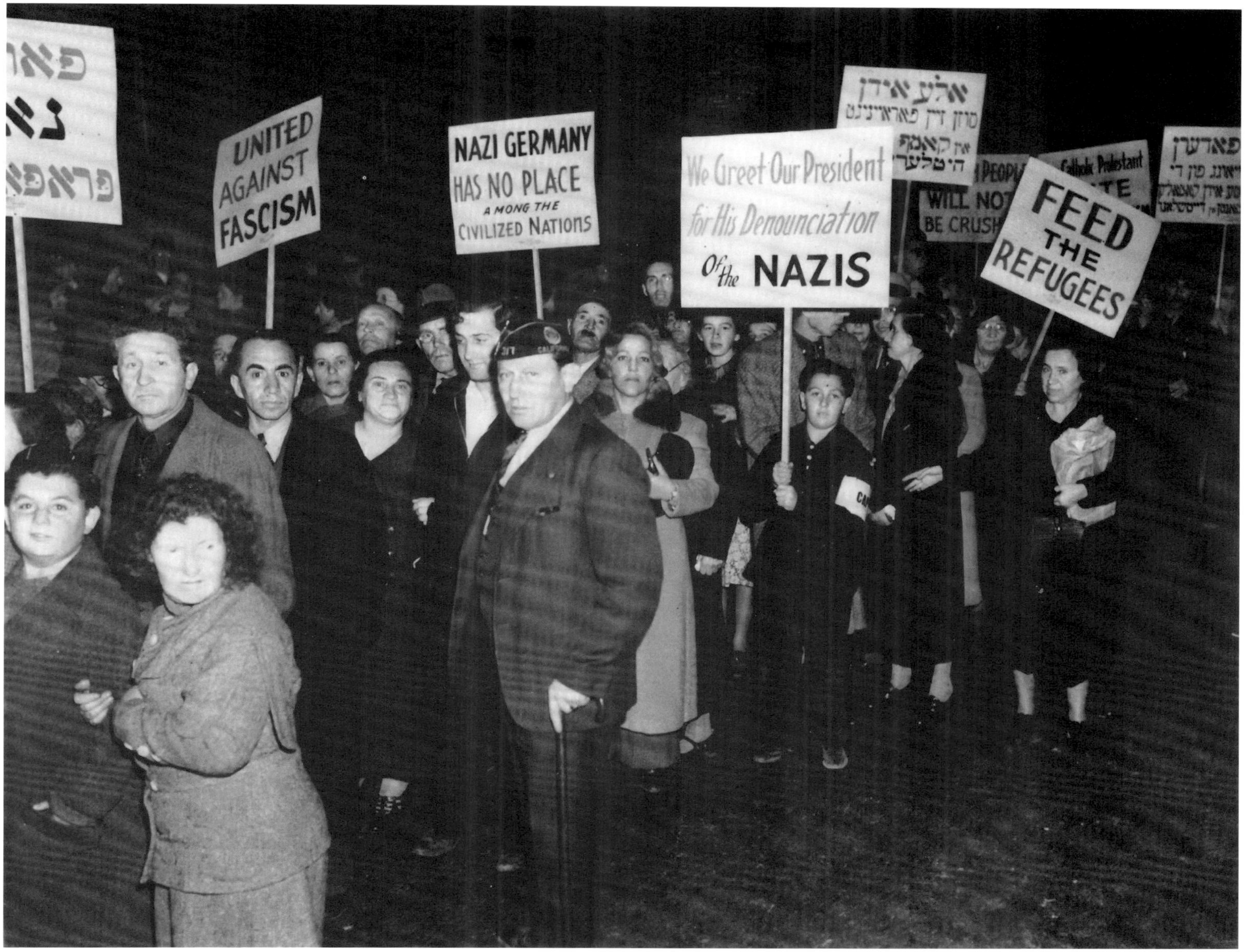

Los Angeles marchers in 1938 carry signs that urge the United States to boycott German imports to protest Nazi Germany's repressive policies toward its Jewish citizens. Worse was yet to come. The terms "Holocaust" and "Shoah" are used to describe the methodical extermination of more than six million Jews killed during World War II as a deliberate ideological policy of genocide by the Nazis.

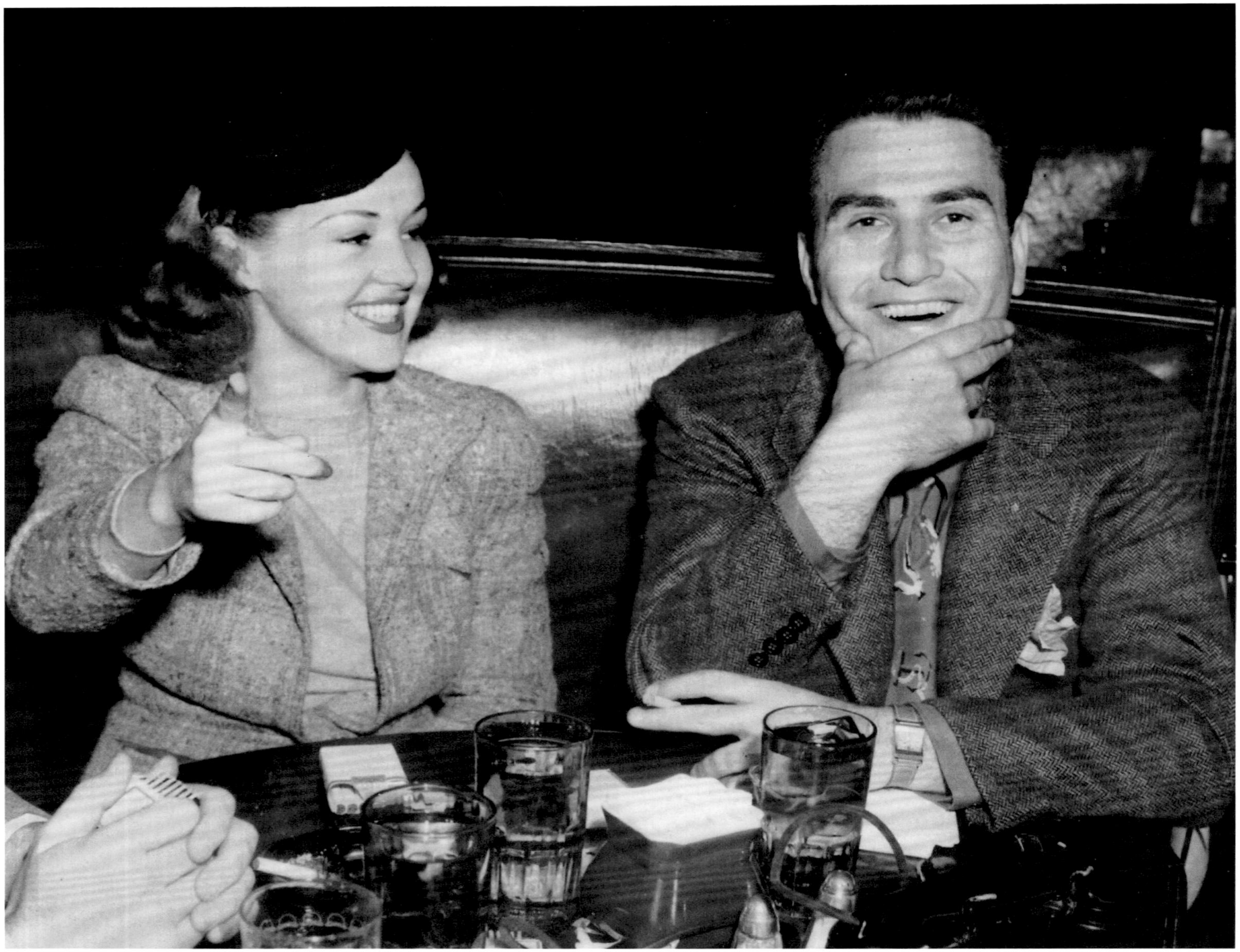

Movie star Betty Grable (1916–1973) and jazz musician Artie Shaw (1910–2004) enjoy each other's company at a Hollywood restaurant in 1939. That year was a watershed for both Hollywood film and Los Angeles writing. *Gone with the Wind* premiered as one of the most profitable films of all time. *The Big Sleep* by Raymond Chandler (1888–1959), his first crime fiction to feature protagonist Philip Marlowe, was published, as was *The Day of the Locust* by Nathanael West (1903–1940), a novelization of West's experiences living in a hotel on Hollywood Boulevard. On September 1, Nazi Germany invaded Poland.

The Second World War and a New Expansion

(1940–1949)

America moved into the 1940s with the worst of the Depression behind it, but apprehensive of the new war in Europe and Japanese aggression in Manchuria and China.

As part of U.S. military preparations, President Roosevelt enacted the Naval Expansion Act on July 19, 1940. This was good news for Los Angeles, as the Act authorized a fleet base for the Long Beach–San Pedro area. The city of Long Beach received one dollar for the rights to an area that had been an Indian burial ground, a shark oil center, a rumrunner's haven during Prohibition, and a fashionable bathing beach. In return, millions of dollars poured into the L.A. area for shipbuilding, sailors and marines, and the supplies to sustain this huge buildup.

However, large numbers of Americans were opposed to the United States getting involved in another war as it did in 1917, and the year 1940 also saw the formation of the America First Committee, a pressure group that lobbied Congress to keep the U.S. out of the war in Europe.

By mid-1940, Nazi Germany conquered most of Europe. Only Great Britain remained defiant and free. Although Roosevelt wanted to help Britain, isolationist sentiment in America was very strong and influential. Charles Lindbergh (1902–1974), a popular aviator celebrity, proclaimed to an antiwar rally at the Hollywood Bowl on June 20, 1940, that the United States' geographic position made it virtually impregnable.

Not quite 18 months later, on December 7, 1941, Japanese aircraft made devastating surprise attacks against Pearl Harbor and other U.S. bases in the Pacific. Three days later, Germany and Italy, in support of their ally Japan, declared war on the United States. Four months later the first work on Navy ships began at Long Beach.

World War II saw Los Angeles literally on the front line, if for only a brief period, due to the destruction of most of the Navy battleships that were at Pearl Harbor. Military experts saw the threat of a Japanese attack on the U.S. West Coast as slight, but it seemed like a very real possibility for the average Angeleno.

L.A. did not grow geographically in this decade, but war and victory increased the city by almost another half million new residents. Los Angeles was now the fourth-largest city in America.

The walls of Alexander Hamilton Junior High School at Long Beach crumbled in the earthquake of 1933. The school was rebuilt as it appears here in 1940, with earthquake-proof windows, constructed by the Public Works Administration. The architecture style is known as Art Deco, a popular international design movement in the 1920s and 1930s that also affected interior and industrial design, as well as fashion, painting, graphic arts, and film.

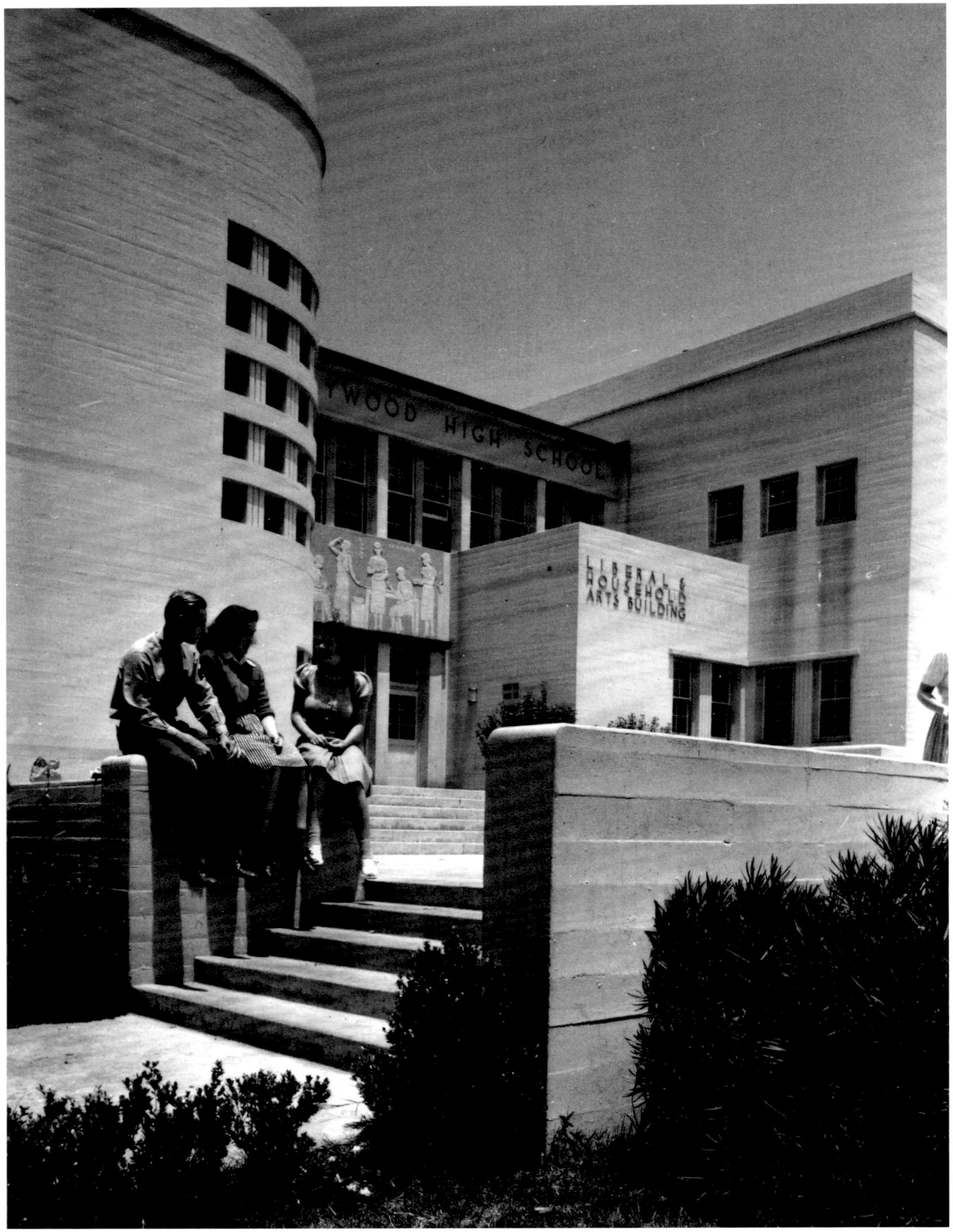

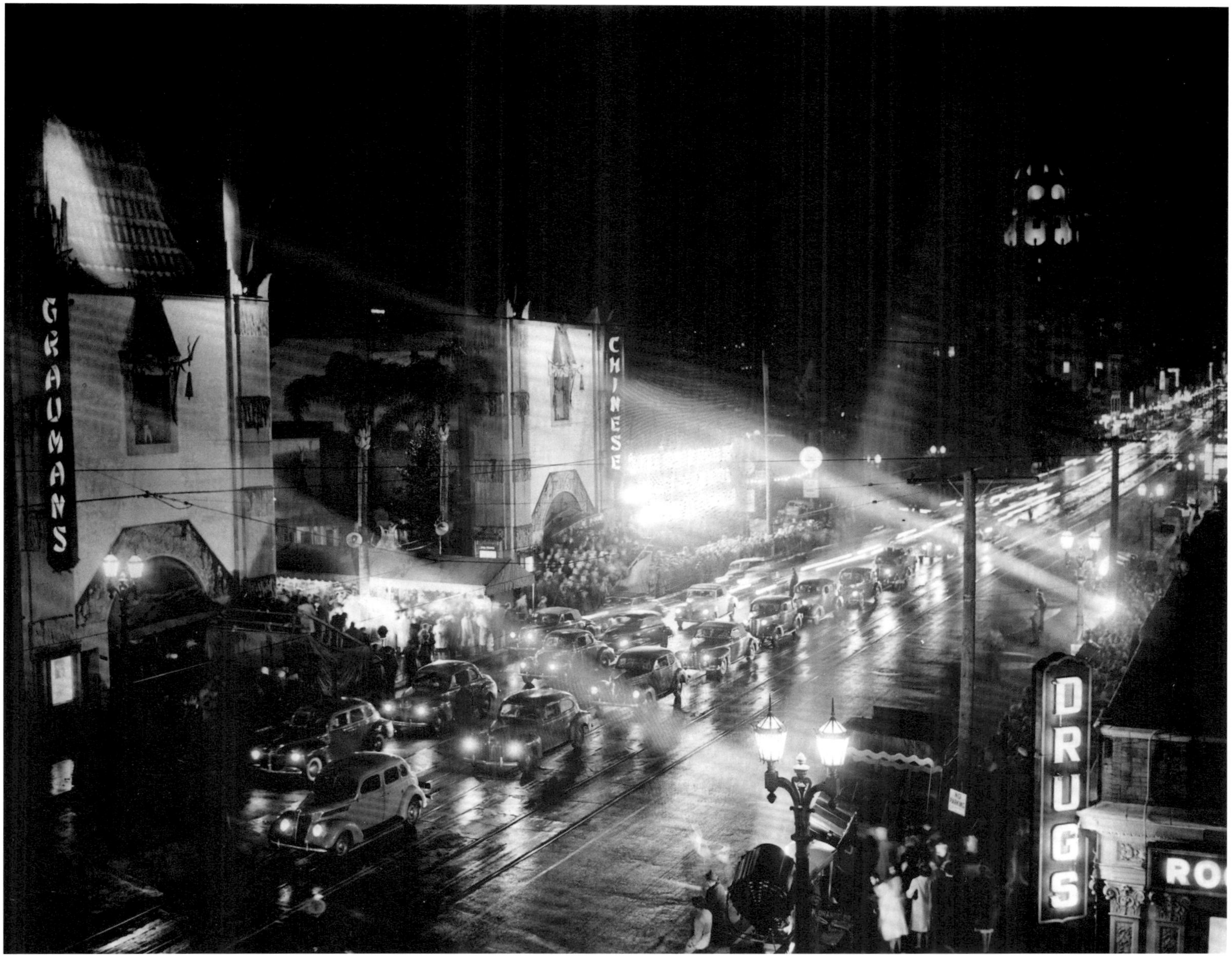

The crowds and traffic at a Grauman's Chinese Theatre premiere attest to Hollywood's continued influence. More than 7,500 movies—95 percent of all American films—were released by the eight leading studios between 1930 and 1945. This period is remembered as Hollywood's golden age, when new genres were formed, the Production Code and B-films were introduced, the first animated feature *Snow White* appeared, and the studio system rose to mammoth status.

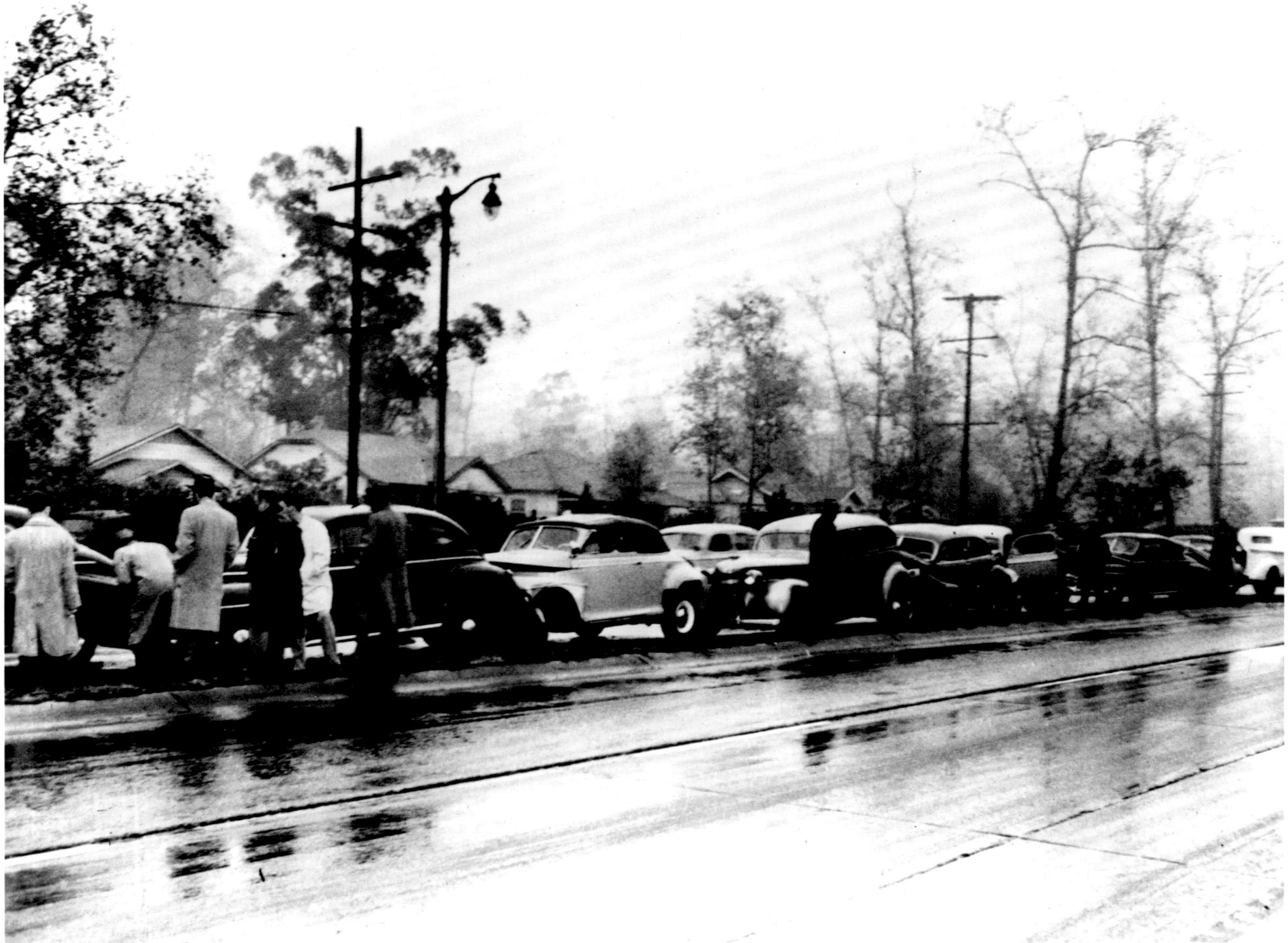

With so many cars, traffic accidents became routine occurrences in Los Angeles. Here, rain-wet Arroyo Seco Parkway (now called the Pasadena Freeway) caused a pileup in which seven people were injured. Arroyo Seco was the first freeway in the West. Because of its engineering significance, it was designated a historic engineering landmark by the American Society of Civil Engineers in 1999.

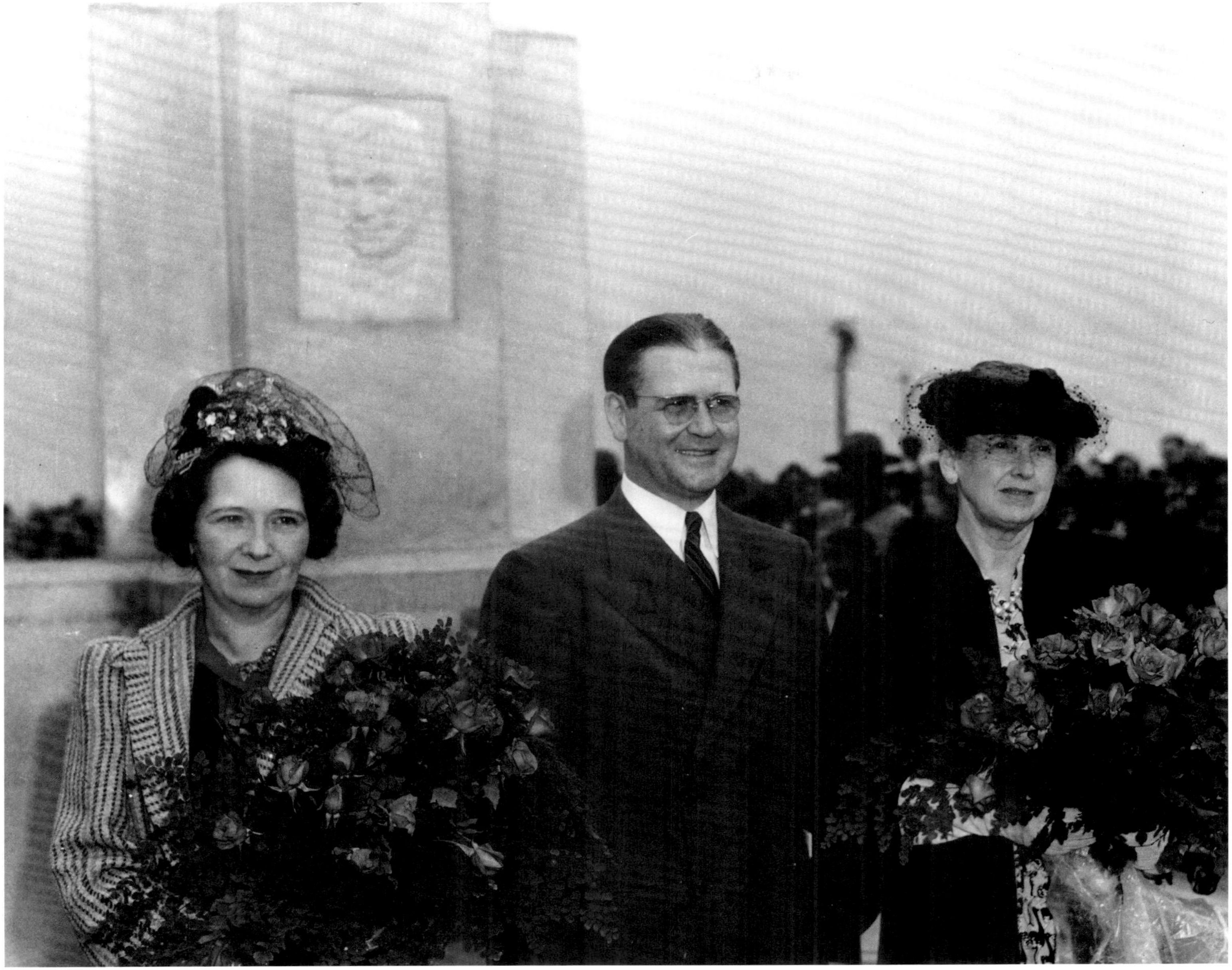

Not quite six years after Will Rogers (1879–1935) died in a plane crash, the Will Rogers Memorial Park and Playground in Southwest Los Angeles was formally dedicated on June 14, 1941. The new play center honoring the popular humorist and actor was sponsored by the County of Los Angeles. The photo shows (left to right) Betty Blake Rogers, widow of the late actor; Gordon McDonough of the County Board of Supervisors; and Mrs. McDonough.

This is the First Street viaduct, west approach, under construction in Los Angeles in 1941. A viaduct is a type of bridge that spans the gap between two high points of land and does not cross any water.

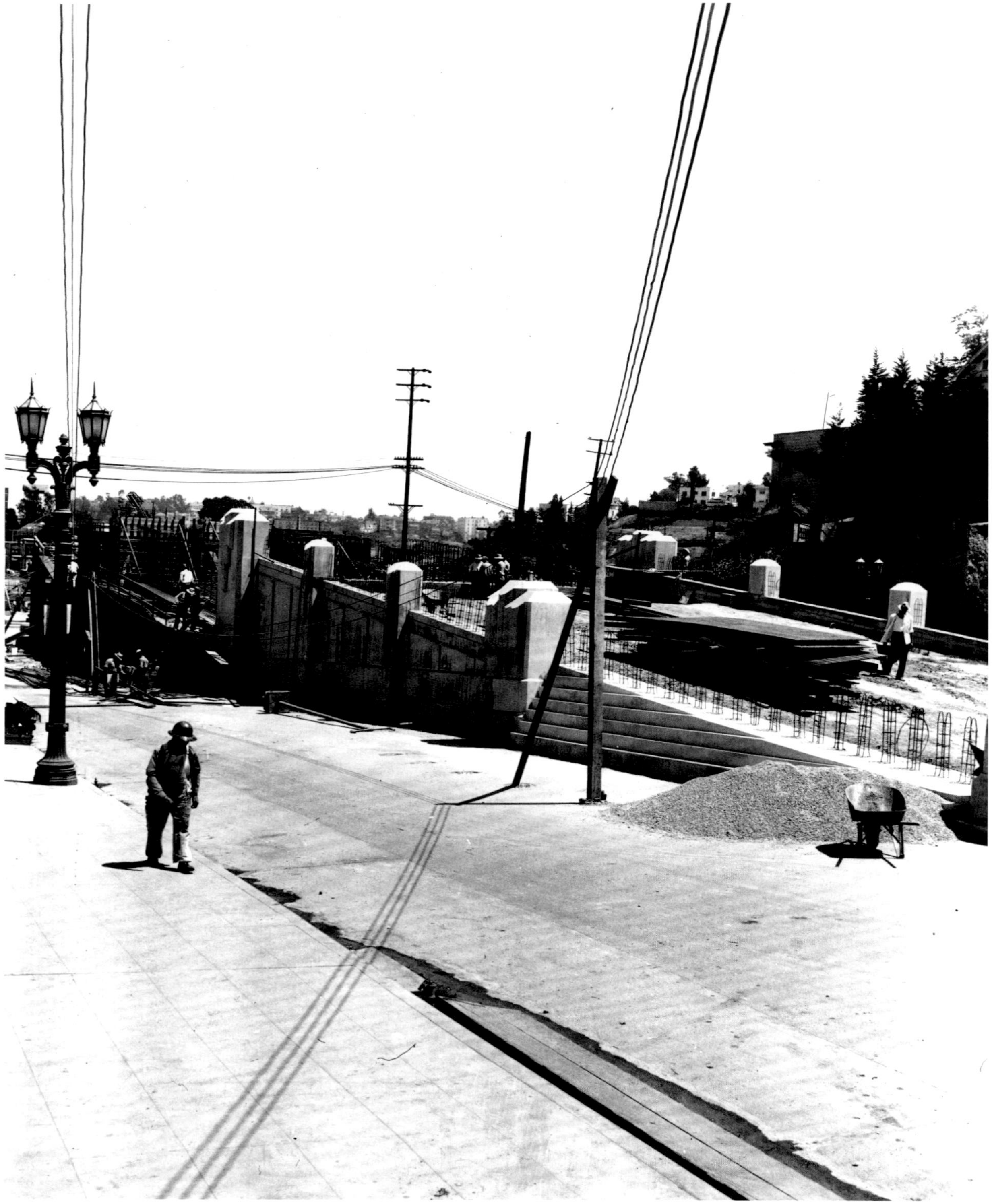

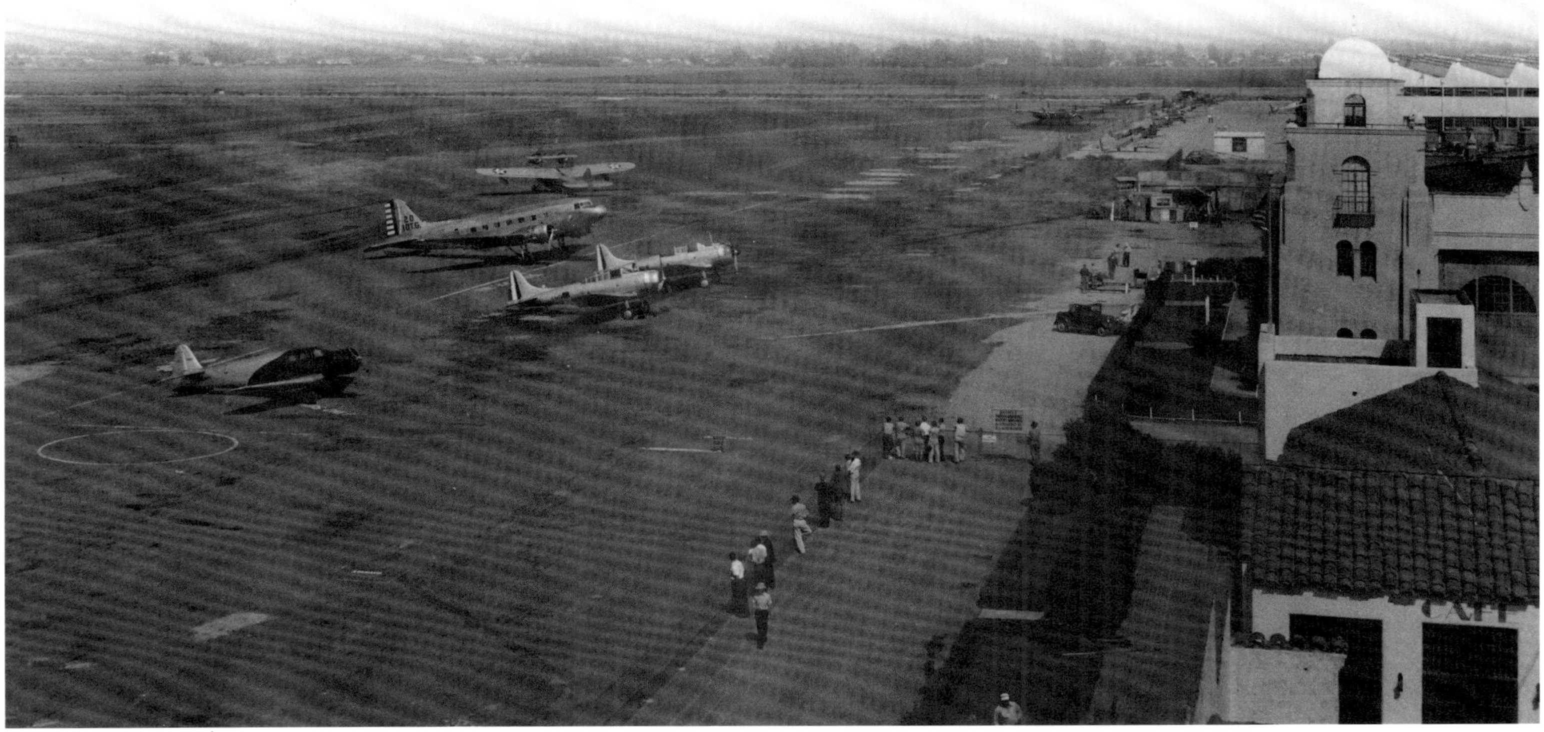

Formerly known as Mines Field, the Los Angeles Municipal Airport was converted into one of the major airports on the Pacific Coast in 1940 as the Work Projects Administration provided 1,600 workers to make improvements. When the National Defense Program was launched, the Mines Field conversion became a priority project. The photo is shot from the central tower.

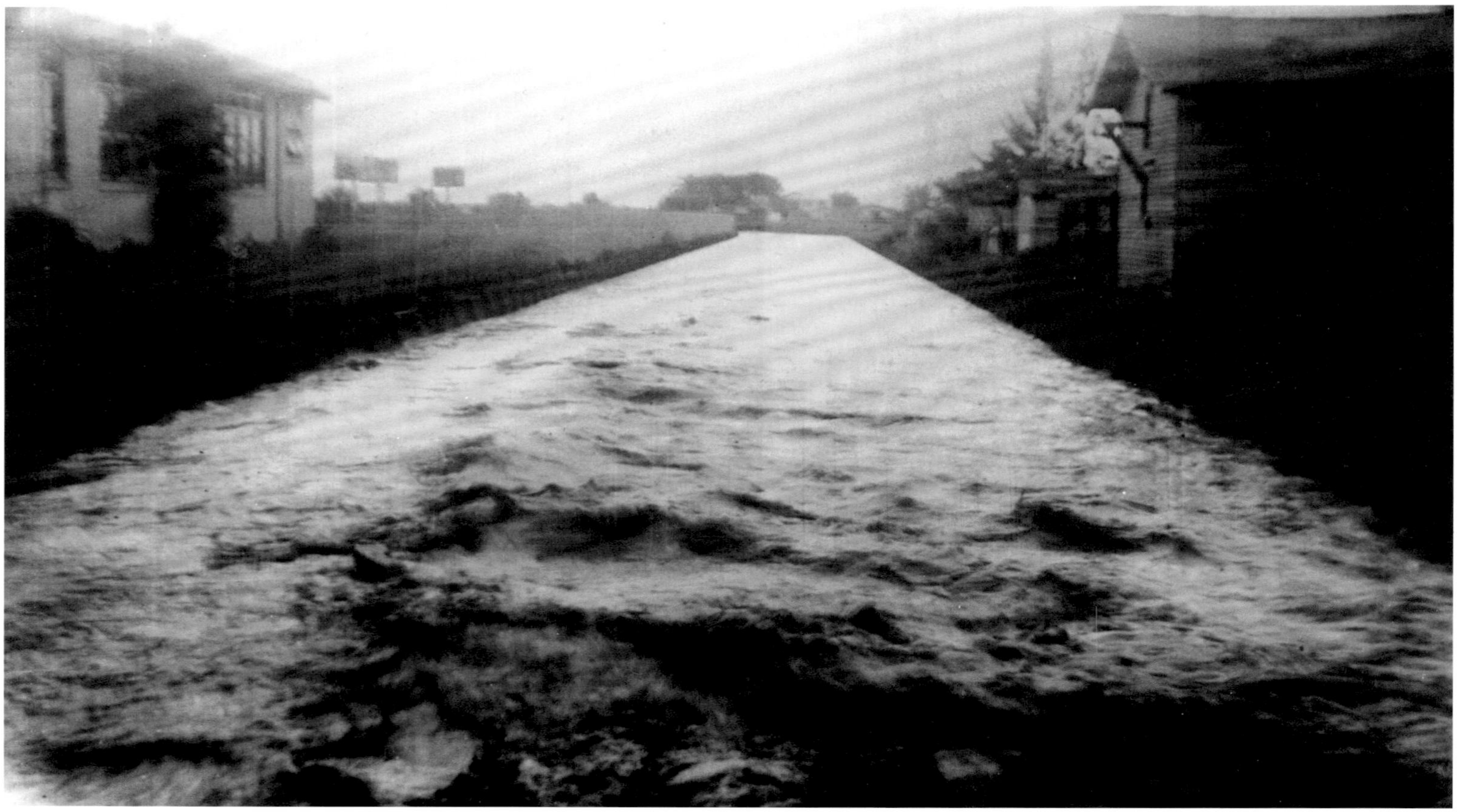

During a 1941 storm, two and a half inches of rain fell in 40 minutes, filling the East Fullerton Relief Channel to a depth of 15 feet. The damage to the Los Angeles area from the year's extraordinary rainfall might have been much worse had the WPA's flood control projects not been completed.

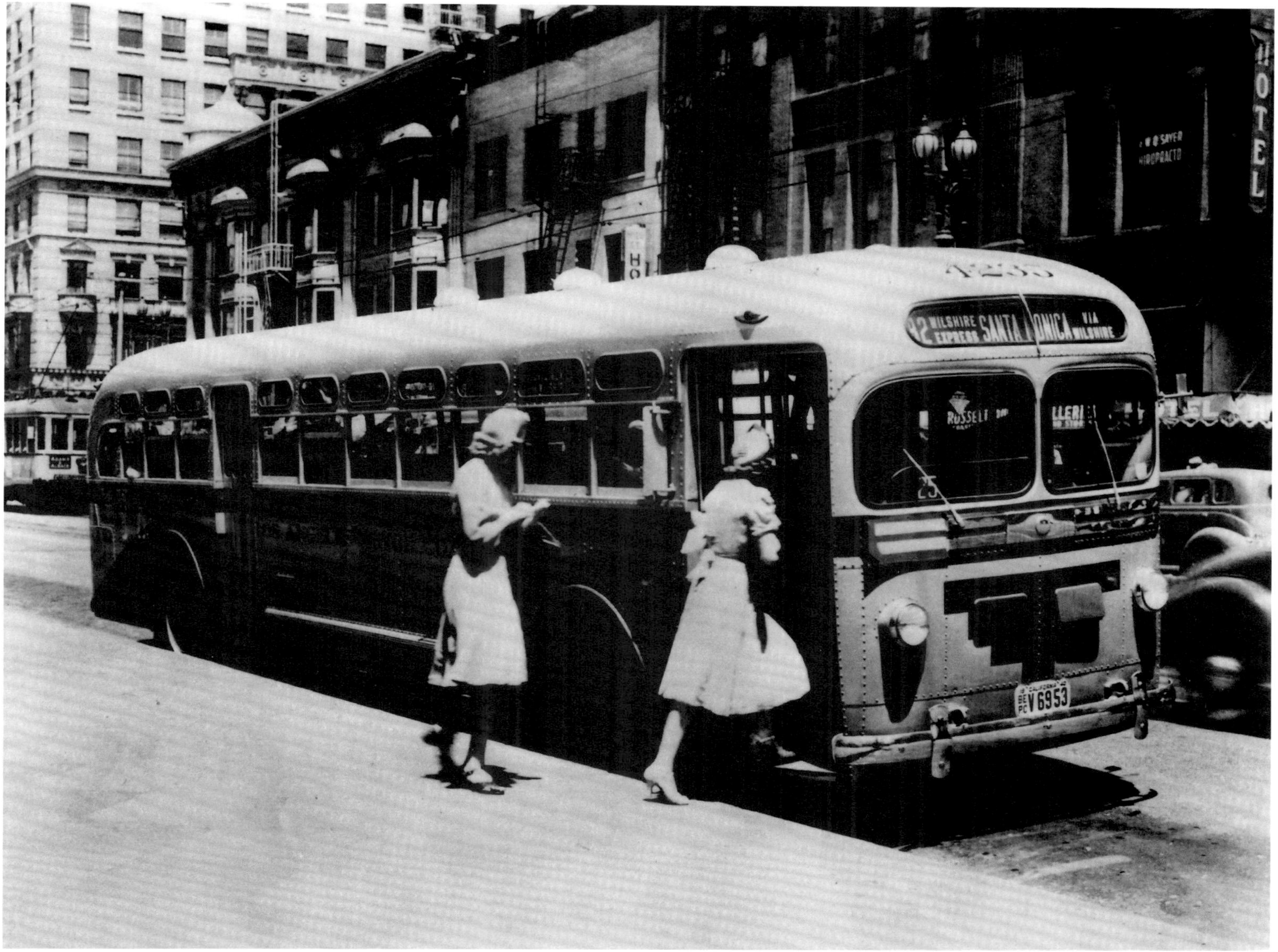

Young women board a bus in Los Angeles. Unlike streetcar lines that required rails, bus routes could be adjusted easily and quickly. World War II halted construction on the parkways and freeways, and gasoline was rationed. For many workers, buses provided a viable transportation alternative to automobiles on L.A.'s crowded roadways.

Benjamin "Bugsy" Siegel is led away by U.S. Marshals in Los Angeles in 1941. Siegel (1906–1947) was famous for his affairs with female Hollywood personalities and for building Las Vegas. In California he ran the illegal transcontinental race wire service and giant prostitution rings, and he also smuggled narcotics across the Mexican border.

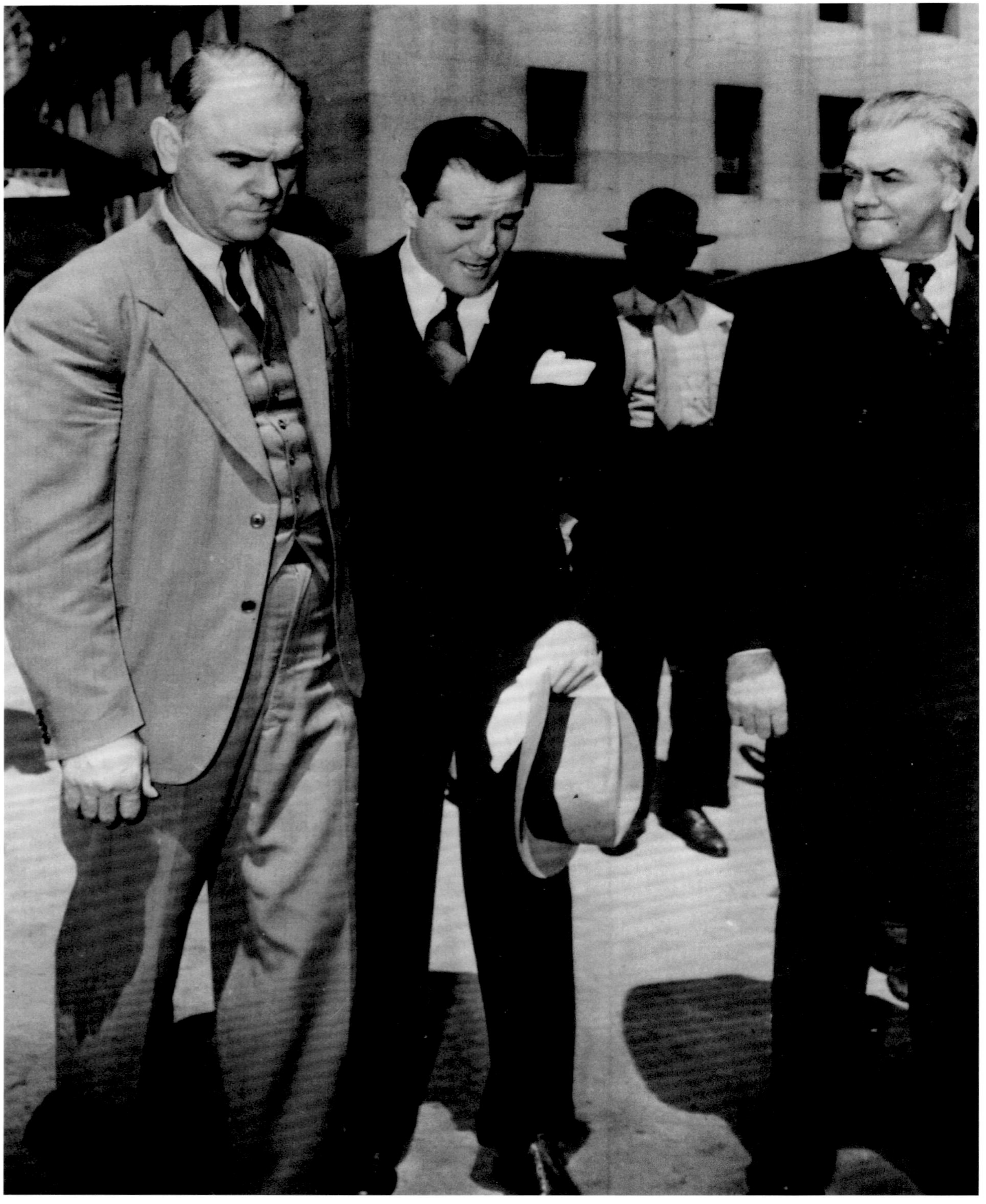

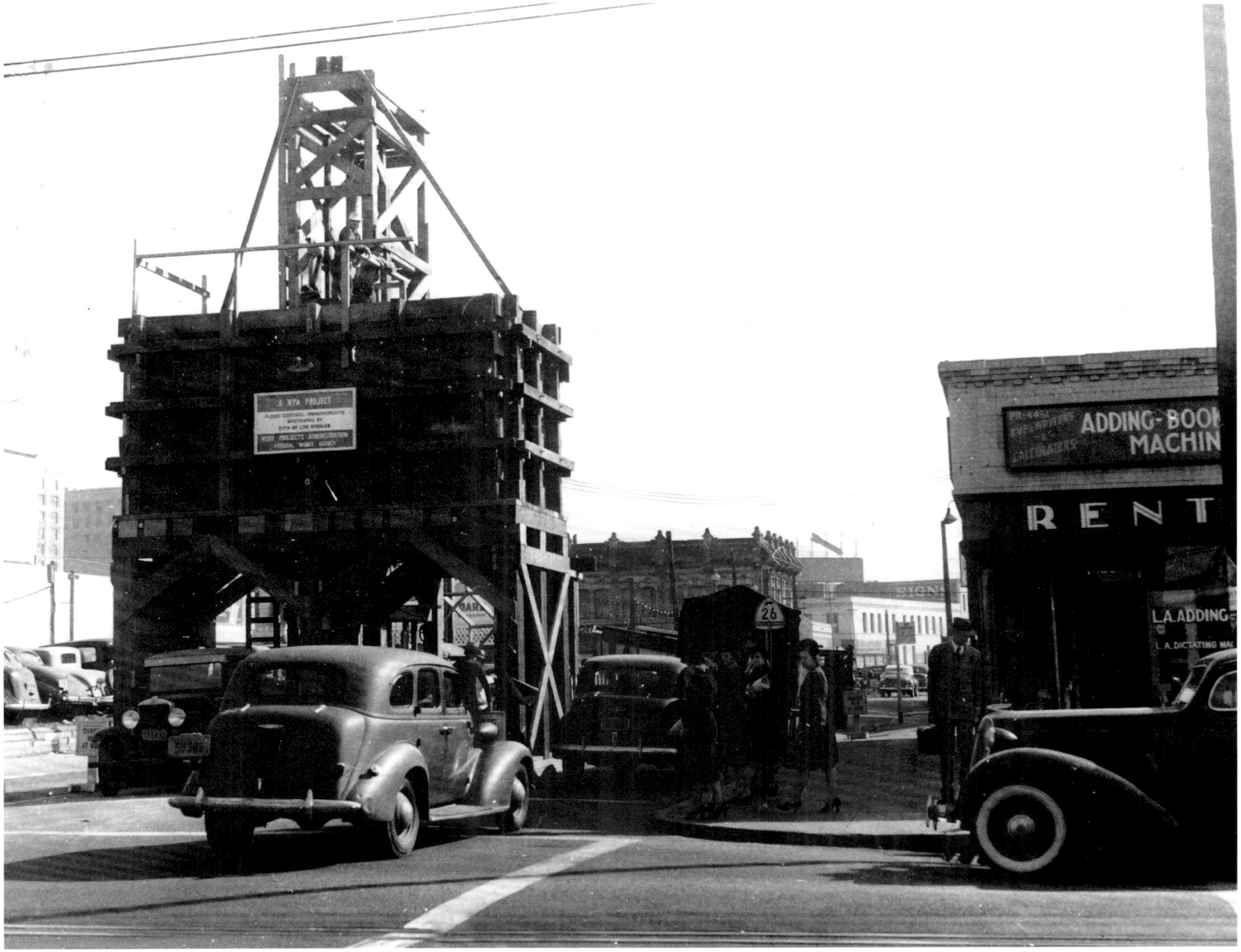

When bad weather did occasionally hit Los Angeles, the city as originally designed was not able to accommodate the sudden influx of water. A 1940 WPA project, the Olympic Boulevard storm drain, shown here, was part of a citywide storm drain system underneath the streets. Its basic structure was a tapered, reinforced-concrete main line with dozens of connecting laterals and catch-basins, making it one of the largest in the West.

Lana Turner (1921–1995), the popular movie femme fatale, shown here just two months before the Japanese attack on Pearl Harbor, inspects the bracelet design embroidered on dressy, lisle cotton mesh hose. During World War II, Turner made tours selling War Bonds. She wrote her own speeches and promised "a sweet kiss" to any man who purchased a bond worth $50,000 or more. "I'm told I increased the defense budget by several million dollars," she said.

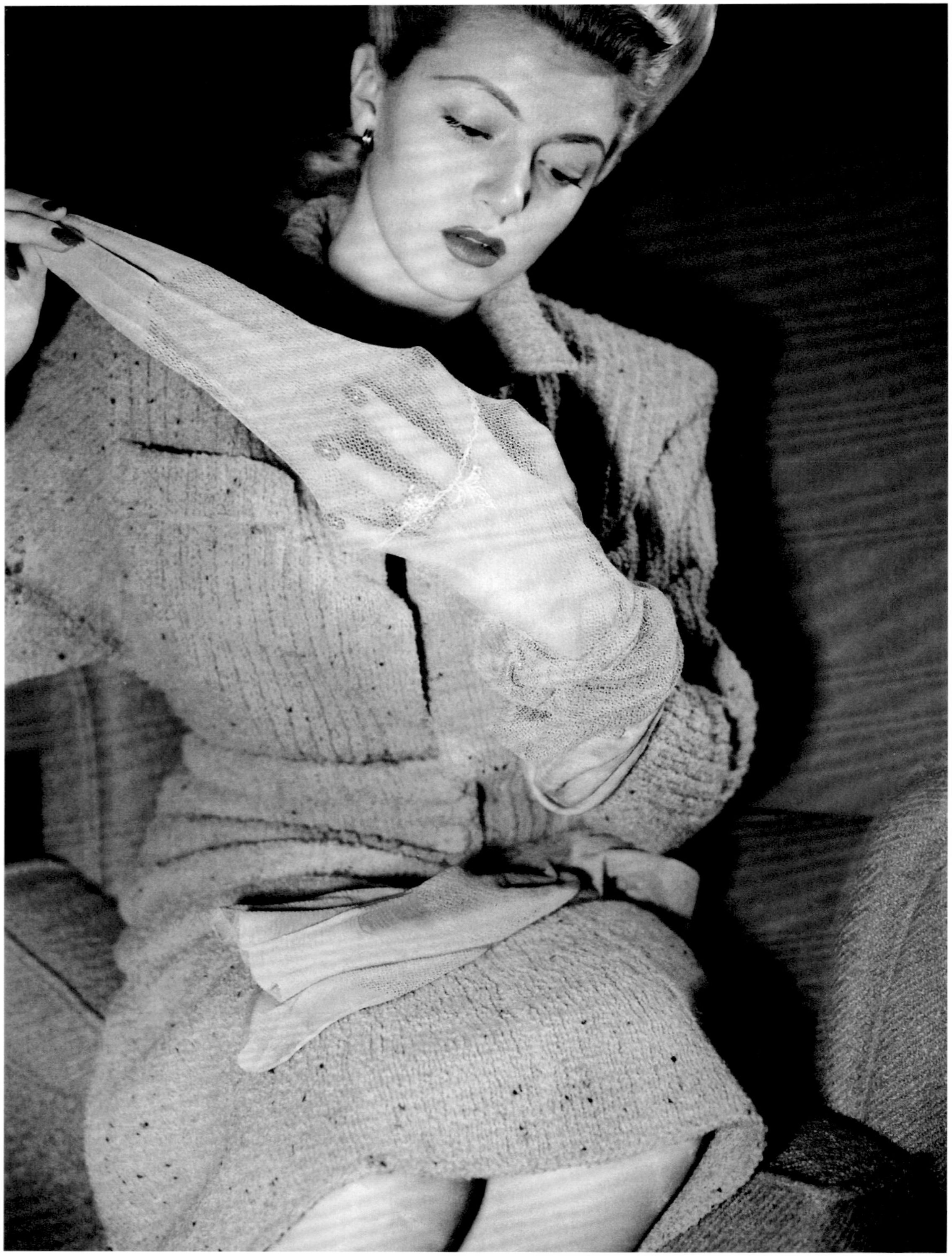

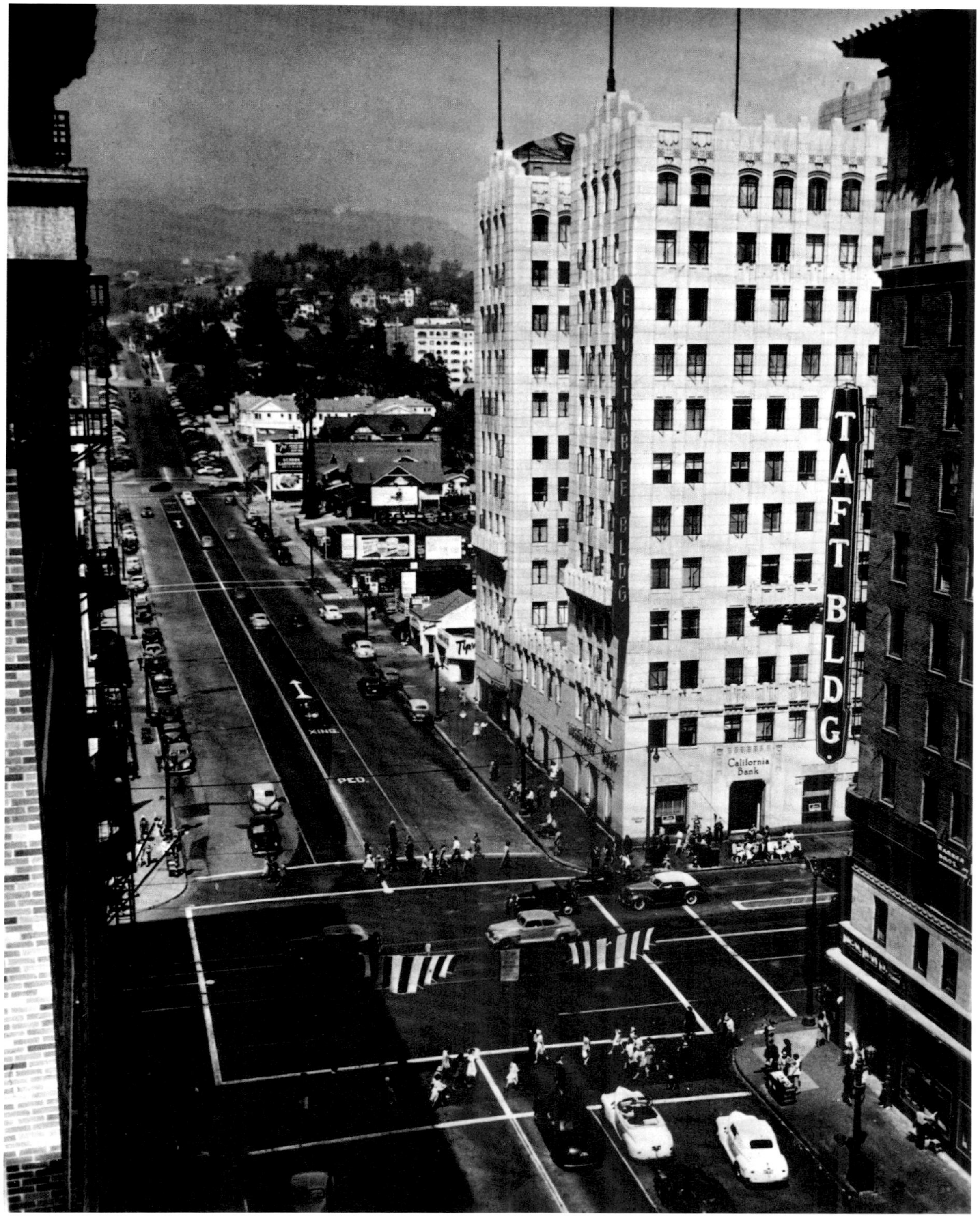

Hollywood and Vine Streets looking north on Vine. This was one of L.A.'s main thoroughfares before the Hollywood Freeway and other superhighways became the primary automobile conveyance. During the 1940s the Pacific Electric Railway "Red Cars" still served the area, but they would disappear during the next decade.

Following Spread: In 1896, Colonel Griffith J. Griffith donated land on Mount Hollywood along with funds to build an observatory, exhibit hall, and planetarium. The structure was finished in 1935. In this 1940s photograph, the front of Griffith Observatory is seen from a nearby trail on the Mount Hollywood hillside. In the background is the city of Hollywood and Pacific Ocean.

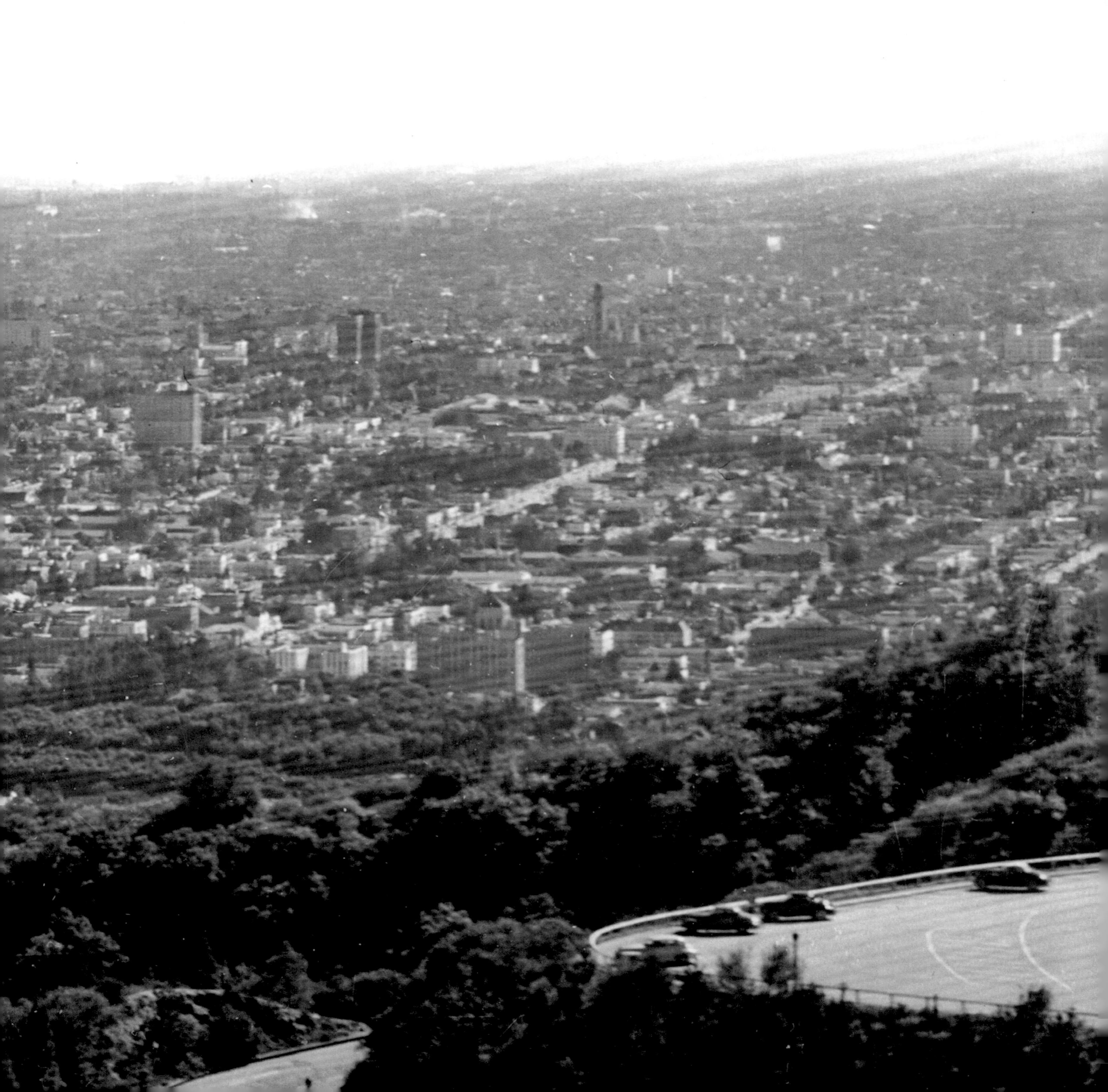

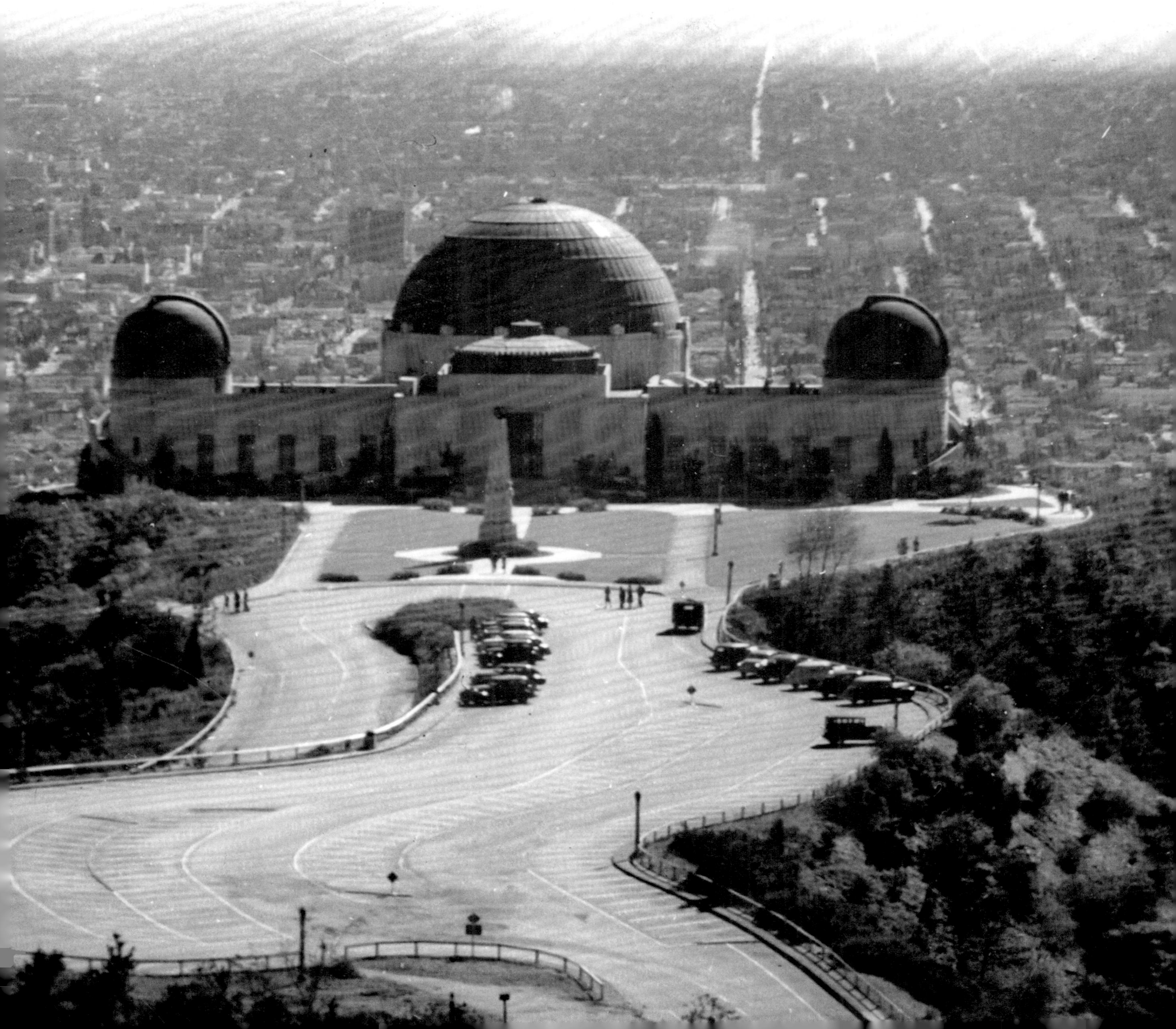

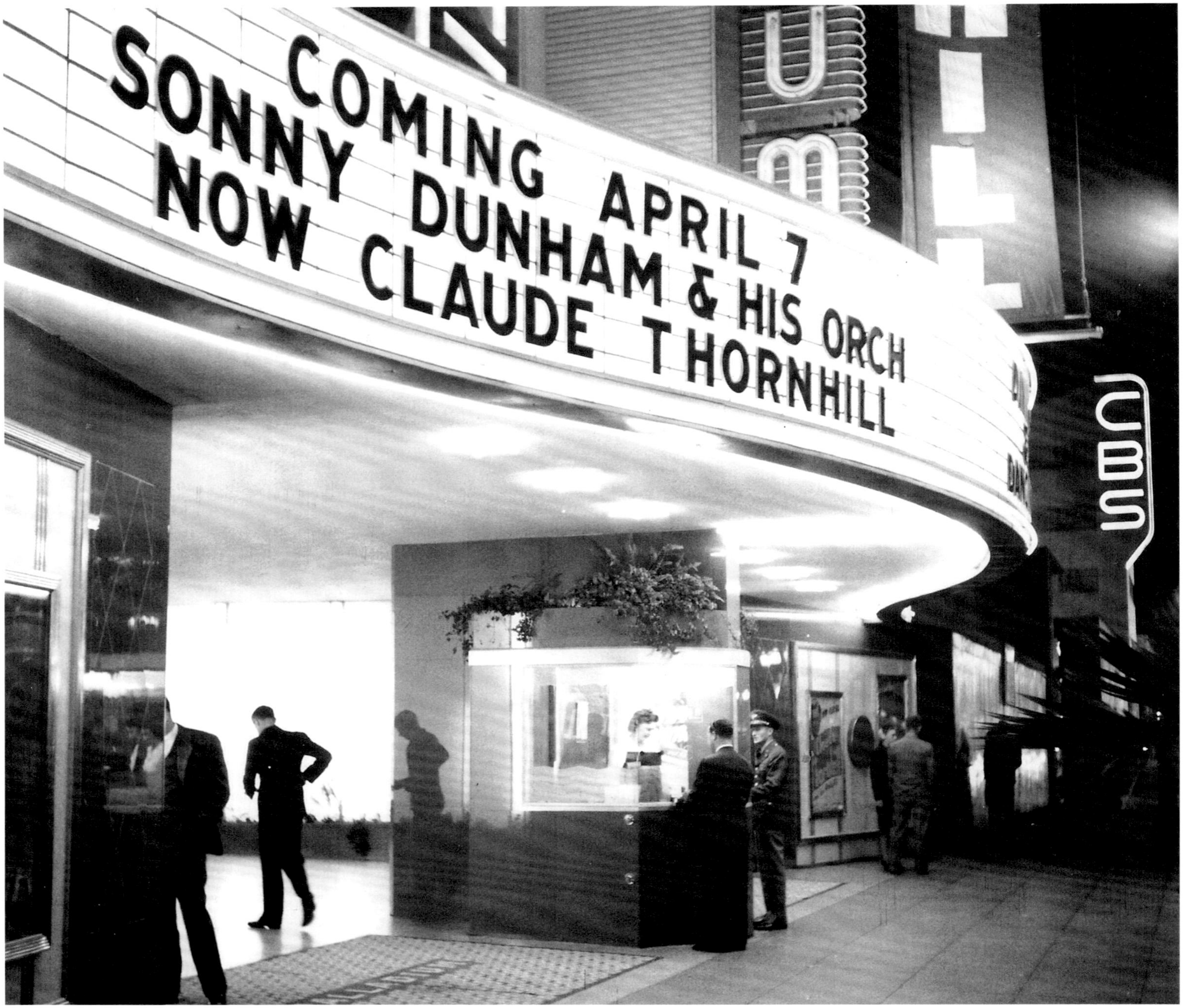

Dance halls existed in American cities since the early 1800s. This sign and ticket window of a large dance palace in Hollywood in April 1942 marks the height of the Swing Era, when big-band swing music was the most popular music in America. Trumpet player Elmer "Sonny" Dunham (1911–1990) was one of the preeminent bandleaders of the 1940s. His band was featured in the 1942 Universal picture *Behind the Eight Ball.*

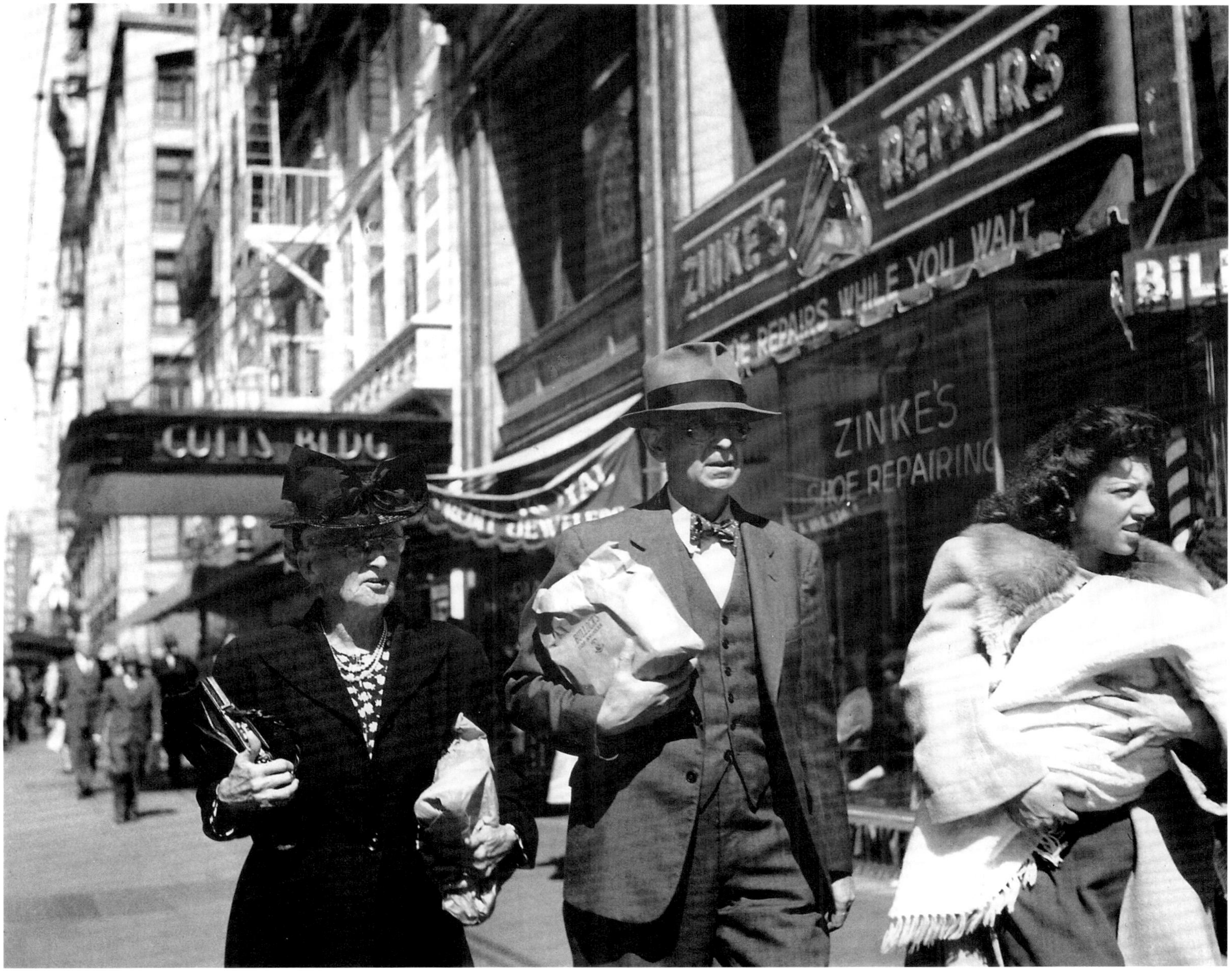

In the spring of 1942, Los Angeles shoppers like these people had to start living with government rationing of food, fuel, and even clothing. Americans were asked to conserve on everything for the duration of the war. The Food Rationing Program provided each citizen with a certain amount of points weekly, using food stamps to purchase meats, butter, oils, etc., and processed foods such as soups, baby food, and catsup. By 1945, about 40 percent of America's vegetables were produced in private "Victory Gardens."

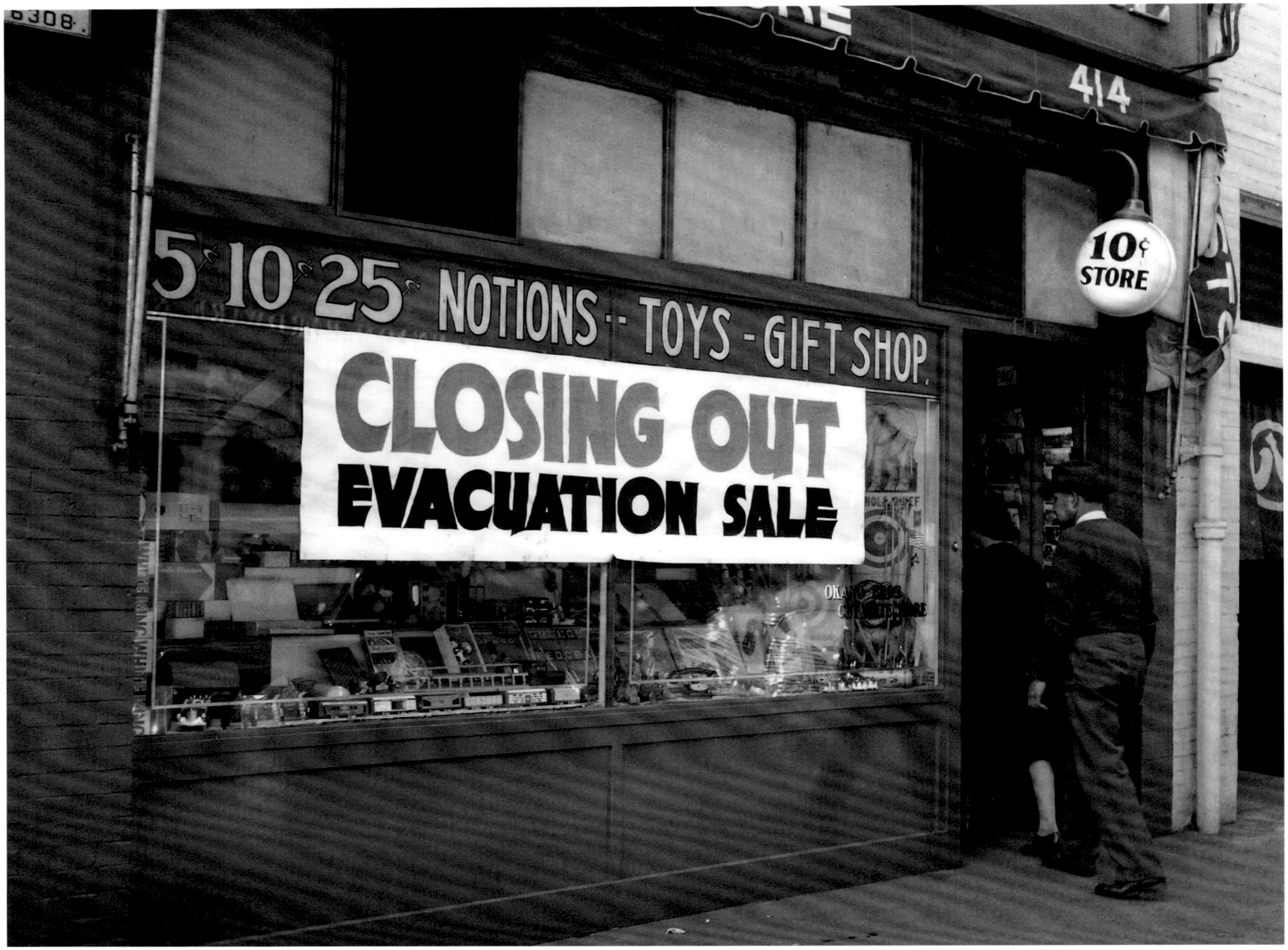

The Japanese surprise attack on Pearl Harbor and rapid conquest of a large portion of Asia and the Pacific caused American civil and military leaders to worry about the loyalty of the more than 100,000 people of Japanese descent living on the West Coast of the United States. Fear of espionage and sabotage, plus racial bias, resulted in President Roosevelt ordering their forced removal to internment camps in April 1942. Here is one of many businesses in L.A.'s Little Tokyo required to close due to the evacuation.

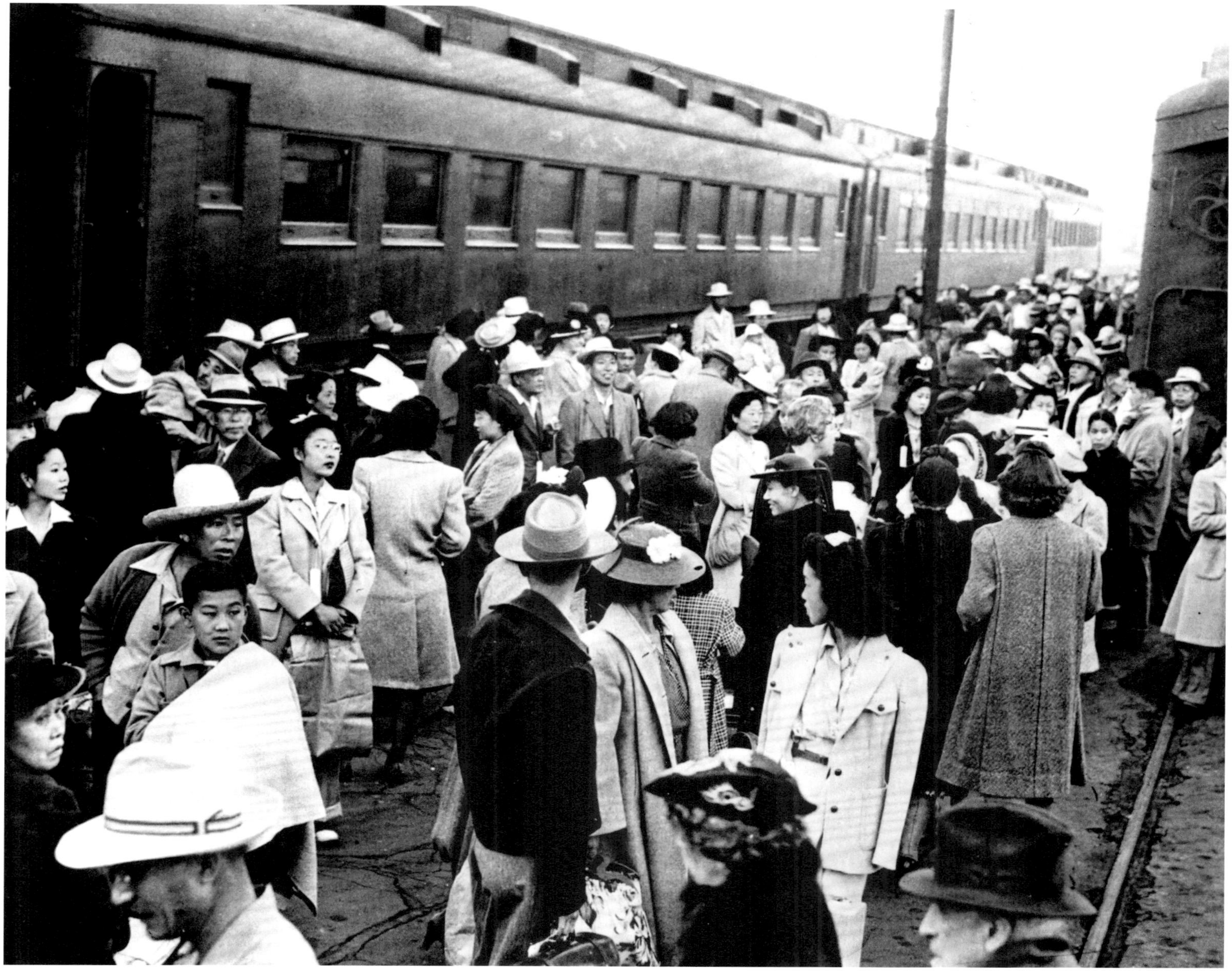

In 1942, 110,000 men, women, and children of Japanese ancestry were sent to camps called "War Relocation Centers" in remote areas of the U.S. Almost two-thirds of them were American citizens, but in 1944, the Supreme Court upheld the constitutionality of the removal and detention, ruling that civil rights of a racial group may be curtailed when there is a "pressing public necessity." These evacuees at a Los Angeles railroad station are waiting to board a train destined for the Santa Anita Assembly Center.

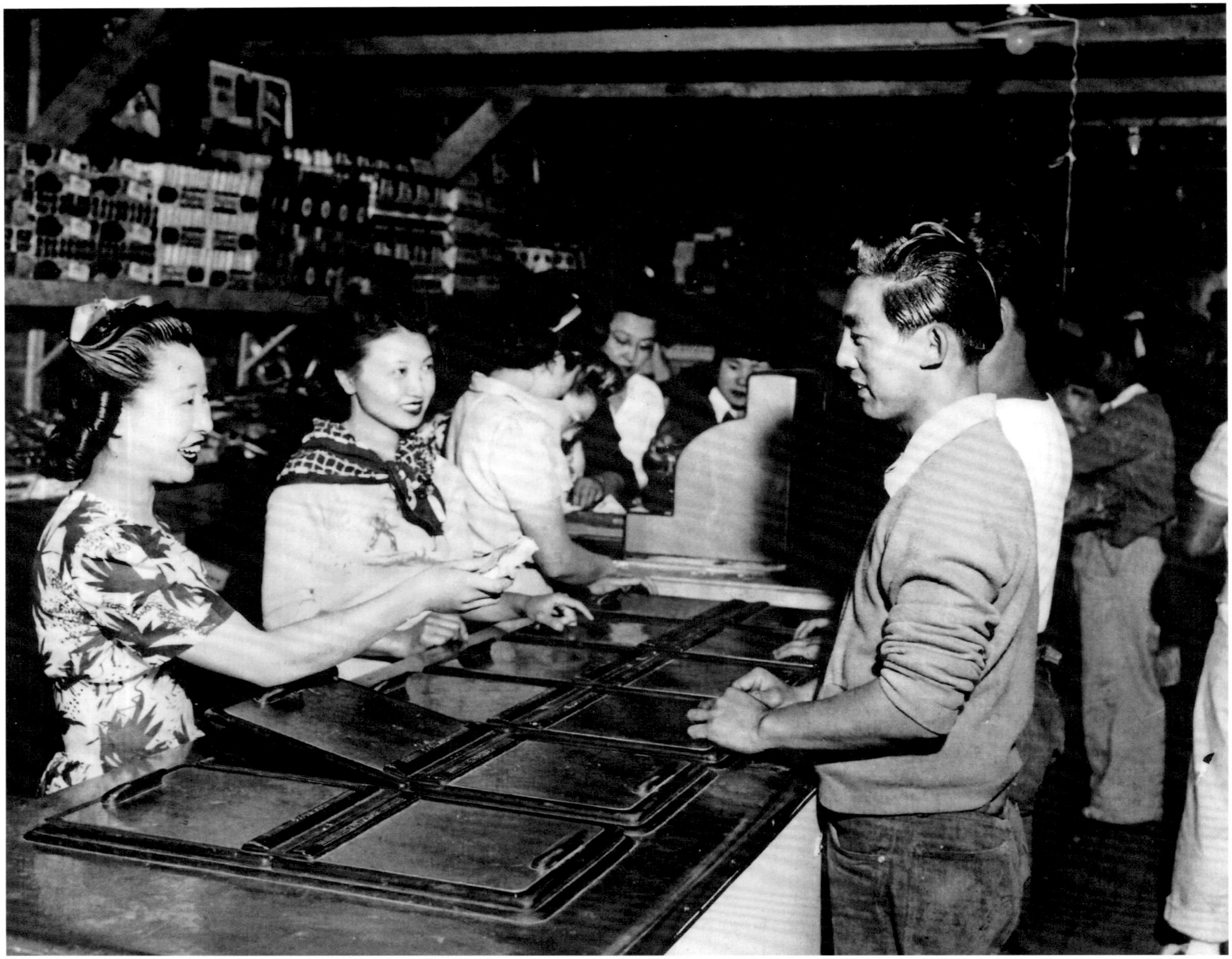

In May 1942, young Japanese American women are shown serving ice cream in a relocation center's community store in Manzanar, California. Some compensation for property losses was paid in 1948, but reparations to surviving internees did not occur until 1990. In 1988, President Ronald Reagan signed legislation that apologized for the internment noting that government actions were based on "race prejudice, war hysteria, and a failure of political leadership."

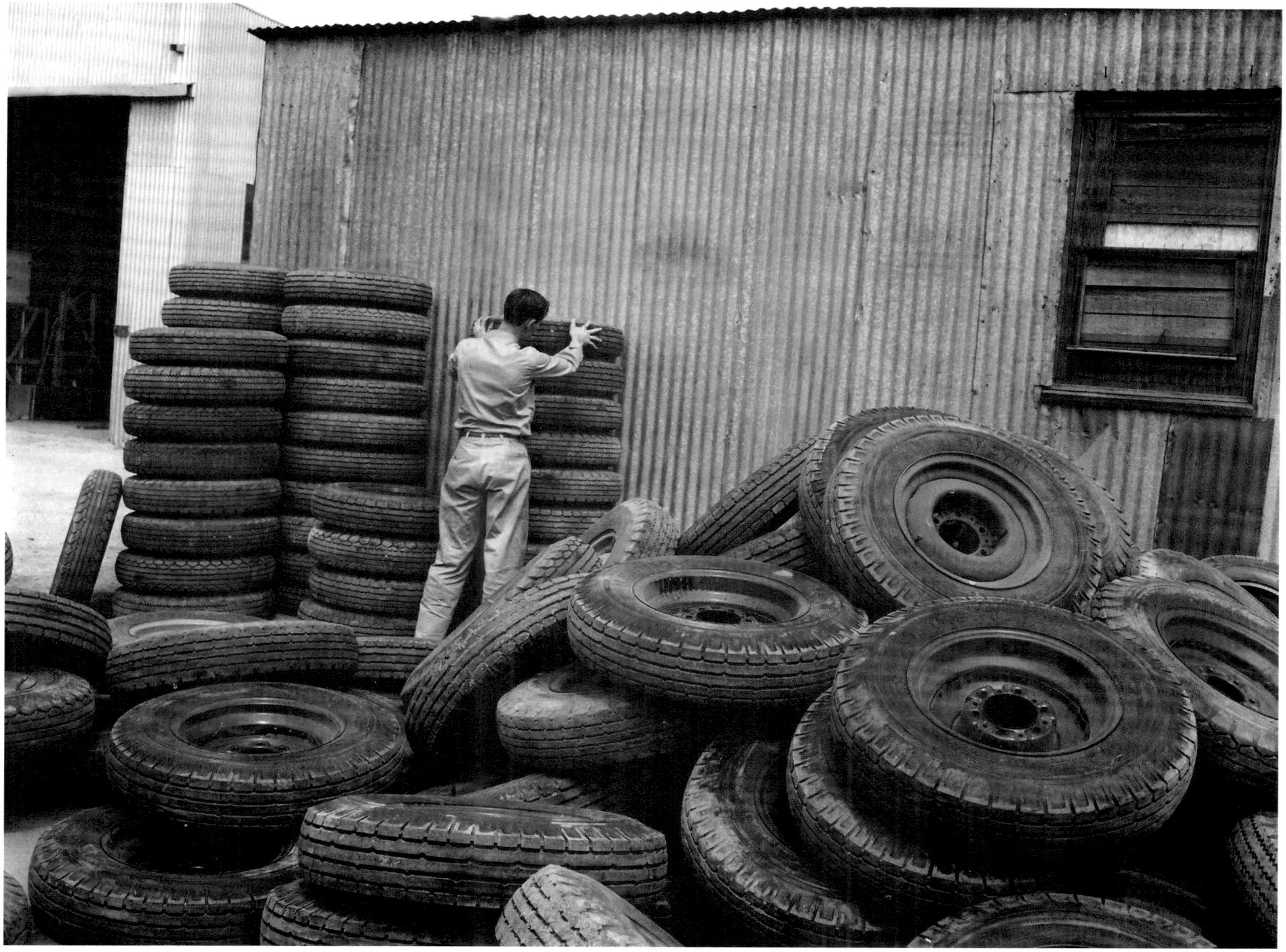

During World War II, Americans were urged to conserve and recycle metal, paper, and rubber. This batch of tires, or "shoes," were removed from trailers that had been delivered from the Los Angeles plant of the Western Trailer Company to war housing areas. Such tires would be registered and recycled for use in other trailers.

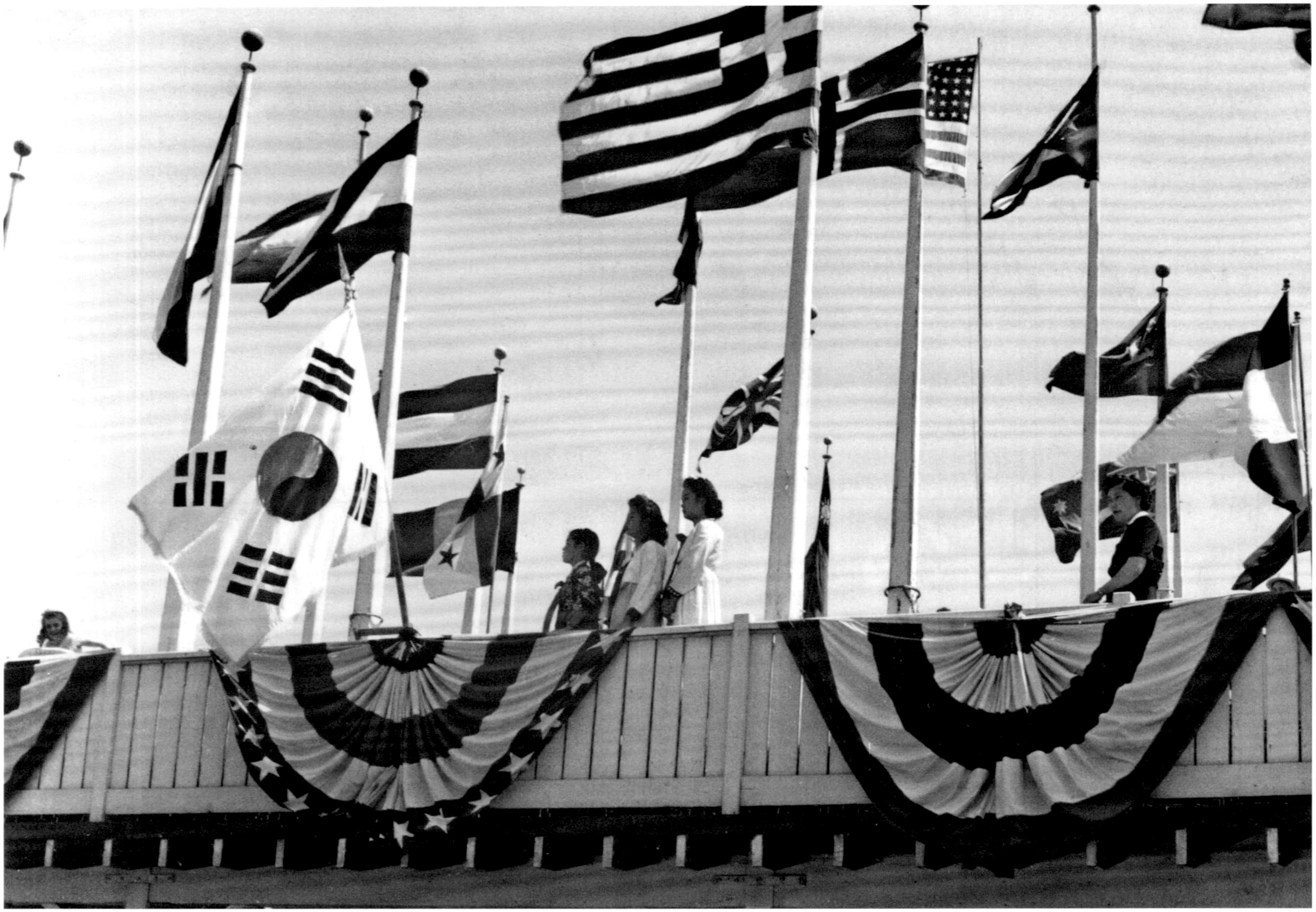

War bonds and stamps were sold to American citizens to provide funds for the government to prosecute the war against the Axis nations in Europe and across the Pacific. This 1942 Los Angeles bond rally and Parade of Nations displays the flag of Korea in the left foreground—the Taegeukgi was made official by the provisional Korean government in exile on June 29 of that year. Most Koreans were unaware of it since their country was under Japanese colonial rule.

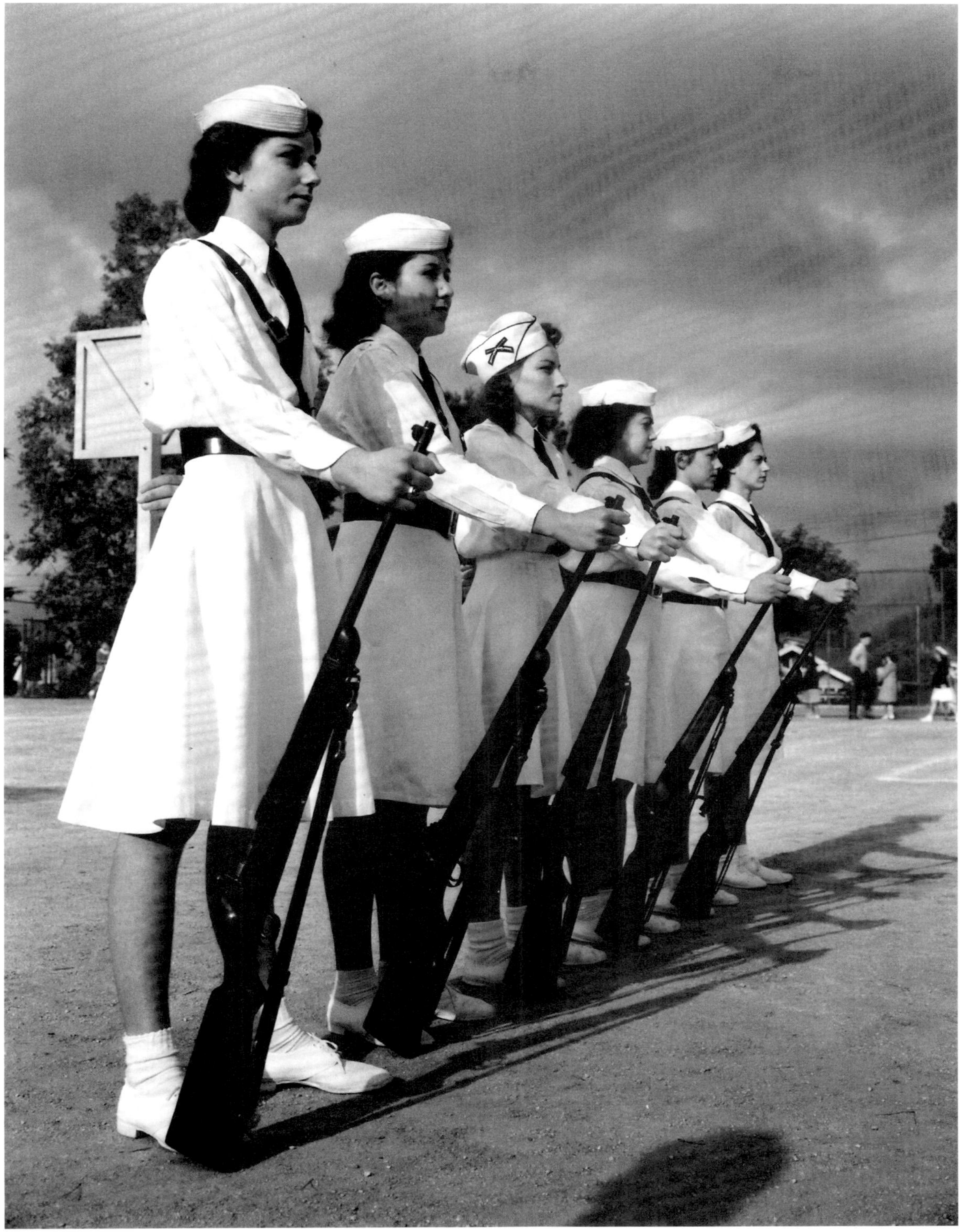

In late 1942, the Victory Corps was created to allow high school students to aid in the war effort. A member needed to participate in a physical fitness program and volunteer for at least one extracurricular wartime activity. These are students at Roosevelt High School in Los Angeles. In 1945, activists at Roosevelt H.S. organized hundreds of other students from local schools to protest against the Board of Education's granting white supremacist Gerald L. K. Smith (1898-1976) a permit to speak at Polytechnic High School.

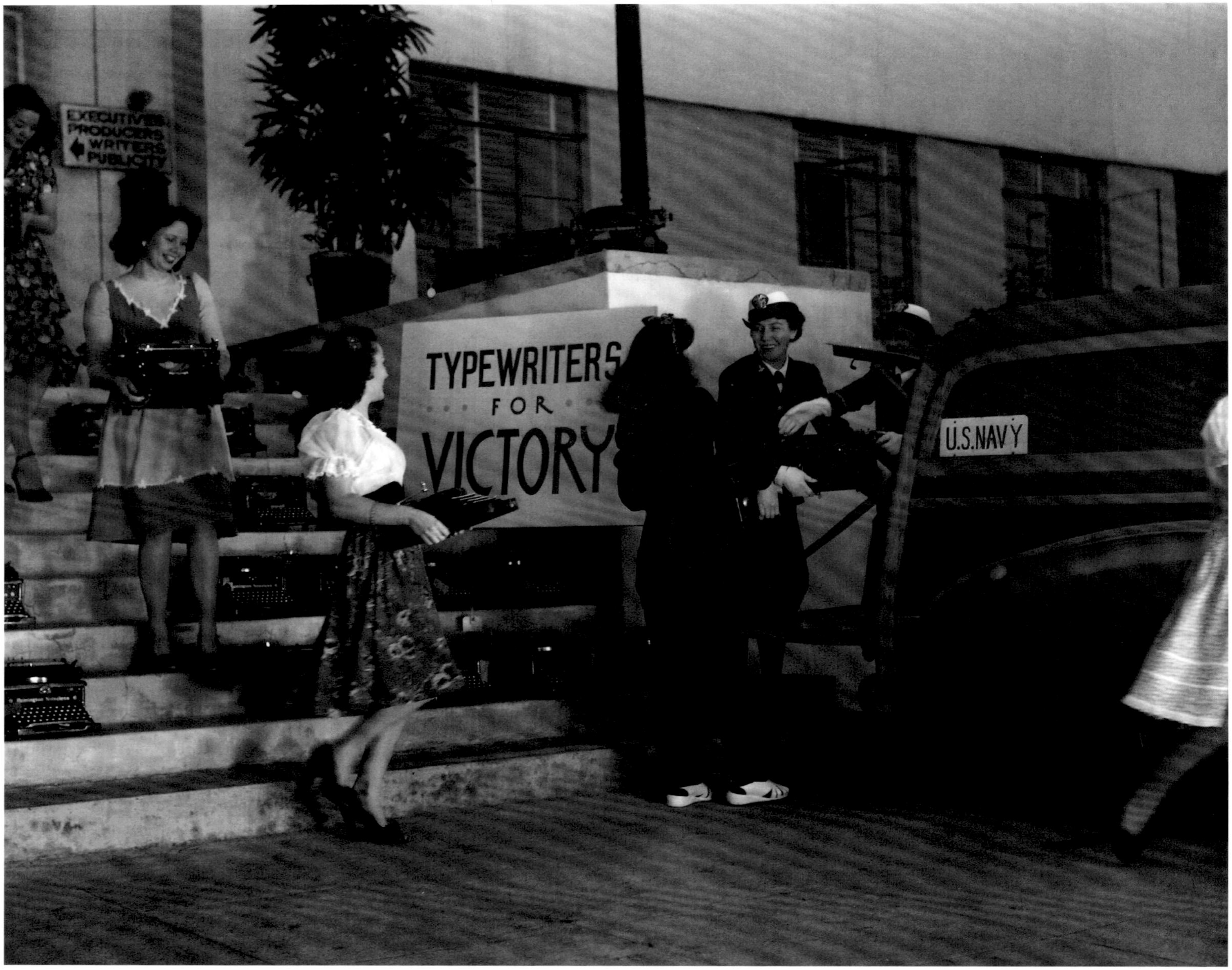

This Office of War Information photo was titled "Hollywood enlists its typewriters for war." In 1942, Hollywood studios responded to the government's urgent call for 600,000 typewriters for the armed services. These machines provided by 20th Century Fox studios were handed off to two U.S. Navy Waves ("Women Accepted for Volunteer Emergency Service"). Women also served with the U.S. Army and Army Air Corps ("Wacs" for Women's Army Corps), and in the Marines Corps as a Women's Reserve.

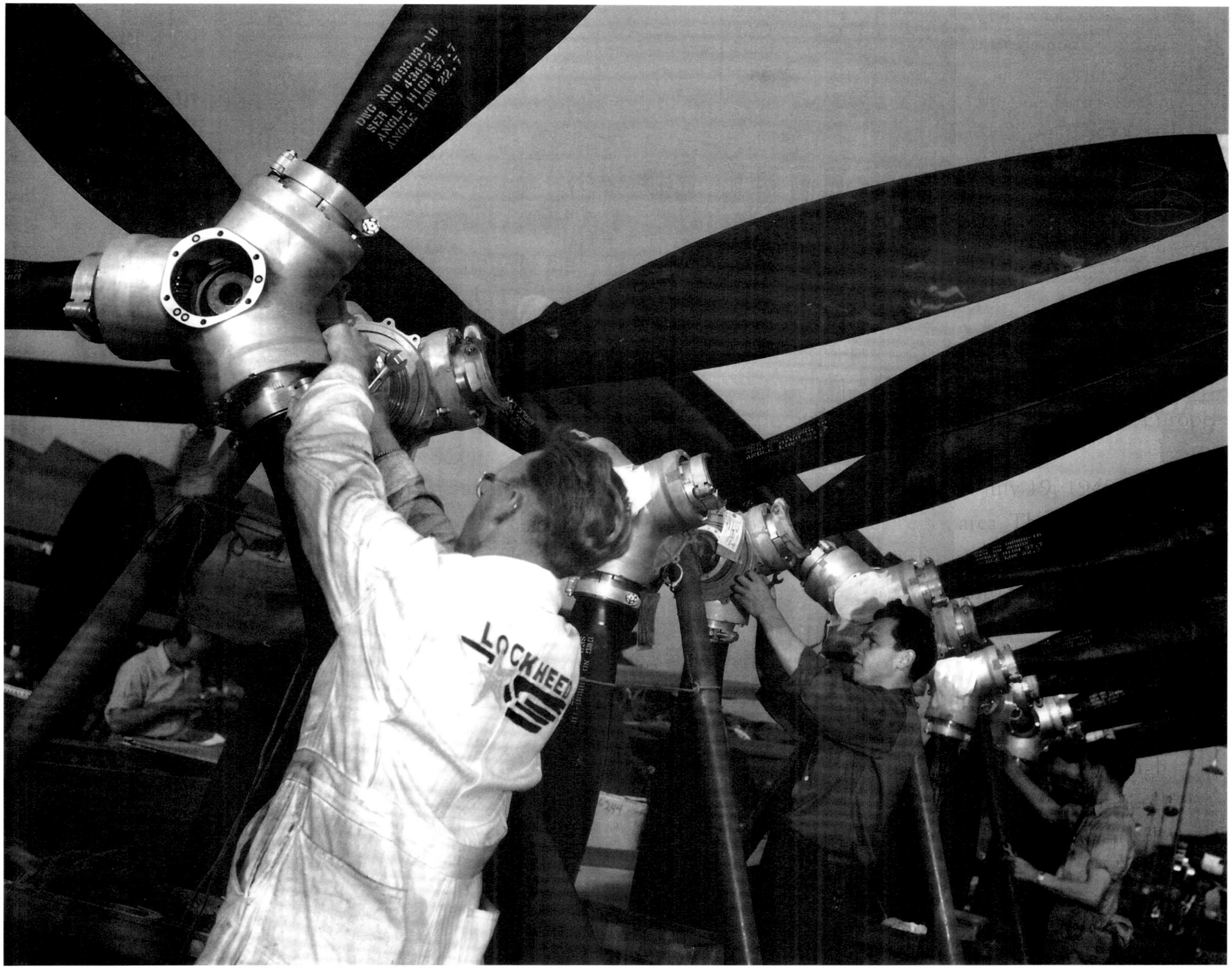

Three-blade, variable-pitch propellers are prepared for installation on Lockheed P-38 pursuit planes at a large Los Angeles aircraft plant in July 1942. That year a unit of eighteen P-38s, outfitted with special long-range fuel tanks, intercepted and shot down the bomber carrying Admiral Isoroku Yamamoto, commander of the Combined Fleet of the Imperial Japanese Navy.

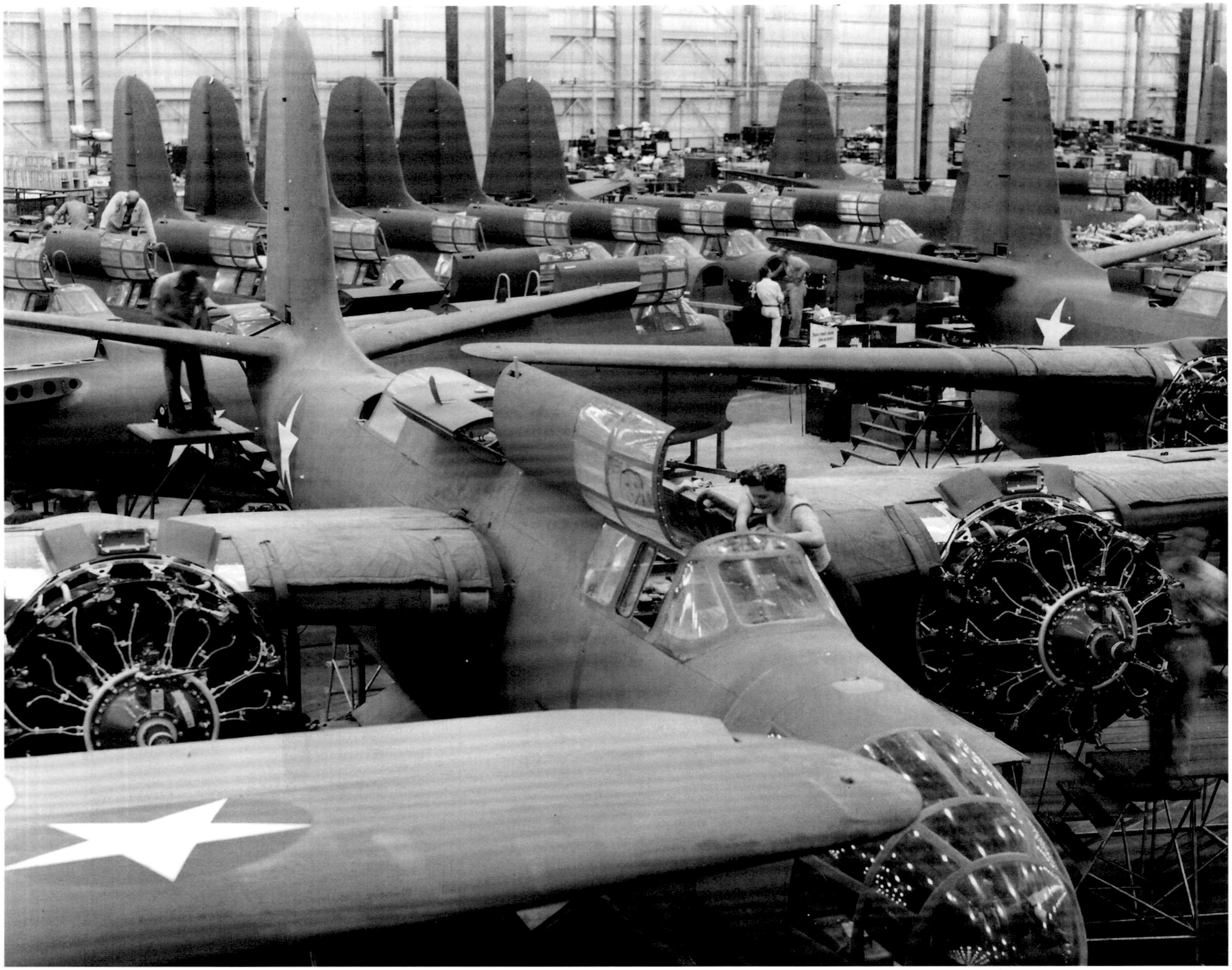

Defense workers at the Douglas Aircraft Company plant in Long Beach in October 1942 assemble DB-7/A-20 "Havoc" medium bombers. The model was called the "Boston" when it was built for England's Royal Air Force. The U.S. produced a staggering 303,713 airplanes during World War II, more than any other nation, and almost more than double that of Germany and Japan combined.

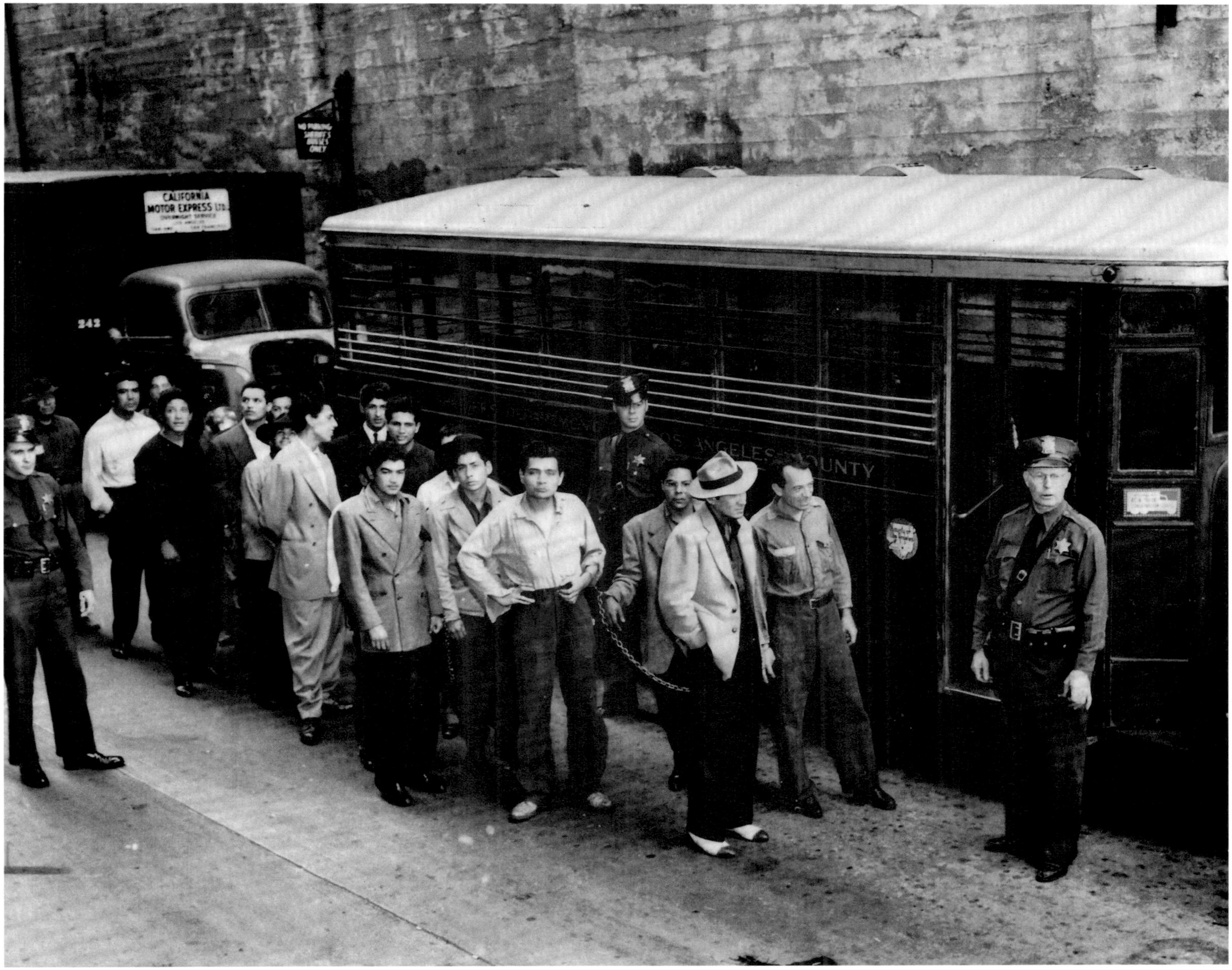

Zoot suiters en route to court after a brawl with sailors that was part of the sporadic anti-Latino "zoot suit riots" in 1942 and 1943. The zoot suit was a style of clothing popularized by African Americans, Mexican Americans, and Italian Americans during the 1930s and 1940s. The violence only subsided when military authorities declared Los Angeles off-limits to all military personnel on June 7, 1943. Of the riots, First Lady Eleanor Roosevelt commented, "The question goes deeper than just [zoot] suits. It is a racial protest."

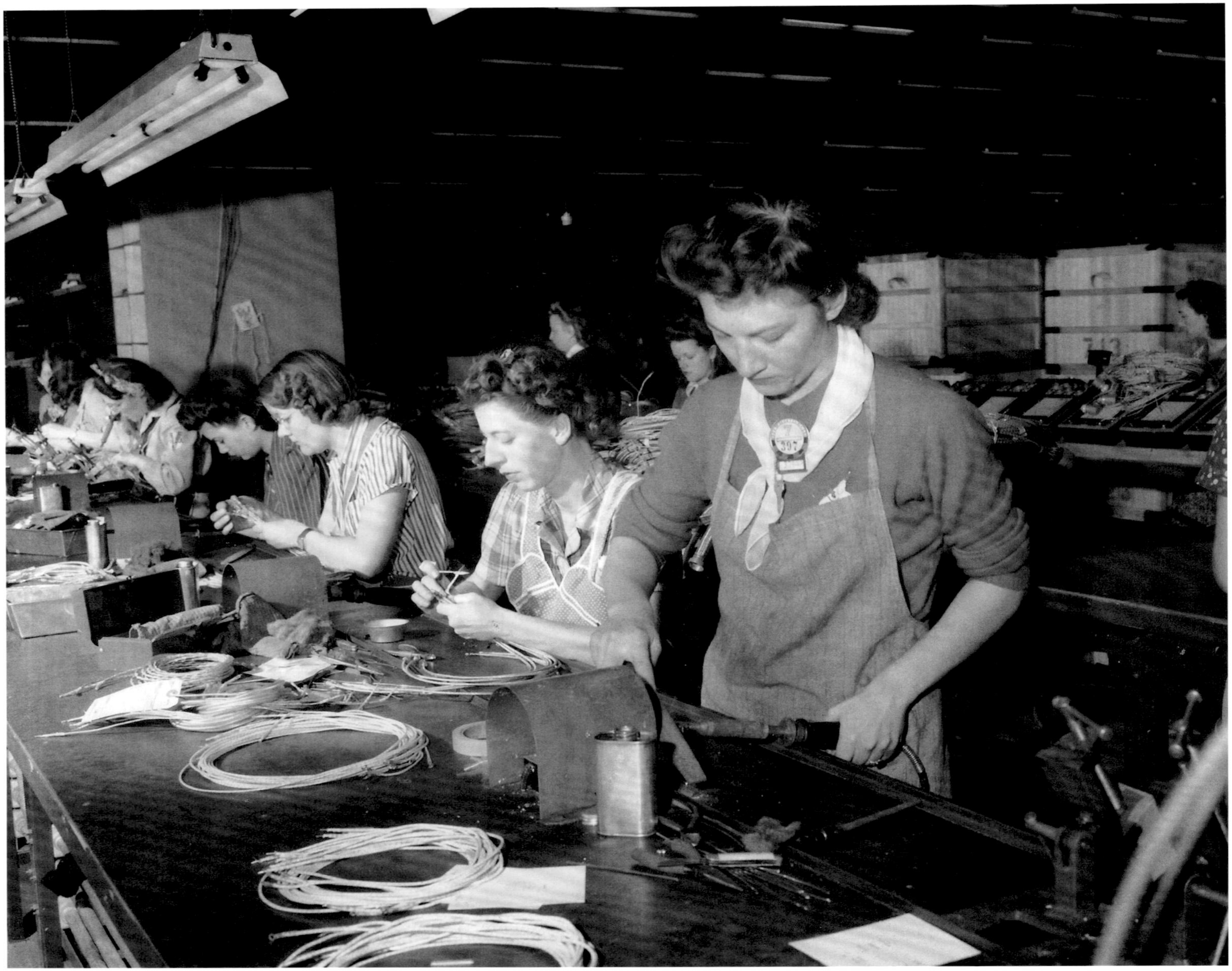

Six million women worked in manufacturing plants that produced munitions and materiel during World War II, such as this assembly line crew making electrical sub-assemblies at an L.A. airplane factory in 1942. Rosie the Riveter symbolized the women who took the places of male workers who were serving in the military. Rosie was a cultural icon of the United States then, and later became a feminist icon for women's economic power.

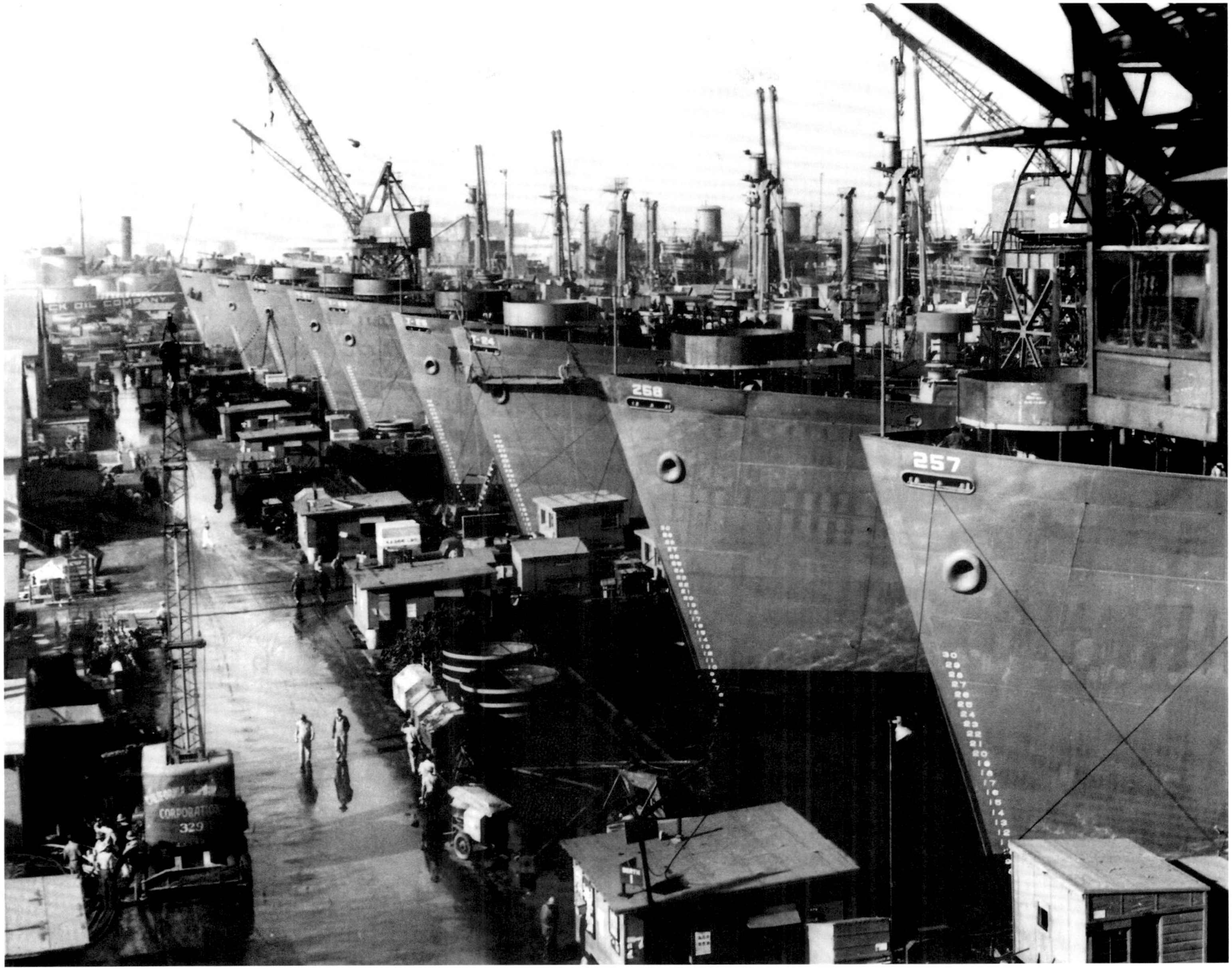

Nine Liberty cargo ships are shown at the docks of the Los Angeles California Shipbuilding Corporation at the end of 1943. During the war, eighteen American shipyards built 2,751 Liberty ships, the most of any single type of vessel in history. It took only 42 days, on average, to build a Liberty ship, using prefabricated sections and welding instead of rivets. The ship came to symbolize America's incredible wartime industrial output.

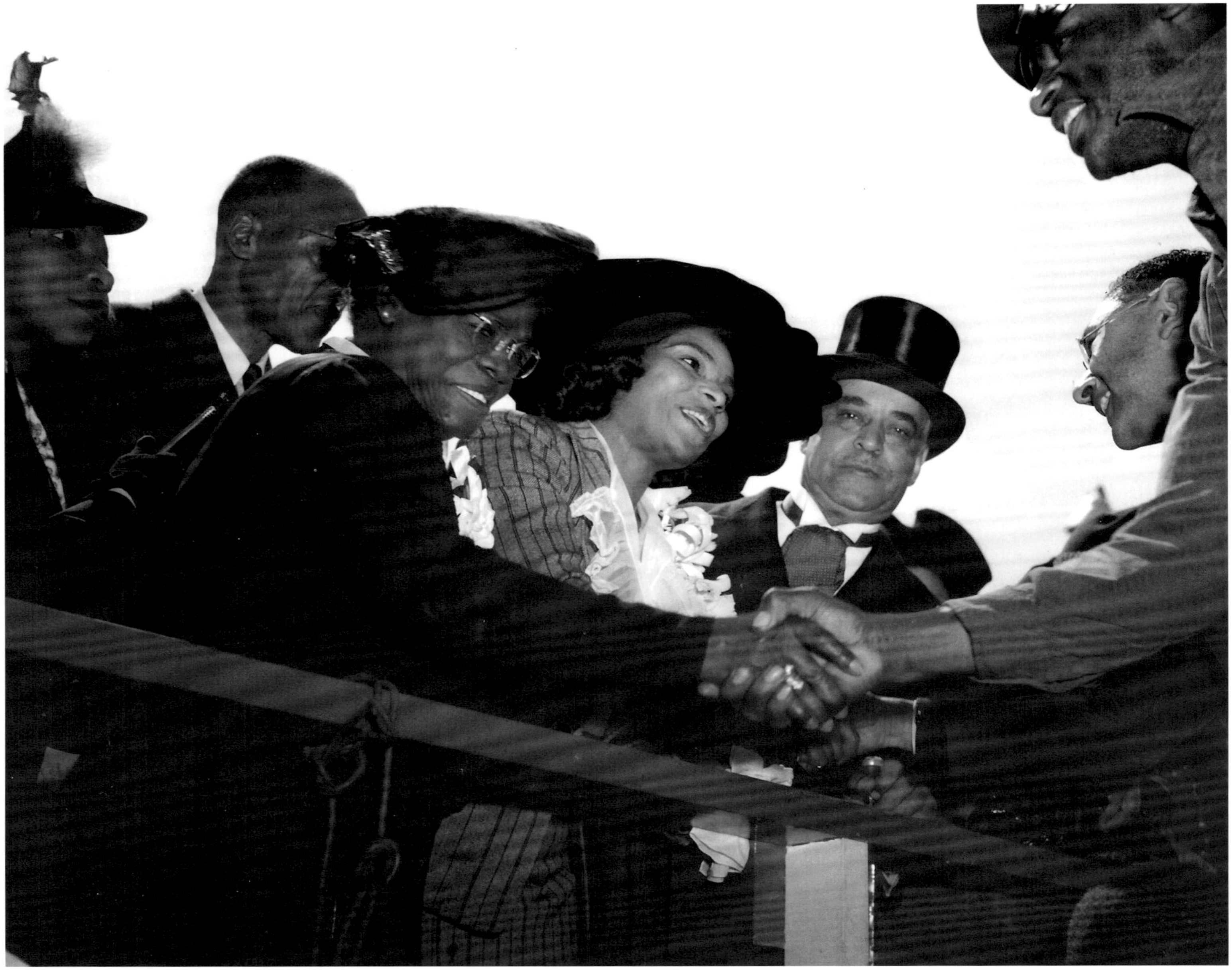

Launched in September 1942, the SS *Booker T. Washington* was the first Liberty ship to be commanded by and named after an African American. Here, Mary McLeod Bethune, Director of Negro Affairs, National Youth Administration; acclaimed singer Marian Anderson; and Dr. William J. Thompkins, Recorder of Deeds, greet workers who helped build the ship.

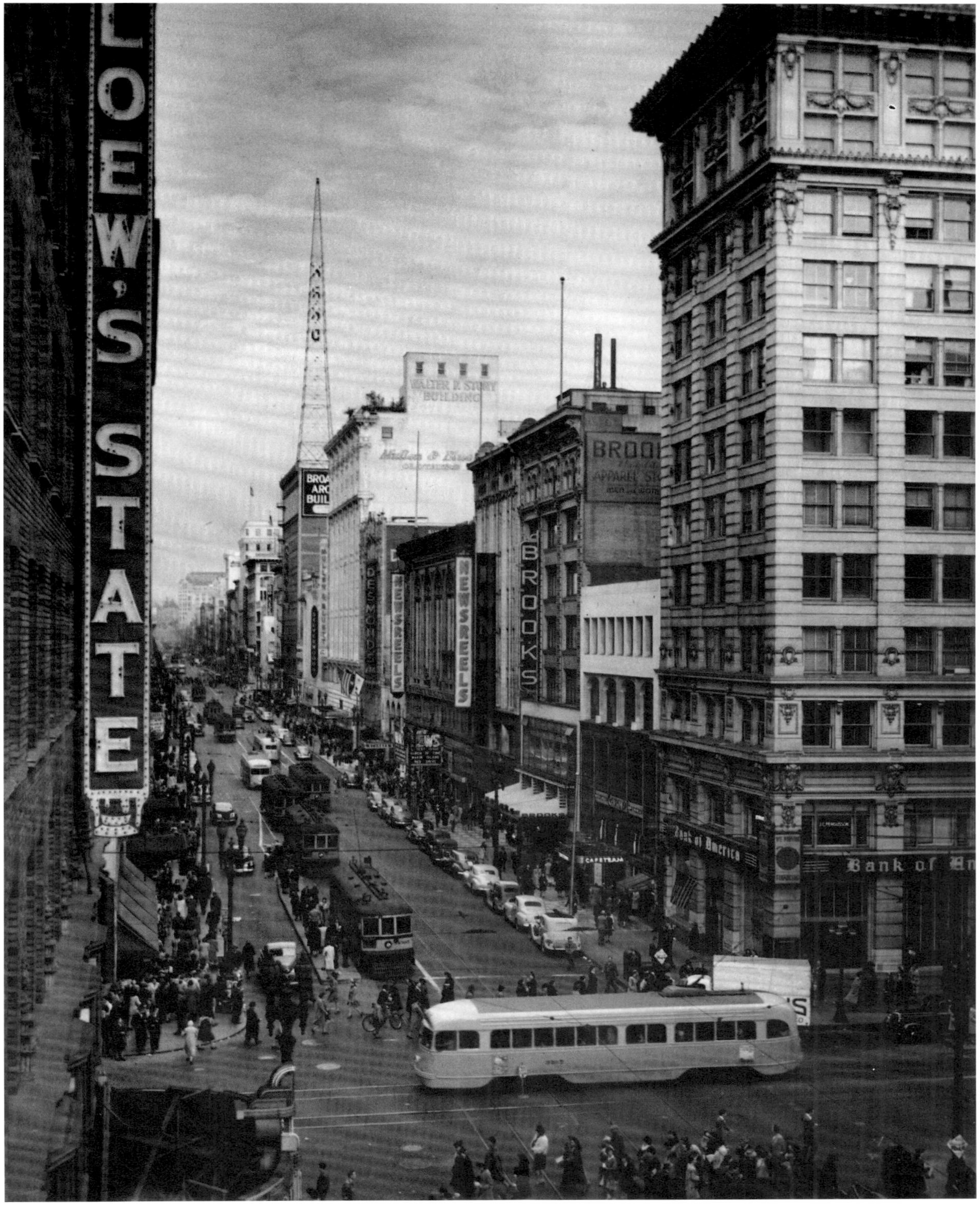

This Spring Street view shows the 1940s financial center of L.A., which held the stock exchange and numerous national business front offices. In addition to the pull of money, many talented writers and artists were lured to Los Angeles by its bohemian lifestyle and other attractions. One of the many British emigrés was Aldous Huxley (1894–1963), who moved to Los Angeles in 1937.

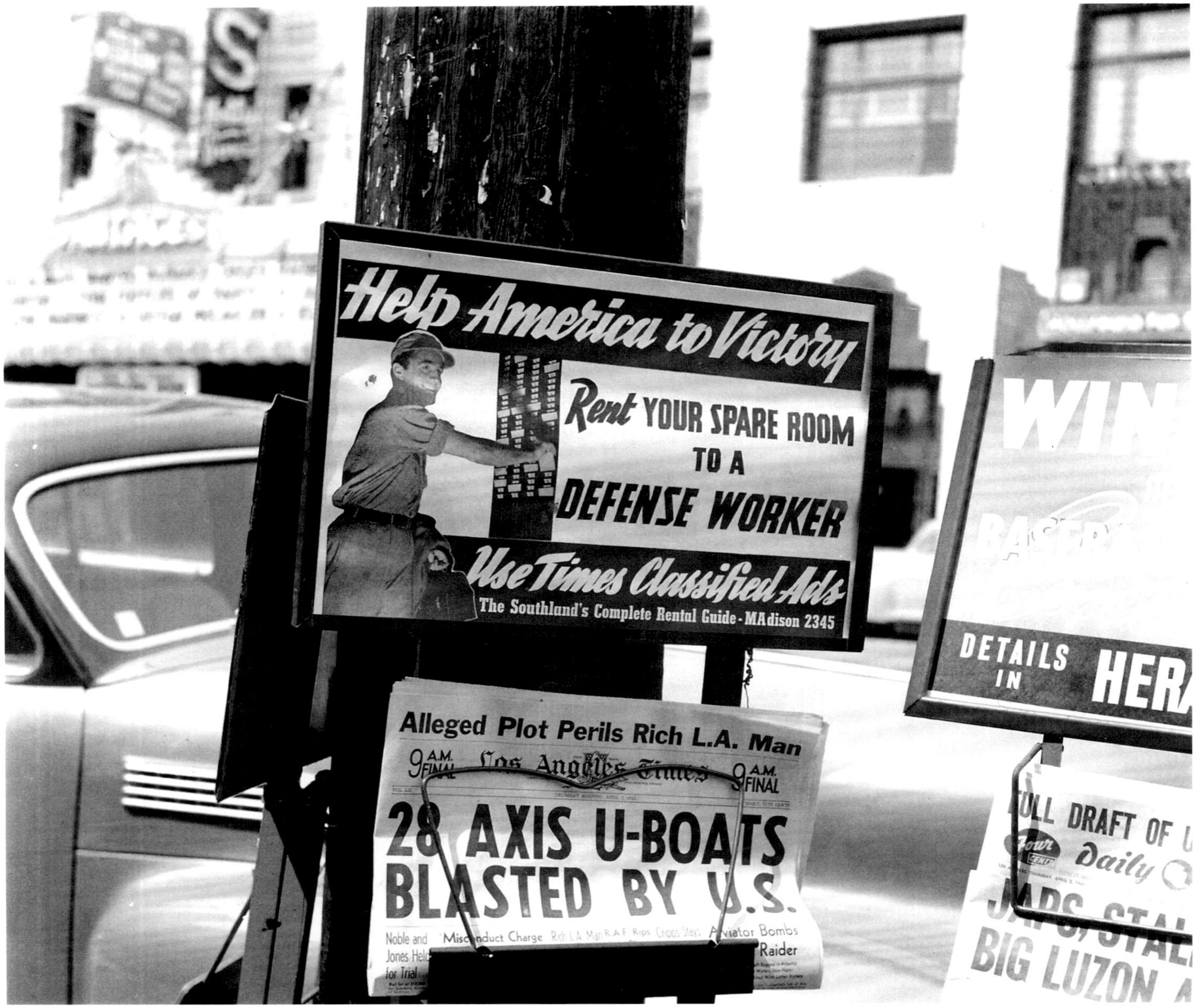

Although war news dominated at this 1942 Los Angeles newsstand, there was plenty of local gossip as well. Budd Schulberg (1914–) summed up all the classic Hollywood stereotypes—the overbearing producer, the naive ingenue, the scheming writer—in his 1941 story "A Table at Ciro's." Schulberg's scathing 1941 book *What Makes Sammy Run?* outraged the film establishment.

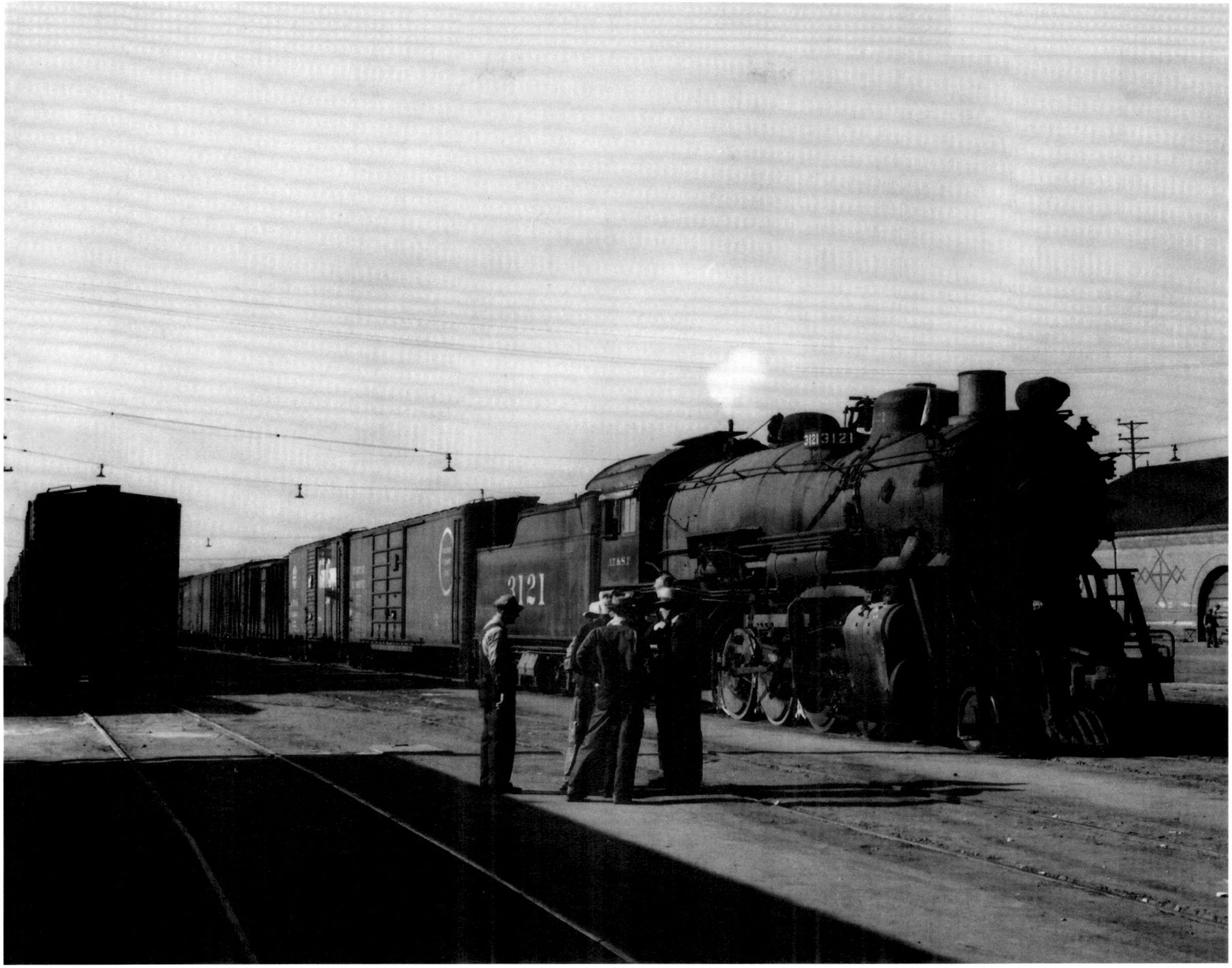

An Atchison, Topeka and Santa Fe freight train prepares to leave the yard in Los Angeles in March 1943. Novelist, poet, and screenwriter William Faulkner (1897–1962) worked in Hollywood but took the train home to Mississippi as often as he could. In a 1945 letter he commented, "I don't like this damn place [L.A.] any better that I ever did." Unlike other Hollywood writers, Faulkner used California as a setting only once, in *Golden Land*, a tale of insidious corruption.

At the Hollywood Canteen in 1943, film star Bette Davis (1908–1989) points out pictures of movie servicemen to German-born singer and actress Marlene Dietrich (1901–1992) and comedian Bob Hope (1903–2003). Hope is most notable for his famous United Service Organizations (USO) tours for American troops overseas. Hope always convinced a handful of talented performers and celebrities to accompany him on these tours that began in 1941 and continued through nearly all of America's conflicts thereafter.

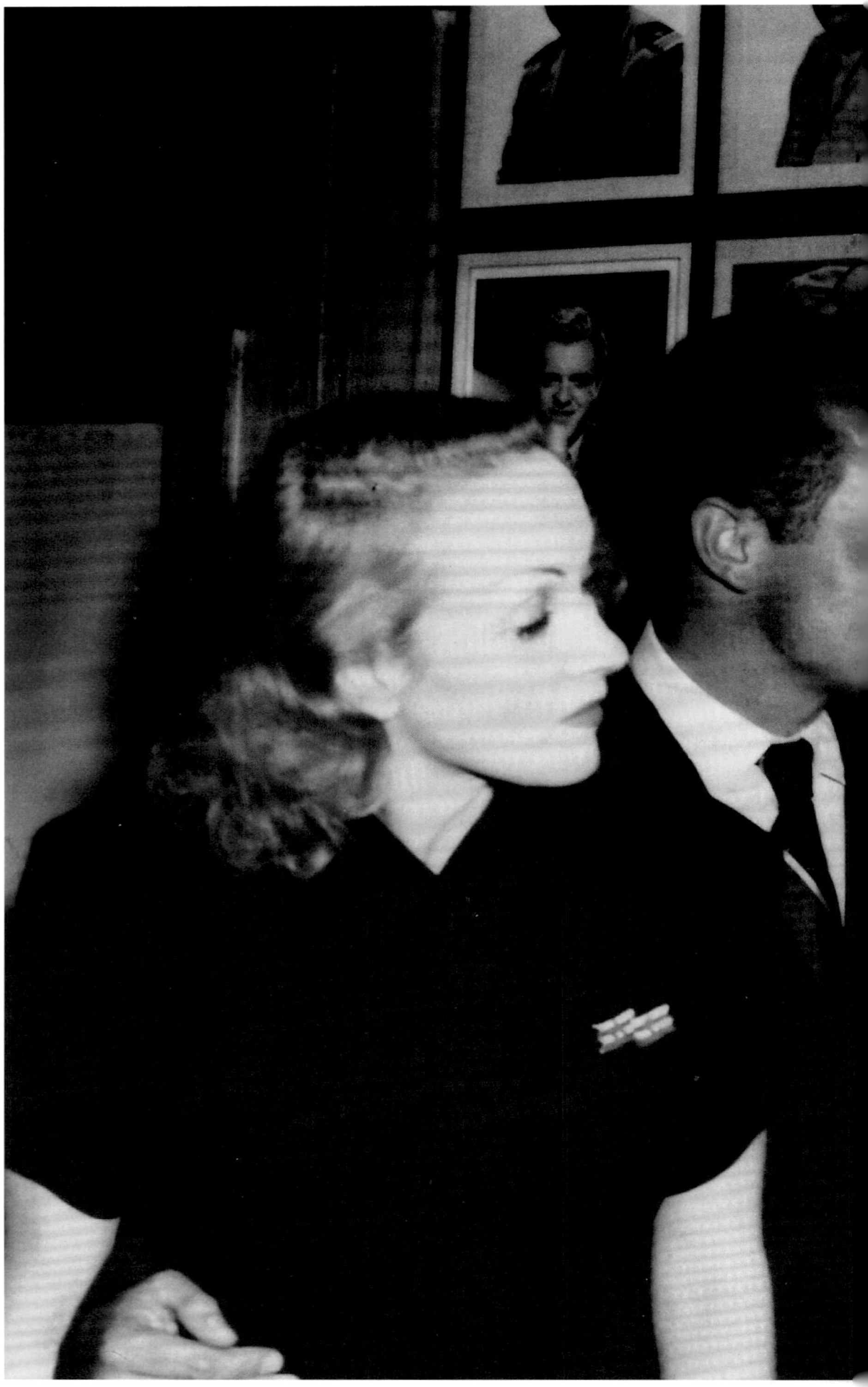

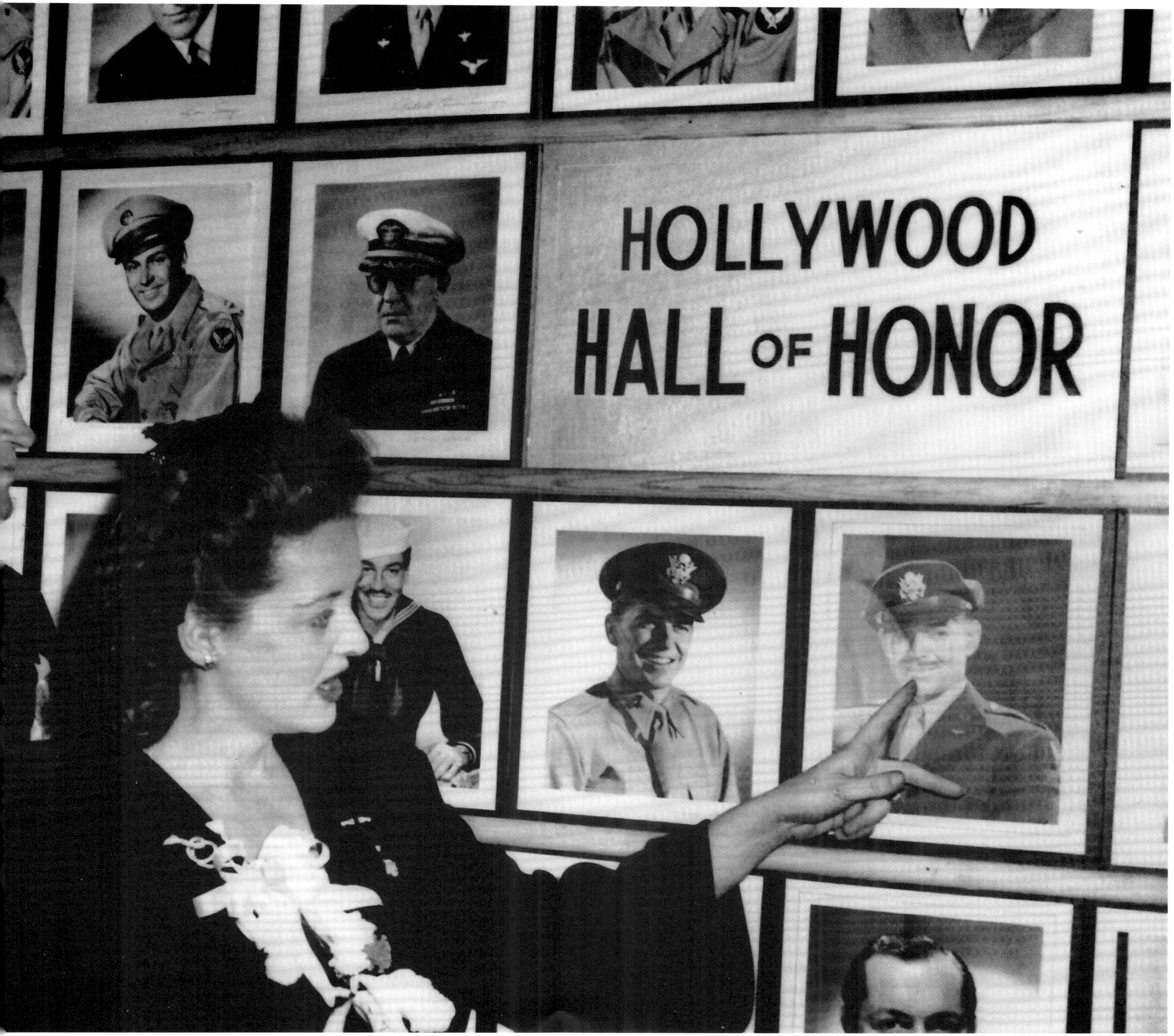
HOLLYWOOD
HALL OF HONOR

A movie theater on the highway between Los Angeles and Santa Monica in 1943 stayed open past midnight to cater to the swing shift workers from the nearby aircraft plants. Theater owners decided they could attract more customers and also save on costs if they offered two movies for the price of one. A typical double bill included trailers, a newsreel, a cartoon and/or a short film, a low-budget second feature (the B-movie), and the high-budget main feature (the A-movie).

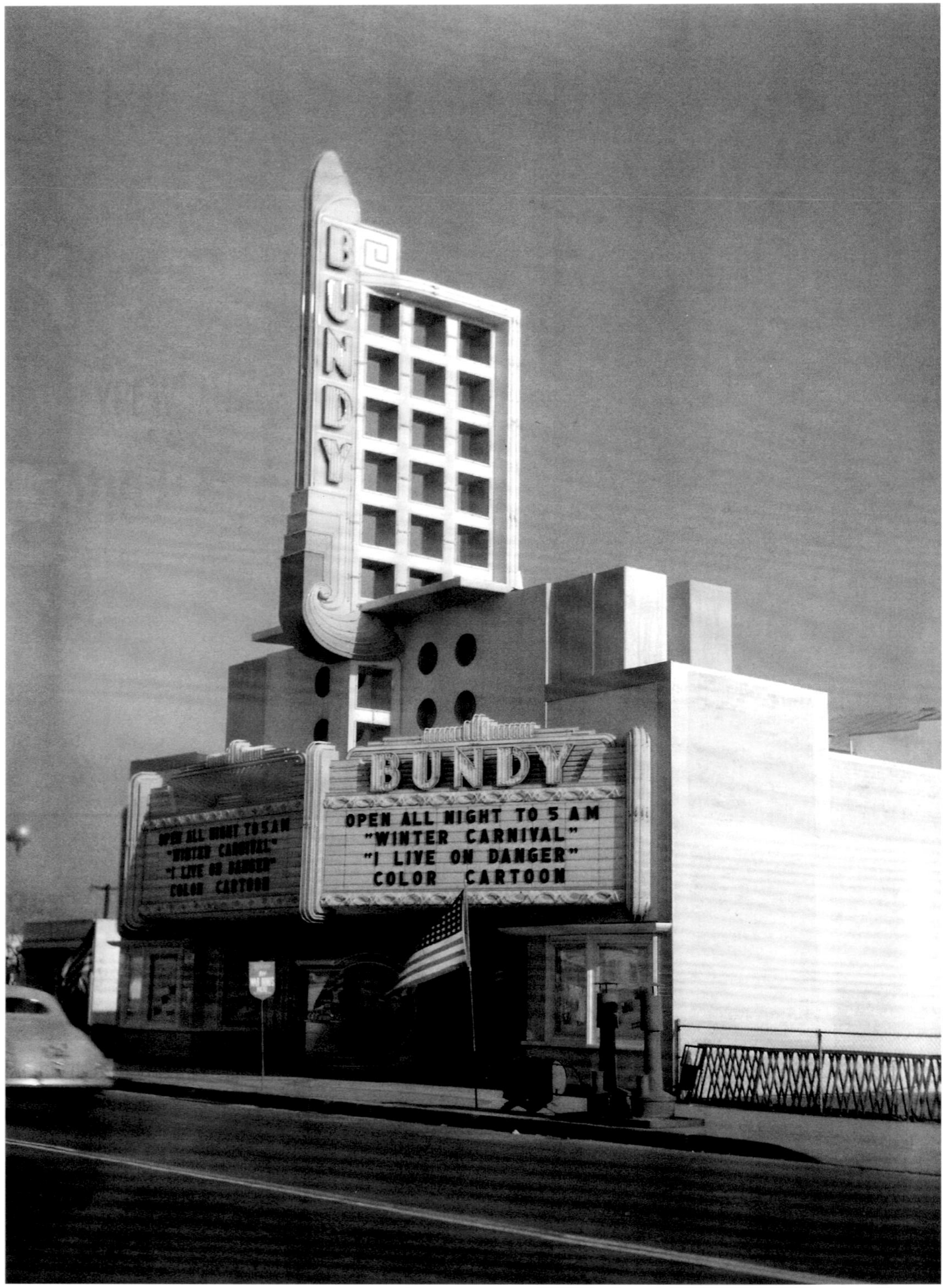

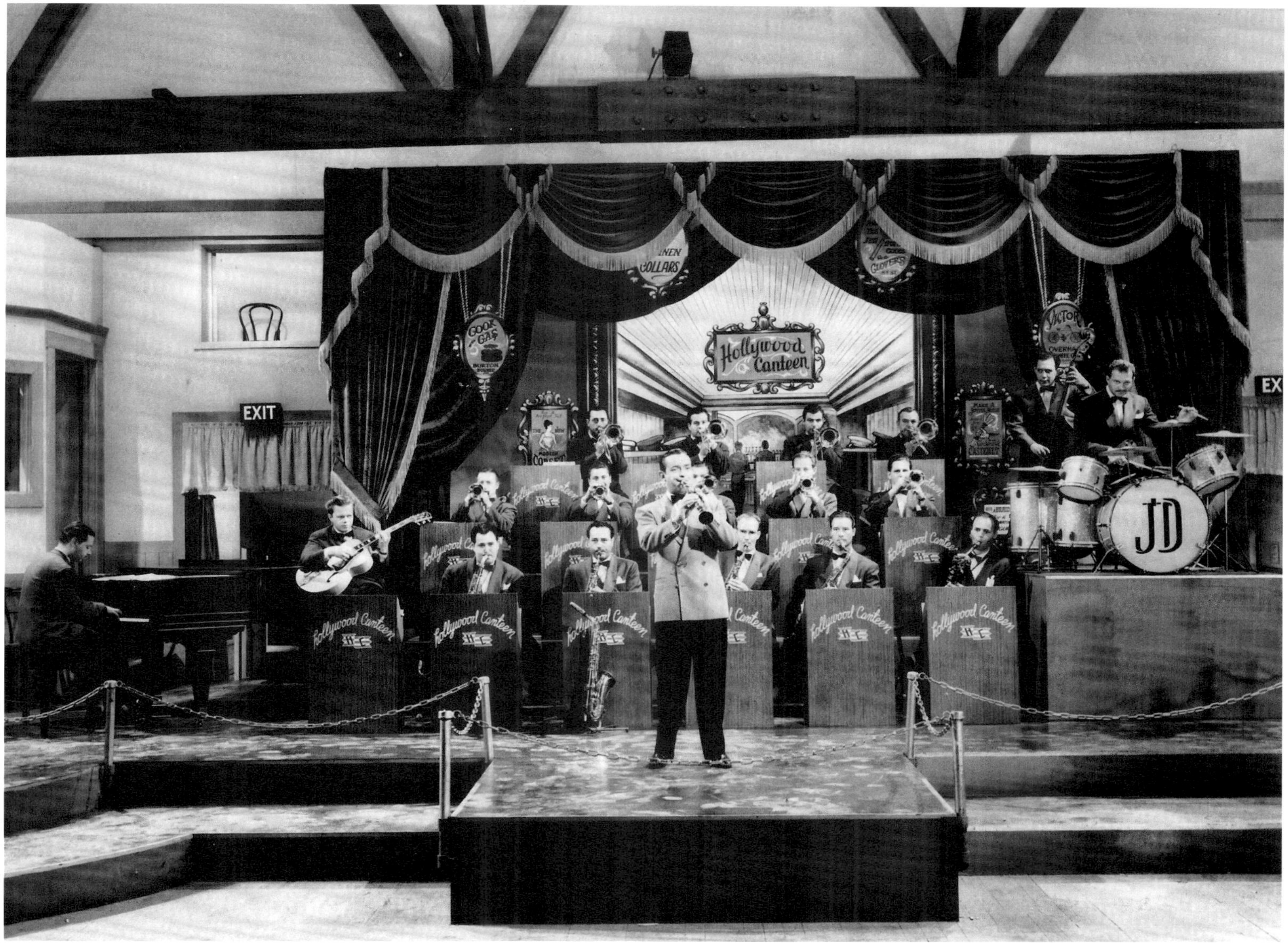

Hollywood was not shy about making movies about itself. Here, big-band leader Jimmy Dorsey (1904–1957) and his orchestra are on stage in a scene from the 1944 film *Hollywood Canteen*, one of several movies in which he appeared. Dorsey is considered one of the outstanding musicians of the pre-bebop jazz era.

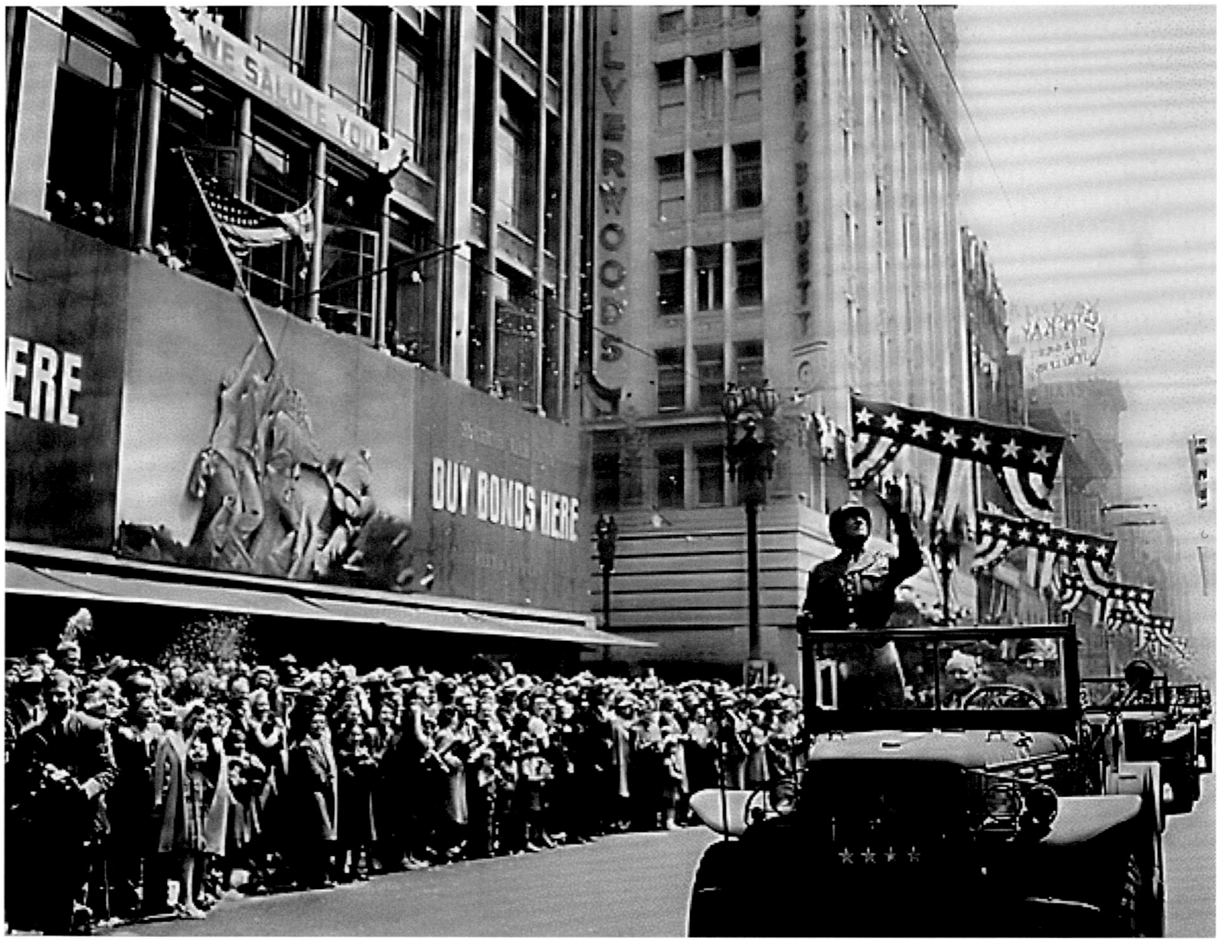

A crowd lining a Los Angeles street cheers for General George S. Patton as he passes by during a visit June 9, 1945, a month after Germany surrendered. The controversial Patton was acknowledged as an outstanding field commander. His Third Army inflicted nearly nine casualties on the German forces for every one it suffered, the best of any Allied army in Northwest Europe during 1944–1945. Hitler called Patton "that crazy cowboy general." Patton died six months after this victory parade as a result of a traffic accident in Germany.

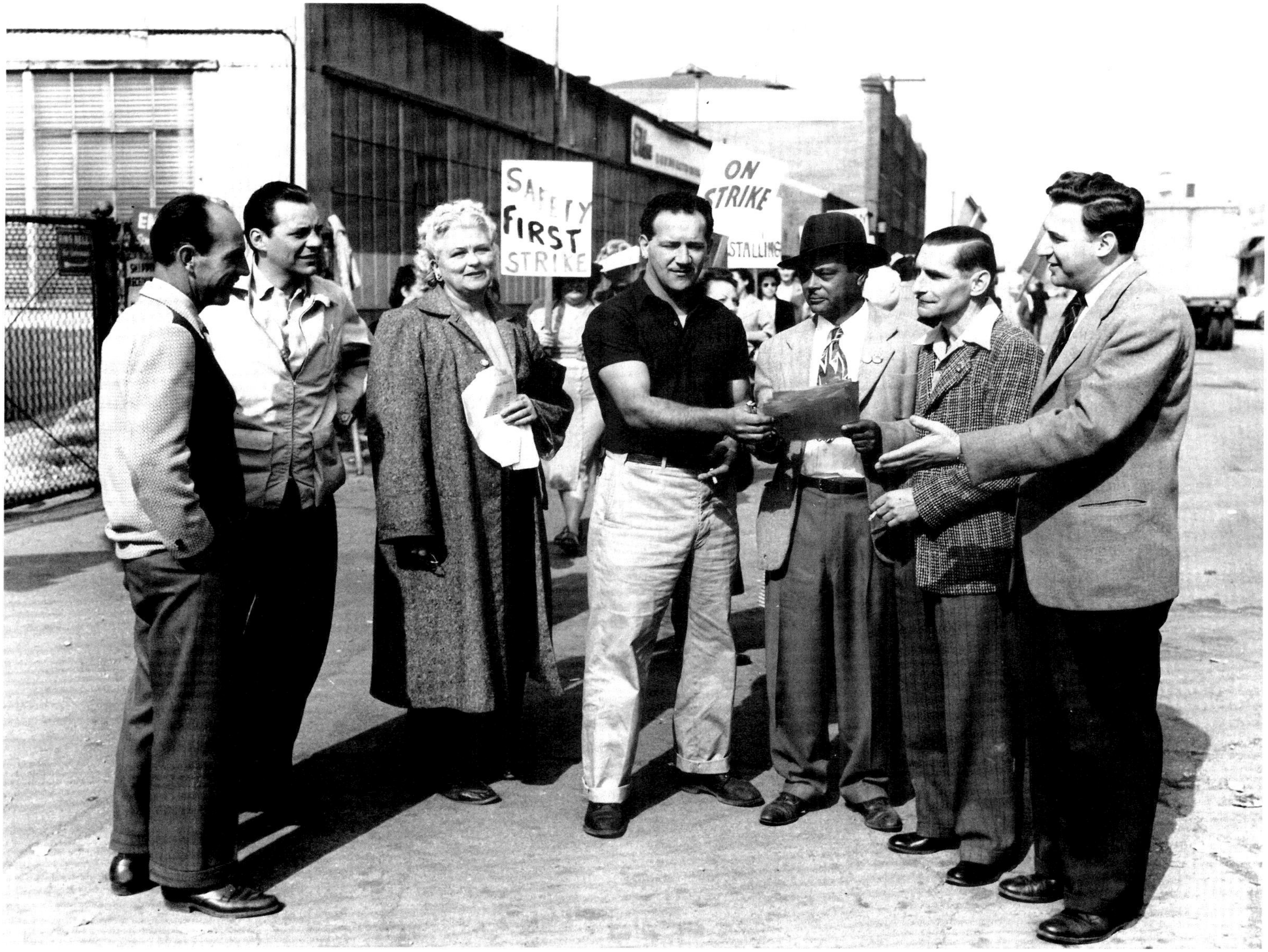

These strikers at Eldon Manufacturing Company on 62nd Street are members of the International Union of Mine, Mill and Smelter Workers. The first successful workers' strike on the West Coast was in 1939 by the Congress of Industrial Organizations (CIO) food processors. That same year the first national Latino civil rights assembly, El Congreso, convened in East L.A., calling for an end to segregation in schools, employment, and housing; the right to join labor unions; and the right for immigrants to work without fear of deportation.

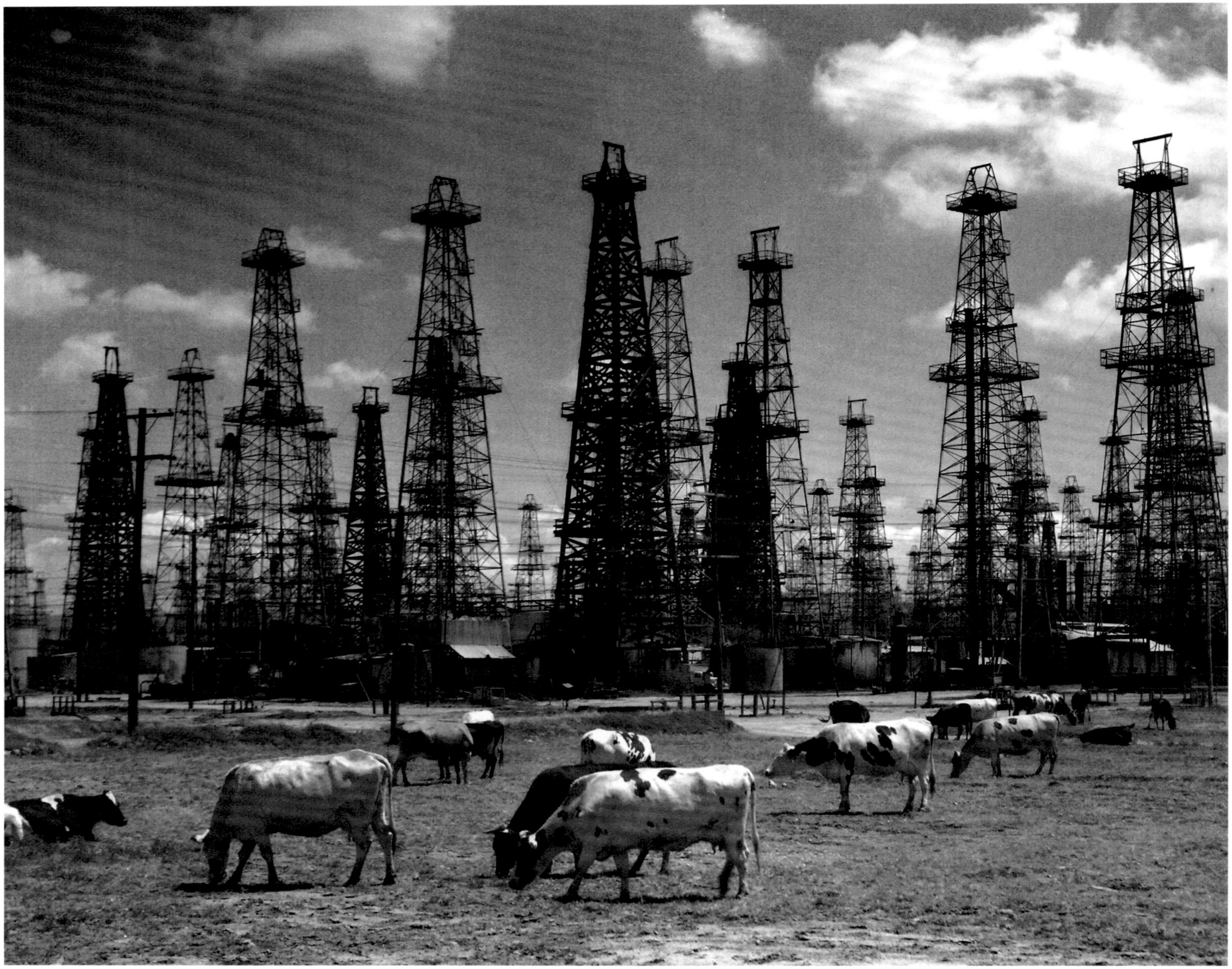

Only seventeen miles from downtown Los Angeles during World War II was the agricultural area of Norwalk and its oil-field backdrop. Like much of Southern California, Norwalk evolved from a rural area with dairy farms to a dense suburb of L.A.

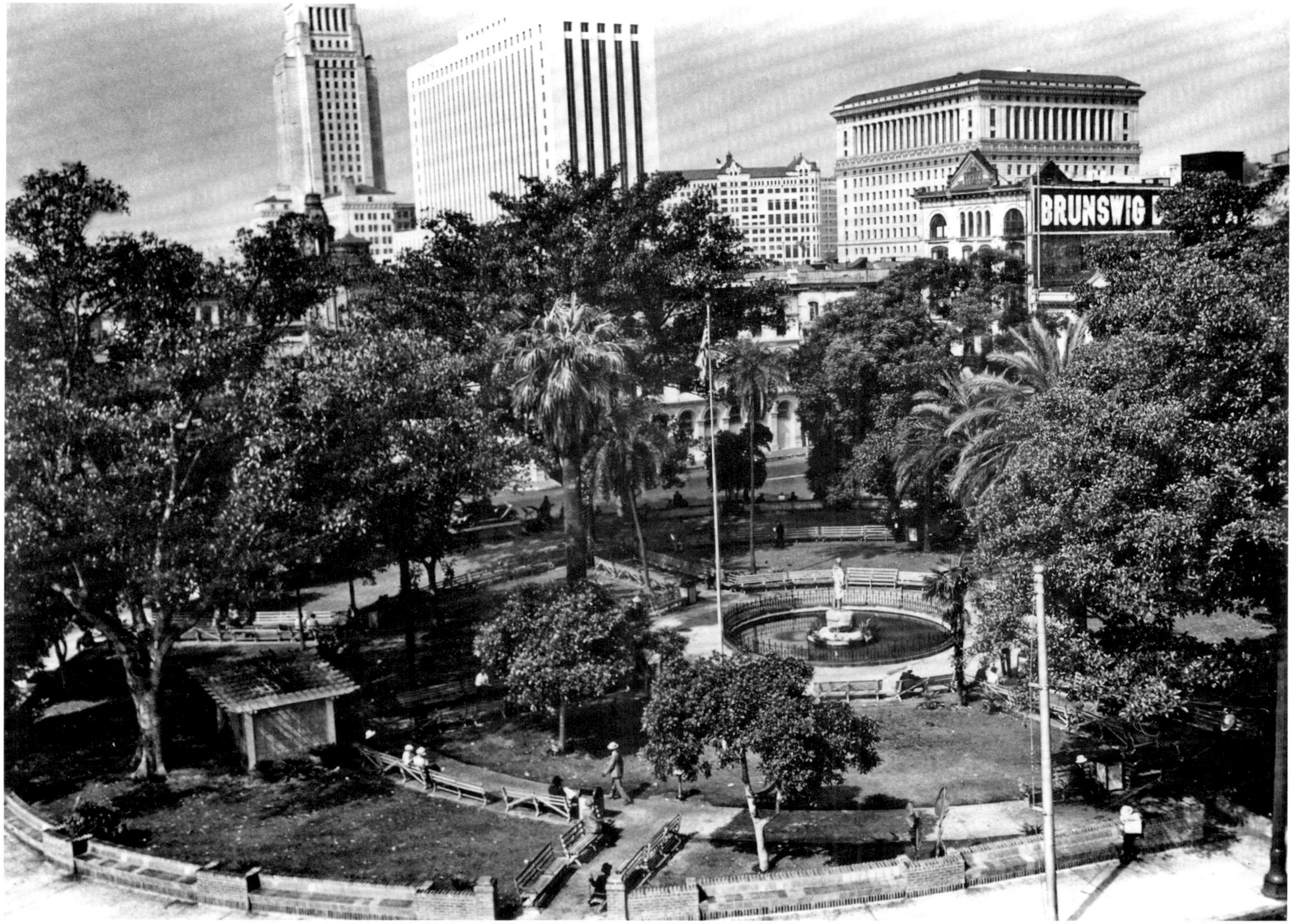

Plaza Park in the 1940s was bounded by Main, Los Angeles, and Marchessault streets, and Ferguson Alley. The fountain statue at center is of the city's founder, Governor Felipe de Neve, who laid out the first plaza in 1781 at a location to the northwest of this one.

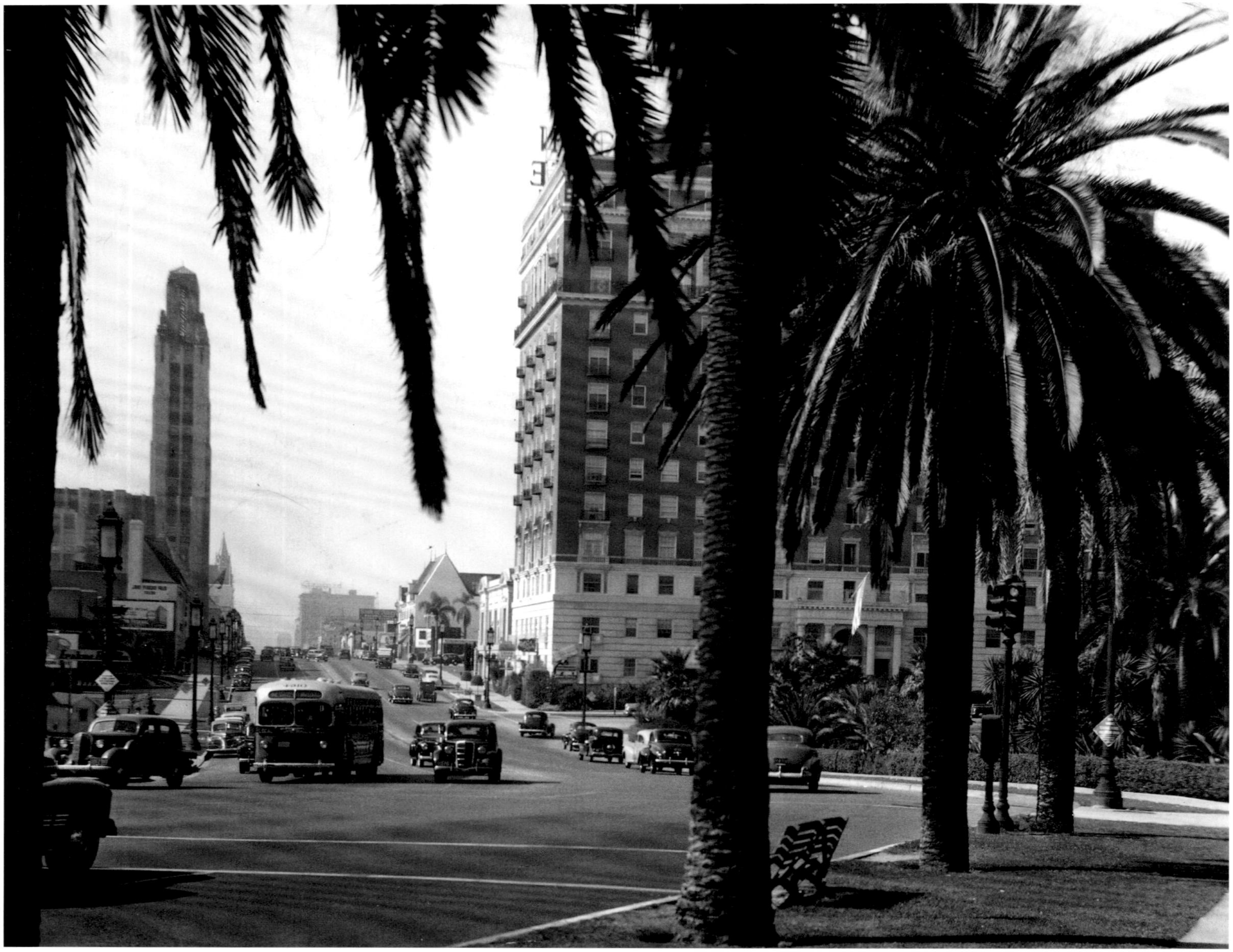

In 1940 L.A. was the fifth-largest city in the United States. By 1950, about the time of this photo, it passed Detroit in population. Writer Truman Capote (1924–1984) visited L.A. just after the war and found it "a dumping ground for all that is most exploitedly American: oil pumps pounding . . . avenues of used-car lots, supermarkets, motels, the . . . gee whiz wham of publicity, the biggest, broadest, best, sprawled and helplessly etherized by immaculate sunshine and sound of sea."

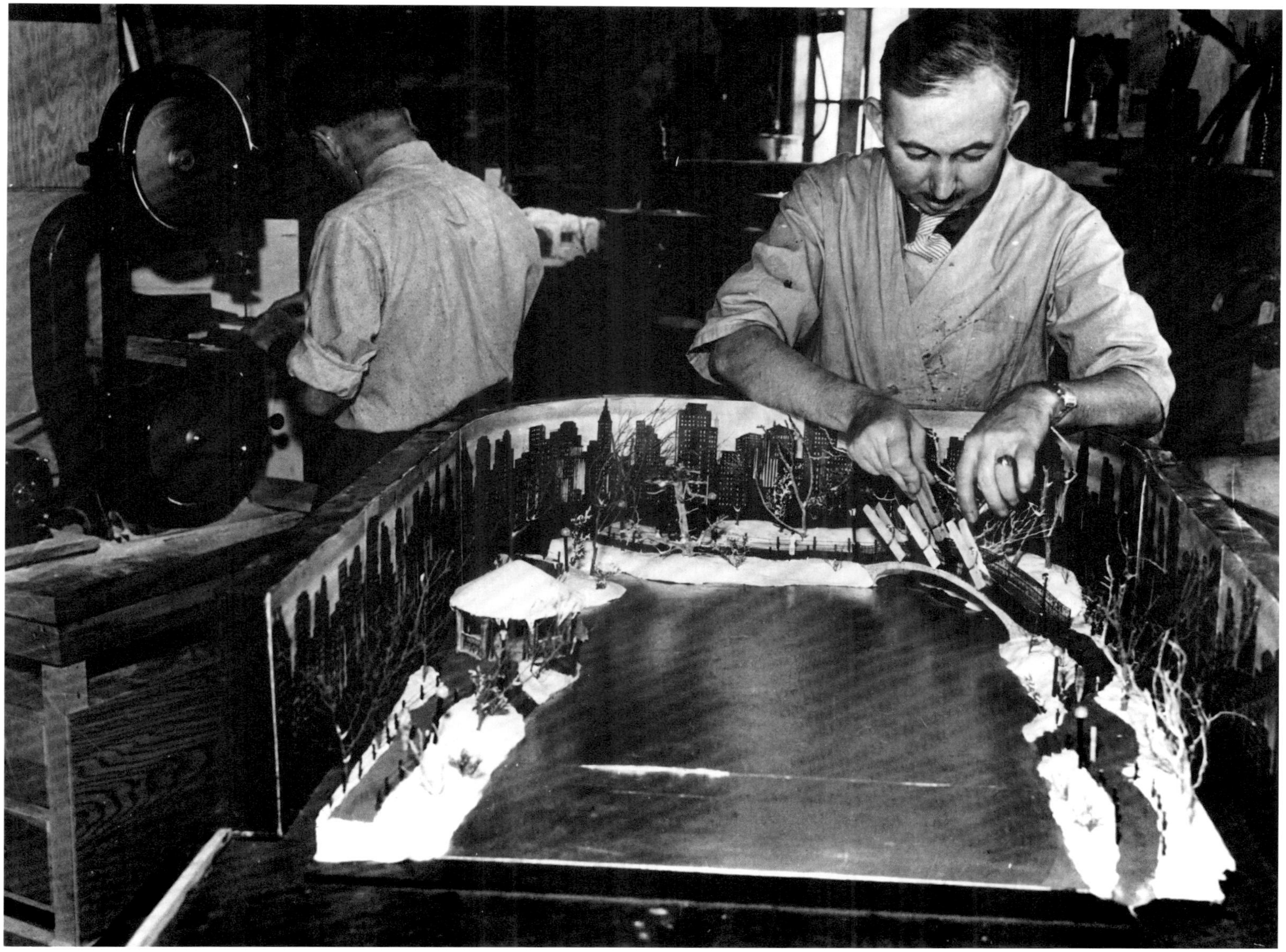

The movie stars, directors, producers, and writers were the most visible celebrities of Hollywood. However, they were outnumbered by an army of supporting workers whose efforts went unnoticed but were essential in the output of the nearly 500 major A- and B-level films each year. Here artists craft a scale replica of a winter scene in New York City's Central Park.

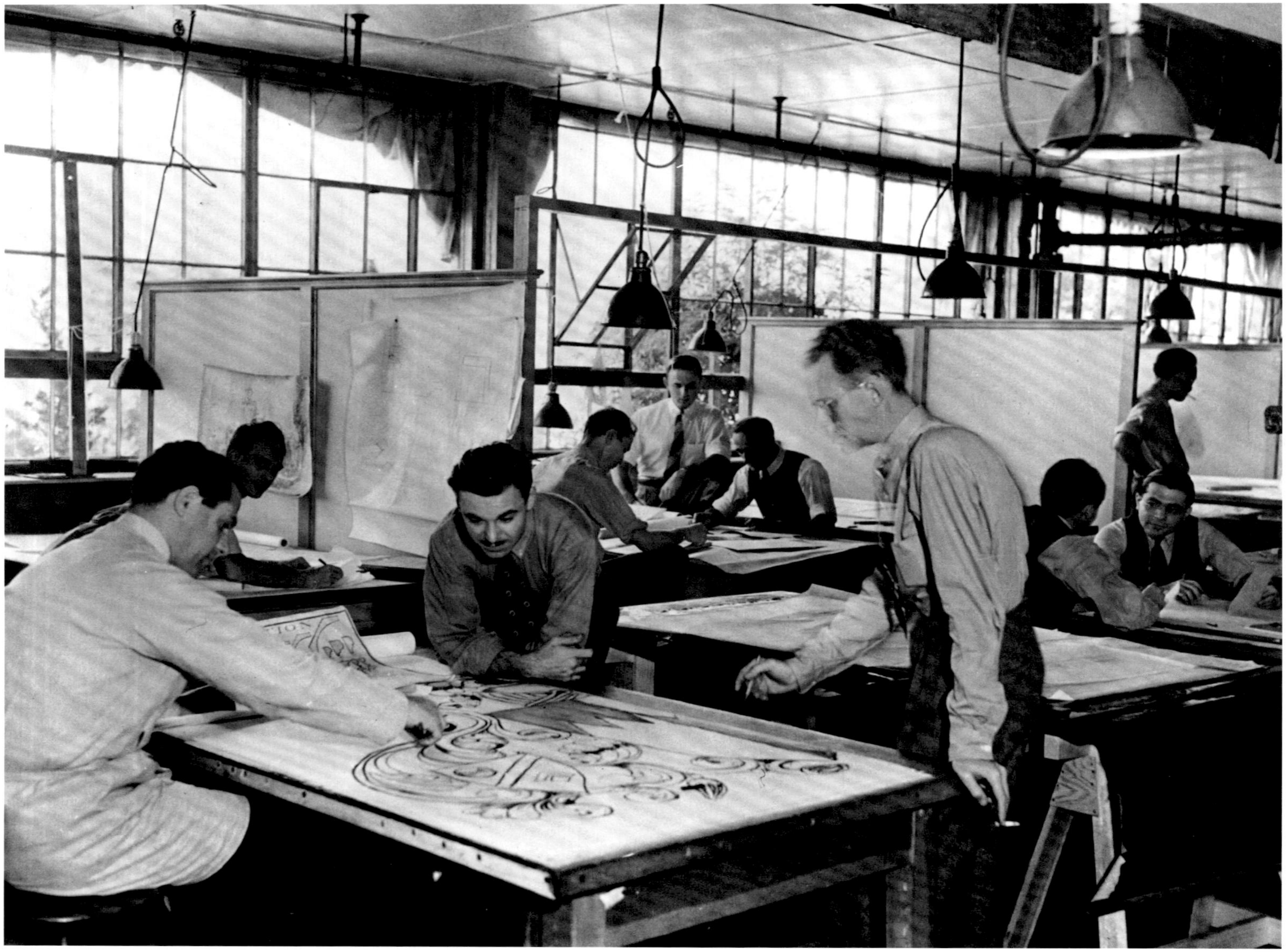

Despite the beautiful weather in Southern California, most films were shot on the studio lots on indoor stage sets. Intricate homes, official buildings, even caves and faux outdoor scenes were created on these sets, often from drawings created in the studio art departments by professionals such as these.

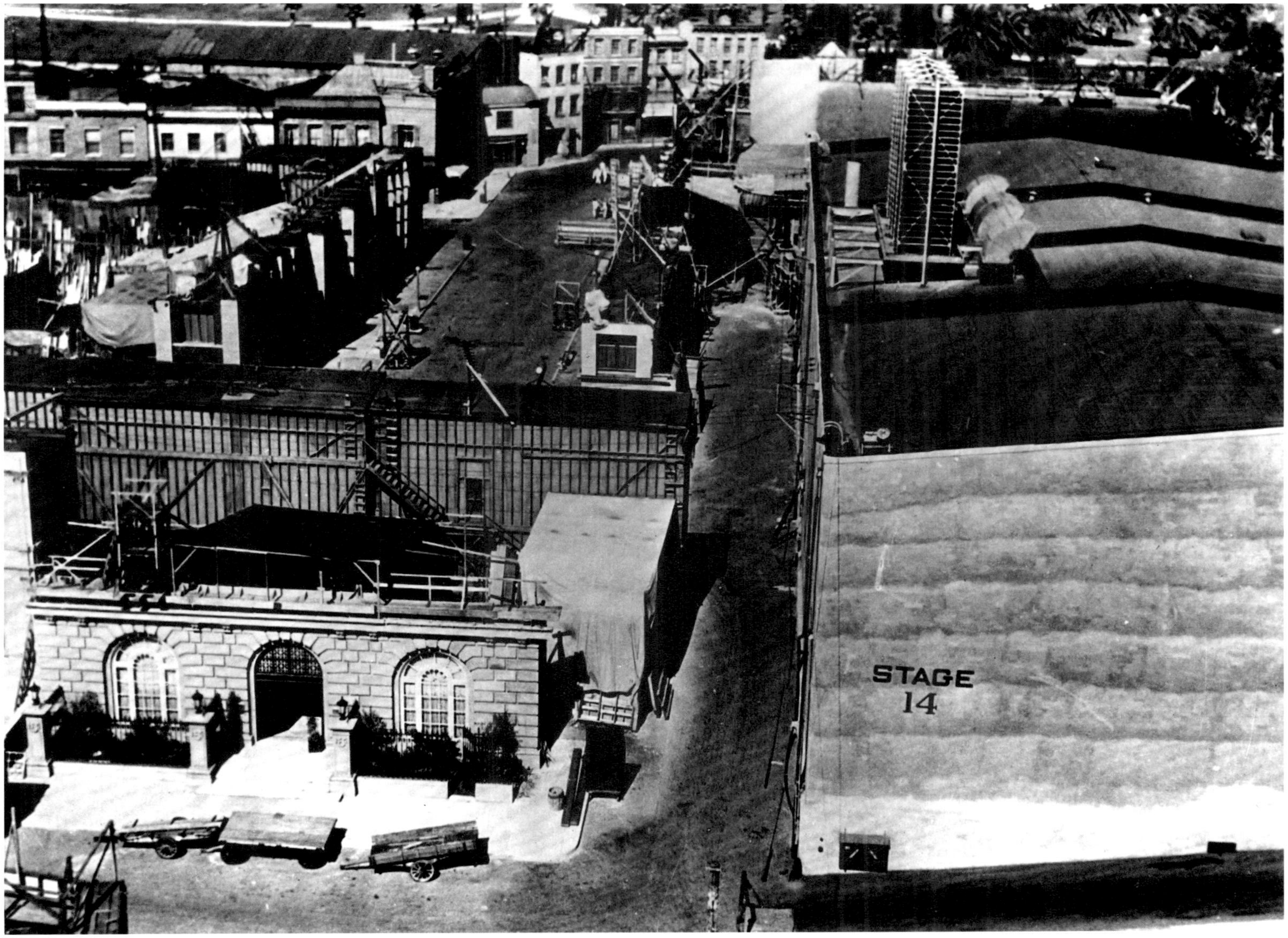

If a movie script required a city street scene, a simulated one was constructed outside on studio property. This overhead photo shows assorted false building fronts and replicated city streets where camera positions could be set up according to the backdrop or scenery required by the script. The "Stage 14" building served for shooting interior scenes.

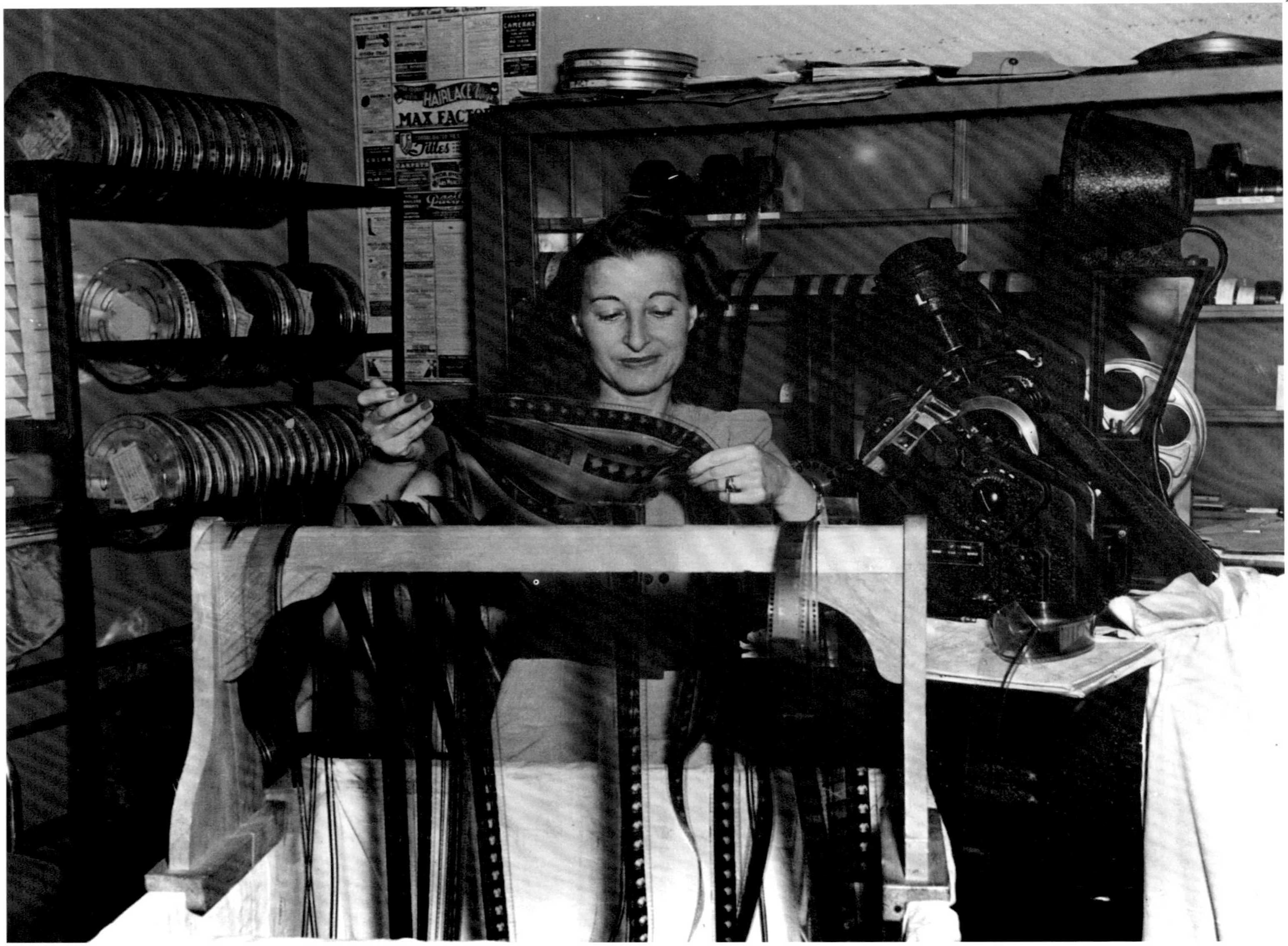

After filming but prior to release, a movie would be edited in a "cutting laboratory" and put into final sequence for projection. At first, moving picture film was shot and projected at various speeds using hand-cranked cameras and projectors. When sound film was introduced in the late 1920s, a constant speed was required, and 24 frames per second was chosen because it was the slowest and therefore cheapest speed that allowed for good sound quality.

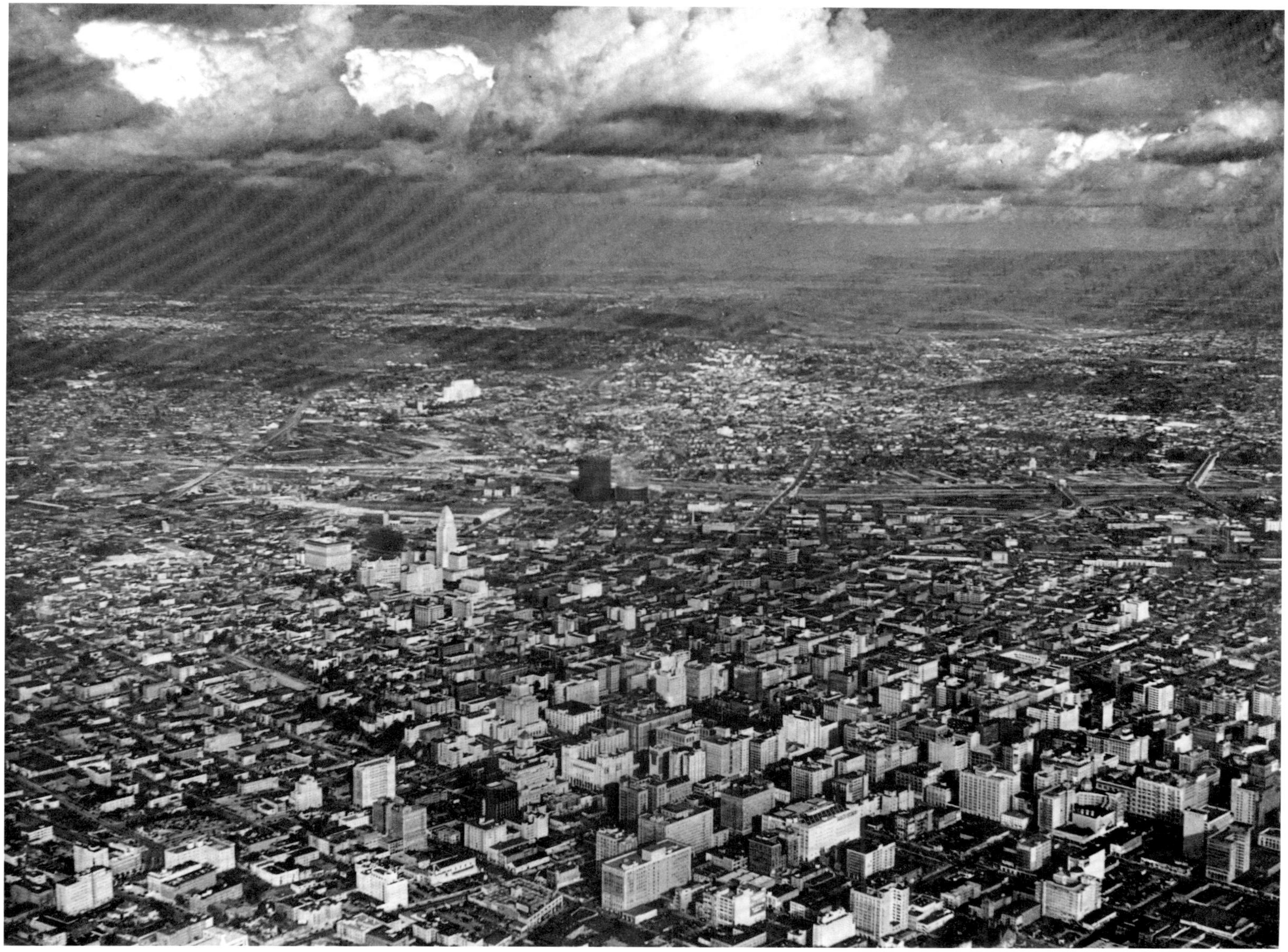

Between 1940 and 1950 the population density within the 400 square miles of Los Angeles was concentrated from downtown to Watts in the south, Inglewood in the west, Beverly Hills and Hollywood in the north, and East L.A. Except for Santa Monica, Long Beach, and Pasadena, the rest of Los Angeles County was sparsely populated. In 1940, nearly 70 percent of the 1.5 million residents lived in Central L.A.

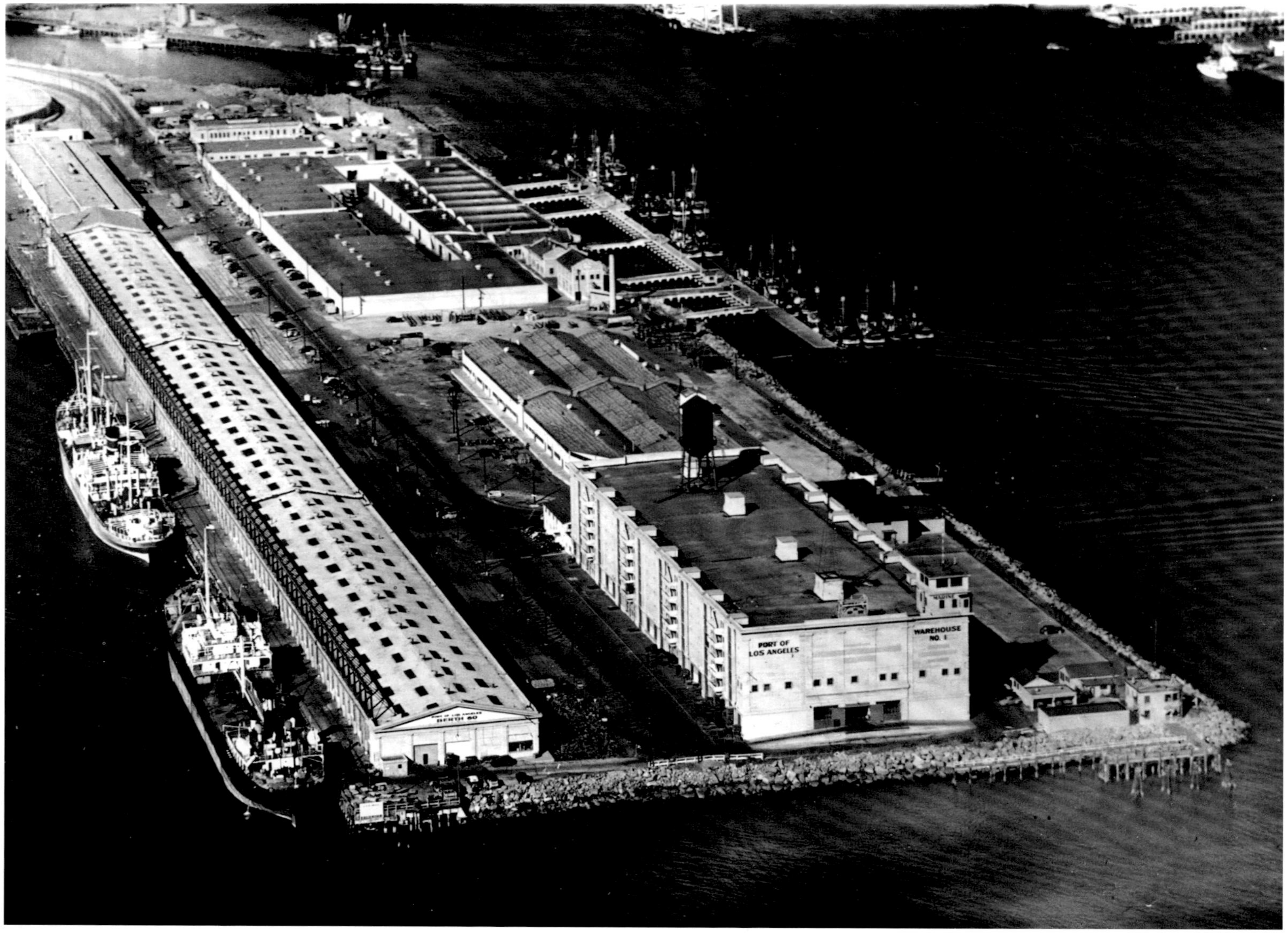

During World War II, San Pedro Bay shipyards employed more than 90,000 workers and produced hundreds of military and merchant vessels. Originally, Los Angeles' poor harbor at San Pedro Bay was a shallow mudflat, too soft to support a wharf. Visiting ships either had to stay far out at anchor and have their goods and passengers ferried to shore, or beach themselves. Dredging began in 1871, and the area was annexed to Los Angeles in 1909.

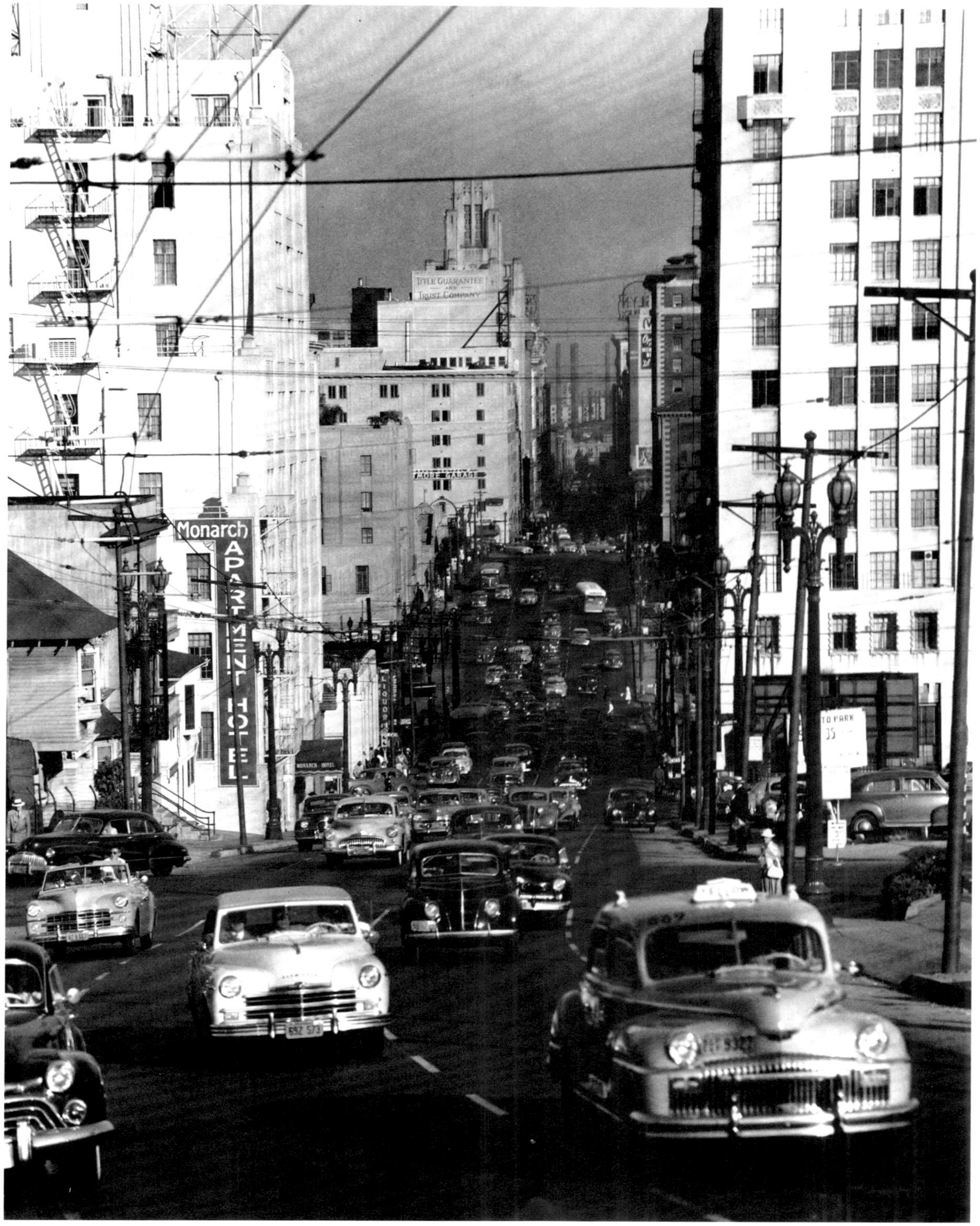

Like many multi-lane Los Angeles streets, this one, seen midtown at the end of the decade, was designated one-way to ease traffic movement. Urban planners also believed that the new freeway system could both engender suburban development and stop the decline of the inner city. In 1947, $300 million was legislated for the metropolitan freeway network, enough to build 105 miles of roadway.

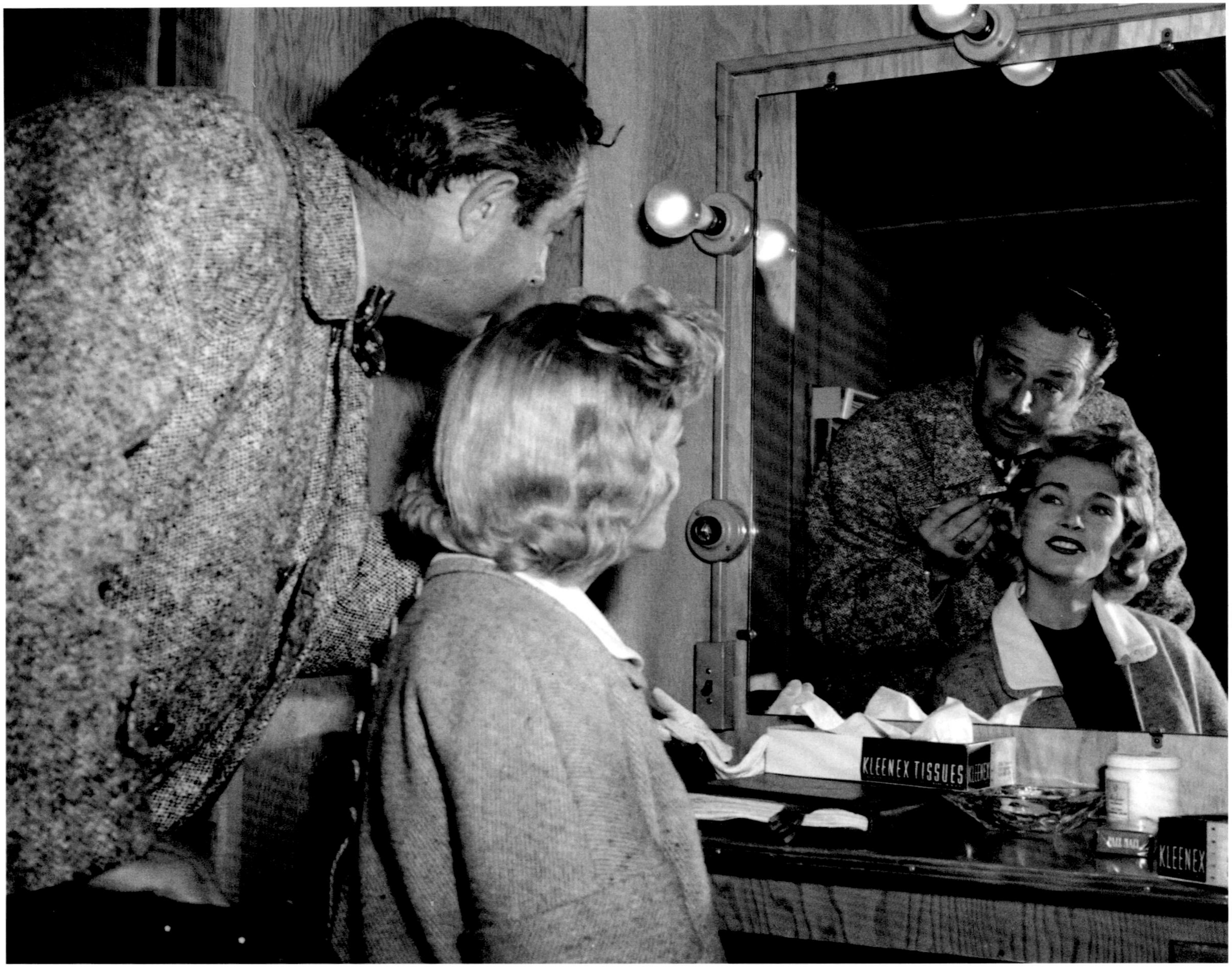

Layne "Shotgun" Britton, a makeup artist and actor in Hollywood from 1939 until 1989, works with Lizabeth Scott during the filming of *The Company She Keeps*, the story of Georgia Durante's days with the Mafia. A willowy blonde with green eyes and a husky, smoky voice, Scott (1922–) excelled as a femme fatale in the genre known as film noir, the dark, angst-ridden films of the post–World War II era.

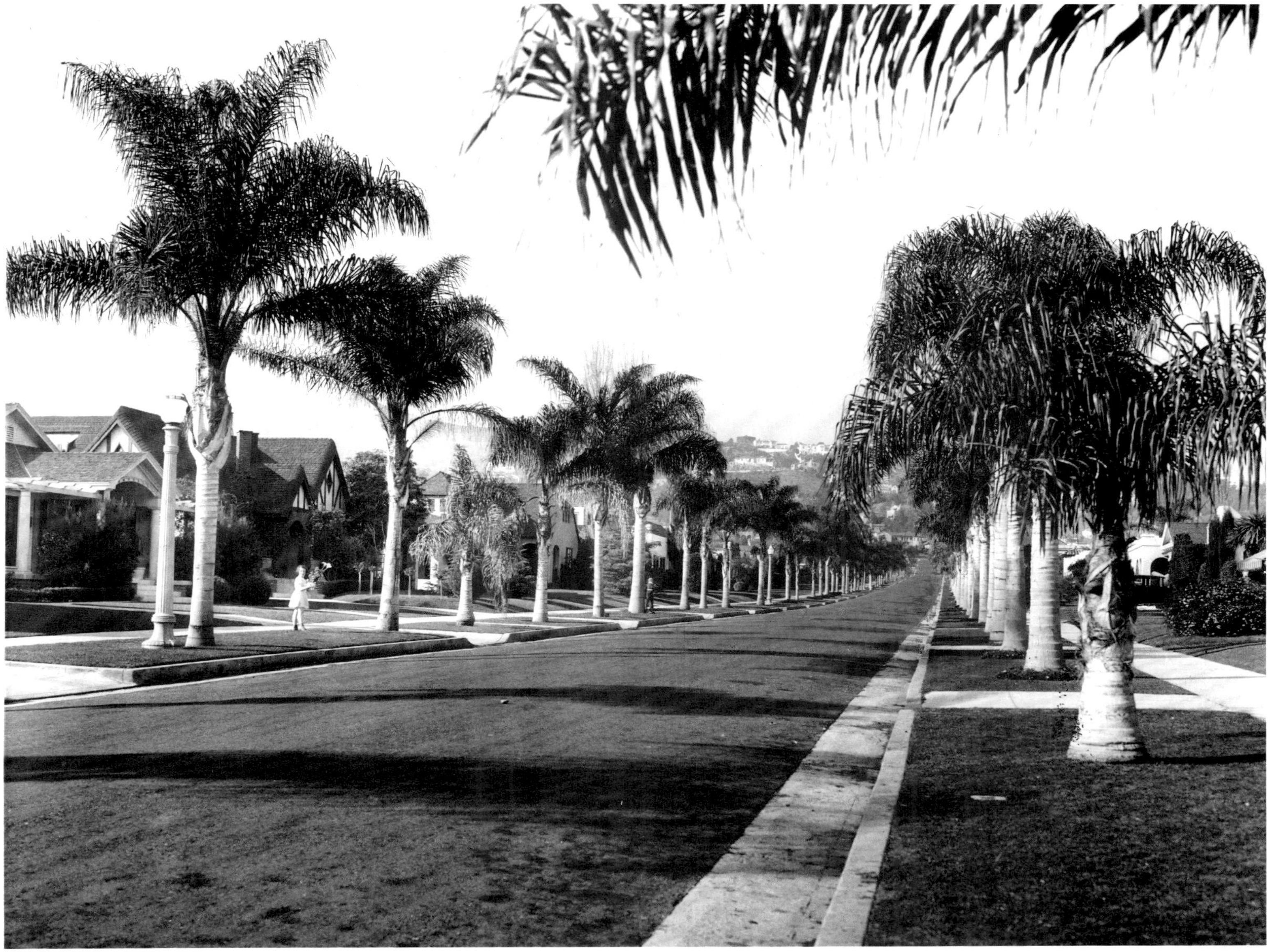

By the 1940s, most of Los Angeles consisted of suburbs such as this Hollywood neighborhood. Simone de Beauvoir (1908–1986) was a French author and philosopher whose 1949 treatise *The Second Sex*, a study of women's oppression, became a cornerstone of modern feminism. In 1947 she visited Los Angeles and wrote, "The city is unlike any other . . . nothing but suburbs. The city slips away like a phantom city . . . Los Angeles is far from possessing the beauty of New York or the depth of Chicago, and I understand why some French people spoke to me about it with such distaste."

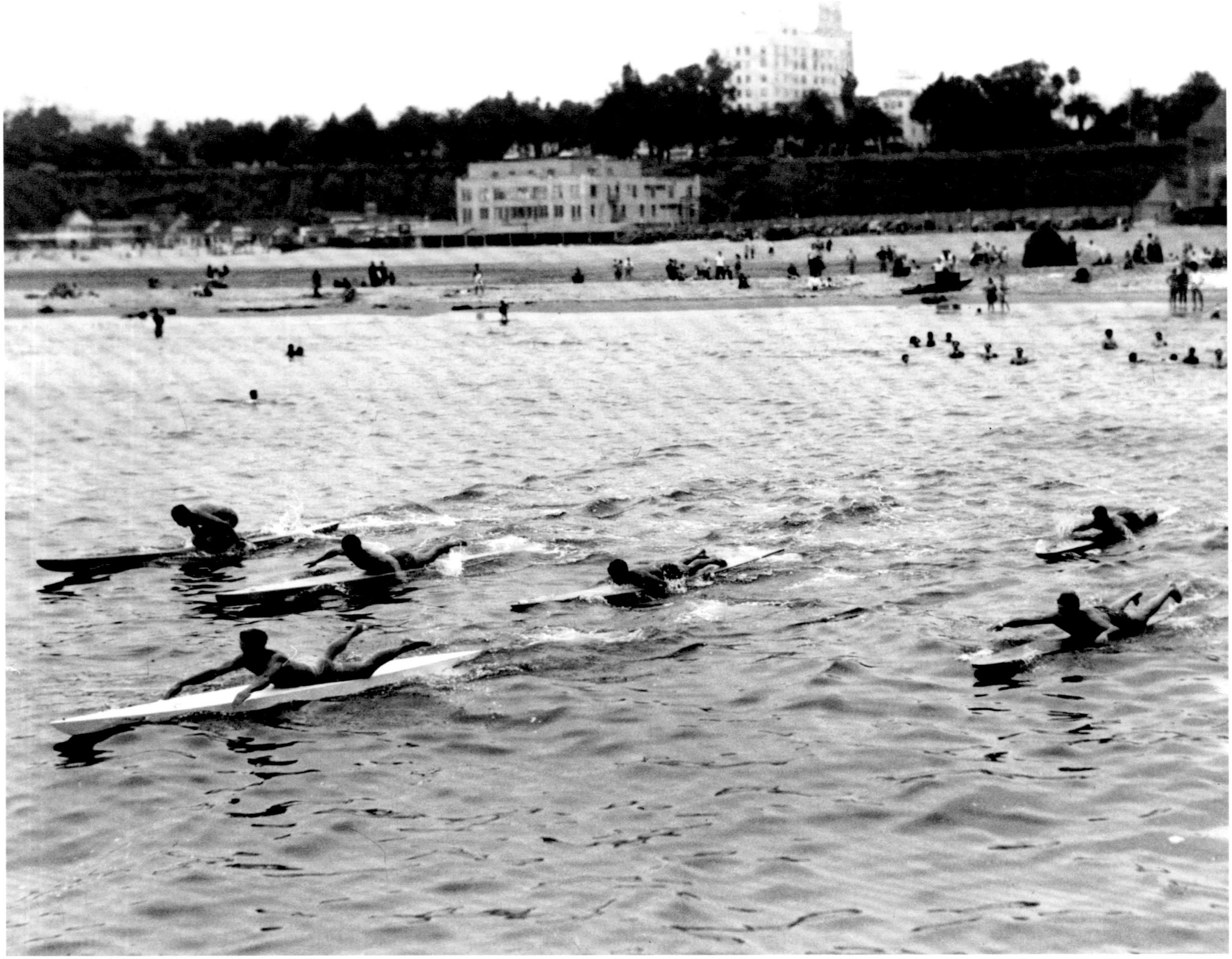

A surfboard race in Santa Monica in 1946. This familiar symbol of Southern California life began in 1907 when author Jack London (1876–1916) spotted George Freeth surfing in Hawaii. London convinced railroad and real estate magnate Henry Huntington to invite Freeth to California, where he put on a demonstration of wave-riding to promote the Redondo–Los Angeles Railway and earned the title of "First Man to Surf in California."

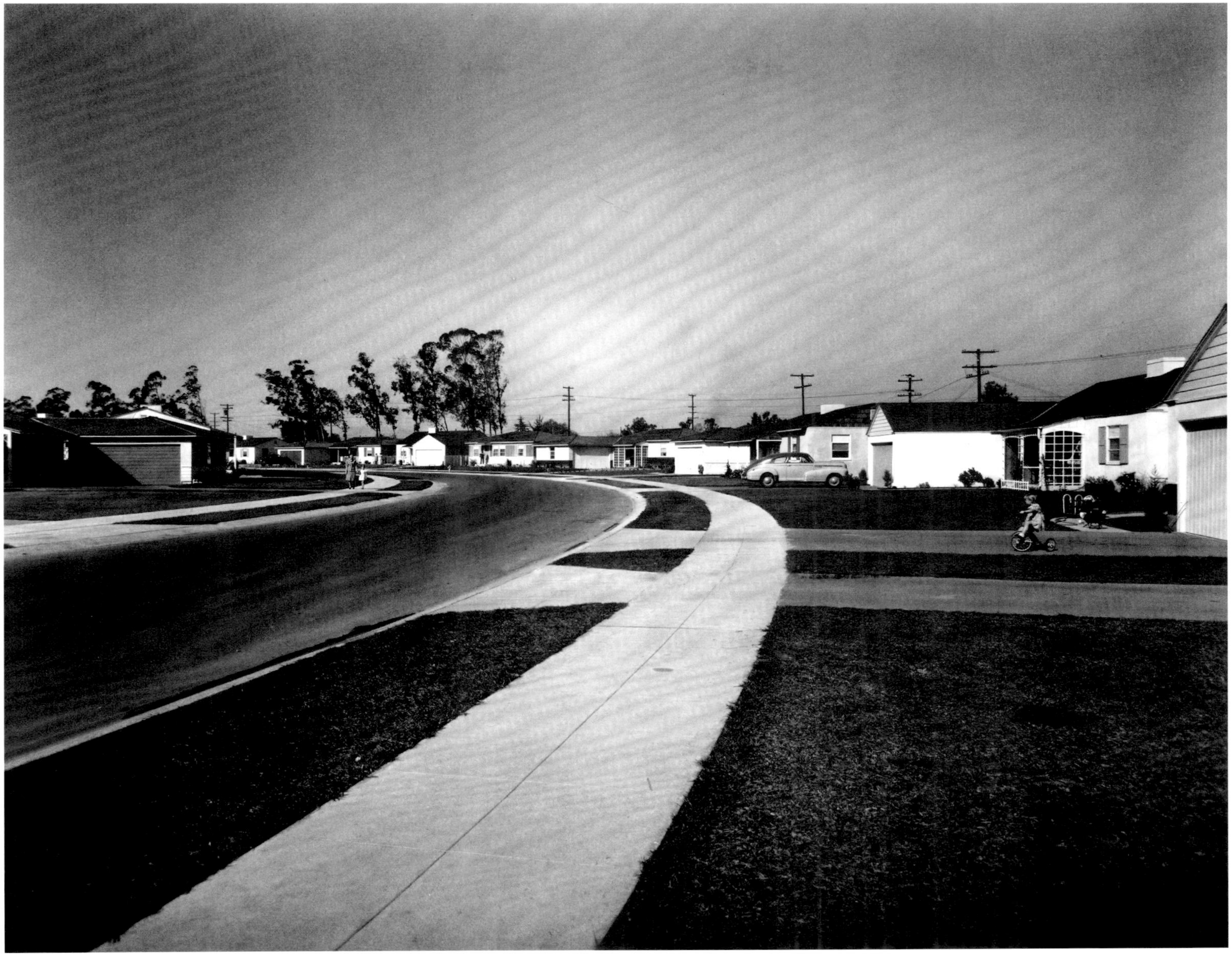

Because of the forty-five fault lines in California, the framed construction used in these "Kaiser Home" houses in the Westchester district provided "seismically sound structures," according to a scholarly study. Such metal-frame houses built in great numbers in Los Angeles in the 1940s and 1950s are considered part of the so-called modern movement in American architecture.

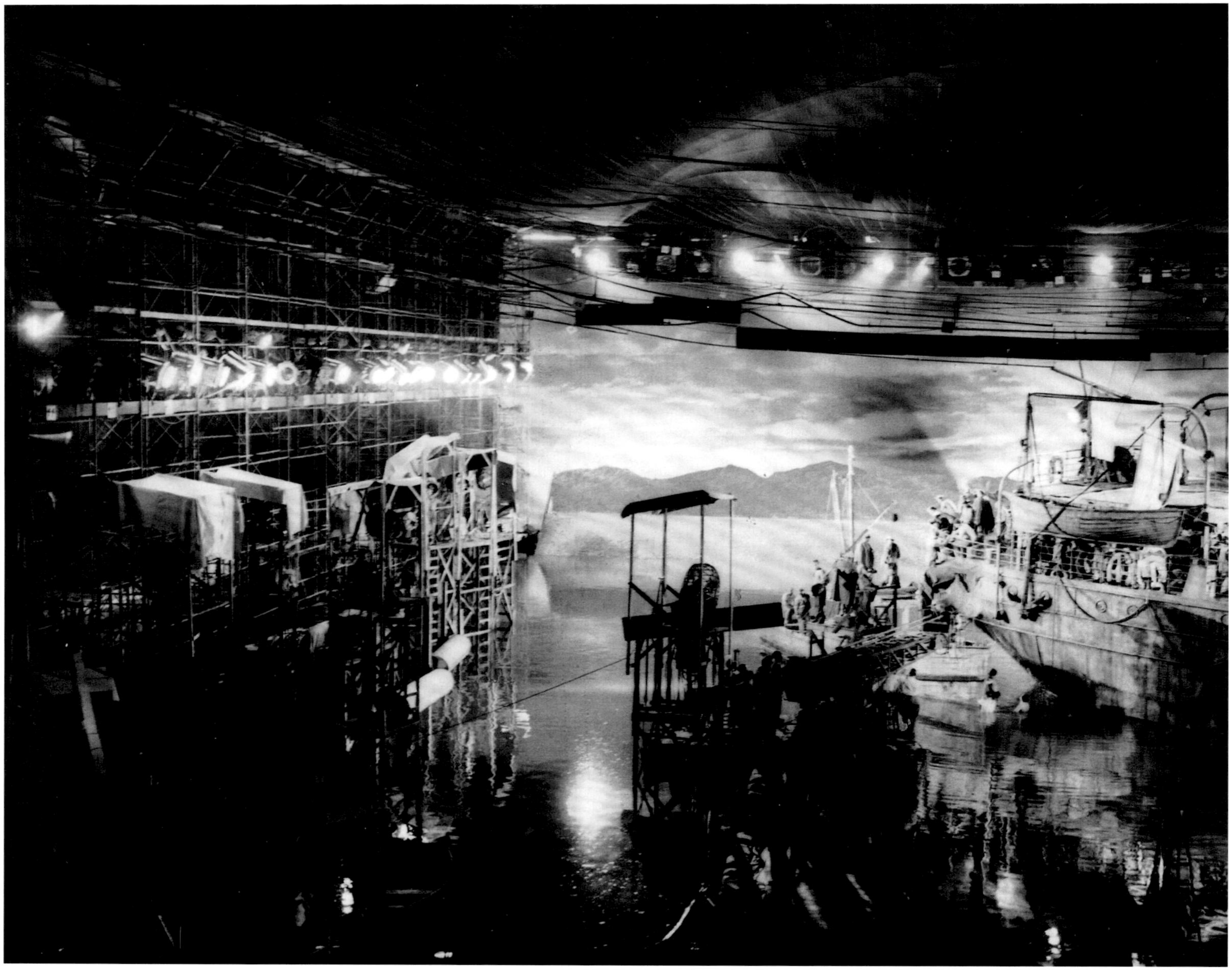

Though not evident from this scene on the Paramount Pictures lot, Hollywood's golden age began to decline in the late 1940s due to television, Hollywood blacklisting, and the newfound freedom of actors to sign with whatever studios they chose. A final blow to the industry's old ways occurred when antitrust suits were filed against the major studios in 1948.

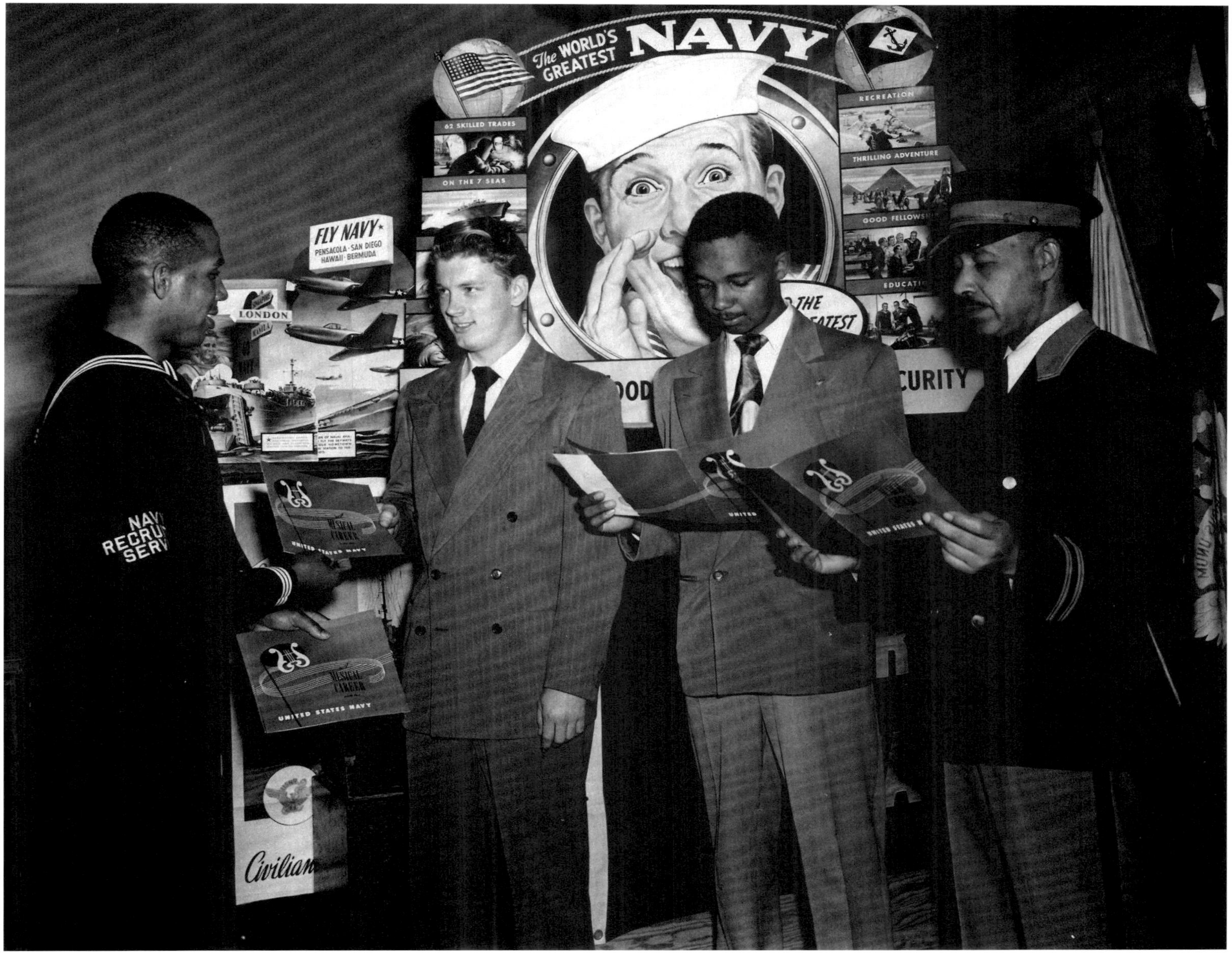

Although World War II was over, the cold war required the U.S. to maintain its armed forces at much higher levels than anything prior to Pearl Harbor. Here, Navy recruiters provide information to potential recruits around 1946. The brochures they hold extol a "musical career with the United States Navy."

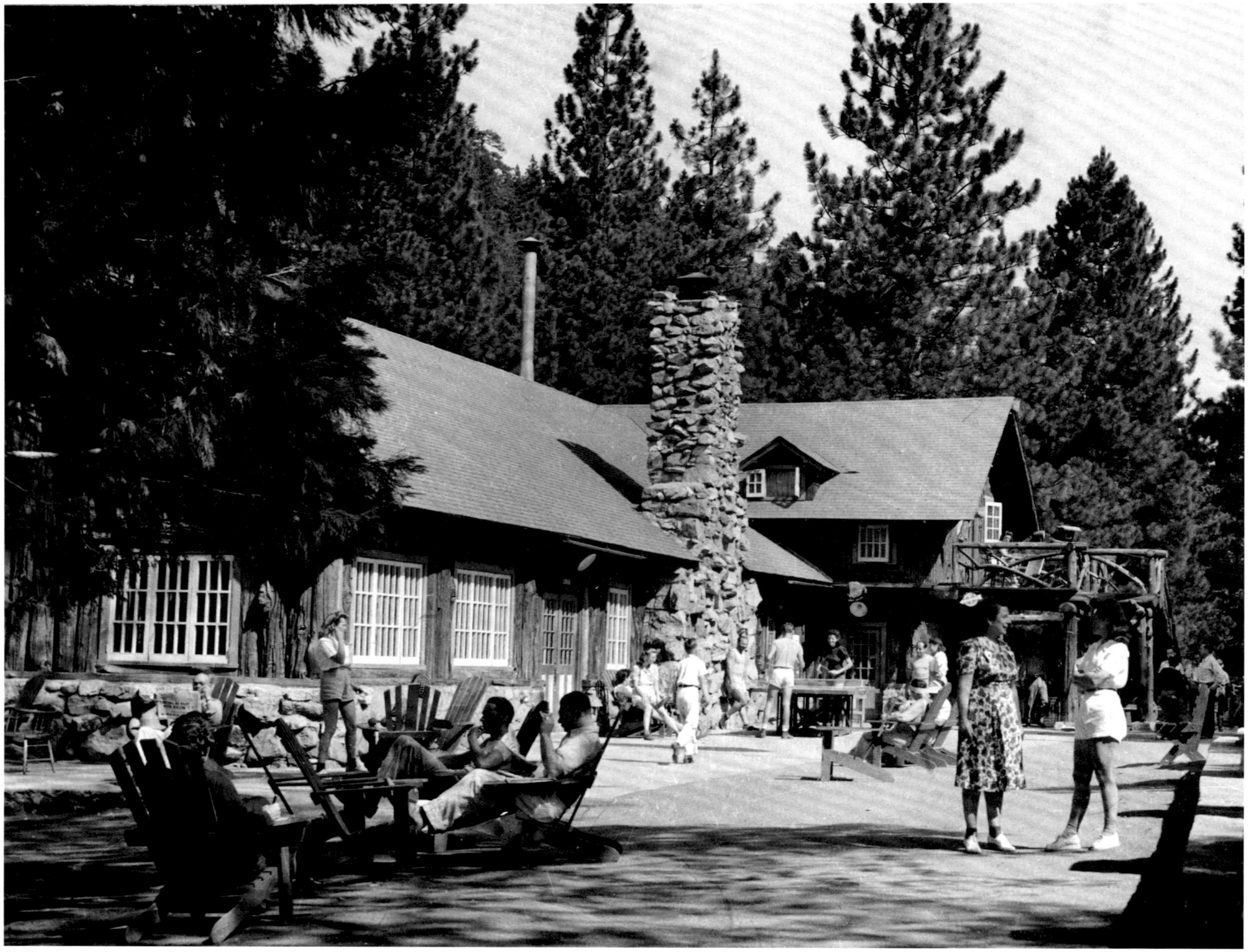

The end of World War II meant an end to rationing and a return to prewar leisure activities. In this case, vacationers relax in the sun and shade of Camp Beeley, one of more than a hundred resorts in the San Bernardino mountains.

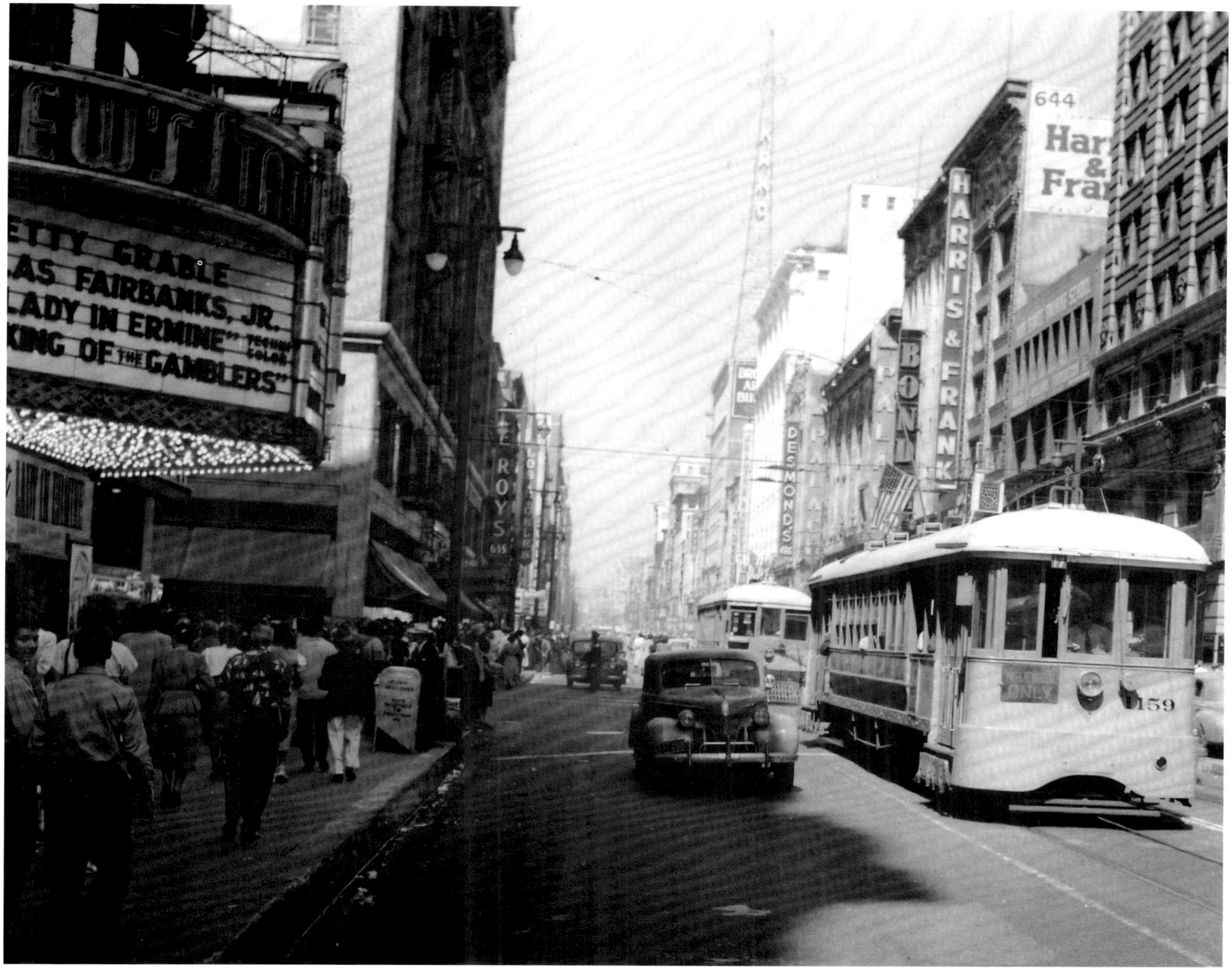

At the corner of 7th and Broadway in Los Angeles in 1948, no parking was permitted against the 10-inch curb. That year the Santa Ana–101 Freeway opened from Aliso Street to Soto Street. Aliso Village was one of the nation's first racially integrated public housing projects. The postwar housing crunch hit L.A. as U.S. servicemen, and Japanese Americans recently permitted to return to Little Tokyo, settled in the area.

Singer and actor Frank Sinatra (1915–1998) is shown getting his fingerprints taken in Hollywood in 1947 after he applied for permission to carry a gun. The popular vocalist became a solo artist with great success in the 1940s and is considered the first teen idol, but his career stalled in the 1950s until he won an Academy Award for Best Supporting Actor in 1954 for his role in the film *From Here to Eternity*.

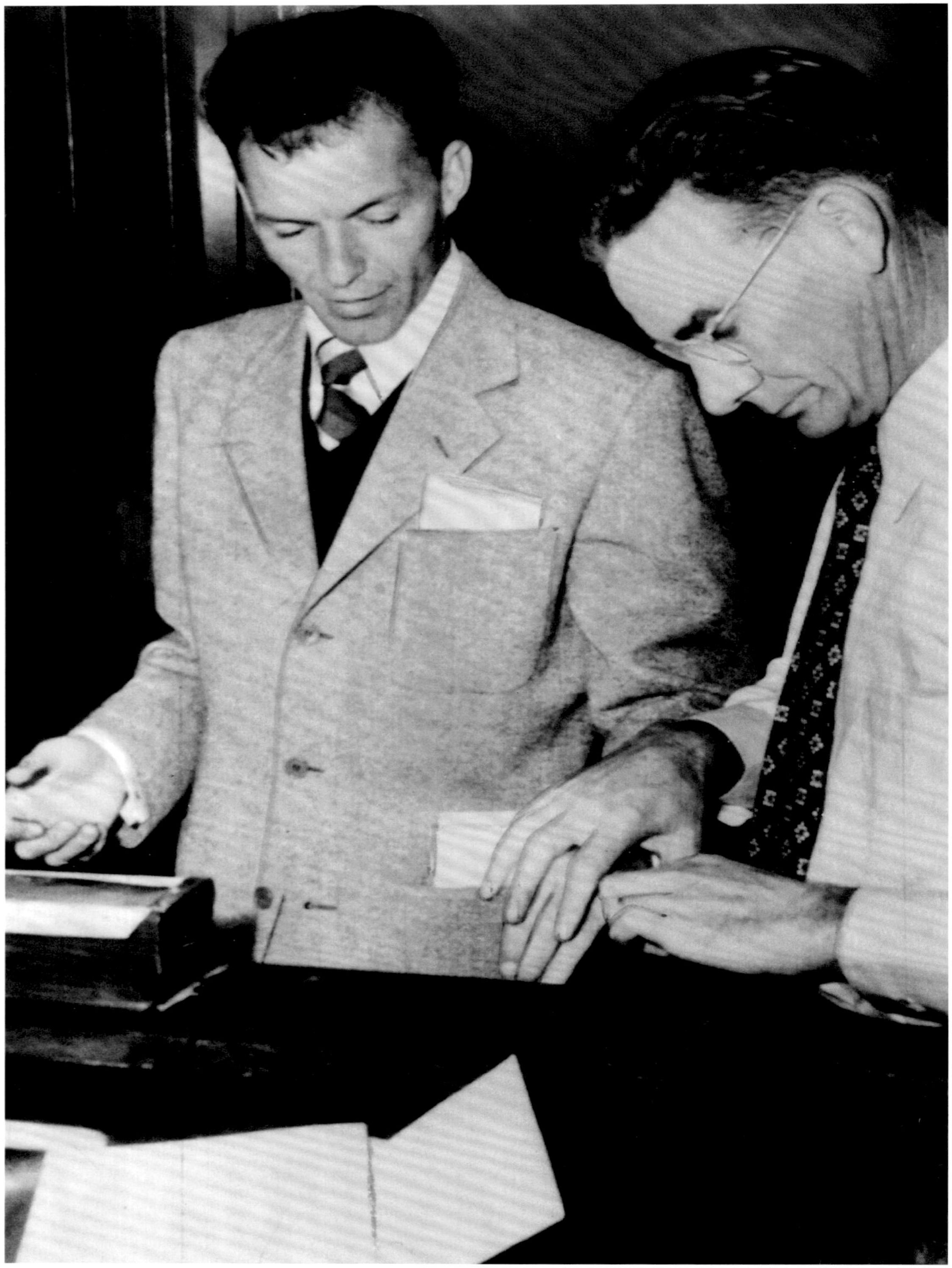

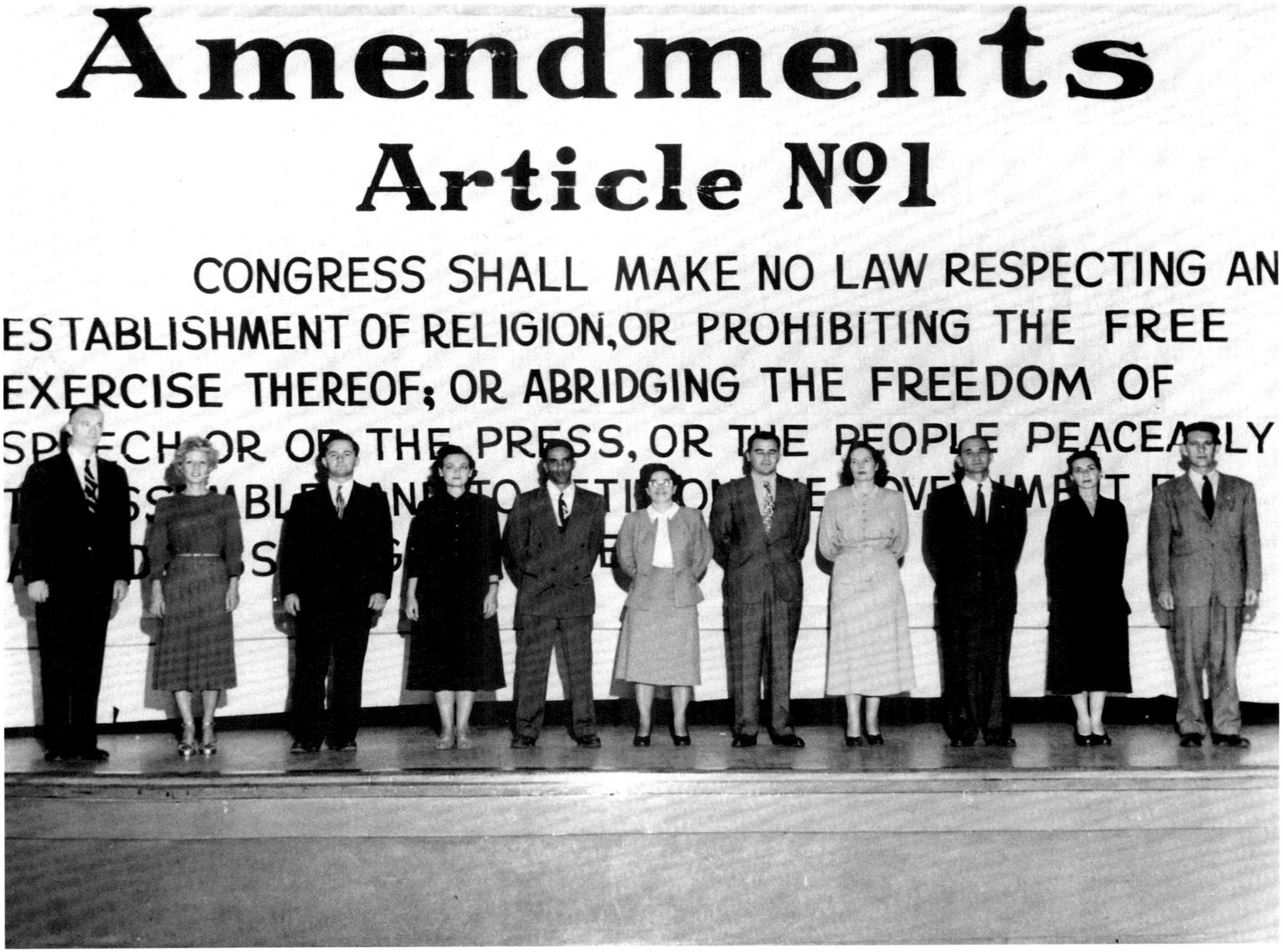

This 1948 photograph shows members of the Los Angeles 21 and their attorney standing in front of a sign with the text of the First Amendment at a rally held on November 9 at Embassy Auditorium. Subpoenaed by a federal grand jury in October, they were asked to discuss their activities in the Communist Party, to name other members of the Communist Party, or they could refuse to testify. These ten and an additional eleven individuals refused to testify, or refused to answer on the grounds of self-incrimination, and were sent to jail.

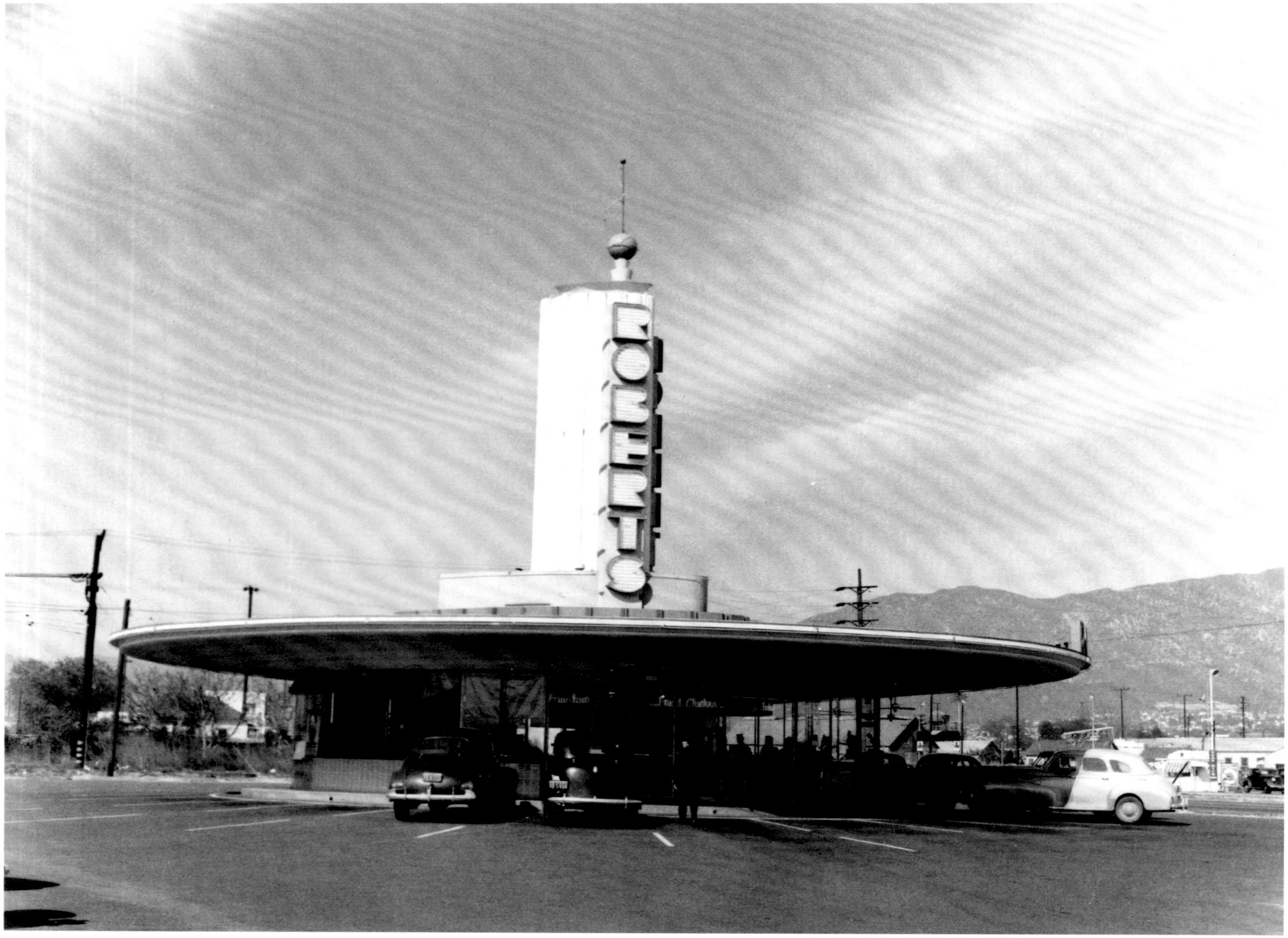

Architect Wayne McAllister (1907–2000) designed the circular Robert's Drive-in, an example of streamline moderne, a late branch of art deco. Also called Googie, populuxe, or doo-wop style, this futurist architecture was influenced by car culture, the space age, and the atomic age. Neon lighting ringed the roof of the drive-in, seen here around the late 1940s.

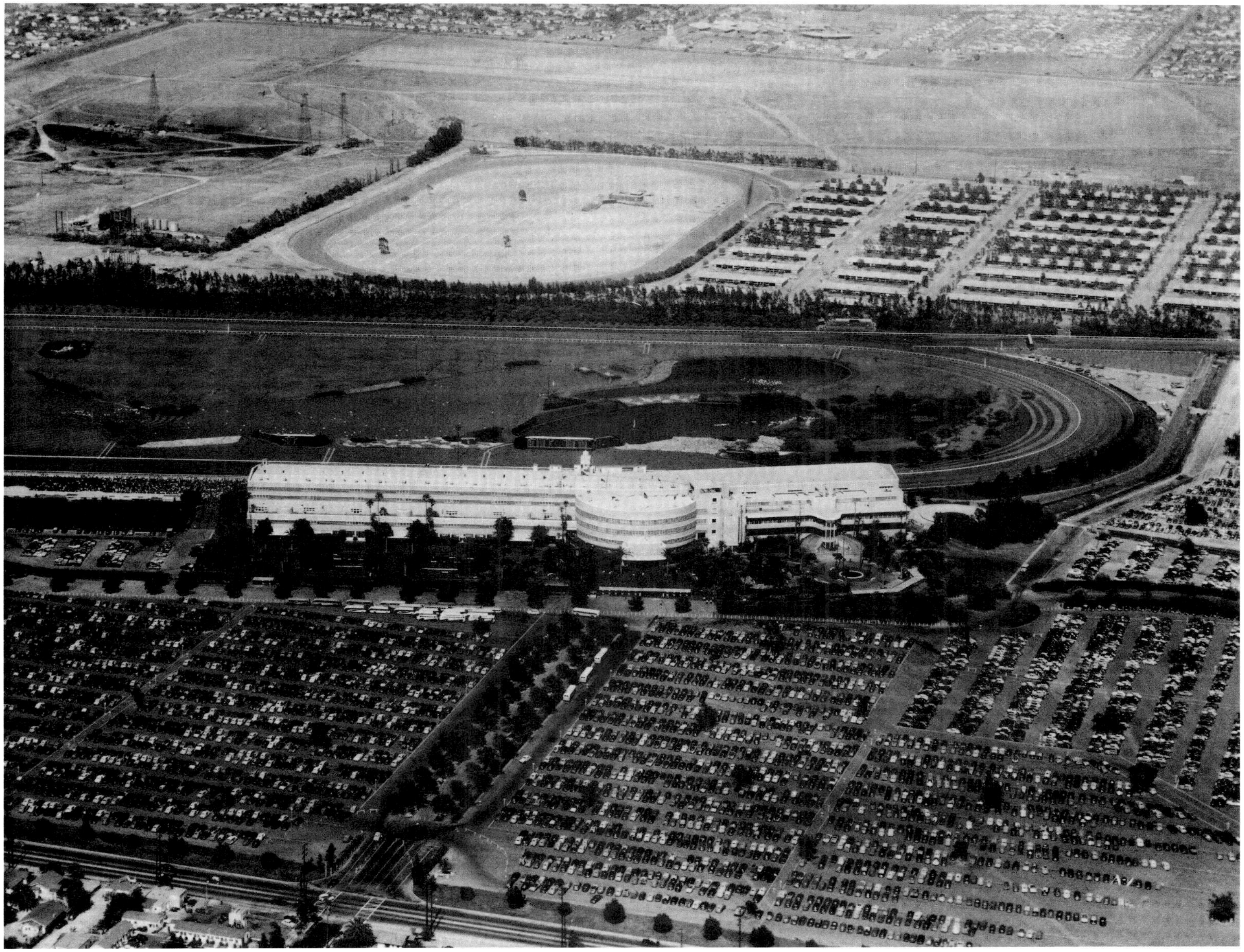

An aerial view of Hollywood Park Race Track. The track was opened in 1938 by the Hollywood Turf Club whose chairman was Jack Warner of Warner Brothers, and its 600 shareholders included many other Hollywood luminaries. It was closed from 1942 to 1944 due to the war, and in 1949 the grandstand and clubhouse were destroyed by a fire, but were rebuilt soon thereafter.

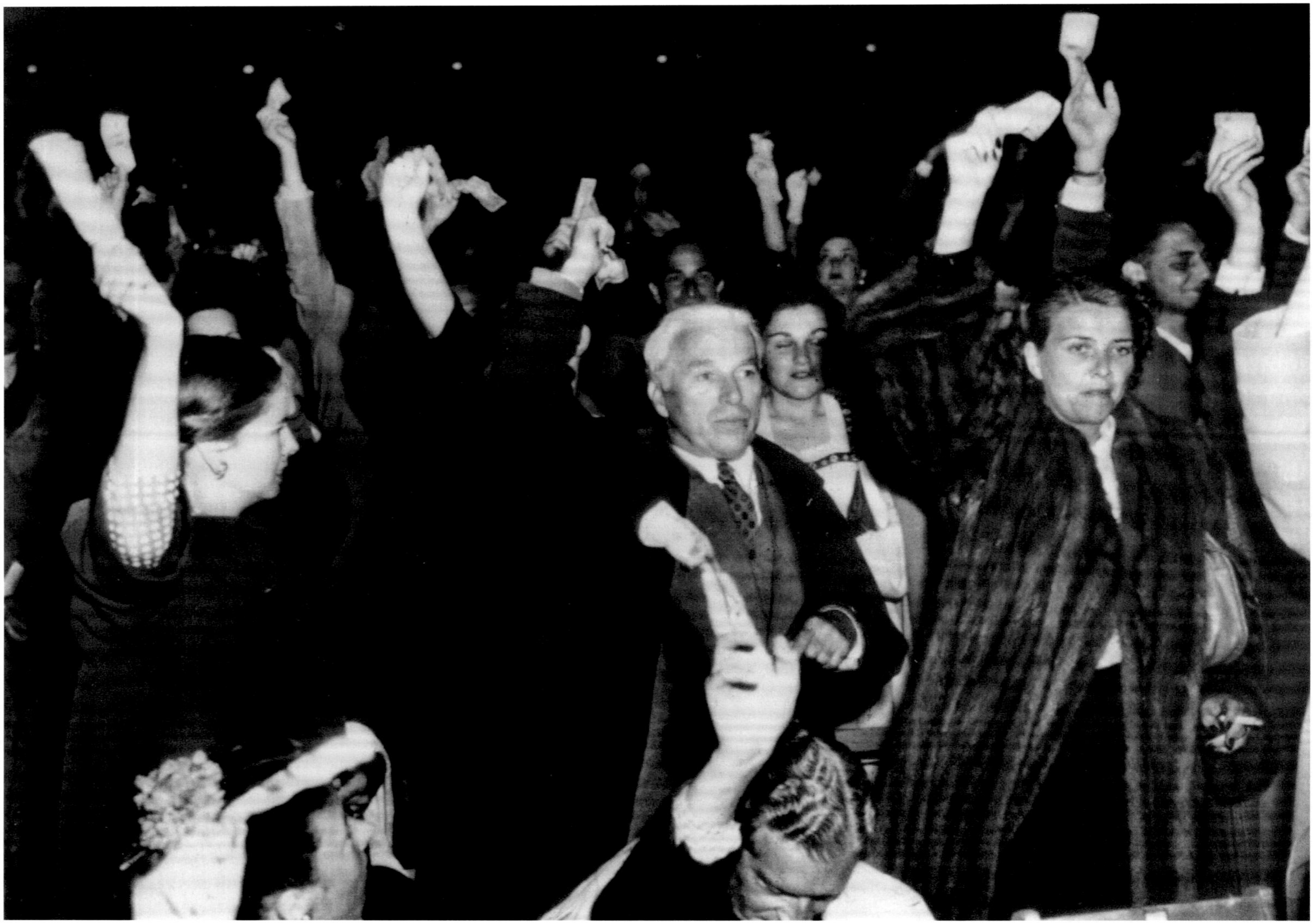

Actor, director, and composer Charlie Chaplin (1889–1977) with his wife Oona at a 1948 rally for the presidential campaign of Henry A. Wallace, the nominee of the Progressive Party. Wallace (1888–1965) was vice-president under Franklin D. Roosevelt from 1941, but Roosevelt replaced him as his running mate in 1944 with Harry S. Truman. Wallace then served as secretary of commerce until 1946 when he was fired by President Truman because of disagreements about U.S. policy towards the Soviet Union.

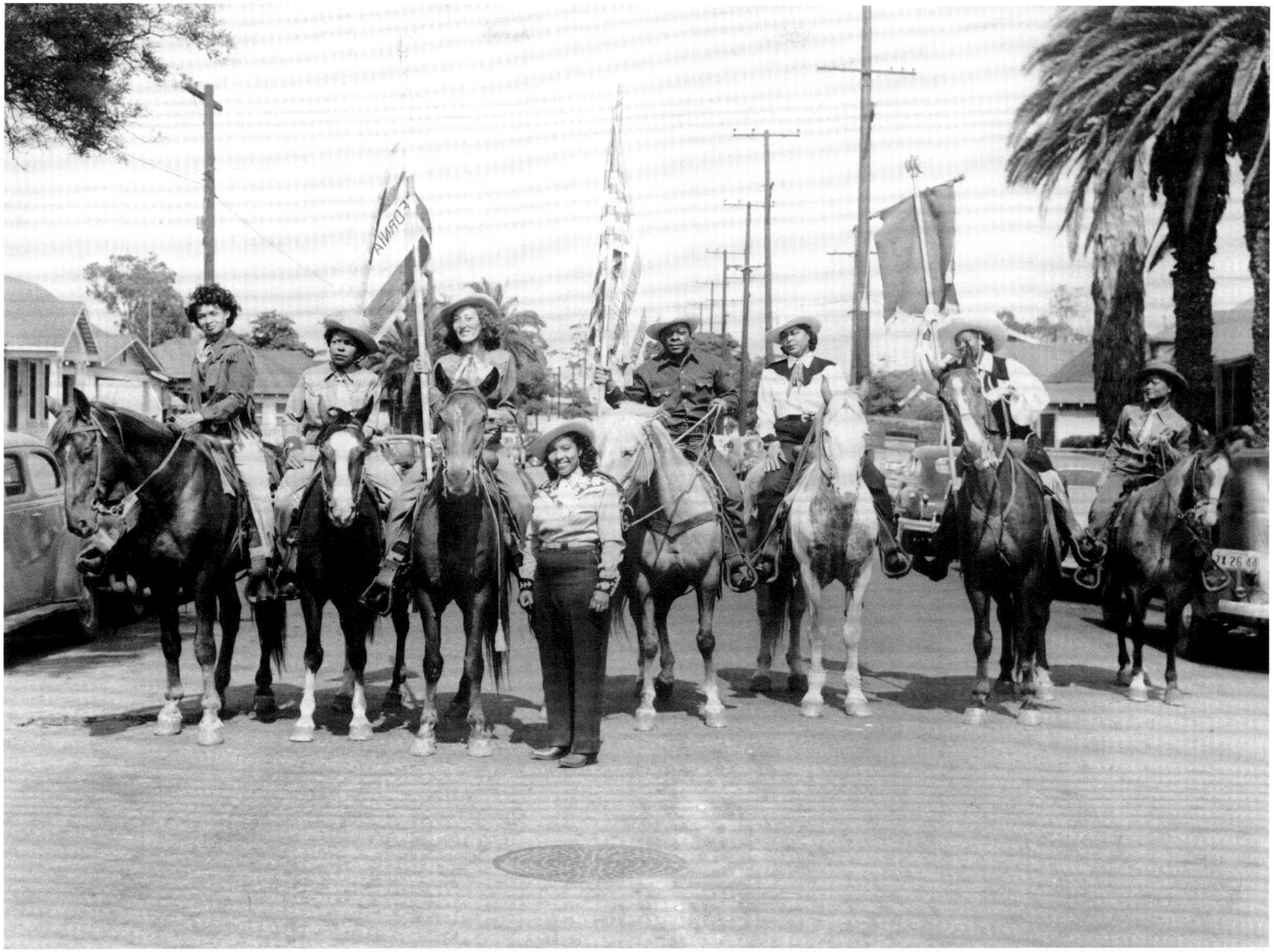

Southern California may be the land of the automobile, but it also fancies itself a part of the Old West, a conviction no doubt encouraged by Hollywood. For nearly every Los Angeles parade, Western-style riders saddle their horses. These are members of the Silver Spurs Riding Club at such an event on June 9, 1949.

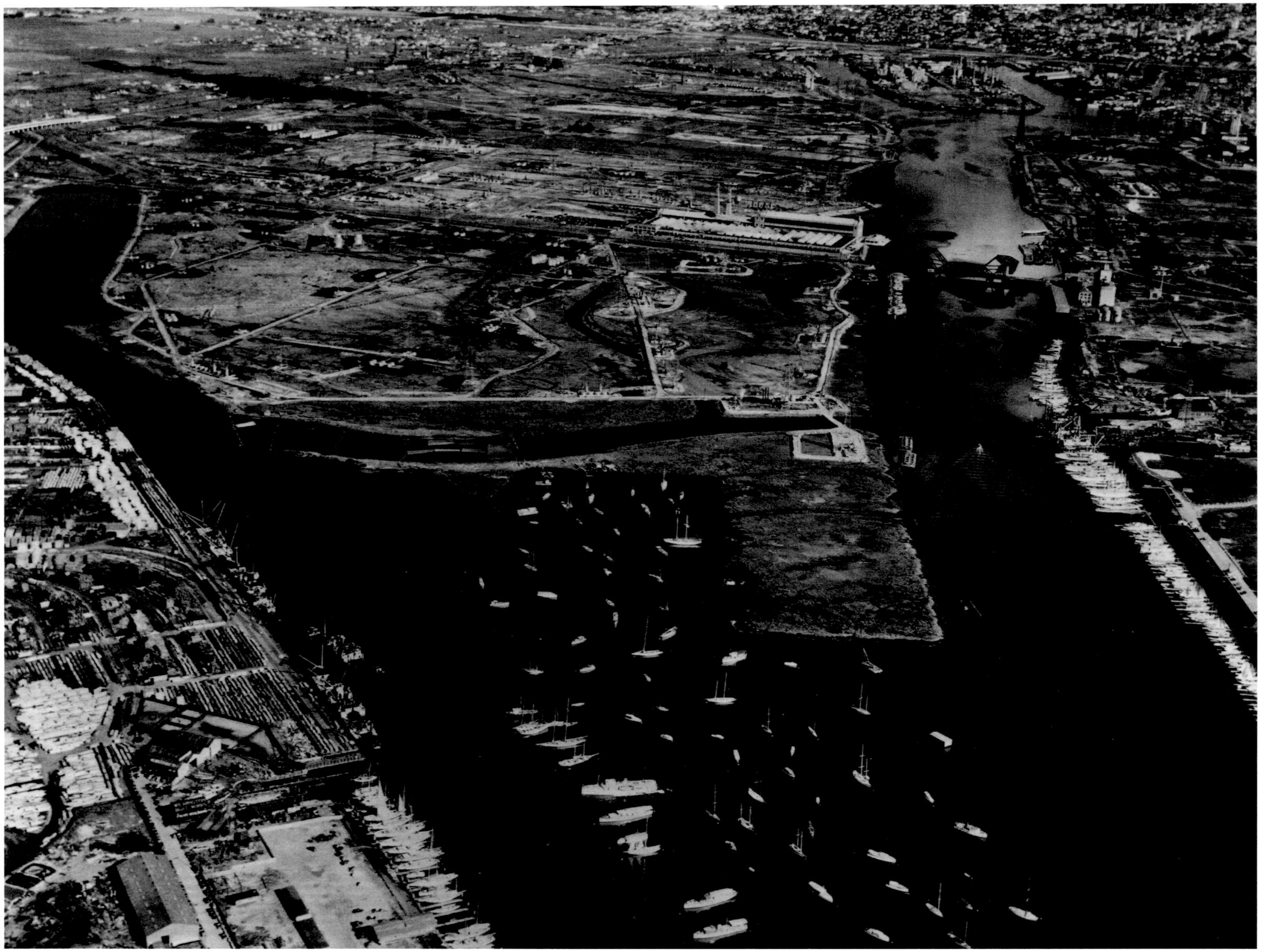

Los Angeles harbor viewed from above in 1949. That year saw the first Mexican American elected to the L.A. City Council in the twentieth century, Edward Roybal, who later represented his area in Congress until 1993.

SUBURBS, FREEWAYS, AND A COLD WAR

(1950–1959)

The World War II alliance between capitalist America, colonial Great Britain, and the communist Soviet Union was a coalition of expediency. With the defeat of Germany and Japan, mutual distrust and competing postwar goals led to a "cold war" between the United States and the Soviet Union. Although during this period there were "hot" conflicts in Korea and the Middle East, the threat of mutual destruction by nuclear weapons prevented a direct confrontation between the world's two new superpowers.

The victory over Japan did not make Los Angeles more secure. With its population grown to nearly 2.5 million people, L.A. became the third largest city in America during the decade of the 1950s—making it a prime target for Soviet long-range weapons. Angelenos learned to live with the daily threat of nuclear extermination.

Fear of communism resulted in repressive measures against anyone suspected of spying for, collaborating with, or helping the "Reds." The Hollywood blacklist denied employment to entertainment professionals because of real or suspected association with, membership in, or sympathy to the American Communist Party. Some people were blacklisted simply because their name came up at the wrong place and time.

Nevertheless, some successes for personal liberties were achieved. In 1952, East L.A. resident Sei Fujii, a Japanese immigrant, challenged the 1913 California Alien Land Law that prevented ownership of property by "aliens ineligible for citizenship." The law was ruled unconstitutional by the state supreme court.

By the 1950s, automobiles and the freeway system were the major means of transport throughout greater L.A., leading to further decentralization and further dramatic growth of the suburbs. A state engineer claimed that three times as many cars could travel at twice previous speeds along the new highways, with a decrease in fatal accidents. For people in love with their cars, surely this was heaven.

The National Broadcasting Company (NBC) building in Hollywood in 1951. In the 1950s, millions of Americans bought TVs, and NBC launched television's first superstar, Milton Berle (1908–2002), whose antics on the *Texaco Star Theater* drew massive audiences. During this decade television became the dominant mass media, and young people watched TV more hours than they went to school, a trend that is still the same in 2008.

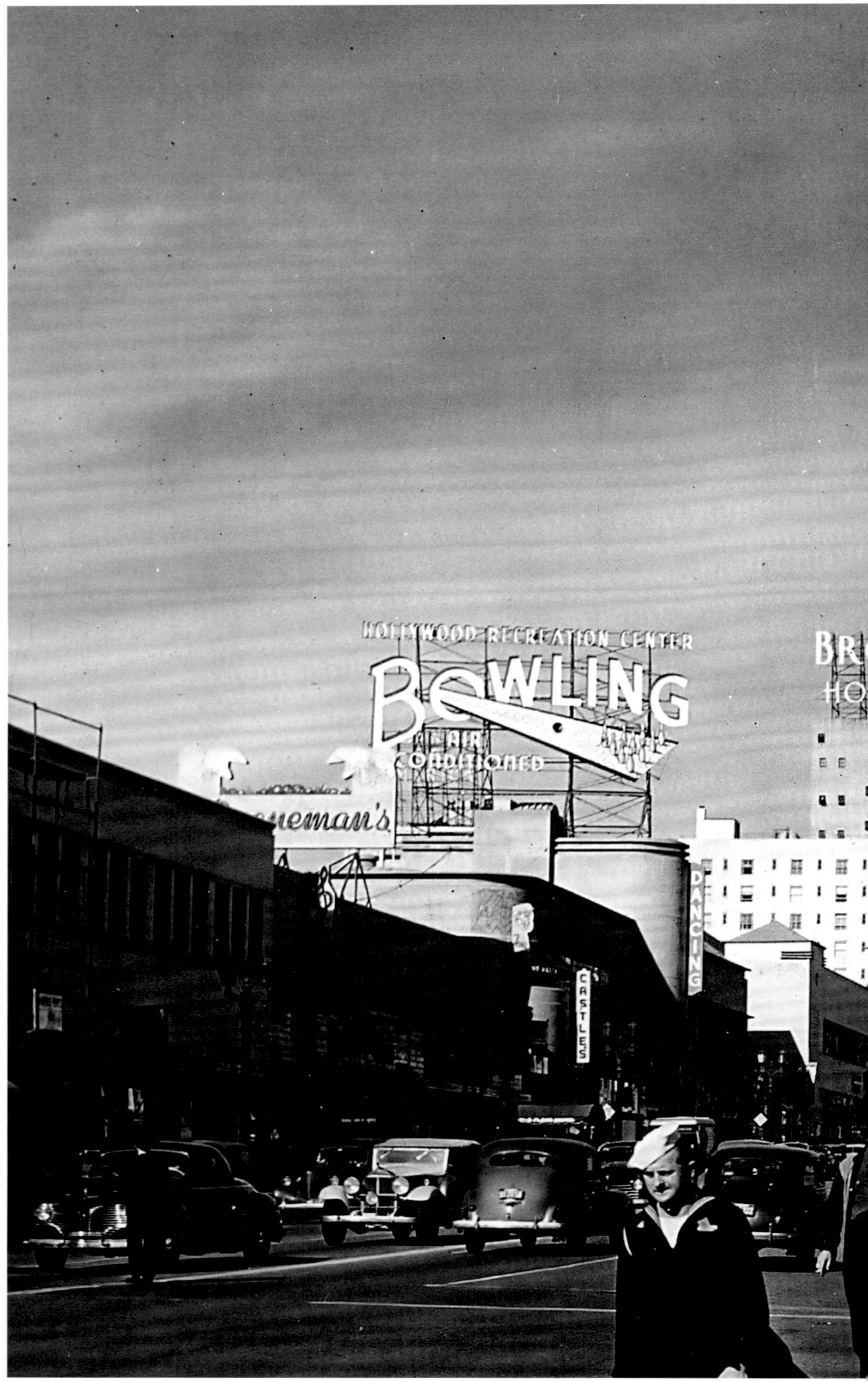

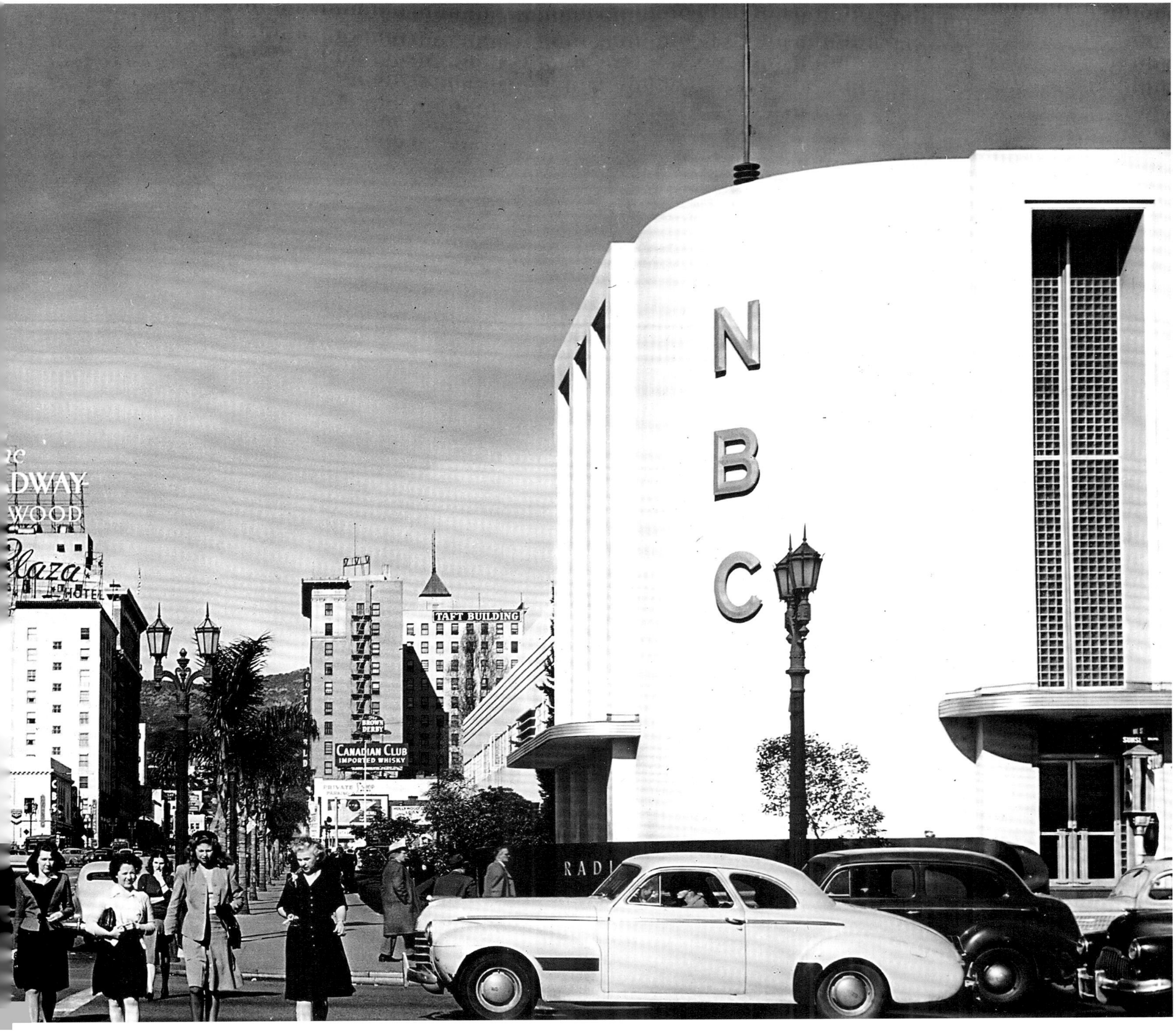
N
B
C
TAFT BUILDING
BROWN DERBY
CANADIAN CLUB
IMPORTED WHISKY
HOTEL

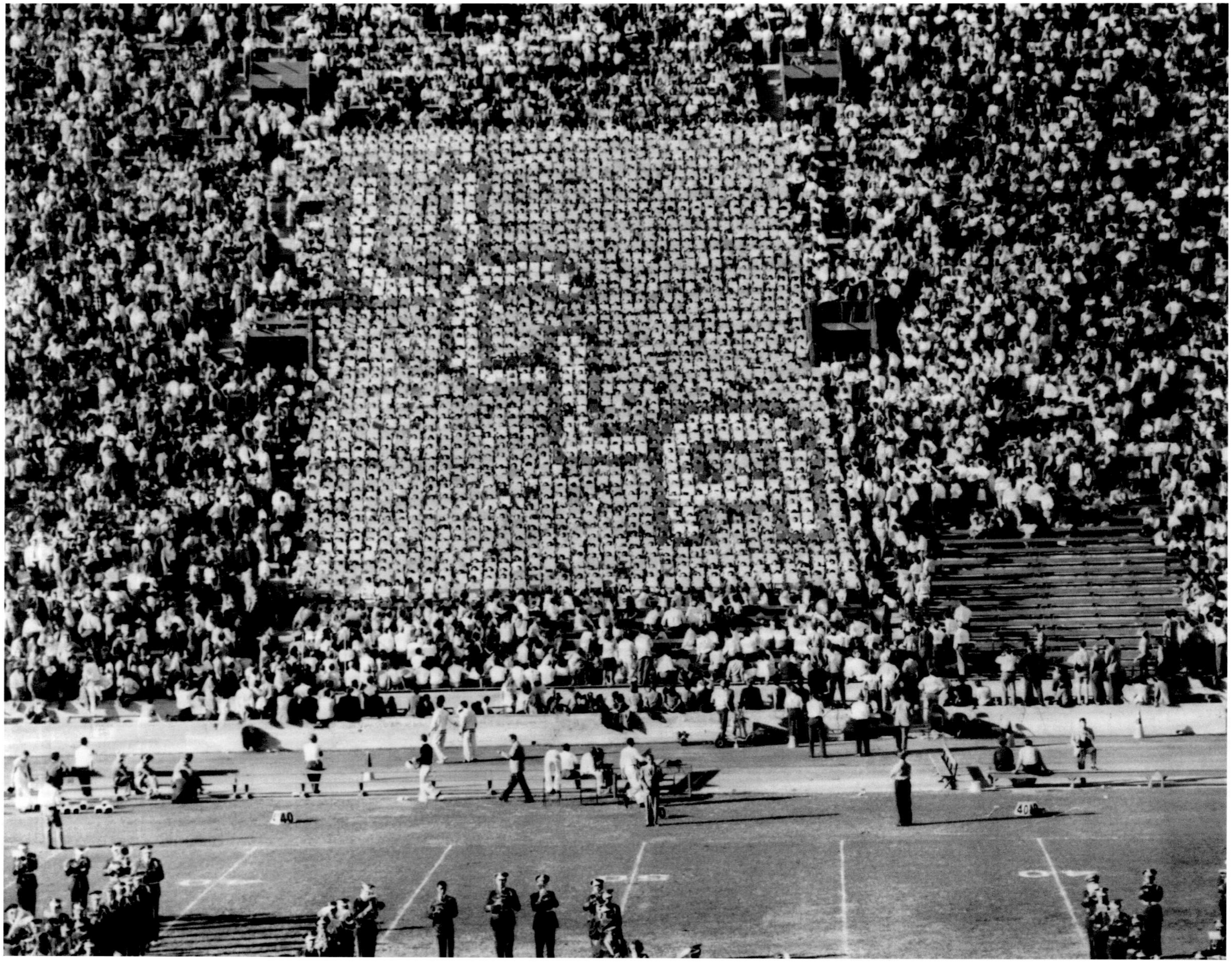

In what appears to be part of a football game halftime extravaganza, 15,000 students hold up cards spelling out "UCLA" in 1950. The University of California, Los Angeles, is a public research university established as a branch of the state university system in 1919. It is the second oldest campus in the UC system and has the largest enrollment of any university in California. In 2008 UCLA had more applicants than any other university in the United States.

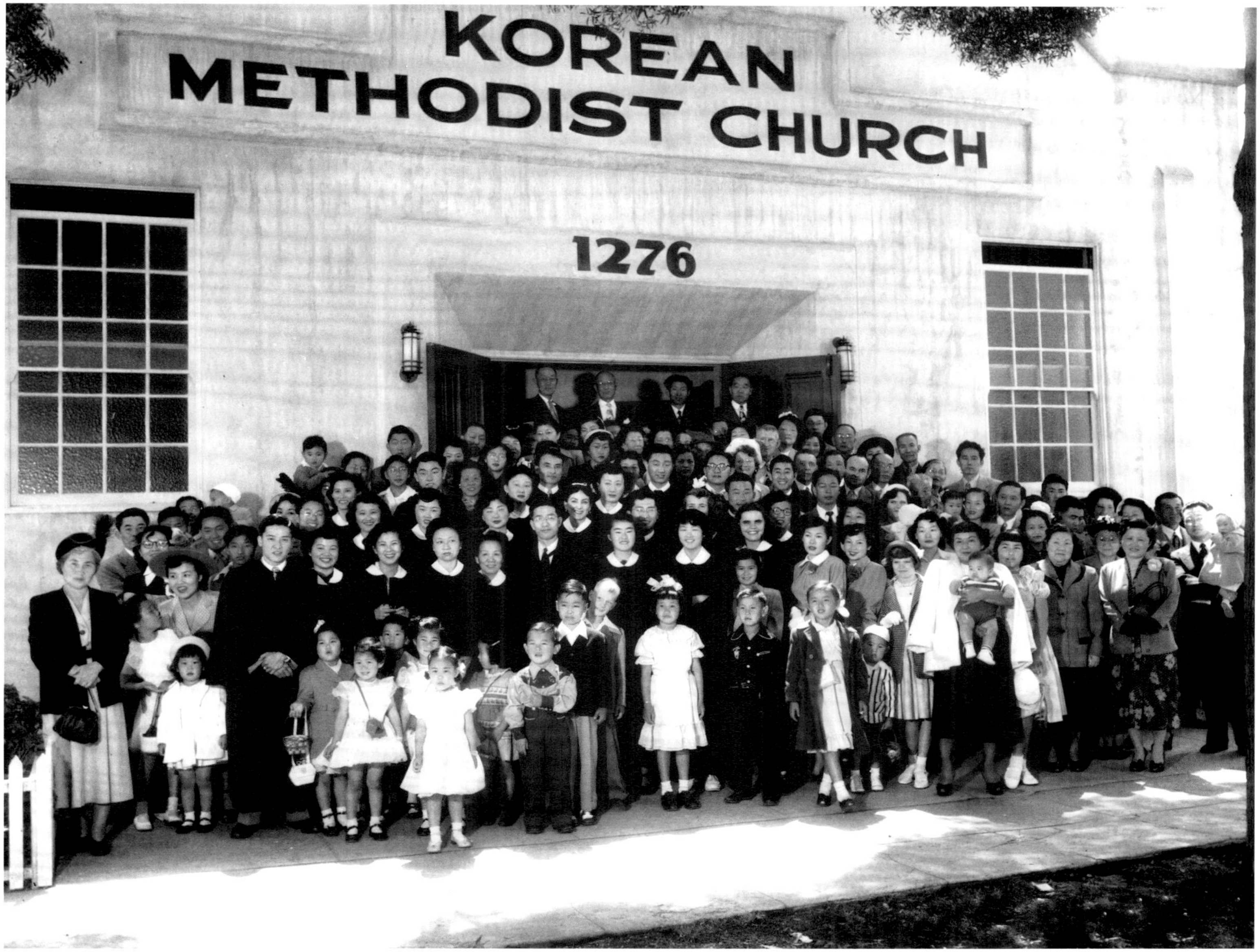

The Korean Methodist Church in Los Angeles in 1950. That year the Korean War broke out when the communist North Korean Army moved into South Korea to attempt to reunite the country that had been divided since 1948. The conflict expanded as the United States and its allies sent military forces to help the South, countered by communist China and the Soviet Union's doing the same for the North. The war lasted from June 25, 1950, until a ceasefire agreement was signed on July 27, 1953.

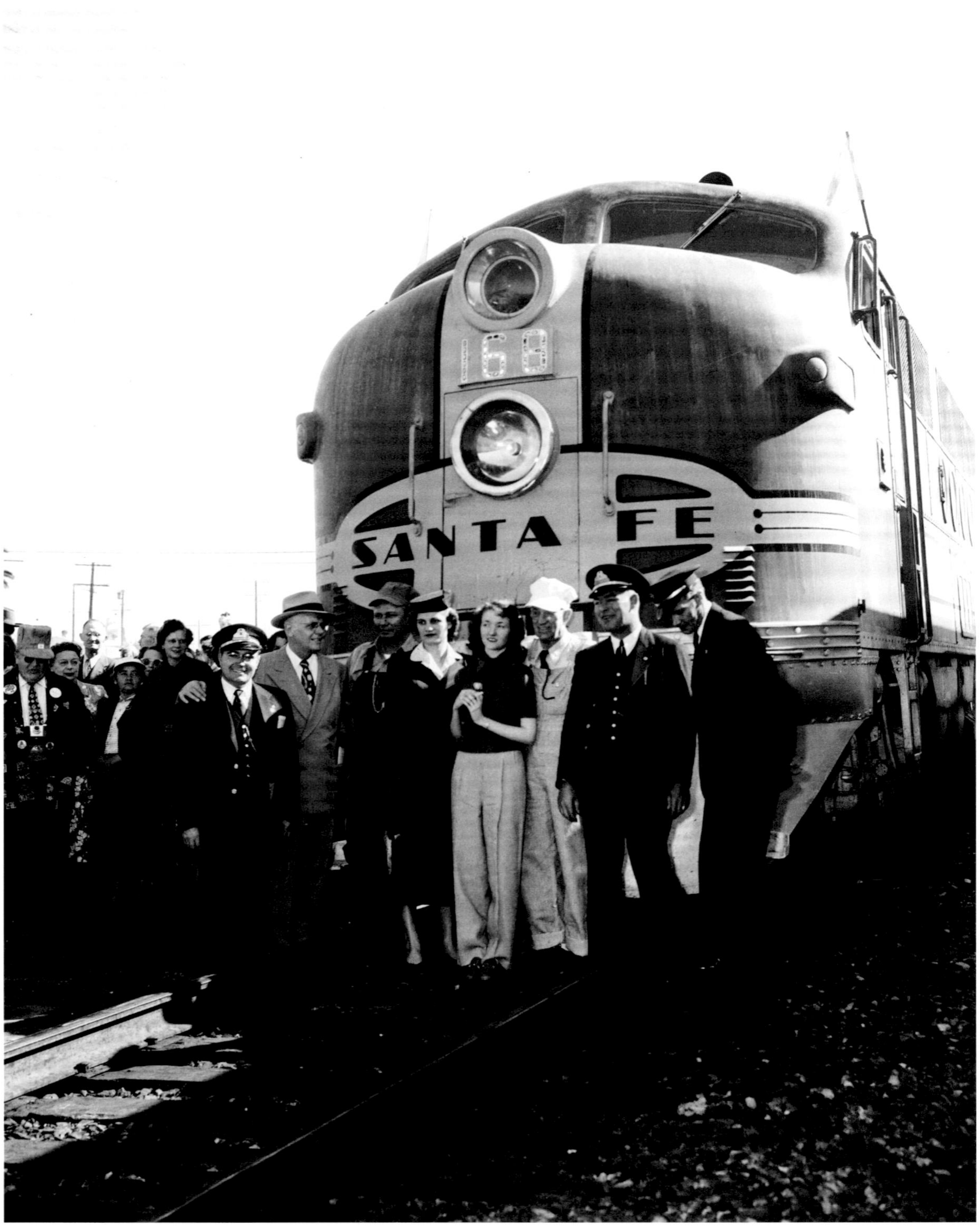

This *Herald-Examiner* photograph of October 28, 1951, shows invalid Jill Miller, who won a "Santa Fe Holiday." The train was the "Super Chief"—the flagship passenger train of the Atchison, Topeka and Santa Fe Railway. It was also called "The Train of the Stars" because it carried many celebrities between Chicago and Los Angeles. The *Herald-Examiner* went out of business in 1989, leaving the *Los Angeles Times* as the only citywide daily newspaper.

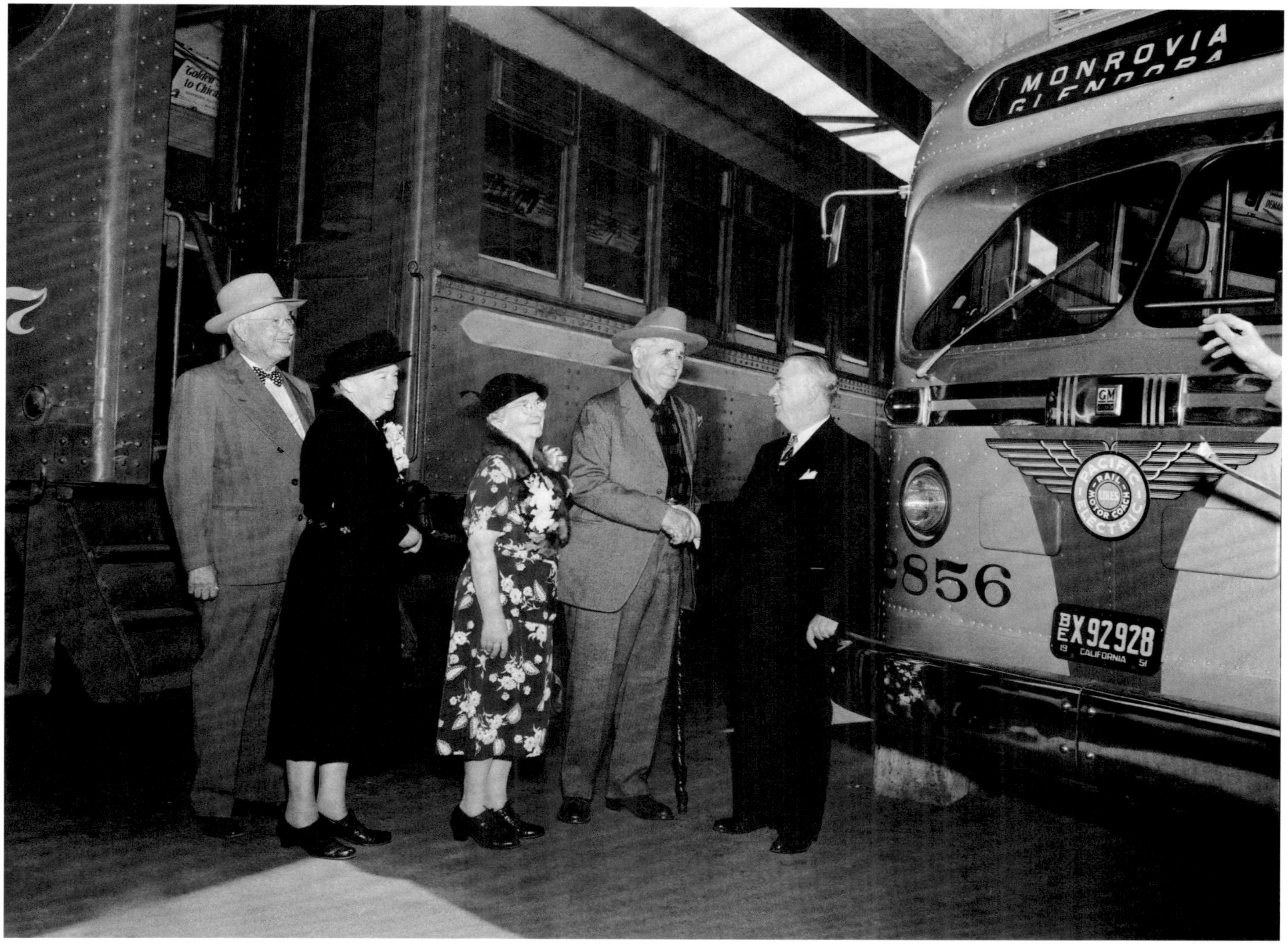

On September 30, 1951, with the "Red Cars" of the Pacific Electric Railway nearing retirement in favor of motor coaches (buses), two pioneer riders who had made the first Pacific Electric run from Monrovia to Los Angeles in 1903 took one of the last rides on the Red Cars, too. At the system's height in 1925, the streetcars and light rail of the Pacific Electric Railway were the city's dominant means of mass transit.

Florist-turned-producer Kenneth McEldowney (1907–2004) and his daughter, Gay, are shown arriving in Los Angeles in 1951 from the Venice Film Festival in Italy, where producer McEldowney won an award for *The River.* Filmed entirely in India, the picture was directed by Jean Renoir (1894–1979) and was Renoir's first color film. McEldowney, who made his fortune in real estate, was encouraged by his wife, a publicist for MGM. McEldowney swore he could make a better film than his wife's company did.

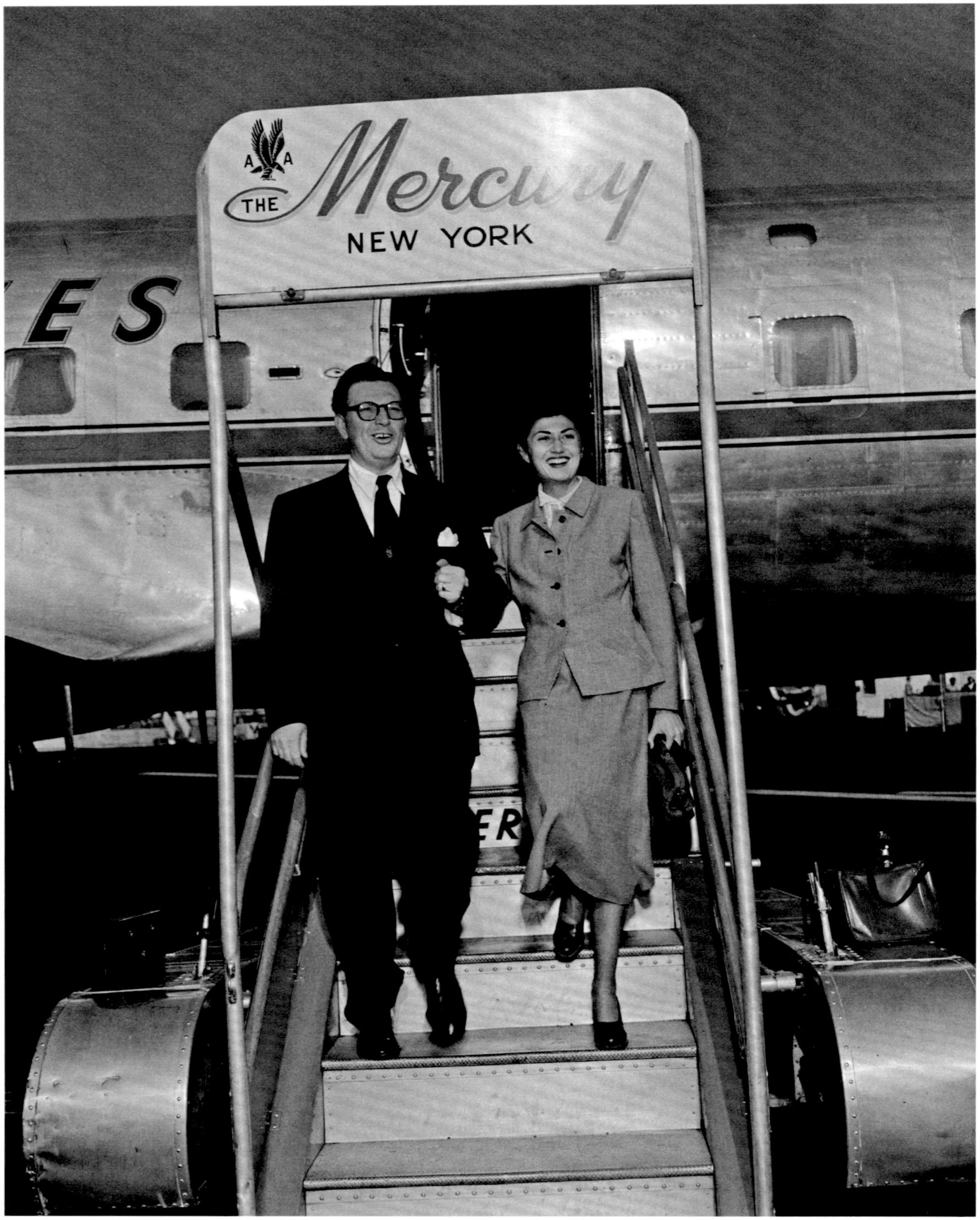

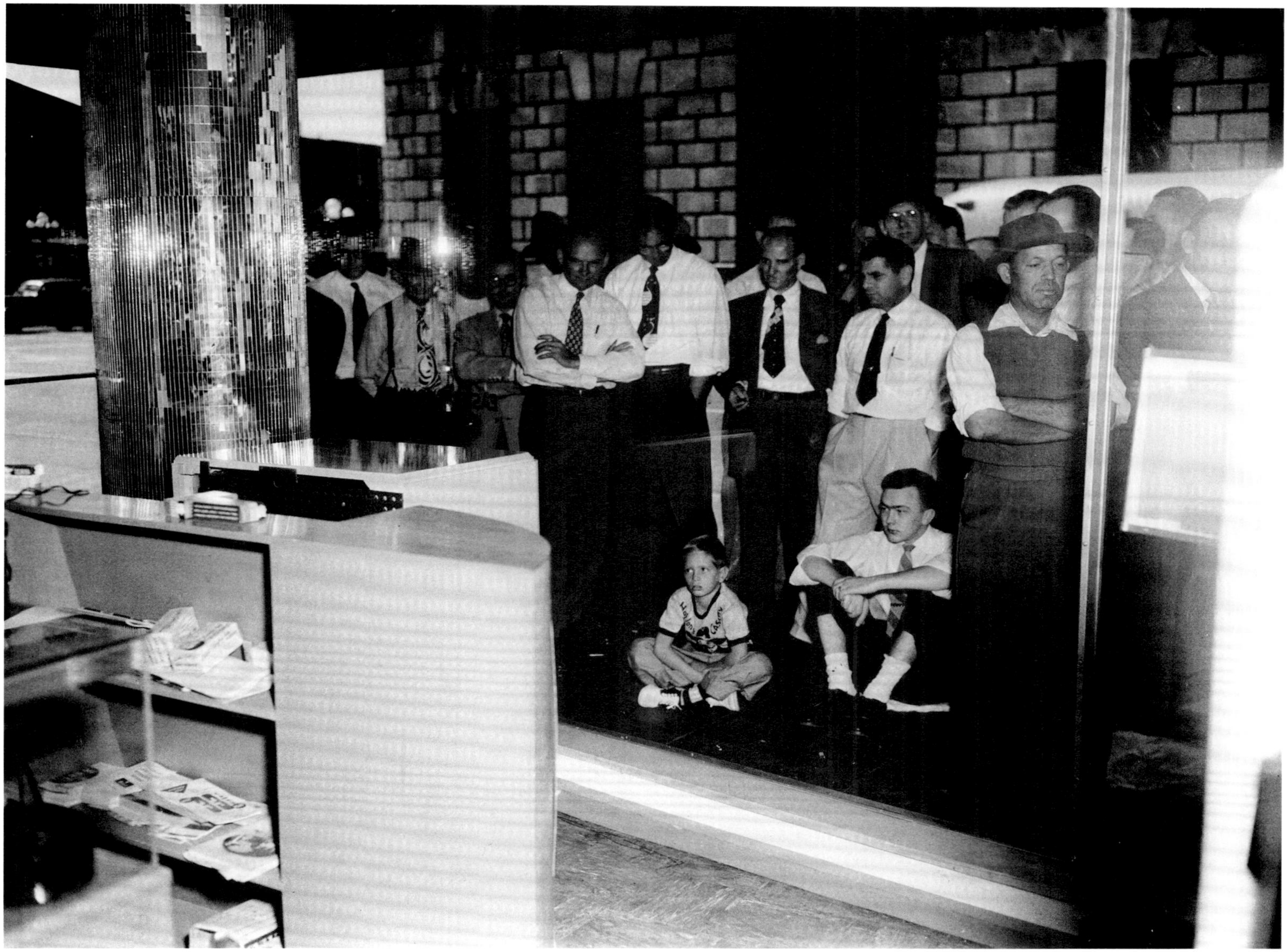

A crowd at the Eastern Columbia Store at Ninth and Hill Streets in Los Angeles watch a televised game between the Brooklyn Dodgers and New York Giants on October 1, 1951. The fourth most populous city in America did not then have a major-league baseball team, but that would change when the Dodgers relocated to Los Angeles for the 1958 season.

The Reverend Billy Graham at the Alexandria Hotel in Los Angeles on October 2, 1951. Born William Franklin Graham Jr. (1918–) he is better known as Billy Graham, a Christian evangelist who became a national religious figure after his 1949 L.A. revival. Graham has preached in person to more than 2.5 million people around the world and has been a spiritual adviser to multiple U.S. presidents. In 2002, his lifetime audience, including radio and television broadcasts, topped two billion.

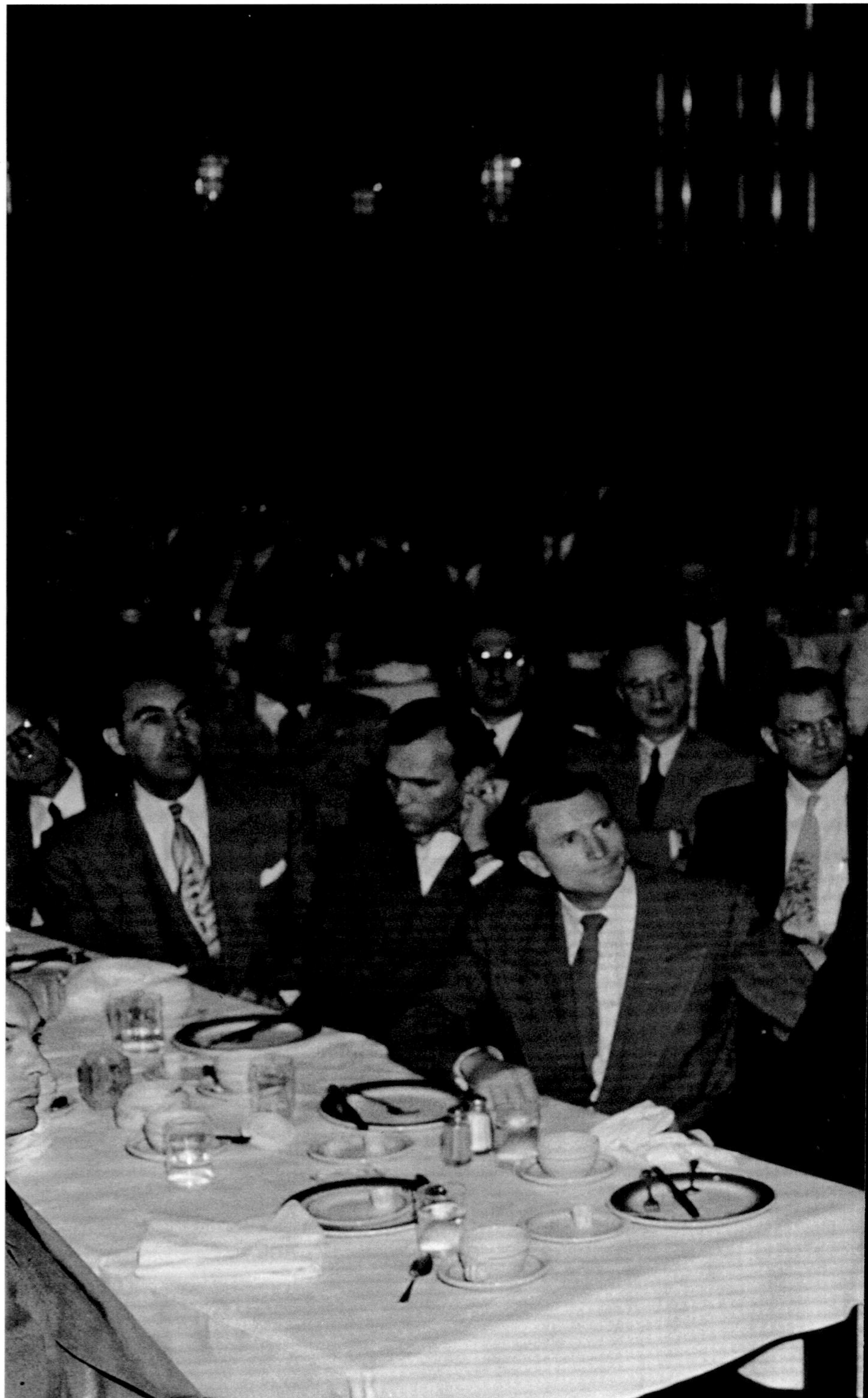

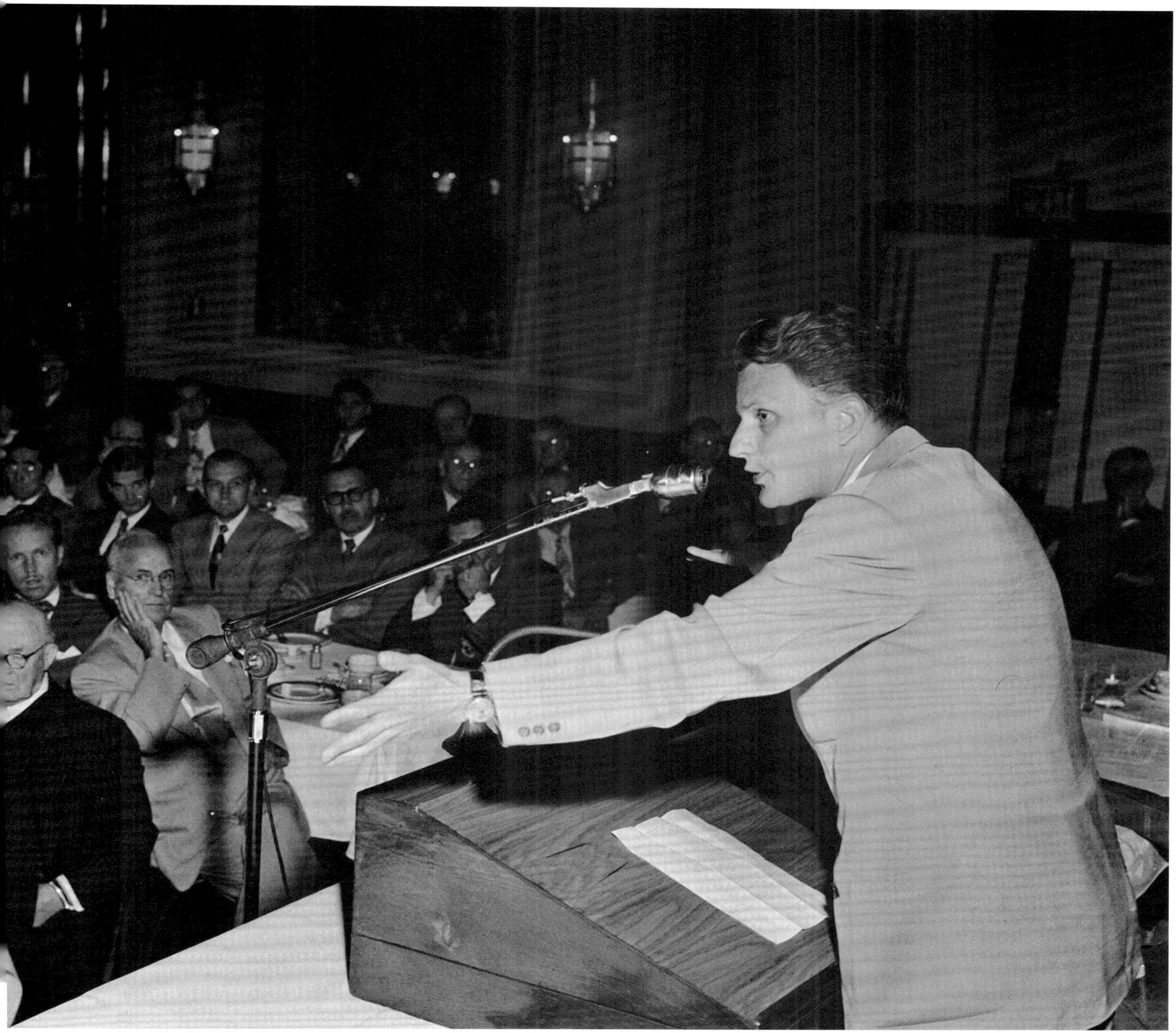

This newspaper photograph shows Joe Sica, a bookie arrested along with three bookie suspects on April 12, 1951. Like Sica, Dominic Brooklier (1914–1984) started his crime career as a bookmaker, but Brooklier, also known as Jimmy Regace, became head of the Los Angeles crime syndicate during the 1970s. In 1978, Brooklier was convicted of racketeering and extortion and died in prison. As of 2008, his son Anthony is a prominent and successful criminal defense attorney in Los Angeles.

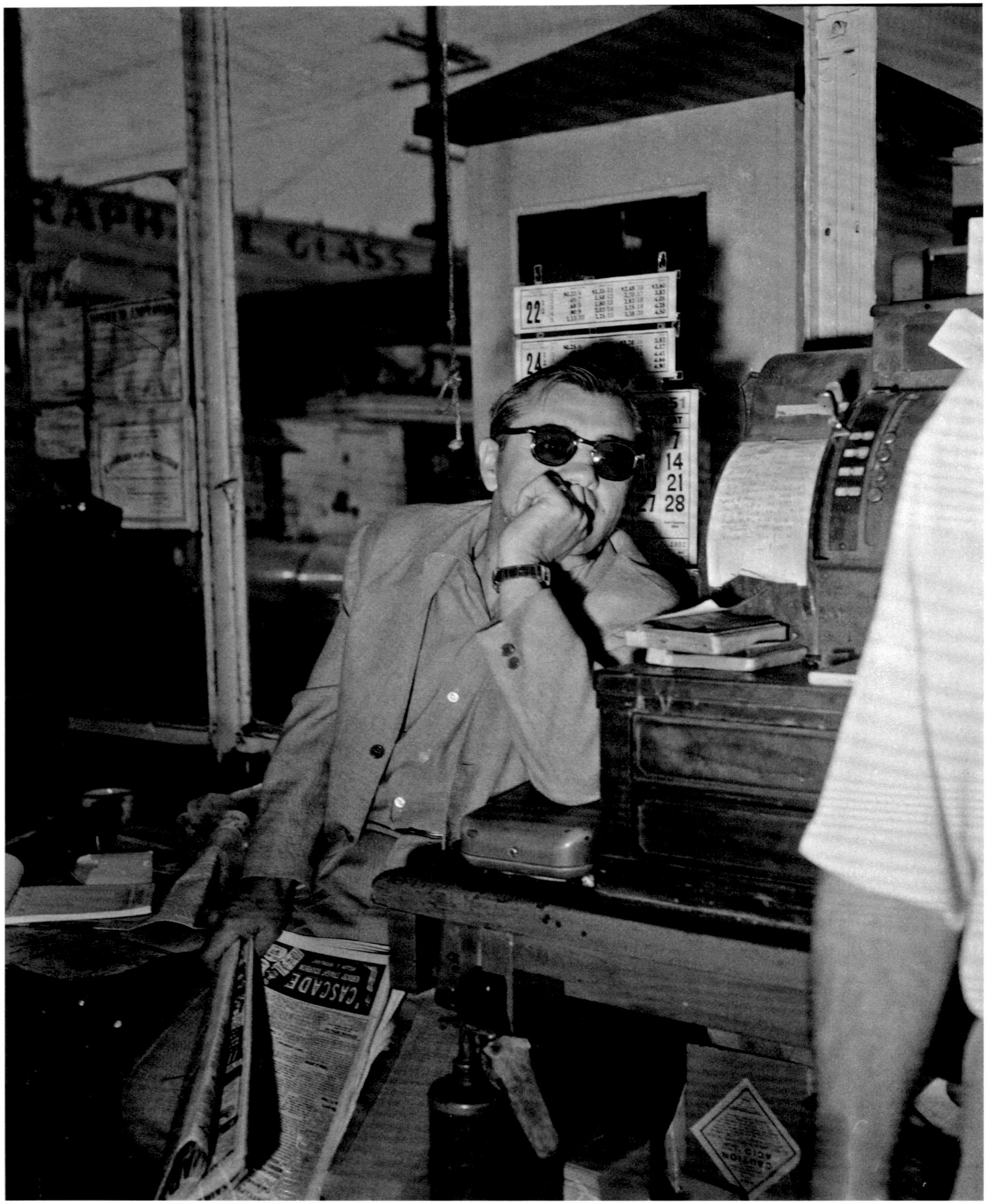

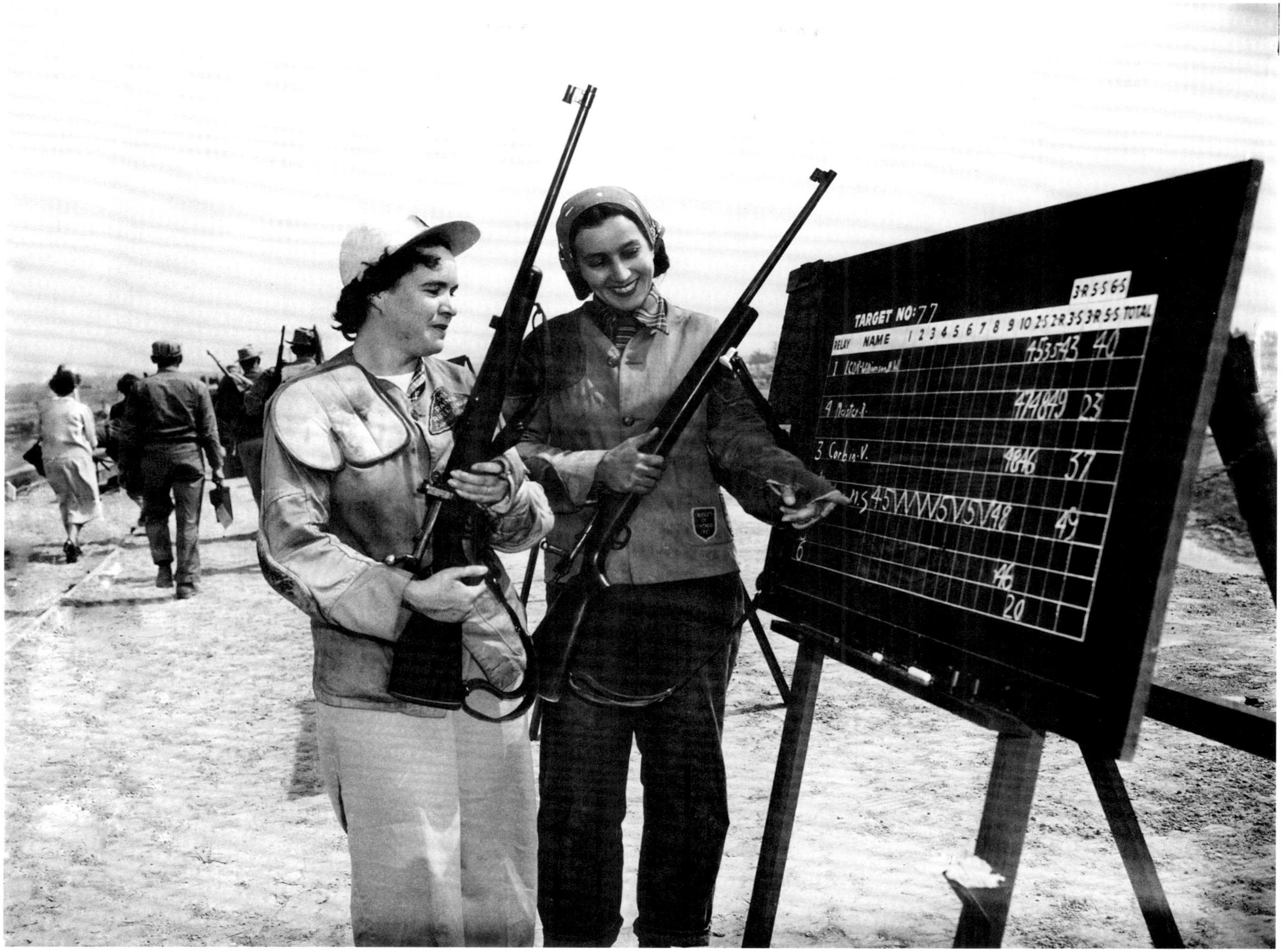

Mrs. Leone Ackerland of Seattle and Mrs. Miralotte Ickes of Berkeley, California, participated in the National Rifle Shoot matches held by the National Rifle Association (NRA) on September 27, 1951. The NRA is a nonprofit group established in 1871 for the promotion of marksmanship, firearm safety, and the protection of hunting and firearm ownership rights based on the principle that gun ownership is a civil liberty protected by the Second Amendment of the Bill of Rights.

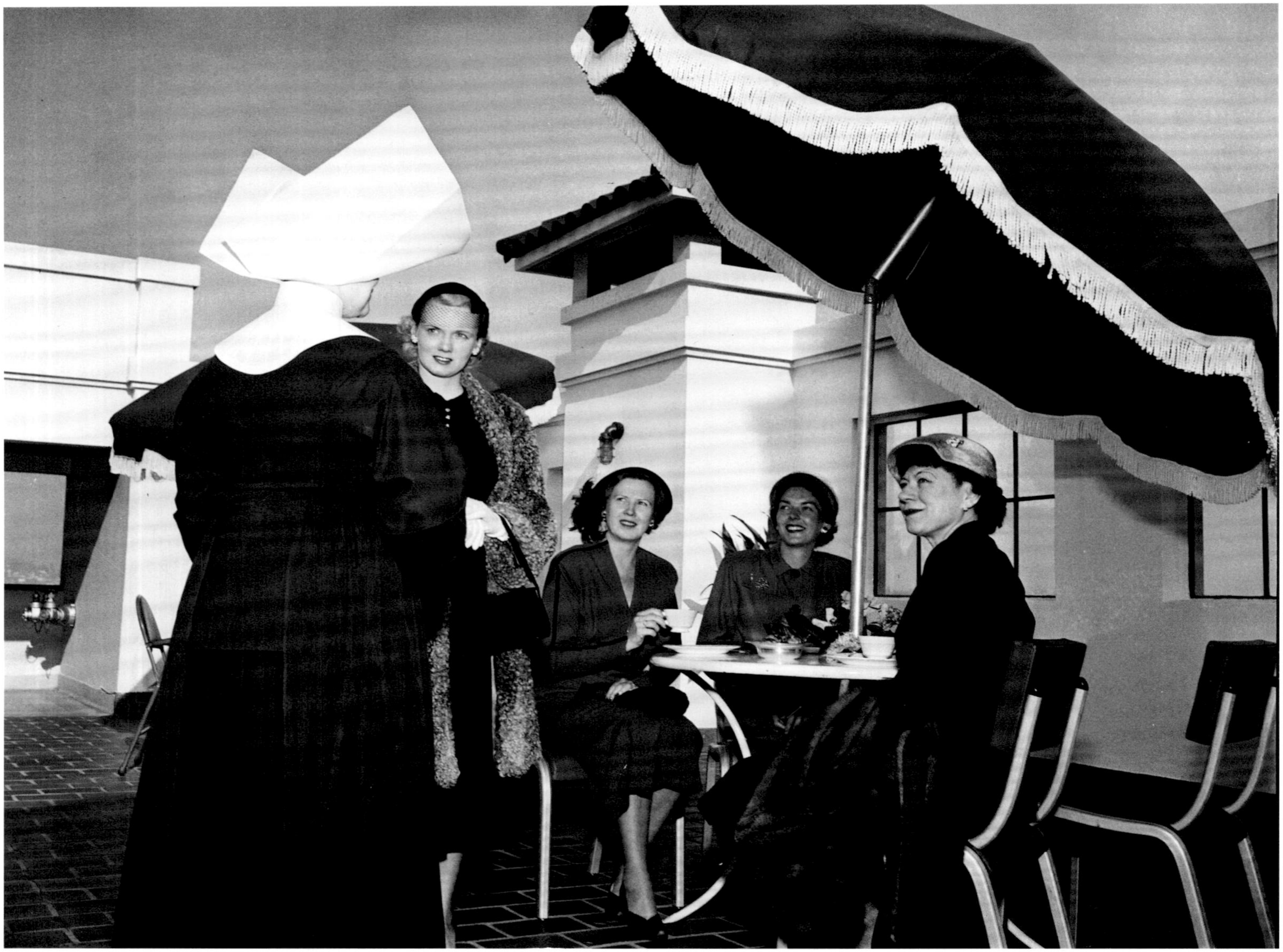

A nun of the Roman Catholic religious order the Daughters of Charity, founded by Saint Vincent de Paul, meets with the Saint Vincent Hospital Women's Auxiliary on November 15, 1951. Her unique headpiece is a cornette that was especially popular in the fifteenth to seventeenth centuries. It is a type of wimple or medieval head garment consisting of a large starched piece of white cloth folded upwards to create the resemblance of horns (in French "cornes").

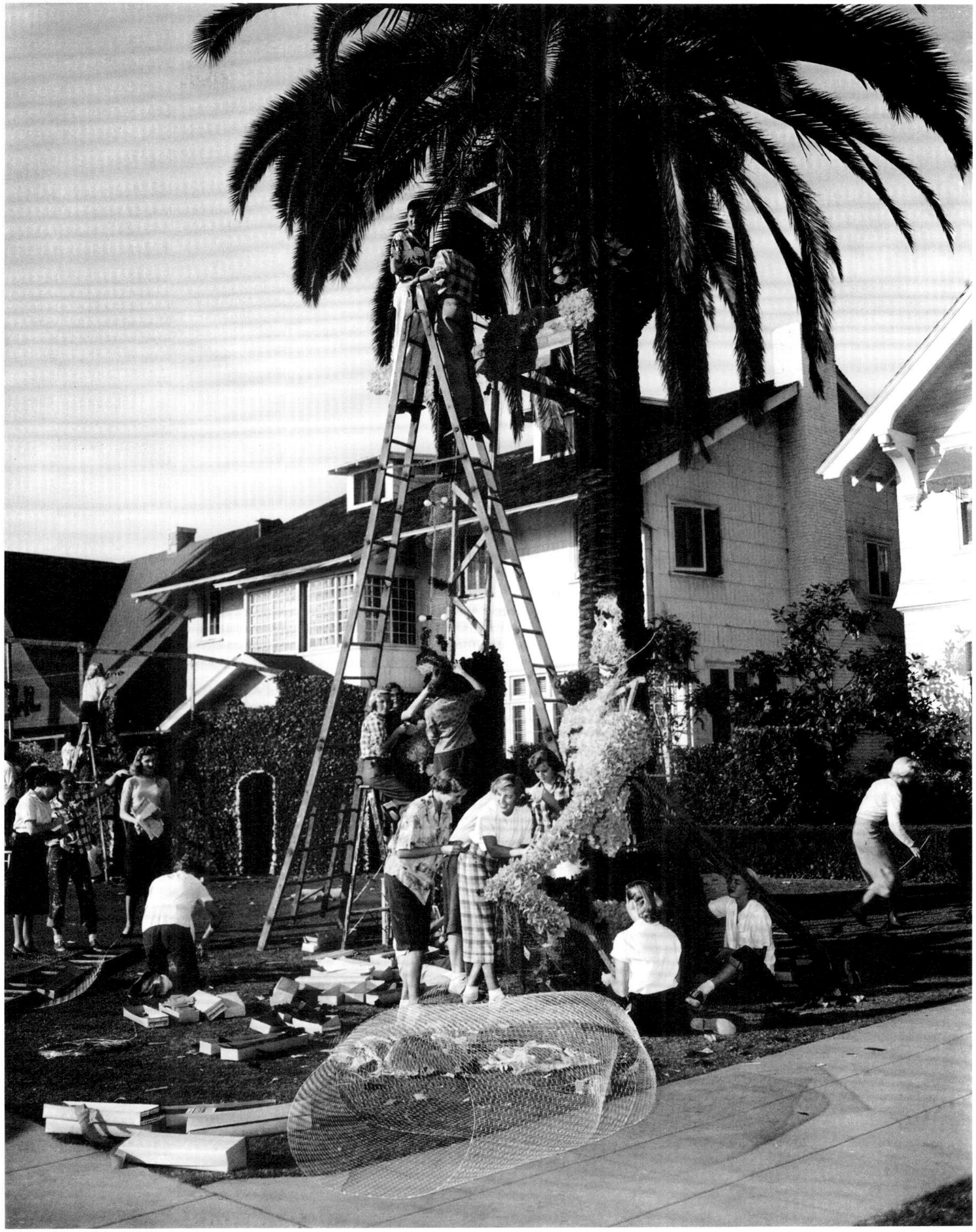

University of Southern California students work on their homecoming float in 1951. USC, a private school, is the main rival of UCLA. The winner of the annual USC-UCLA football contest keeps a Victory Bell trophy for the next year and paints it the school's color: "true blue" for UCLA, or "cardinal red" for USC. The Victory Bell is a 295-pound brass bell that originally was affixed to a Southern Pacific railroad locomotive.

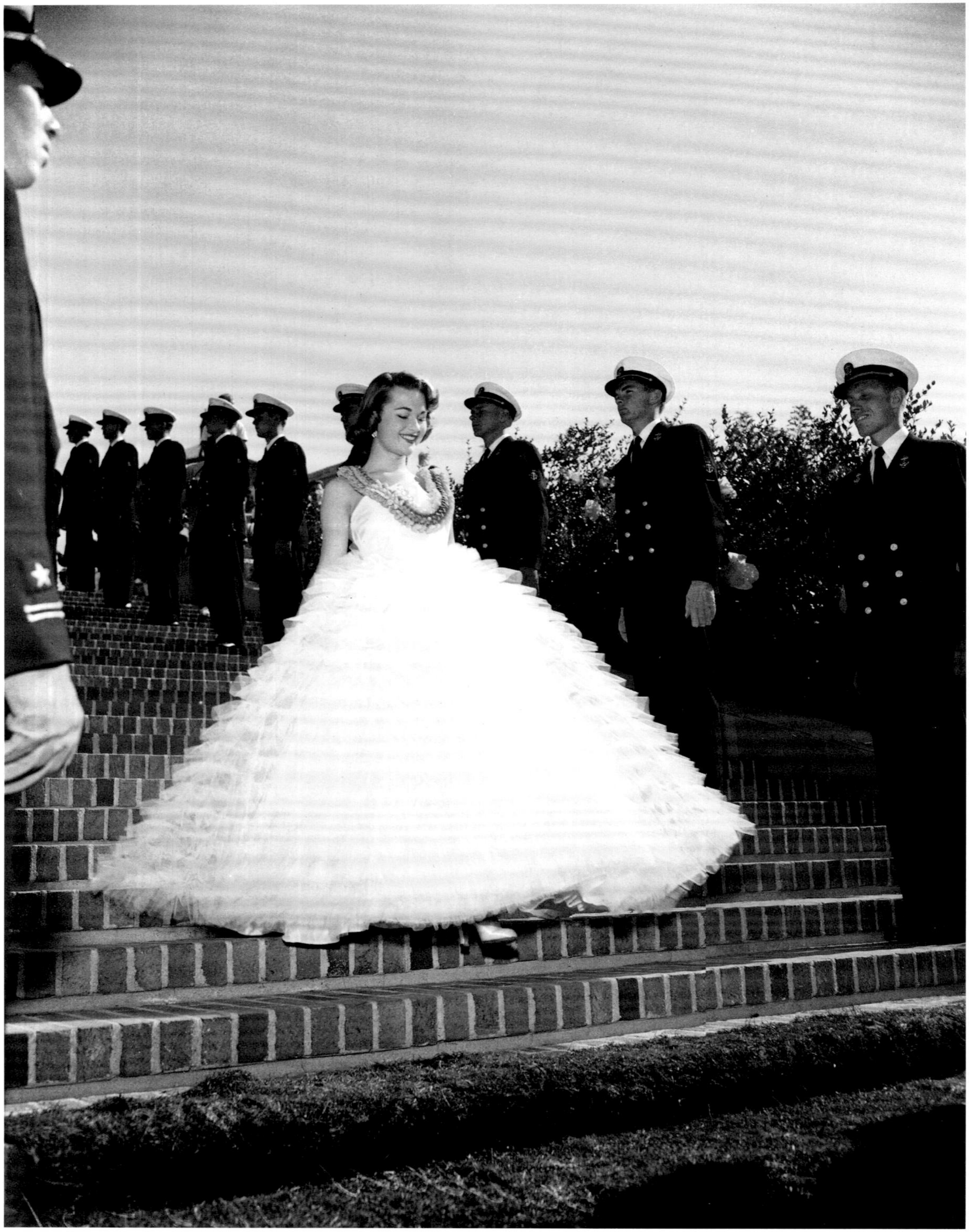

At the 1951 celebration, UCLA Homecoming Queen Evalyne Miller is surrounded by men in uniform. Homecoming is an annual American tradition where people, towns, high schools, and colleges come together, usually in late September or October, to welcome back former residents and alumni. The tradition of homecoming most likely evolved from alumni football games held at colleges and universities since the late 1800s.

Thomas Fastenmyer (the suspect) and L.A. Detective Sergeant J. H. Hooper watch as an assistant helps a diver looking for a stolen jewel in Long Beach Harbor on May 25, 1951. Like Los Angeles crime novelist Raymond Chandler, author Ross Macdonald (1915–1983) wrote about his detective hero's escapades in a city of sprawling suburbs, two-car garages, and private beach clubs. Macdonald's itinerant characters change worlds and their identities simply by driving from one suburb to another.

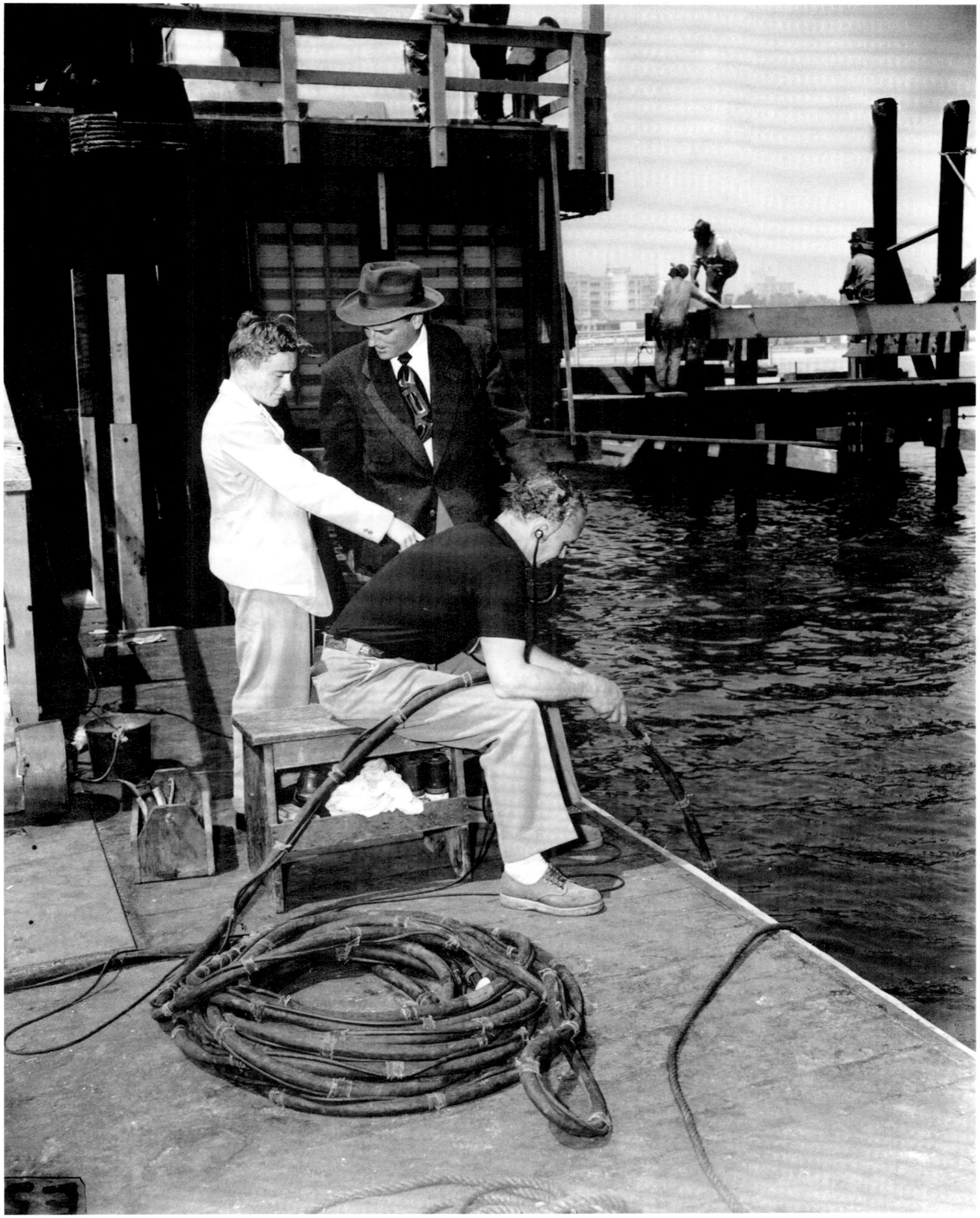

Two officers subdue a young bull that was on the loose in West Los Angeles, May 26, 1951. There is a stereotype of L.A. as an artificial landscape, but it actually has many natural areas, including Griffith Park, just northwest of downtown. The park's 4,210 acres include wildlife, hiking trails, the Griffith Observatory, the Los Angeles Zoo, and more.

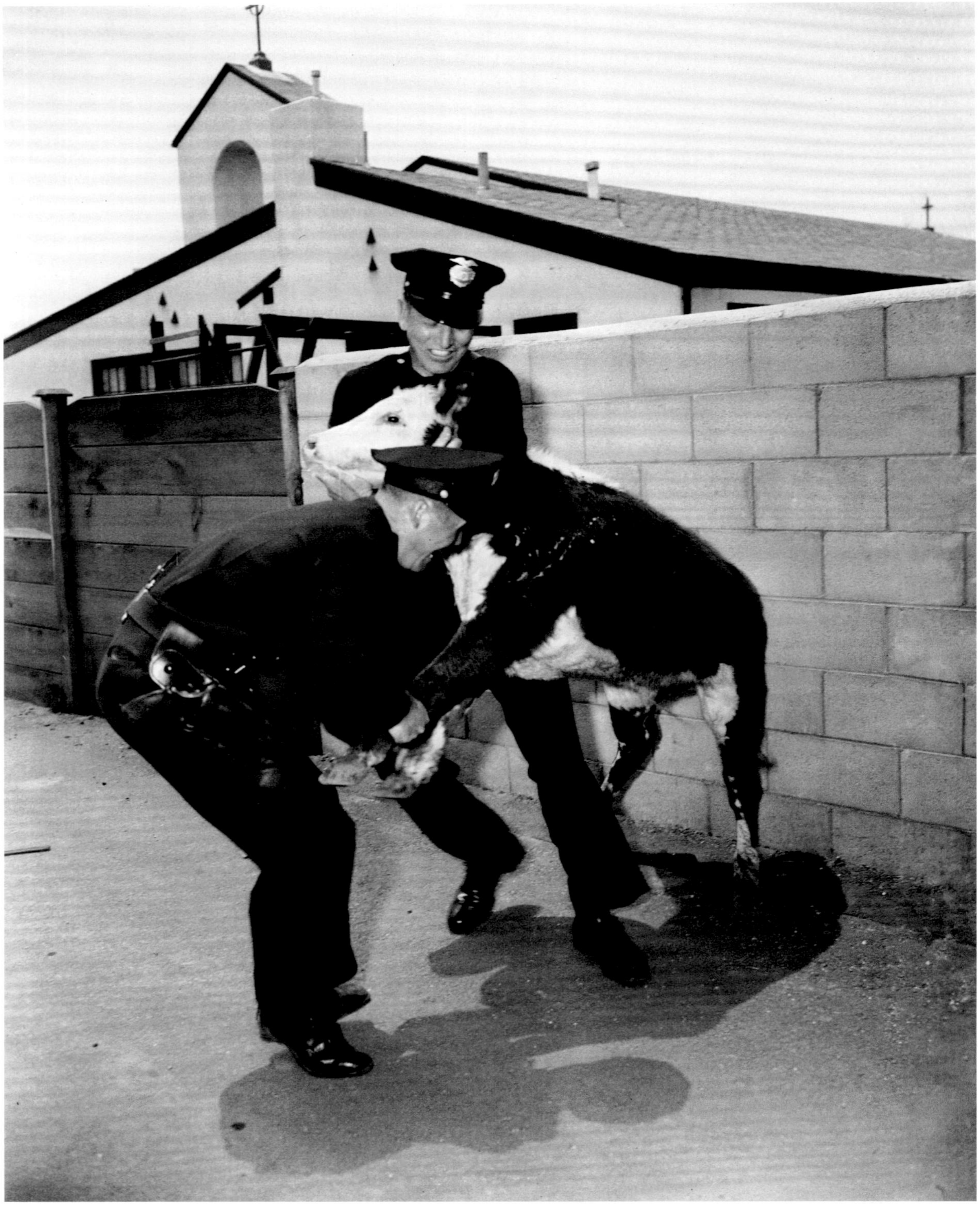

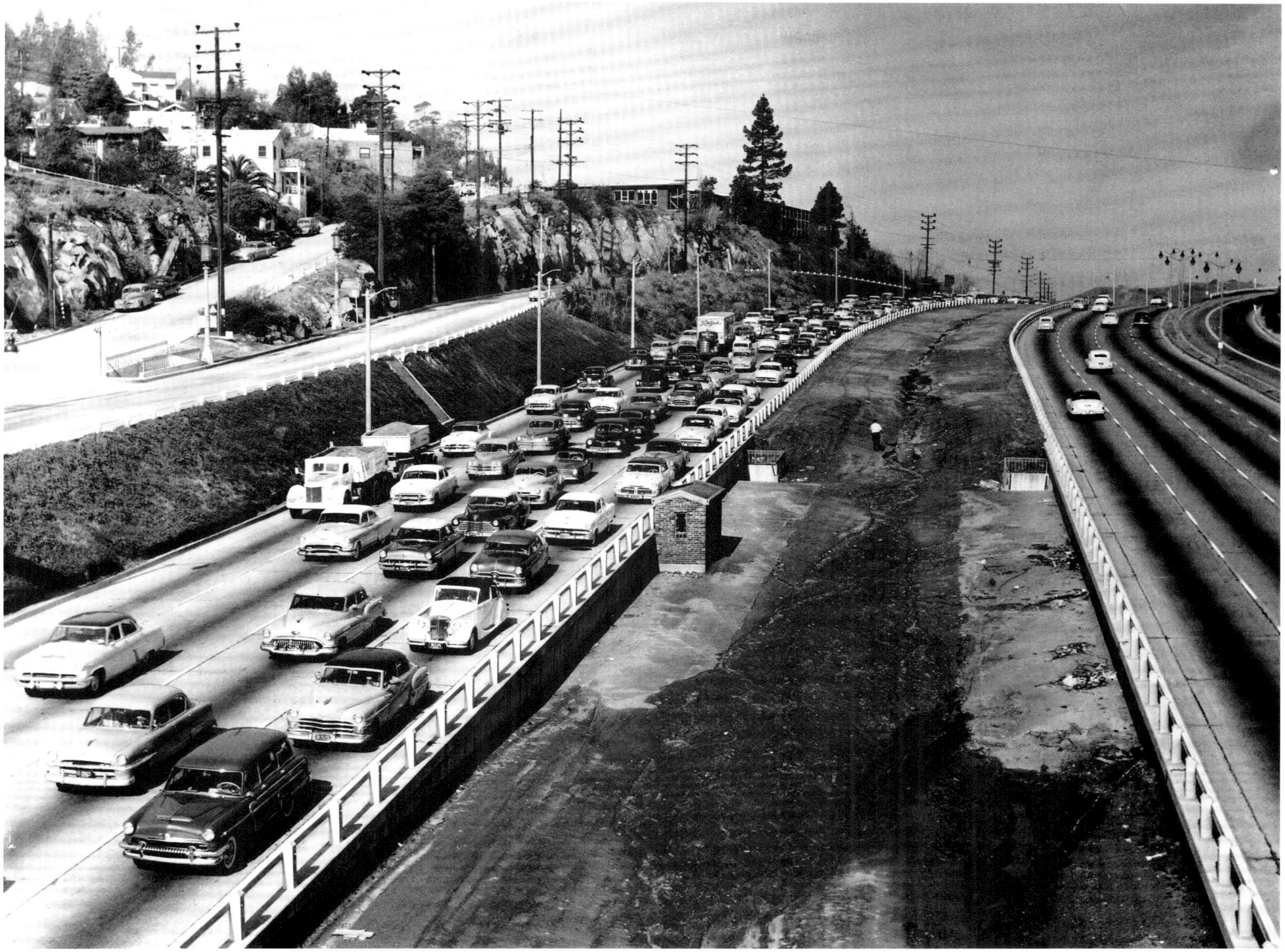

Much as today, an accident could back up traffic on the freeways quickly in1955, as in this view north from the Mulholland Drive bridge. The freeways may be a trademark of Los Angeles, but there are actually fewer lane-miles per capita than most large metropolitan areas. In 1999, L.A. had 0.419 lane-miles per 1,000 people, only slightly more than New York City and fewer than Boston or the San Francisco Bay Area. Angelenos idiomatically refer to their freeways with the definite article, such as "the 10" instead of I-10 or simply 10.

Elizabeth Rosemond Taylor (1932–) kisses Captain Robert N. McFarland, commander of the recently recommissioned heavy cruiser *Los Angeles*. Twice the winner of an Academy Award, Taylor is an English American actress known for her acting skills as well as for her Hollywood lifestyle of many marriages. She is considered one of the great celebrities of Hollywood history. The American Film Institute named Taylor seventh among female stars on its "100 Years . . . 100 Stars" list.

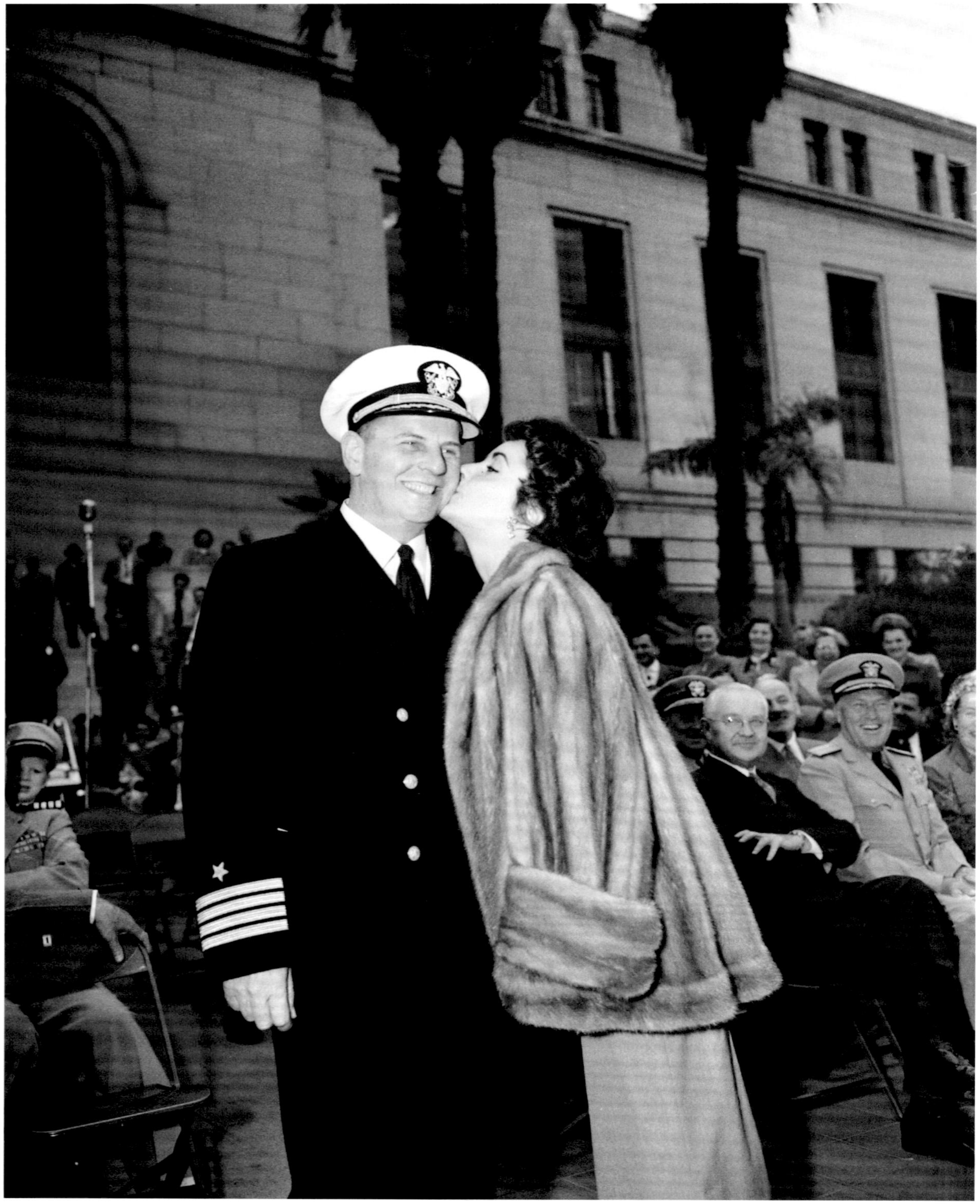

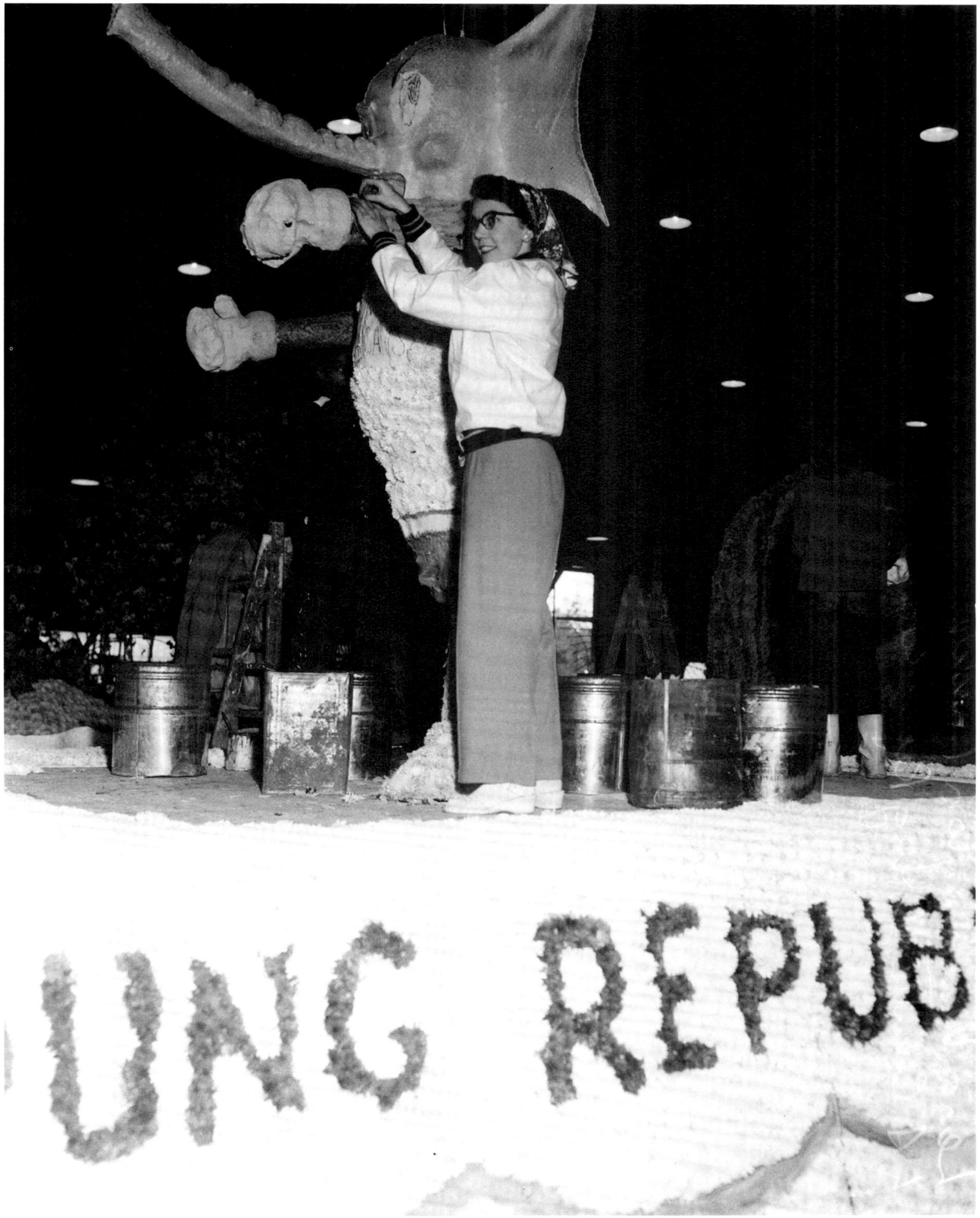

Young Republicans prepare their float for the January 1, 1952, Rose Parade. To ring in the New Year, Pasadena began hosting the Rose Parade in 1890. The first Rose Bowl football game was played in 1902. Called "the granddaddy of them all" by the venerable sportscaster Keith Jackson (1928–), the Rose Bowl is the oldest of the bowl games.

Sailor James Hovey almost misses his ship the *Los Angeles*, leaving the namesake city on April 16, 1951. The third Navy warship to carry the name *Los Angeles* (CA-135) was a Baltimore-class heavy cruiser, commissioned too late to see combat in World War II. The ship fought as part of the American response to communist aggression against the Republic of South Korea after the North Korean Army invaded ten months prior to this photo.

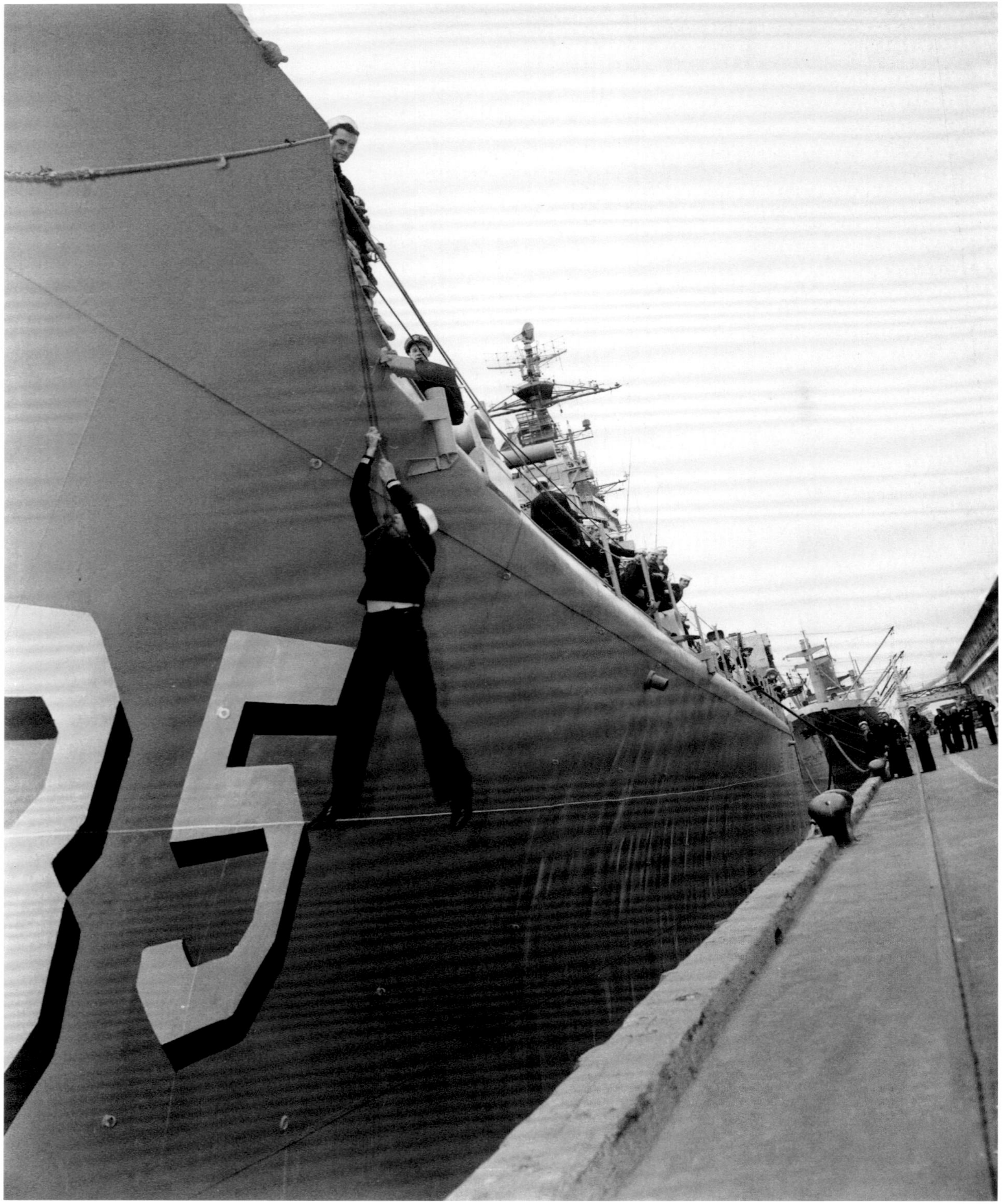

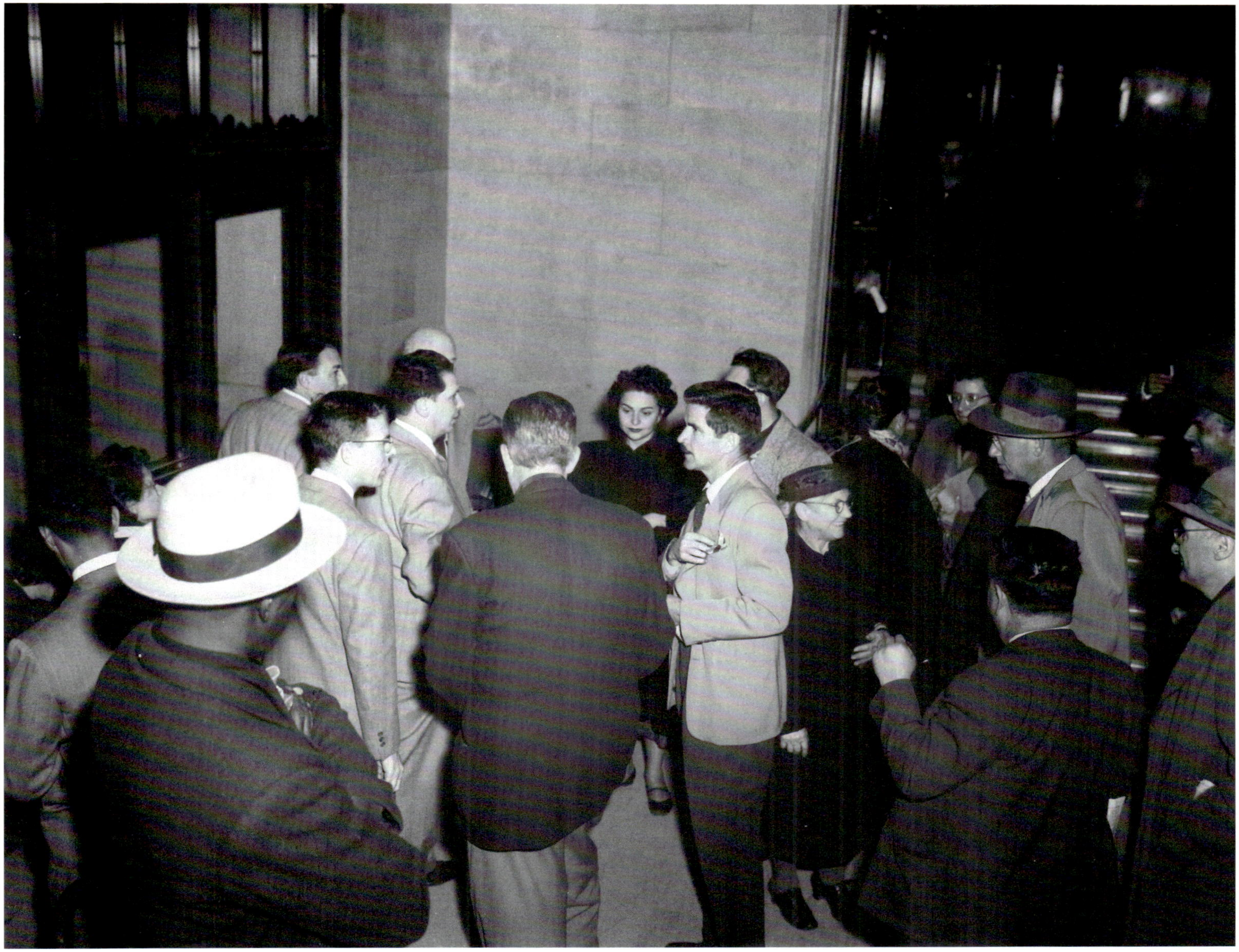

People wait at the downtown Federal Building for the December 1951 release of Communist Party members who were jailed for violating the Smith Act that made it illegal to advocate the overthrow of any United States government by force or violence. In the 1950s, Senator Joseph Raymond McCarthy (1908–1957) became infamous for making claims that there were large numbers of communists and Soviet spies and sympathizers inside the federal government and elsewhere. The term "McCarthyism" was coined to describe demagogic, reckless, and unsubstantiated accusations.

A public swimming pool of the Playground and Recreation Department in Compton. Los Angeles is not usually noted for such normal activities as diving at a public pool, but instead has been referred to as "La-La-Land," an expression that pokes fun at the supposed eccentricities of the city's residents.

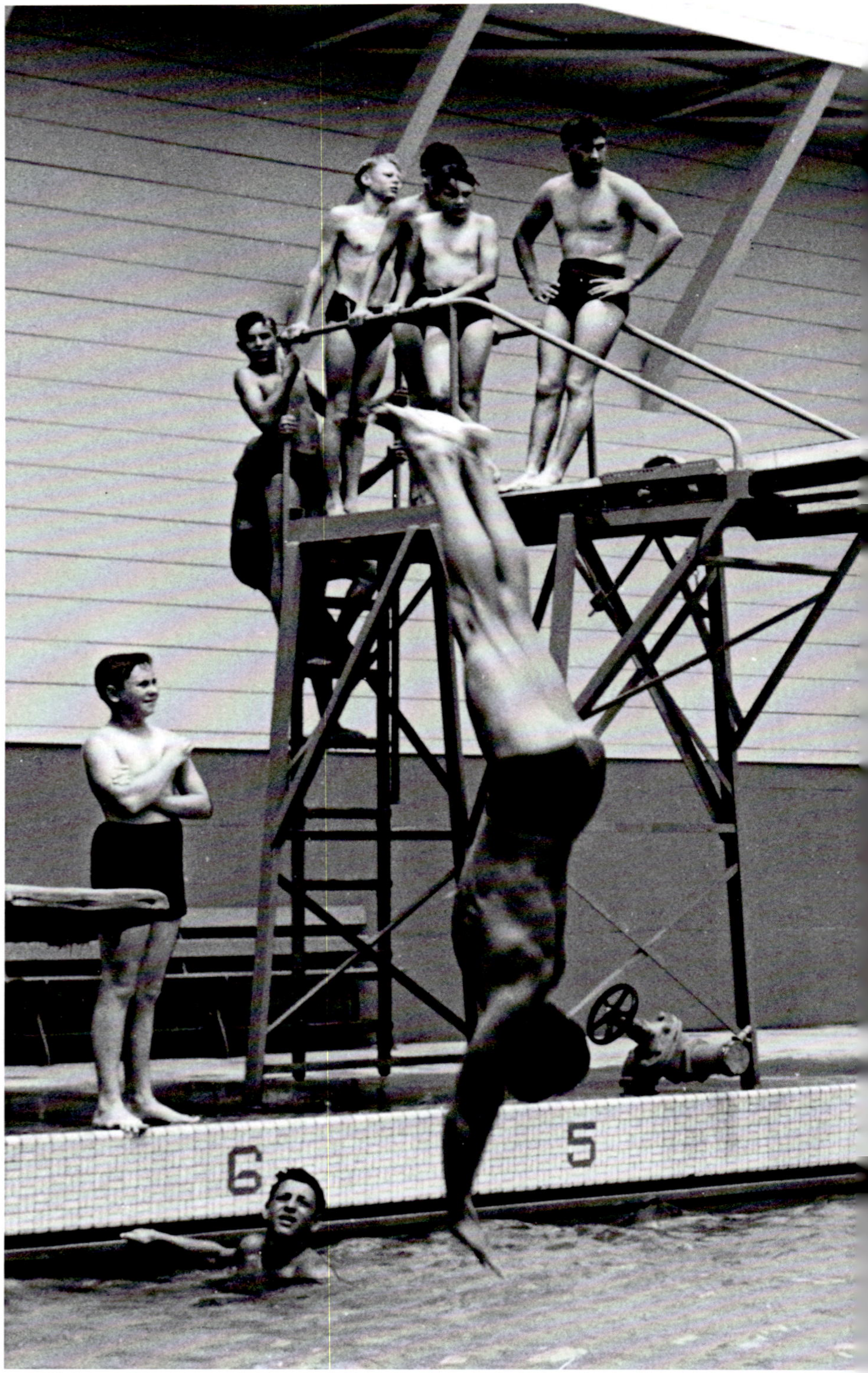

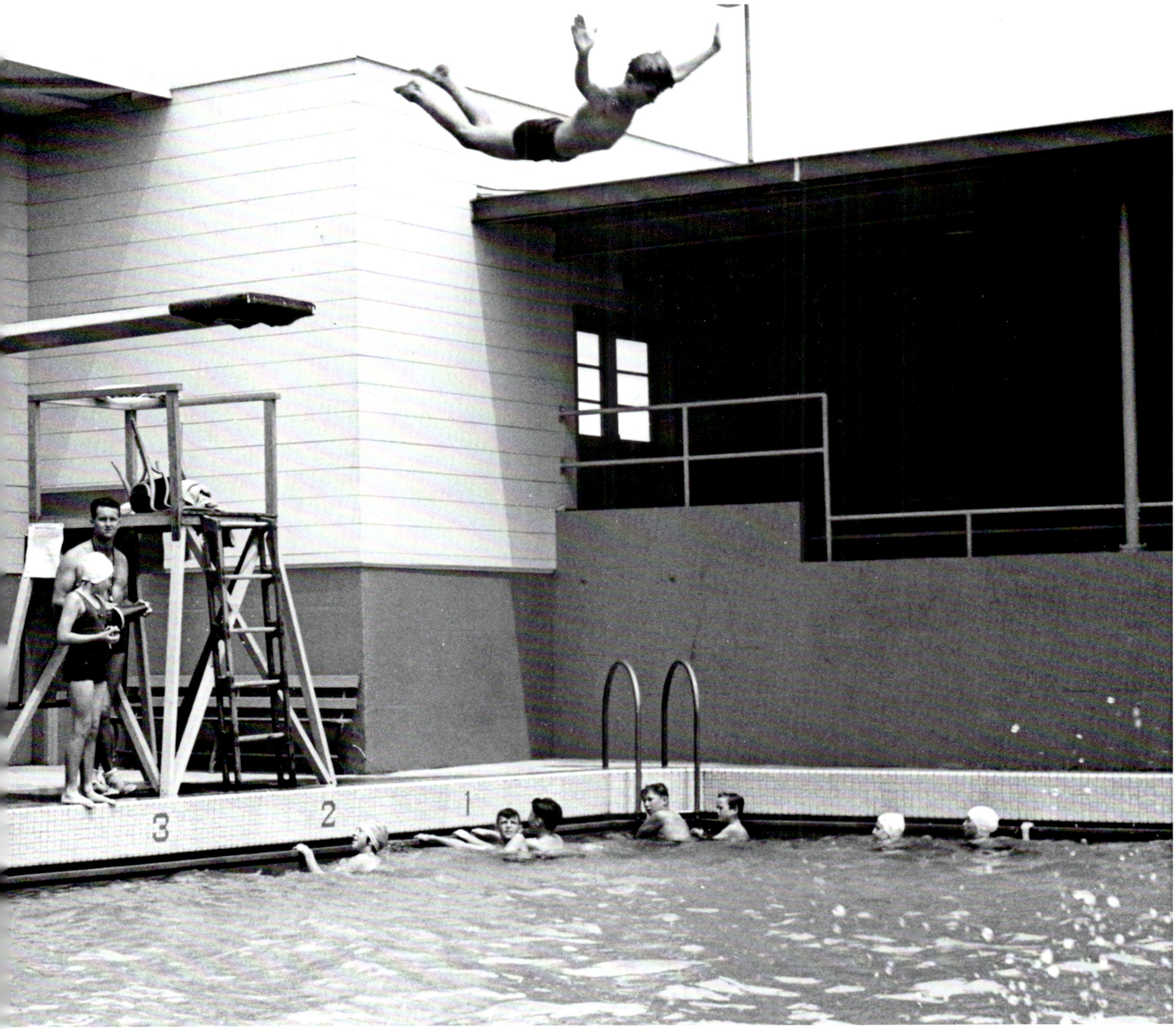
3
2
1

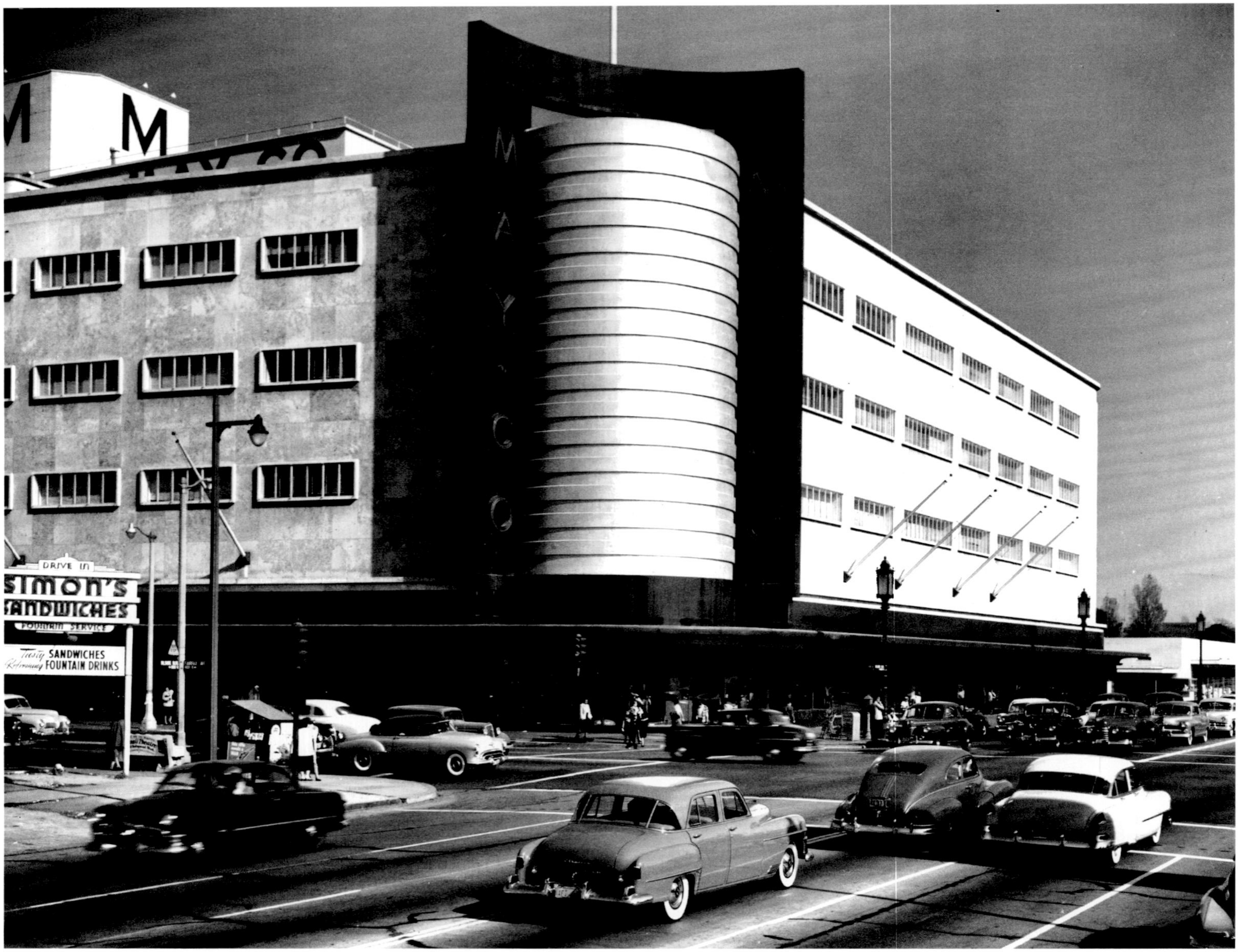

The May Company department store, seen here in 1956, was part of the Miracle Mile, the name given to the "super-modern" retail and service establishments along Wilshire Boulevard. In the early 1920s, Wilshire west of Western Avenue was an unpaved farm road. Developer A. W. Ross developed Wilshire as a car-oriented shopping district to compete with downtown Los Angeles. It was named Miracle Mile for its unprecedented and unlikely commercial success.

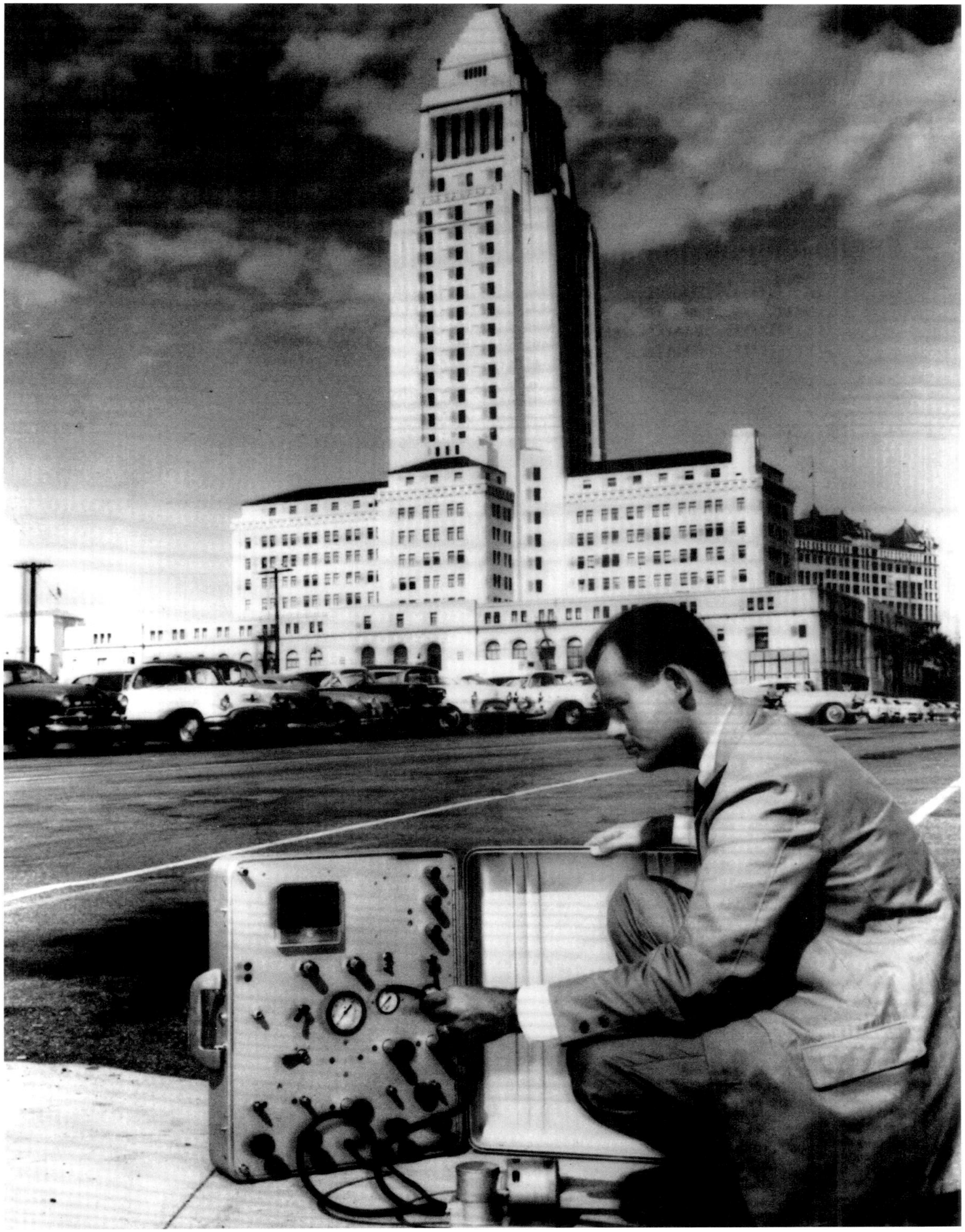

In October 1954, heavy smog shut down schools and industry in Los Angeles for most of the month. Historically, the word "smog" meant a blend of smoke and fog, but it became synonymous with automobile-exhaust air pollution in L.A. Here, engineer Newell Claudy measures carbon impurities in the L.A. atmosphere of 1959. Los Angeles City Hall is in the background.

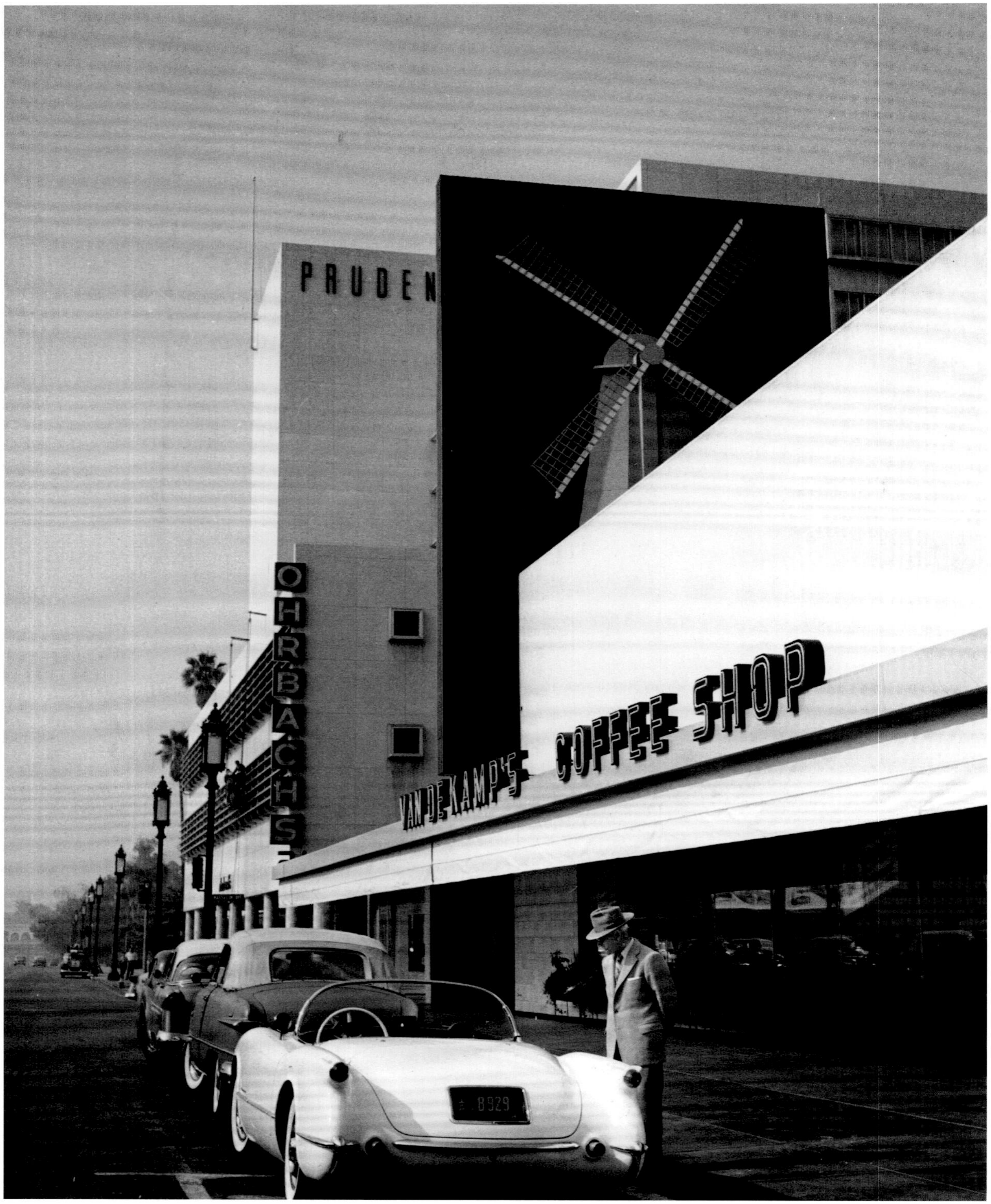

Parked in the foreground outside the Van De Kamp Coffee Shop, down the block from the Prudential Insurance Building, on Wilshire Boulevard in Hollywood is a Chevrolet Corvette, the first all-American sports car, whose initial model ran from 1953 to 1962. The scene is 1956, but this is a pre-1956 Corvette with the early body design.

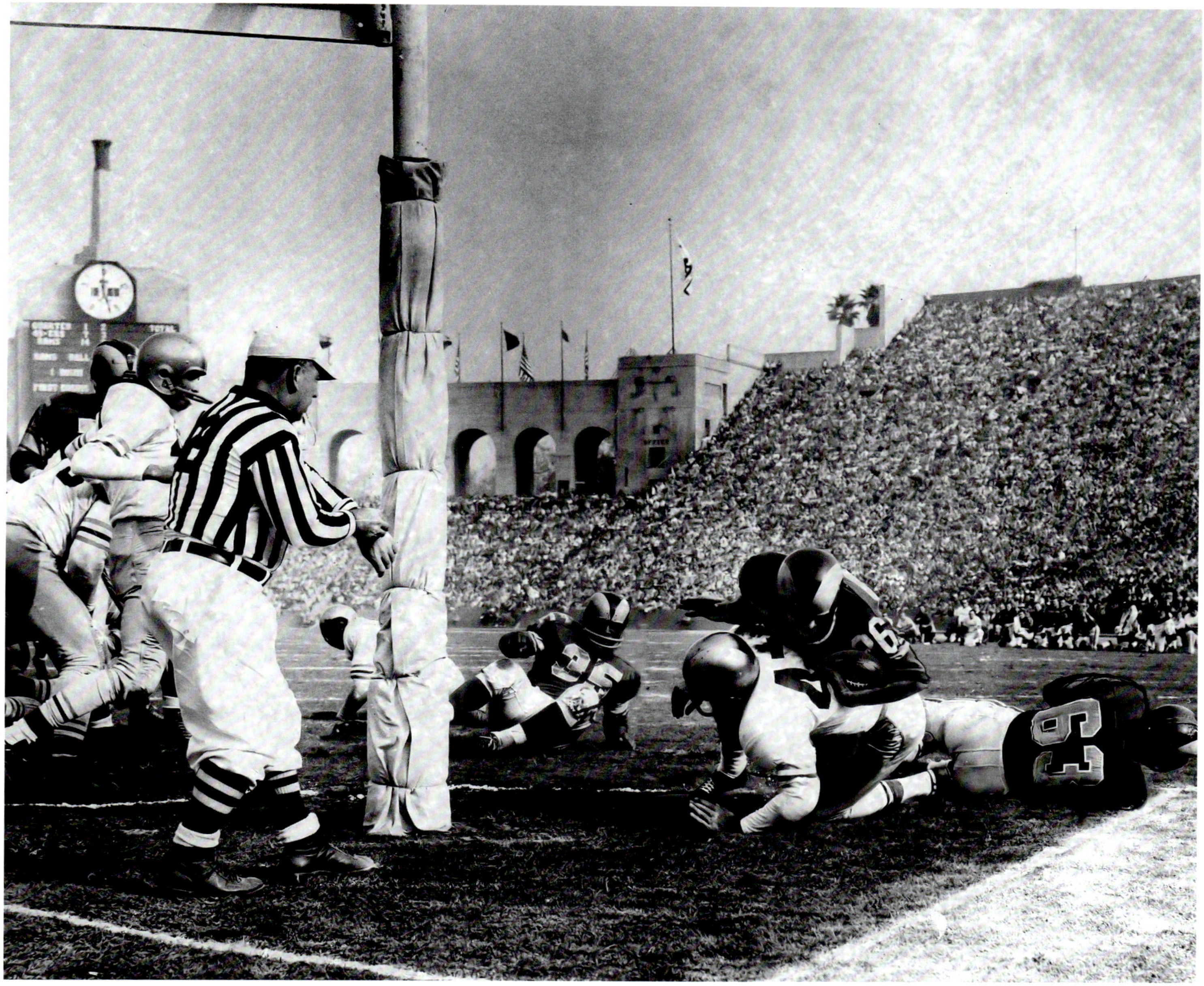

The Cleveland Rams moved to Los Angeles in 1946. This game between the Rams and the San Francisco 49ers was played on November 10, 1957, in Los Angeles Coliseum before 102,368 fans, the largest crowd in National Football League history until 1994. Jon Arnett is shown scoring a touchdown in the Rams victory, but San Francisco won the conference championship that year.

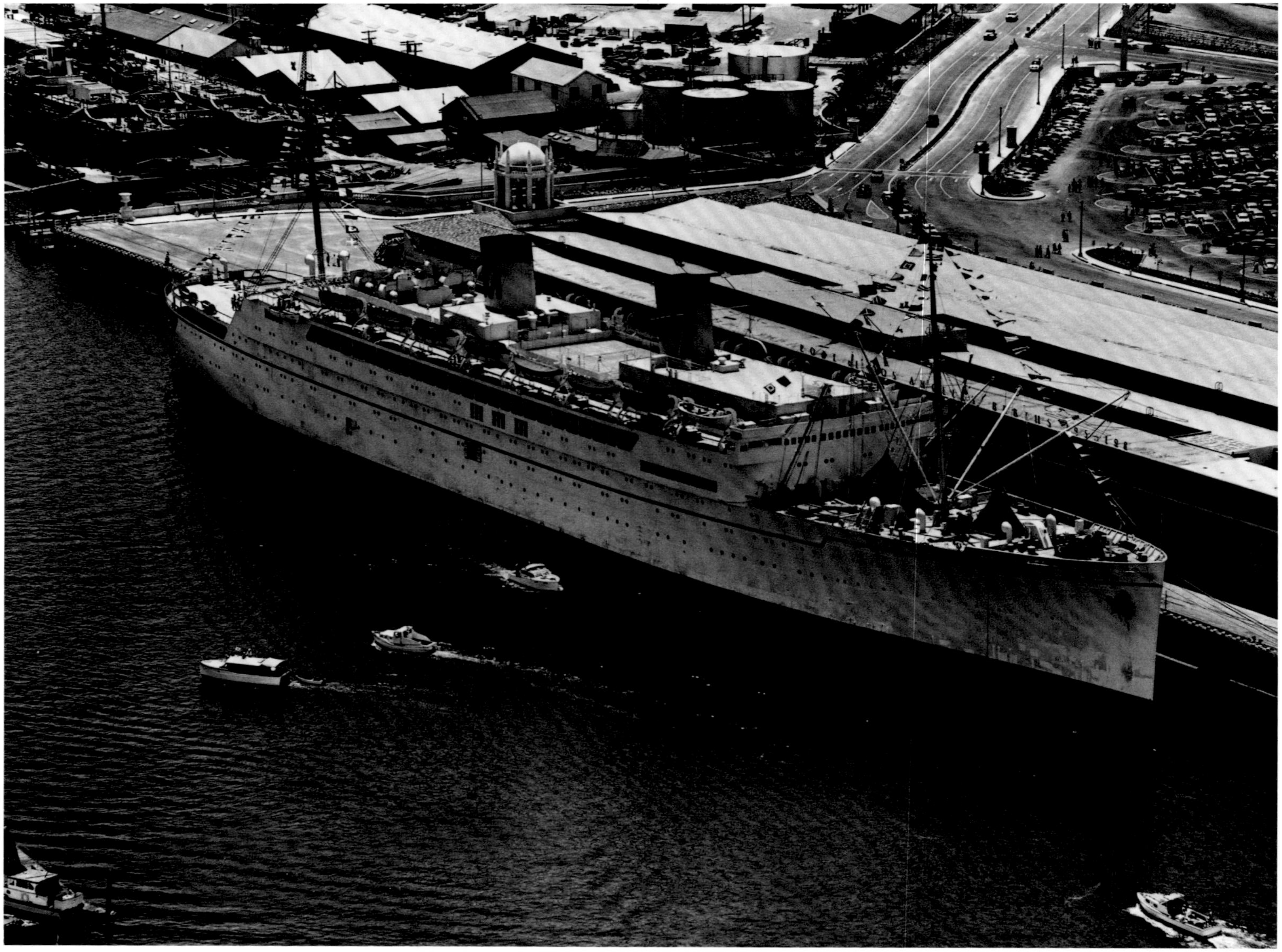

The passenger ship *Lurline* rests alongside the 70-foot wharf of the 48-acre terminal assigned to Matson Navigation Company during the 1950s. The *Lurline* was christened in 1931 and sailed the San Francisco, Honolulu, and Sydney, Australia, route. During World War II, the *Lurline* carried thousands of troops. After the war, and until 1970, the *Lurline* returned to passenger service as one of the four Matson luxury liners called "white ships" because of their color.

Social Unrest, Social Change

(1960–1969)

In 1960, Los Angeles was the third largest city in the United States. By 1964, California surpassed New York to become the most populous state. One reason for this may be that more immigrants settle in California than in any other state—more than one-third of the nation's total in 1994.

The 1960s were an incredibly tumultuous decade in America. In Los Angeles, as in other major cities, long-unresolved racial problems erupted in the 1960s and 1970s. Los Angeles was wracked by the Watts riots in 1965, the high-school walkout by Chicano students in 1968, and the 1970 Chicano moratorium.

Television prices continued to drop, and more homes had TV sets. Millions of Americans watched as the first men walked on the Moon in 1969. Television also brought news of the assassinations of President John F. Kennedy, his brother Robert, and civil rights leader Martin Luther King Jr.; scenes of the violence at the Democratic Convention in 1968; and the daily reports of casualties from the Vietnam War.

Radio was no longer the entertainment medium it was in the 1930s and 1940s, but radio ownership grew from 80 million in 1949 to 228 million during the 1960s. The motion picture studio system declined further in this decade, and the following decades saw changes in the production and style of film.

As of 2008, Los Angeles is the most populous county in the United States. Los Angeles was built by a variety of intriguing people who had big dreams for the "City of Angels." Unfortunately, most of these big dreams simply succeeded in making Los Angeles big. If L.A. is sometimes found lacking in comparison to other major American cities, Angelenos can take comfort in a metropolis that is generally bathed in sunshine, constantly in transition, and always interesting.

At a Biltmore Hotel reception on July 10, 1960, Senator Lyndon B. Johnson, with his wife beside him, campaigns for the Democratic nomination for president. The Democratic Convention was held in Los Angeles at the L.A. Memorial Sports Arena. Senator John F. Kennedy won the presidential nomination and asked Johnson to be his running mate, despite clashes between them during the primary elections. Kennedy needed Johnson's political strength in the South.

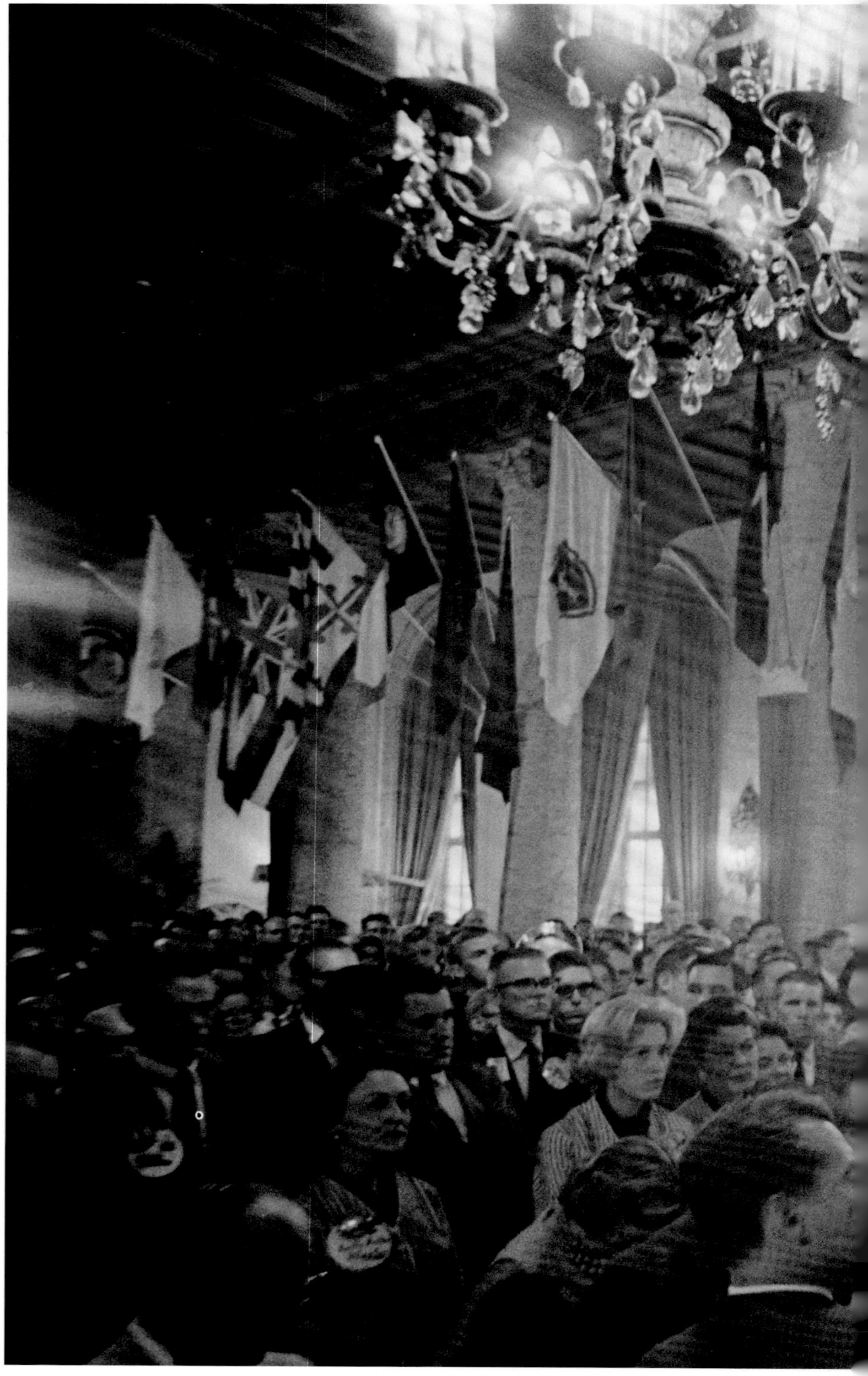

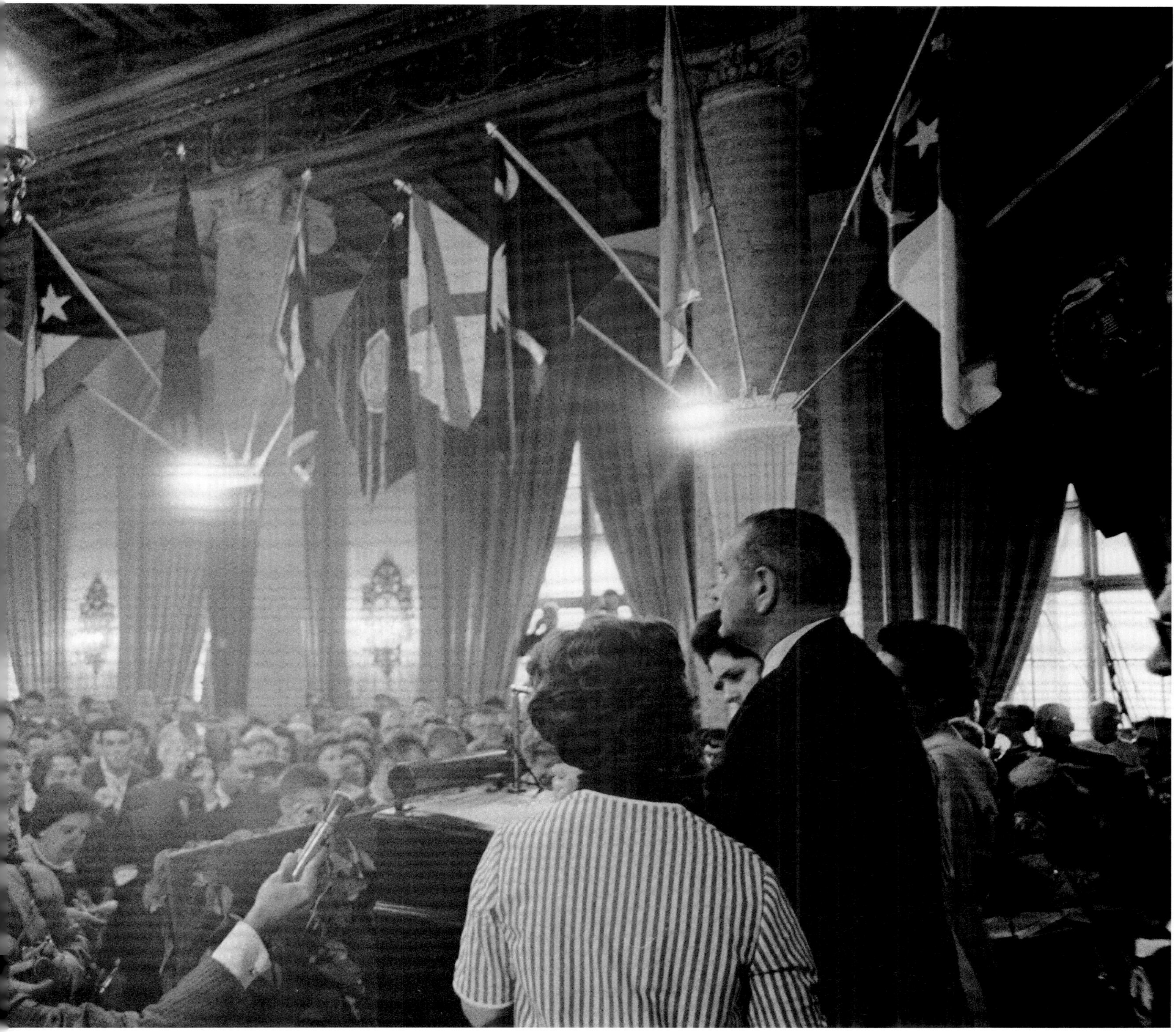

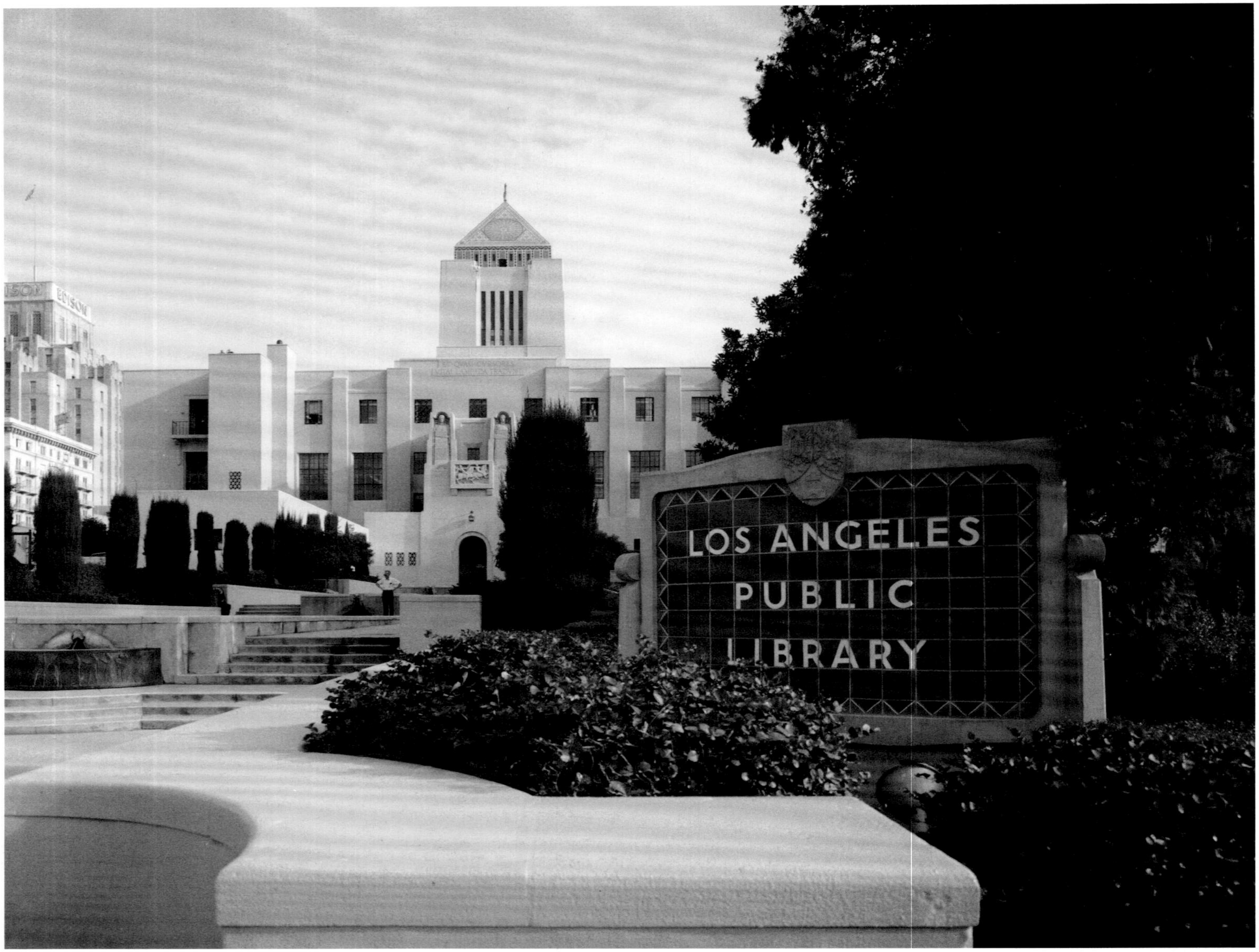

The Los Angeles Public Library, initially constructed in 1926, is a downtown landmark. In 2008 it is the third largest public library in the United States in terms of book and periodical holdings.

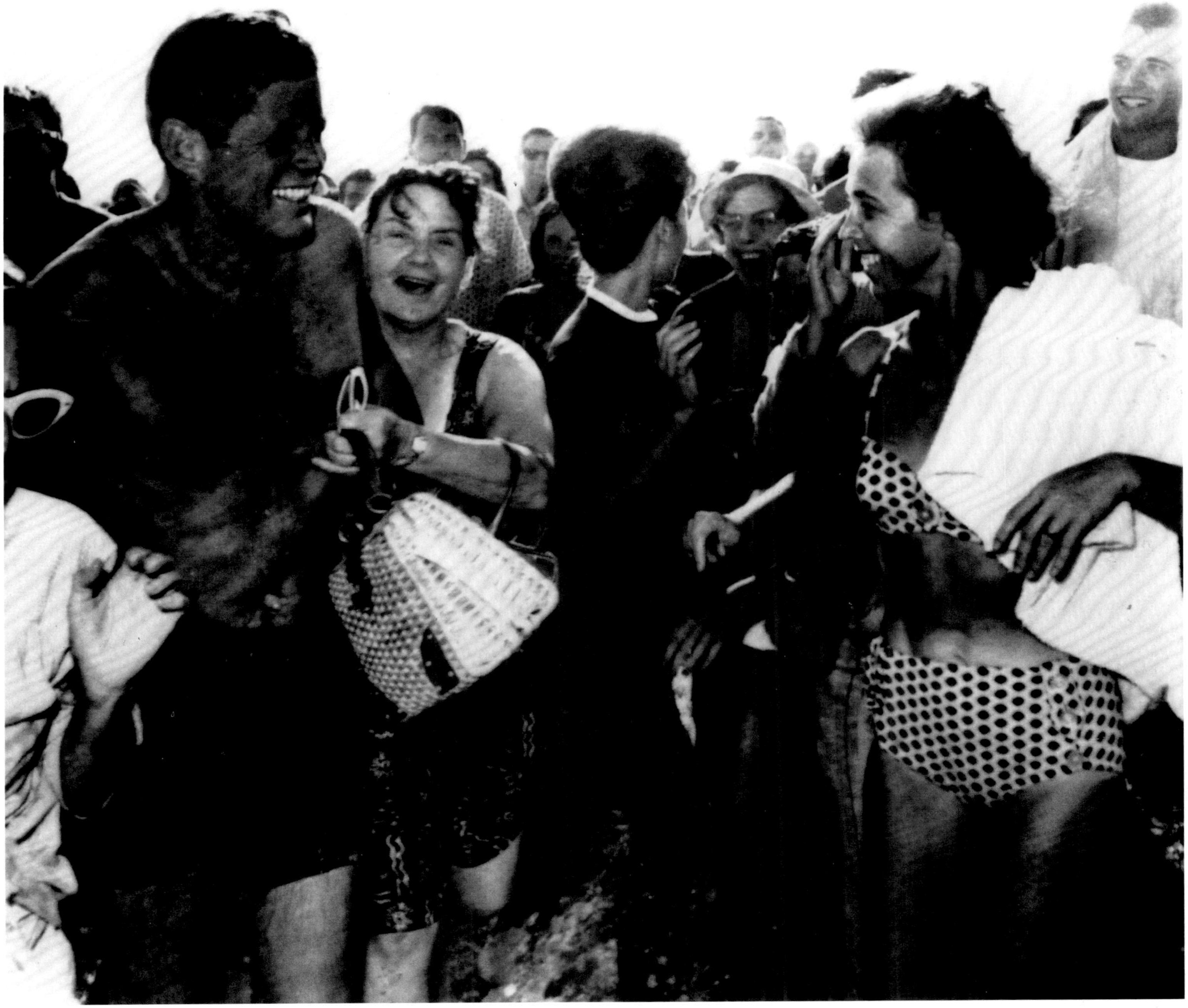

A splashing crowd surrounds President John F. Kennedy as he leaves the water for the beach behind the Santa Monica home of actor Peter Lawford, August 19, 1962. Fifteen months later the president was assassinated in Dallas, Texas. Kennedy's most famous line may be from his inaugural address, when he asked Americans to "Ask not what your country can do for you; ask what you can do for your country."

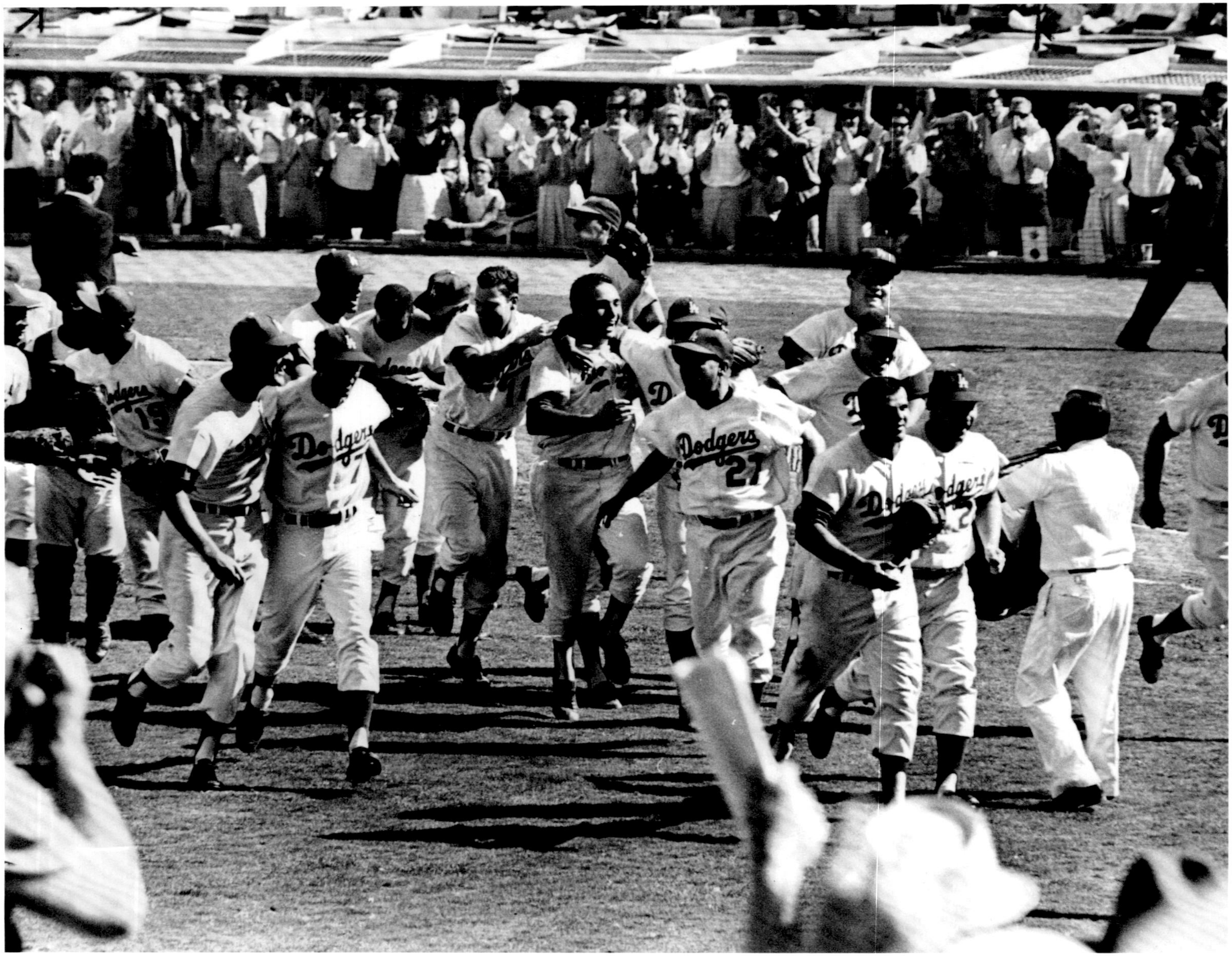

The Los Angeles Dodgers celebrate their sweep over the defending champion New York Yankees in the 1963 World Series. Pitcher Sandy Koufax (with a teammate's arm around his neck) was the hero of this game. Koufax (1935–), one of Major League Baseball's greatest left-handed pitchers, is also notable as one of the outstanding Jewish athletes of his era.

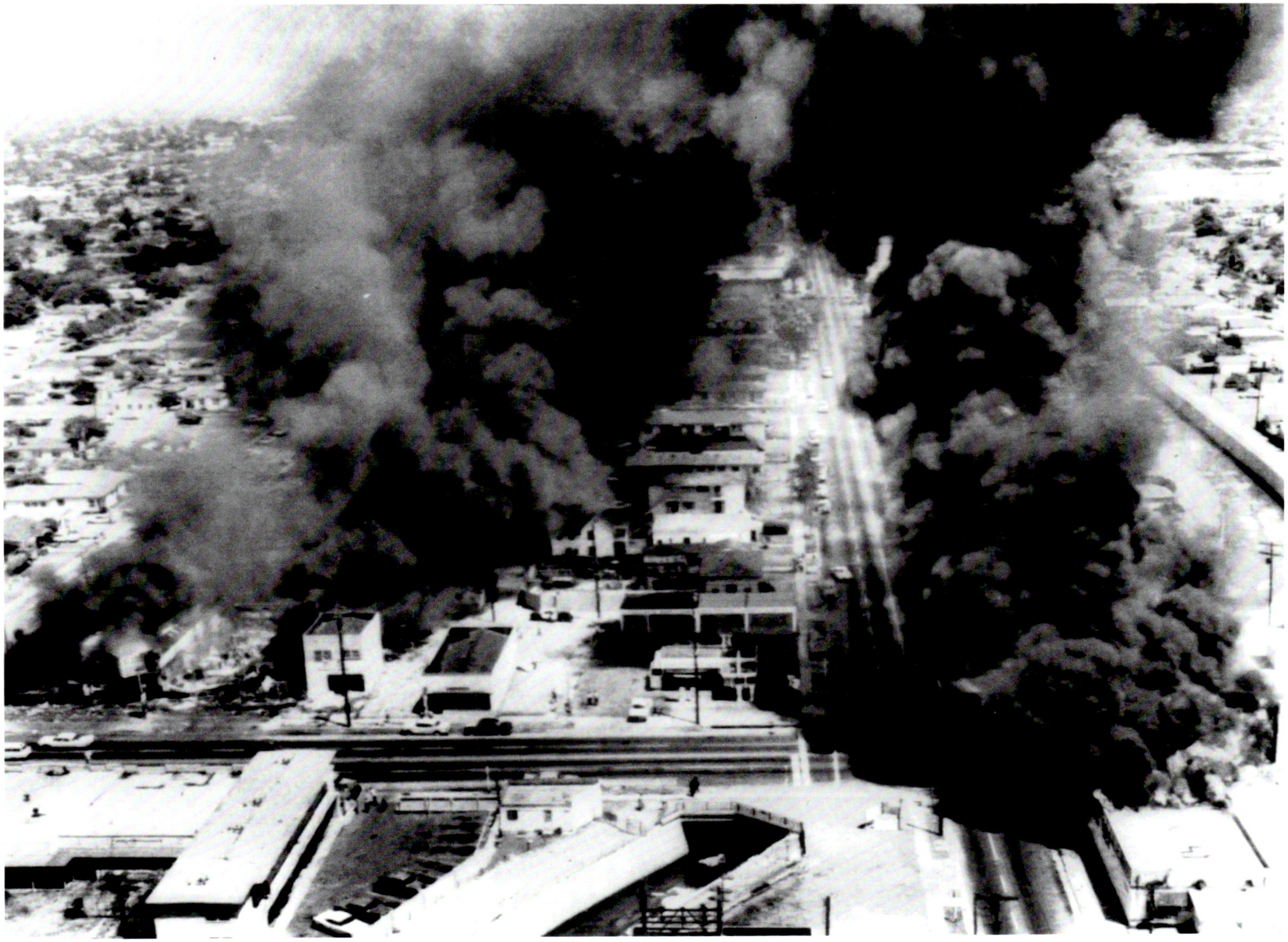

Buildings burn on Avalon Boulevard during the six days of looting and rioting in the Watts section of Los Angeles in August 1965. The violence killed 34 people, injured 1,034, and caused $40 million in damages. Chester Himes (1909–1984), a novelist who wrote *Cotton Comes to Harlem*, moved to Los Angeles from Missouri but found that the racism in L.A. "hurt me racially as much as any city I have ever known—much more than any city I remember in the South."

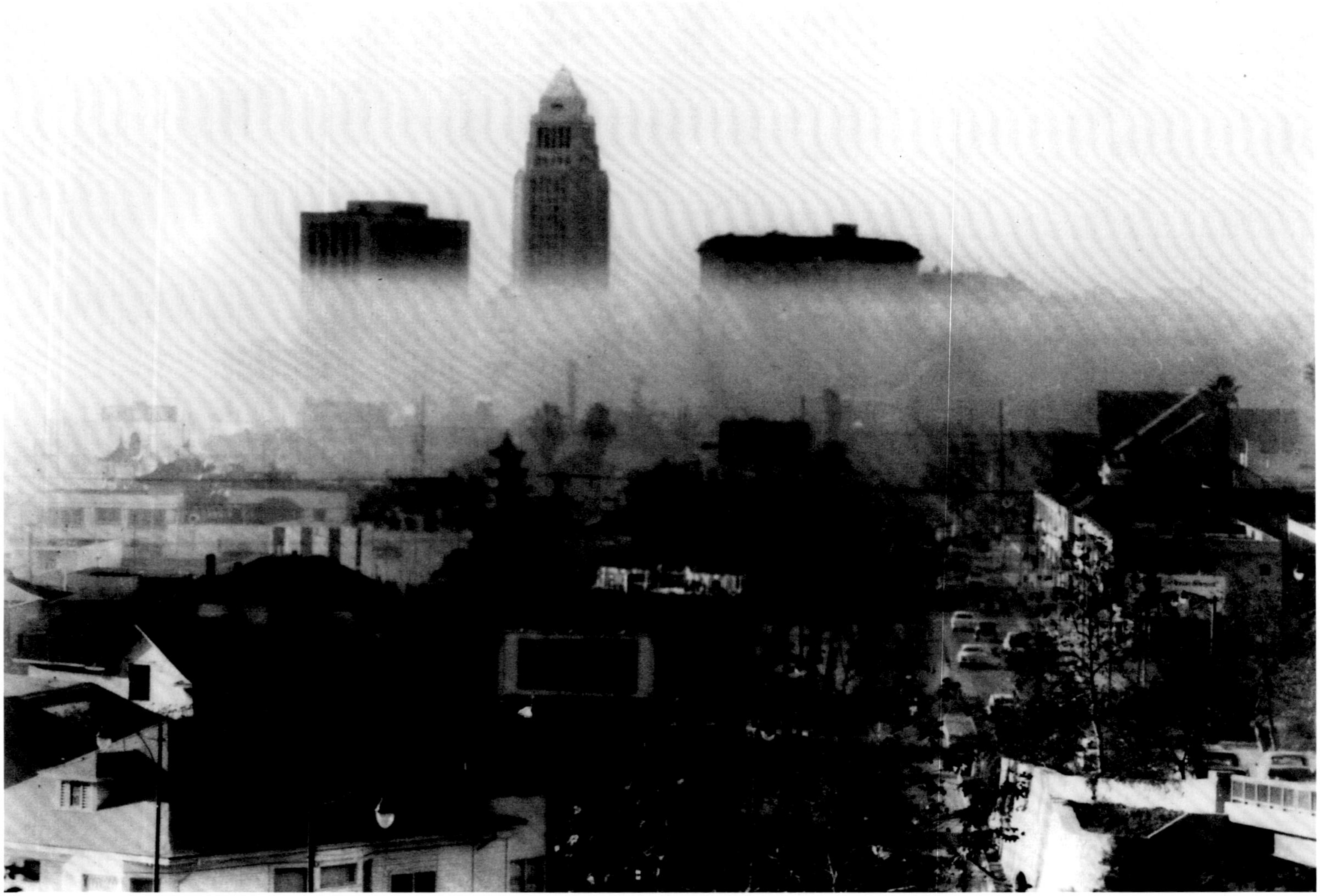

Smog engulfs downtown L.A. in 1966. For decades air pollution created beautiful sunsets in Los Angeles but also caused numerous health problems, even sudden death, for people who lived in the incessant haze from automobile exhaust. The 1950s and 1960s were the heyday of "Autopia"—a term that British architecture critic Reyner Banham (1922–1988) coined to describe L.A. in his 1971 book *Los Angeles: The Architecture of Four Ecologies.*

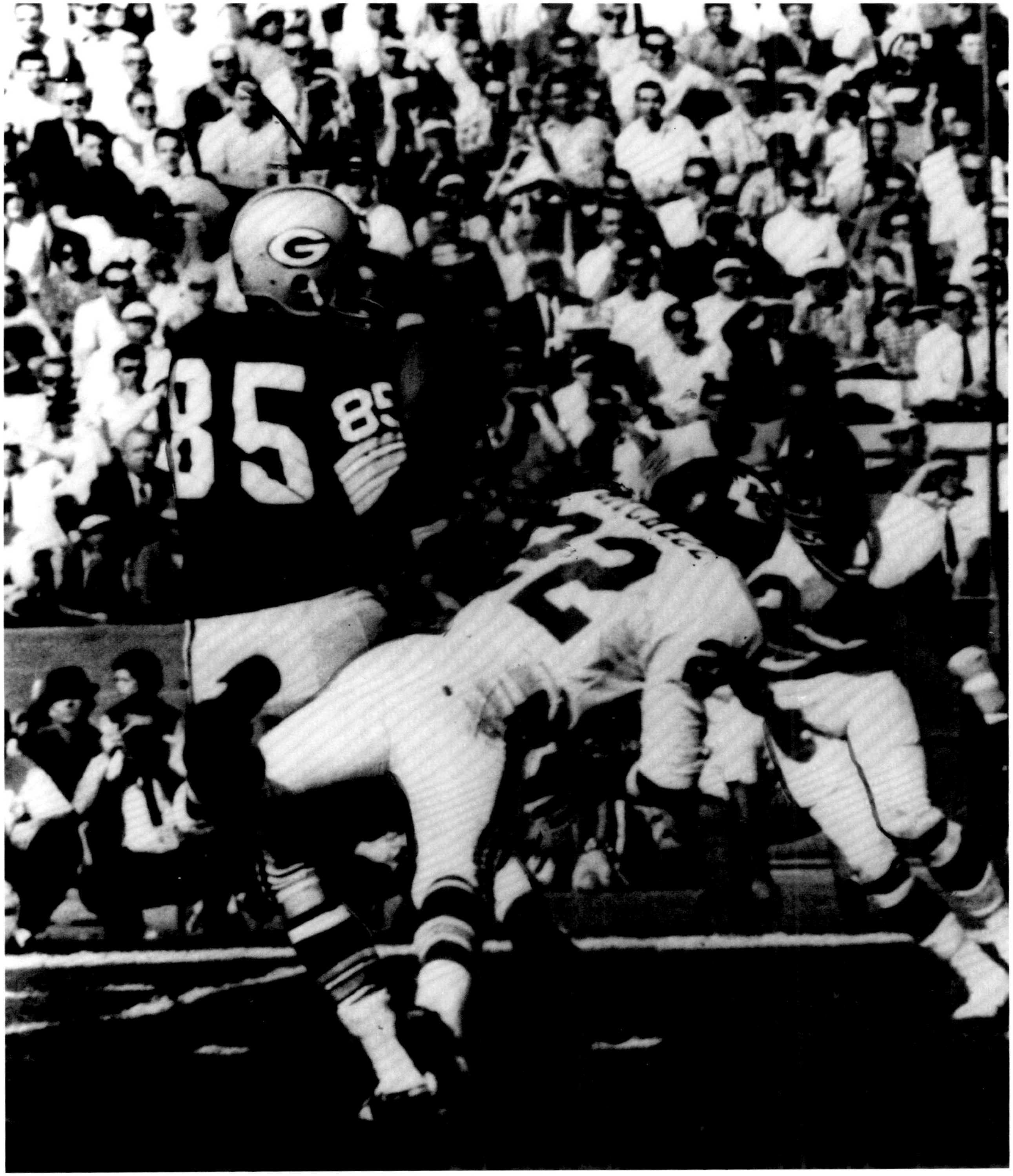

The first Super Bowl was played in Los Angeles Coliseum in 1967. The Green Bay Packers, coached by Vince Lombardi (1913–1970), defeated the Kansas City Chiefs. The Chiefs went on to win Super Bowl IV. The Super Bowl was created as part of the merger agreement between the National Football League (NFL) and its competitive rival, the American Football League (AFL). After Lombardi's death in 1970, the Super Bowl trophy was named for him.

Notes on the Photographs

These notes, listed by page number, attempt to include all aspects known of the photographs. Each of the photographs is identified by the page number, photograph's title or description, photographer and collection, archive, and call or box number when applicable. Although every attempt was made to collect all available data, in some cases complete data was unavailable due to the age and condition of some of the photographs and records.

II **Bathing Beauties**
Library of Congress
LC-USZ62-97741

VI **Fifth Street**
Library of Congress
LC-USZ62-108344

X **Automobile Course**
National Archives
950-A1

2 **Frontier Town**
National Archives
306-NT-950-X-5

3 **First Los Angeles Streetcar**
Courtesy of The Bancroft Library
University of California, Berkeley
1964.056:8-PIC
BRK00008035_24A

4 **Wolfskill Orange Grove**
Courtesy of The Bancroft Library
University of California, Berkeley
1905.06211:18-PIC
BRK00008041_24A

6 **Main and Requena Streets**
Courtesy of The Bancroft Library
University of California, Berkeley
1964.056:15-PIC
BRK00008036_24A

7 **St. Vibiana's Catholic Cathedral**
Library of Congress
HABS CAL, 19-LOSAN, 16-

8 **Church of Our Lady**
Courtesy of The Bancroft Library
University of California, Berkeley
1962.005:16-PIC
BRK00008044_24A

9 **Mount Lowe Incline**
Courtesy of The Bancroft Library
University of California, Berkeley
1964.056:27-PIC
BRK00008037_24A

10 **Victorian Mansion in Los Angeles**
Courtesy of The Bancroft Library
University of California, Berkeley
1960.010Ser2:0744-NEG
BRK00016811_31B

11 **L.A.'s First Park**
National Archives
50-2103

12 **Los Angeles View**
Library of Congress
Prints & Photographs Division
Detroit Publishing Company Collection
LC-D4-10077

13 **Spring Street**
Library of Congress
LC-USZ62-57368

14 **Yuma Land Claims**
Library of Congress
LC-DIG-ggbain-04541

16 **Los Angeles Train Station**
Library of Congress
Prints & Photographs Division
Detroit Publishing Company Collection
LC-D4-8691

18 **President William McKinley**
Library of Congress
LC-USZ62-122820

19 **Los Angeles Court House and Hall of Records**
Library of Congress
Prints & Photographs Division
Detroit Publishing Company Collection
LC-USZ62-65776

20 **St. Vincent's College**
Library of Congress
PAN 6A02098

22 **Aerial Swallow**
Courtesy of The Bancroft Library
University of California, Berkeley
1964.056:29-PIC
BRK00008038_24A

23 **Broadway Looking from 4th Street**
Library of Congress
Prints & Photographs Division
Detroit Publishing Company Collection
LC-USZ62-65774

24 **Venice Street Scene**
Library of Congress
Prints & Photographs Division
Detroit Publishing Company Collection
LC-D418-68093

26 **Stereo-Card View of Broadway**
Library of Congress
LC-USZ62-75150

28 **Los Angeles Times Building Wreckage**
Library of Congress
LC-DIG-ggbain-08499

29 **Talesmen**
Library of Congress
LC-DIG-ggbain-09902

30 **Louis Paulhan**
Library of Congress
LC-USZ61-1752

31 **Tar Pit in Hancock Park**
Security Pacific Collecton/
Los Angeles Public Library
00010548

32 **Redondo Beach**
Library of Congress
PAN 6A01753

33 **Crossing the Los Angeles Aqueduct**
National Archives
9098

34 **Barefoot Newsie**
Library of Congress
LC-DIG-NCLC-03967

35 **Heavy-Maintenance Squad**
National Archives
13032

36 **Medium and Heavyweight Auto Race**
Library of Congress
PAN 6A28954

38 **C. A. Coey and His Bride**
Library of Congress
LC-DIG-ggbain-03245

39 **First Division Reunion Display**
National Archives
111-SC-90017

40 **Presentation of Colors at USC**
National Archives
111-SC-55071

42 **University of Southern California**
National Archives
111-SC-55069

43 **Target Diving**
Library of Congress
LC-USZ62-128405

44 **2nd and Los Angeles Streets**
Courtesy of The Bancroft Library
University of California, Berkeley
1988.052:235-PIC
BRK00008042_24A

45 **Fountain on Olvera Street**
Library of Congress
LC-USZ62-98846

46 **Lincoln Park**
Library of Congress
LC-USZ62-98842

47 **Aviation Pioneer Glenn Martin**
Library of Congress
LC-USZ62-402977

48 **Central Park**
Library of Congress
Prints & Photographs Division
Detroit Publishing Company Collection
LC-D418-68546

50 **Double-Decker Motor Bus**
Library of Congress
LC-USZ62-105766

51 **Port of Los Angeles**
National Archives
P-898-B

52 **Congressional Visit**
National Archives
P-898-B

54 **Broadway at 8th Street**
Library of Congress
LC-USZ62-105757

55 **Artist on Avenue of the Palms**
National Archives
306-NT-950-X-7

56 **Marines Guarding Mail Truck**
National Archives
603-NT-950-L-1

57 **Lemons Coming from the Washer**
Library of Congress
LC-DIG-PPMSCA-09646

58 **Los Angeles Harbor**
National Archives
306-NT-950-R-4

59 **Canoes at Westlake Park**
Library of Congress
LC-USZ62-113430

60 **Pershing Square and Biltmore Hotel**
Library of Congress
LC-USZ62-102731

61 **Redcaps**
Photo courtesy of the Southern California Library for Social Studies and Research
SCL-M0366

62 **Bullock's**
National Archives
306-NT-950-E-3

63 **Elks Convention**
National Archives
950-K3

64 **Grauman's Chinese Theatre**
Library of Congress
LC-USZ62-120535

66 **Hollywood**
National Archives
56-4489

67 **Church of the Little Flower**
National Archives
306-NT-950-G-2

68 **Los Angeles Olympic Stadium**
National Archives
LX10101

69 **Queen of La Fiesta**
National Archives
306-NT-950-V-10

70 **Los Angeles Street Scene**
National Archives
306-NT-950-X-14

72 **Telephone Exchange**
National Archives
950-U1

73 **Night Event at Olympic Stadium**
National Archives
306-NT-950-U-8

74 **Deportation**
Herald Examiner Collection/
Los Angeles Public Library
00058837

75 **Works Progress Administration**
National Archives
IMG090

76 **Russian Fishermen**
National Archives
306-NT-950-R-3

77 **Pershing Place**
National Archives
306-NT-950-X-6

78 **Earthquake at Long Beach**
Security Pacific Collection/
Los Angeles Public Library
00058873

79 **Broadway Looking North**
National Archives
42-490

80 **The Terminus of Ramona Boulevard**
National Archives
46-467

81 **Mae West**
Library of Congress
LC-USZ62-111081

82 **The Masonic Temple Number 42**
Library of Congress
HABS CAL,19-LOSAN,4-

83 **Wilshire Boulevard**
National Archives
208-LU-148-3

84 **Bandini Underpass**
National Archives
46-1006

85 **Stock Exchange Home Office**
Library of Congress
LC-USZ62-83257

86 **Sheriff's Barbecue**
Library of Congress
LC-DIG-PMSCA-08752

88 **MacArthur Park**
National Archives
49-10690

89 **Run Little Chillun**
National Archives
19645-C

90 **Hollywood Bowl**
National Archives
69-N-30075

91 **Morris Hutchins Ruger and Gastone Usigli**
National Archives
17106-C

92 **The Brown Derby**
Photo by Fred William Carter
Security Pacific Collection/
Los Angeles Public Library
0008674

93 **Vega Aircraft Corporation in Burbank**
Library of Congress
LC-USW3-058461-C

94 **Students at Long Beach Marine Stadium**
National Archives
20274-C

95 **Los Angeles Protesters**
Library of Congress
LC-USZ62-117023

96 **Betty Grable and Artie Shaw**
Library of Congress
LC-USZ62-130043

98 **Alexander Hamilton Junior High School**
National Archives
P-3126

99 **Grauman's Chinese Theatre**
National Archives
50-6671

100 **Traffic Accident**
National Archives
50-5901

101 **Will Rogers Memorial Park**
National Archives
165-1-07-188

102 **First Street Viaduct**
National Archives
165-1-07-101

103 **Mines Field**
National Archives
5782-C

104 **East Fullerton Relief Channel**
National Archives
69-NS-5M-1

105 **Women Boarding Bus**
Library of Congress
LC-USZ62-92933

106 **Benjamin "Bugsy" Siegel**
Library of Congress
LC-USZ62-120733

107 **Olympic Boulevard Storm Drain**
National Archives
261-A

108 **Lana Turner**
Library of Congress
LC-USE6-D-001605

109 **Hollywood and Vine**
National Archives
07-13902

110 **Mount Hollywood**
Los Angeles Public Library
00010385

112 **Dance Palace**
Library of Congress
LC-USW3-022822-E

113 **Los Angeles Shoppers**
Library of Congress
LC-USW3-022814-E

114 **Little Tokyo Evacuation Sale**
Library of Congress
LC-USF34-072375-D

115 **Evacuees at Los Angeles Railroad Station**
Library of Congress
LC-USZ62-133822

116 **Japanese American Women Serving Ice Cream**
Library of Congress
LC-USZ62-117354

117 **Batch of Tires**
Library of Congress
LC-USE6-D-004614

118 **Los Angeles Bond Rally**
Courtesy of Korean Heritage
Library, University of
Southern California
KADA-M13930
KADA-HahnG-201

119 VICTORY CORPS
Library of Congress
LC-USE6-D-007633

120 HOLLYWOOD ENLISTS TYPEWRITERS FOR WAR
Library of Congress
LC-USE6-D-008372

121 THREE-BLADE PROPELLERS
Library of Congress
LC-USE6-D-006921

122 DEFENSE WORKERS
Library of Congress
LC-USE6-D-008141

123 ZOOT SUITERS EN ROUTE TO COURT
Library of Congress
LC-USZ62-113319

124 ROSIE THE RIVETER
Library of Congress
LC-USE6-D-004076

125 LIBERTY CARGO SHIPS
Library of Congress
LC-USZ62-92190

126 MARY MCLEOD BETHUNE
Library of Congress
LC-USE6-D-007662

127 SPRING STREET VIEW
National Archives
306-P5-50-1954

128 LOS ANGELES NEWSSTAND
Library of Congress
LC-USW3-002827

129 ATCHISON, TOPEKA AND SANTA FE FREIGHT TRAIN
Library of Congress
LC-USW3-022247-D

130 BETTE DAVIS, MARLENE DIETRICH, AND BOB HOPE
Library of Congress
LC-USZ62-112143

132 MOVIE THEATER
Library of Congress
LC-USW3-035297-D

133 JIMMY DORSEY
Library of Congress
LC-USZ62-130047

134 GENERAL GEORGE S. PATTON
National Archives
208-PU-154F(5)

135 STRIKERS AT ELDON MANUFACTURING COMPANY
Photo courtesy of the Southern California Library for Social Studies and Research
SCL-M0392

136 AGRICULTURAL AREA OF NORWALK
Library of Congress
LC-USE6-D-000971

137 PLAZA PARK
National Archives
14E-4

138 LOS ANGELES STREET VIEW
National Archives
49-10045

139 MOVIE SUPPORT WORKERS
National Archives
48-1950

140 STUDIO ART DEPARTMENT
National Archives
48-1948

141 STAGE 14 BUILDING
National Archives
48-1944

142 CUTTING LABORATORY
National Archives
48-2005

143 BIRD'S-EYE VIEW OF LOS ANGELES
National Archives
49-11765

144 SAN PEDRO BAY SHIPYARDS
National Archives
49-10693

145 MIDTOWN ONE-WAY STREET
National Archives
50-761

146 LAYNE "SHOTGUN" BRITTON AND LIZABETH SCOTT
National Archives
50-9455

147 RESIDENTIAL STREET
National Archives
50-6672

148 SURFBOARD RACE
Herald Examiner Collection/ Los Angeles Public Library
00022047

149 "KAISER HOME" HOUSES
National Archives
50-2917

150 PARAMOUNT PICTURES LOT
Library of Congress
LC-USZ62-127768

151 NAVY RECRUITERS PROVIDING INFORMATION
Photo courtesy of the Southern California Library for Social Studies and Research
SCL-M0271

152 CAMP BEELEY
National Archives
48-1333

153 CORNER OF 7TH AND BROADWAY
National Archives
48-1623

154 FRANK SINATRA
Library of Congress
LC-USZ62-127356

155 MEMBERS OF THE LOS ANGELES 21 AND ATTORNEY
Photo courtesy of the Southern California Library for Social Studies and Research
SCL-M0340

156 ROBERT'S DRIVE-IN
Los Angeles Public Library
00044921

157 HOLLYWOOD PARK RACE TRACK
National Archives
49-11802

158 CHARLIE CHAPLIN AND WIFE OONA
Library of Congress
LC-USZ62-116246

159 SILVER SPURS RIDING CLUB
Photo courtesy of the Southern California Library for Social Studies and Research
SCL-M0303

160 Los Angeles Harbor
National Archives
15-1947

162 National Broadcasting Company
National Archives
51-13903

164 UCLA Football Game
Library of Congress
LC-USZ62-53242

165 Korean Methodist Church
Courtesy of Korean Heritage Library, University of Southern California
KADA-M13767
KADA-KimLe-001

166 Super Chief
Courtesy of University of Southern California, on behalf of the USC Special Collections
EXM-N-9374-006-1

167 Red Cars
Courtesy of University of Southern California, on behalf of the USC Special Collections
EXM-N-9342-008

168 Kenneth McEldowney
Courtesy of University of Southern California, on behalf of the USC Special Collections
EXM-N-9344-008

169 Watching Television
Courtesy of University of Southern California, on behalf of the USC Special Collections
EXM-N-9344-014-1

170 Reverend Billy Graham
Courtesy of University of Southern California, on behalf of the USC Special Collections
EXM-N-9345-020-1

172 Joe Sica
Courtesy of University of Southern California, on behalf of the USC Special Collections
EXM-N-9128-012-8

173 National Rifle Shoot
Courtesy of University of Southern California, on behalf of the USC Special Collections
EXM-N-9342-006-1

174 Nun of the Daughters of Charity
Courtesy of University of Southern California, on behalf of the USC Special Collections
EXM-N-9386-030-1

175 USC Students Work On Homecoming Float
Courtesy of University of Southern California, on behalf of the USC Special Collections
EXM-N-9387-022-1

176 UCLA Homecoming Queen
Courtesy of University of Southern California, on behalf of the USC Special Collections
EXM-N-9382-023

177 Detective and Suspect
Courtesy of University of Southern California, on behalf of the USC Special Collections
EXM-N-9169-014-1

178 Two Officers Subdue a Young Bull
Courtesy of University of Southern California, on behalf of the USC Special Collections
EXM-N-9169-008

179 Freeway Traffic
Herald Examiner Collection/ Los Angeles Public Library
00041129

180 Elizabeth Taylor
Courtesy of University of Southern California, on behalf of the USC Special Collections
EXM-N-9153-006-3

181 Young Republicans Prepare Their Float
Courtesy of University of Southern California, on behalf of the USC Special Collections
EXM-N-9471-026-7

182 Sailor James Hovey
Courtesy of University of Southern California, on behalf of the USC Special Collections
EXM-N-9126-013-2

183 Awaiting Release of Communist Party Members at Federal Building
Photo courtesy of the Southern California Library for Social Studies and Research
SCL-M0349

184 Public Swimming Pool
National Archives
#9

186 May Company
National Archives
56-8614

187 Measuring Carbon Impurities
Library of Congress
LC-USZ62-114382

188 Van De Kamp Coffee Shop
National Archives
56-8613

189 Los Angeles Rams
Herald Examiner Collection/ Los Angeles Public Library
00053674

190 Passenger Ship Lurline
National Archives
55-10397

192 **SENATOR LYNDON B. JOHNSON**
Library of Congress
LC-U9-4667E-19

194 **LOS ANGELES PUBLIC LIBRARY**
Library of Congress
HABS CAL, 19-LOSAN, 65

195 **PRESIDENT JOHN F. KENNEDY**
Library of Congress
LC-USZ62-133122

196 **LOS ANGELES DODGERS**
Hollywood Citizen News Collection/Los Angeles Public Library
00053504

197 **WATTS RIOT**
Library of Congress
LC-USZ62-11364

198 **SMOG ENGULFS DOWNTOWN LOS ANGELES**
Library of Congress
LC-USZ62-114345

199 **THE FIRST SUPER BOWL**
Library of Congress
LC-USZ62-121407